Manchester Medieval Sources Series

series advisers Rosemary Horrox and Janet L. Nelson

This series aims to meet a growing need among students and teachers of medieval history for translations of key sources that are directly usable in students' own work. It provides texts central to medieval studies courses and focuses upon the diverse cultural and social as well as political conditions that affected the functioning of all levels of medieval society. The basic premise of the series is that translations must be accompanied by sufficient introductory and explanatory material, and each volume, therefore, includes a comprehensive guide to the sources' interpretation, including discussion of critical linguistic problems and an assessment of the most recent research on the topics being covered.

already published in the series

Mark Bailey *The English Manor c. 1200–c. 1500*

Malcom Barber and Keith Bate *The Templars*

Simon Barton and Richard Fletcher *The world of El Cid: Chronicles of the Spanish Reconquest*

J. A. Boyle *Genghis Khan: History of the world conquerer*

Trevor Dean *The towns of Italy in the later Middle Ages*

P. J. P. Goldberg *Women in England, c. 1275–1525*

Janet Hamilton and Bernard Hamilton *Christian dualist heresies in the Byzantine world c. 650–c. 1450*

Rosemary Horrox *The Black Death*

Graham A. Loud and Thomas Wiedemann *The history of the tyrants of Sicily by 'Hugo Falcandus', 1153–69*

Michael Staunton *The lives of Thomas Becket*

R. N. Swanson *Catholic England: Faith, religion and observance before the Reformation*

Elisabeth van Houts *The Normans in Europe*

David Warner *Ottonian Germany*

POPULAR PROTEST IN LATE MEDIEVAL EUROPE

Published in our
centenary year
2004
MANCHESTER
UNIVERSITY
PRESS

MedievalSources*online*

Complementing the printed editions of the Medieval Sources series, Manchester University Press has developed a web-based learning resource which is now available on a yearly subscription basis.

Medieval Sources*online* brings quality history source material to the desktops of students and teachers and allows them open and unrestricted access throughout the entire college or university campus. Designed to be fully integrated with academic courses, this is a one-stop answer for many medieval history students, academics and researchers keeping thousands of pages of source material 'in print' over the Internet for research and teaching.

titles available now at Medieval Sources*online include*

John Edwards *The Jews in Western Europe, 1400–1600*

Paul Fouracre and Richard A. Gerberding *Late Merovingian France: History and hagiography 640–720*

Chris Given-Wilson *Chronicles of the Revolution 1397–1400: The reign of Richard II*

P. J. P. Goldberg *Women in England,* c. *1275–1525*

Janet Hamilton and Bernard Hamilton *Christian dualist heresies in the Byzantine world* c. *650*–c. *1450*

Rosemary Horrox *The Black Death*

Graham A. Loud and Thomas Wiedemann *The history of the tyrants of Sicily by 'Hugo Falcandus', 1153–69*

Janet L. Nelson *The Annals of St-Bertin: Ninth-century histories, volume I*

Timothy Reuter *The Annals of Fulda: Ninth-century histories, volume II*

R. N. Swanson *Catholic England: Faith, religion and observance before the Reformation*

Jennifer Ward *Women of the English nobility and gentry, 1066–1500*

Visit the site at *www.medievalsources.co.uk* for further information and subscription prices.

POPULAR PROTEST
IN LATE MEDIEVAL EUROPE
Italy, France, and Flanders

selected sources translated and annotated
by Samuel K. Cohn, Jr

Manchester University Press
Manchester and New York

distributed exclusively in the USA by Palgrave

Copyright © Samuel K. Cohn, Jr. 2004

The right of Samuel K. Cohn, Jr. to be identified as the editor of this work has been asserted by him in accordance with the Copyright, Designs and Patents Act 1988.

Published by Manchester University Press
Oxford Road, Manchester M13 9NR, UK
and Room 400, 175 Fifth Avenue, New York, NY 10010, USA
www.manchesteruniversitypress.co.uk

Distributed exclusively in the USA by
Palgrave, 175 Fifth Avenue, New York NY 10010, USA

Distributed exclusively in Canada by
UBC Press, University of British Columbia, 2029 West Mall, Vancouver, BC, Canada V6T 1Z2

British Library Cataloguing-in-Publication Data
A catalogue record for this book is available from the British Library

Library of Congress Cataloging-in-Publication Data
A catalog record for this book is available from the Library of Congress

ISBN 978 0 7190 6730 3 *hardback*
ISBN 978 0 7190 6731 0 *paperback*

First published by Manchester University Press 2004

First digital paperback edition published 2012

Printed by Lightning Source

To Malcolm and Henry

CONTENTS

Series editor's foreword	*page* xv
Acknowledgements	xvi
List of maps	xvii
Notes to the reader	xviii
Introduction	1

I: BEFORE THE BLACK DEATH, 1245–1348   15

Flanders and Northern France   19

1 A crusade of shepherds and many children, 1251   19
2 Legislation against strikes in Douai in 1245   20
3 Strikes and disturbances to work in Douai, 1266   20
4 Sentences against cloth workers on strike in Douai, 1280   20
5 Inquest at Poperinghe, after the rebellion of textile workers in Ypres (Ieper), 3 April 1280   21
6 The Count of Flanders fines the drapers after the revolt of textile workers, known as the Cockeruelle, Ypres, 1281   21
7 Revolt against the mayor and city council of Rouen in 1281   22
8 Weavers' revolt in Tournai, 1281   22
9 Legislation against strikes for higher wages; argument for the swift repression of revolts; advice against overtaxing the poor, Clermont-en-Beauvaisis, *c.* 1283   23
10 Revolt of commoners against their masters and the officials of the king, Rouen, 1291   24
11 Revolt in Flanders of the people of little wealth, 1297   25
12 Revolt in Bruges and Ghent against the patricians and taxes, 1301   26
13 An Italian's account of the revolt of Bruges, 1299-1301   27
14 Commoners revolt against changes in currency and the rise of rents in Paris, 1307   30
15 Tax revolt in Tournai, 1307   32
16 Revolt of fullers, Tournai, 1307   35
17 Shepherds' movement, 1320   35
18 Revolt of Flanders, 1323–28: *Chronicon comitum Flandrensium*   36
19 Revolt of Flanders, 1324–28: *Anciennes Chroniques de Flandre*   38
20 Revolt of Bruges, 1323: an Italian view   40
21 'A general rebellion' against new taxes, Rouen, 1347   40

Southern France   41

22 Two clerics accused of heresy for leading a revolt in Carcassonne, 1306   41

Central and Northern Italy		42
23	The rise of the *Primo Popolo*: the people's victory over the aristocracy, Florence, 1250	44
24	Tax revolt in Venice, 1266	46
25	*Gran tumulto* in Viterbo, 1282: the people chase the nobility out of the city	47
26	Magnates versus merchants and the 'weak': the first anti-magnate laws in Florence, 1293	49
27	The revolt of 'the people without underpants', Bologna, 1289	50
28	Aristocratic backlash in Florence, 1295	51
29	'How the magnates of Florence instigated a revolt to break the People', 1295	53
30	Revolt of disenfranchised gentlemen, Venice, 1299	55
31	Fra Dolcino's heretical kingdom, 1305-7	55
32	A Sienese account of Fra Dolcino's movement	56
33	A riot of butchers and blacksmiths, Siena, 1318	57
34	Student solidarity, Bologna, 1321	60
35	'Of the riots and great turmoil that occurred in the city of Pisa', 1322	61
36	A match of fisticuffs explodes into city-wide riots in Siena, 1324	62
37	The political consequences of food shortages in Rome, 1328	64
38	How the Florentines avoided food riots, 1328-30	65
39	Florentine craftsmen start up clubs and have parties, 1333	66
40	The people topple the Doges in Genoa and Savona, 1339	67
41	The people of Ancona hound out their Magnates, 1342	68
42	A revolution from above: the Duke of Athens sides with the lowliest artisans and workers of Florence, 1342-43	68
43	The Duke of Athens flies the banner of the people in a last-ditch attempt to placate them	70
44	A mad lord rouses wool carders to revolt against taxes and the fat cats, Florence, 1343	70
45	A street-corner revolt, Florence, 1343	72
46	A riot of wool carders and the lower classes [*gente minuta*] explodes in Florence, 1343	73
47	A union of wool workers with a strike fund, Florence, 1345	74
48	The *popolo minuto* of Siena organise secret meetings and revolt	75
49	The Podestà of Florence condemns the insurgents of Siena, 1346	77
50	Cola di Rienzo's revolt of Rome and his rise as champion [*tribuno*] of the People, 1347	79
51	Farm workers in the *contado* of Florence go on strike, 1347	81
Southern Italy		82
52	Rural and small-town insurrections in southern Italy, 1310-28	82
53	The villagers of Lauria, Basilicata, overthrow their governor, 1317	85
54	Tax revolt in Ascoli-Piceno, Marche, 1269	85
55	A peace march by small children in Naples, 1347	86

CONTENTS

II: FROM THE BLACK DEATH TO 1378   87

Northern France and Flanders   93

56 The merchants' revolt against new royal taxes, Rouen, 1351   93
57 Seizure of the royal castle at Rouen, 1358   93
58 Internecine artisan conflict in Bruges and its resolution, 1359   94
59 The weavers and fullers of Flanders unite, 1360   96
60 Tax revolt in Tournai, 1365   96

Southern France   99

61 The Tuchins: a retrospective view from the north   99
62 Locals try to rid their region of a band of Tuchins, 1367   101
63 The Tuchins and personal antagonisms in a village outside Saint-Flour   102
64 Tuchins, cattle raids, and the gang of Guillaume Gracia   104
65 Village assassins and the early training of a Tuchin   105
66 Conflict between aristocrats and commoners in the region of Toulouse, 1364   106
67 The people of Carcassonne attack a royal castle, 1364   107

Italy   109

68 A tavern riot over earlier election results, 1348   109
69 A riot of the 'people' cut down to size by the Bentivoglio of Bologna, 1350   110
70 The Roman people [*popolo*] kick Luca Savelli out of town, 1353   111
71 The *popolo minuto*, magnates, and the emperor boot the Nine out of Siena, 1355   112
72 The organisation of the guilds in the new regime of the Twelve, Siena, 1355   117
73 Tax revolt in Ravenna, 1357   118
74 Taxes beyond measure, Bologna, 1357   120
75 Conspiracy of artisans, workers, priests, and friars, Pisa, 1360   121
76 Independence and resistance of a subject town, Montalcino, 1359   122
77 Riot over the cardinal's pretty little dog, Viterbo, 1367   123
78 A grain riot in Florence because of the high price of bread, 1368   124
79 Regime change in Siena, six governments in five months, 1368-69   126
80 A failed conspiracy of artisans, Lucca, 1369: a chronicler's view   129
81 A failed conspiracy of artisans, Lucca, 1369: the judicial records   130
82 Revolt of the wool workers in Perugia, 1371   132
83 Wool workers and carders of Siena clash with their bosses over wages: the revolt of the Club of the Caterpillar, 1371   133
84 Domestic servants of the Governor of Cortona attempt to kill him and overthrow the government, 1371   135
85 A subject town rebels, Galliano, Lucchesia, 1372   135
86 Overthrow of Papal authority in Cento, 1375   136

87	The city of Fermo rebels against the Papacy and creates a government of the People, 1375	137
88	Revolt of mountain men against the cardinal legate of Bologna, 1376: the story from the judicial records	137
89	The same: the chroniclers' view	140
90	Ascoli creates a government of the People and rebels against the Church, 1377	141

III: THE JACQUERIE 143

91	A view from the church elite: Jean le Bel	150
92	An aristocrat's view: Froissart	155
93	A view from the Norman clergy	158
94	A view of a provincial knight	163
95	The official view of the king's chronicler	166
96	Another view close to the royal councillors: the chronicler of the abbey of Saint-Denis	169
97	The view of a Carmelite: the chronicle of the supposed Jean de Venette	170
98	An outsider's view from the north of England	172
99	An outsider's view from Florence	173
100	A minor courtier's view	176
101	Letter of Étienne Marcel to the Communes of Picardy and Flanders	177
102	A soldier's view: the testimony of Bascot de Mauléon in 1388	178
103	Letters of remission: annulment of penalties meted out to the city of Paris	179
104	Authorisation given to the chapter of Meaux to close the gates of a street, July 1358	181
105	Remission granted to Jean de Congi, bourgeois of the Marché of Meaux	182
106	Remission granted to Guillaume de Chavenoil, priest and canon of Meaux	183
107	Remission granted to Jean Chandelier, draper, resident of the Marché of Meaux	183
108	Remission granted to Hue of Sailleville, elected by the villagers of Angicourt as their captain	184
109	Remission granted to Colart du Four, a rebel of the Beauvaisis	185
110	Remission granted to Jean Hersent, who announced Étienne Marcel's order to assemble all the men of the region to arm themselves	186
111	General remission granted to the villagers of Bettancourt and Vroil	187
112	Remission granted to Jean Morel, curate of Blacy, who had been forced to follow his parishioners to an assembly of commoners	188
113	Fragment of a letter of remission mentioning an attempt by Pierre de Montfort to spread revolutionary propaganda in the city of Caen	189

CONTENTS xi

114 Remission granted to Jean Flageolet of Favresse, elected as
 leader of several villages of Perthois 190
115 Remission granted to Mahieu de Leurel, mason, condemned
 as an accomplice to the execution of Jean Bernier 191
116 Remission granted to Guillaume le Févre, bourgeois of Paris
 and fishmonger, giving the false reasons for the Parisians
 revolt against the king 192
117 Letter of Charles, granting to the marshal of Boucicaut the use
 rights of all properties which had belonged personally to Robert
 le Coq, bishop of Laon 194
118 Letter of pardon of King John II to the Parisians involved
 in the revolt 195
119 Remission granted to the inhabitants of Amiens, concerning
 various crimes and excesses they committed 197
120 Remission granted to those rebels who planned to seize the city
 of Paris 199

IV: THE REVOLT OF THE CIOMPI, 1378–82 201

121 A diary of the Ciompi by an anonymous Florentine, 1378–82 206
122 Petitions granted to artisans and other workers, 21 July 1378 238
123 On Michele di Lando 240
124 Economic and social policies of the Ciompi 242
125 On the Eight of Santa Maria Novella, 27 August 1378 243
126 The revolution betrayed, 27–29 August 1378 244
127 Criminal proceedings against the Ciompi and the radicals of the
 Eight of Santa Maria Novella, August 1378 245
128 The laws transforming the government of the Ciompi to that
 of the Minor Guilds 249
129 The chronicle of a worker 251
130 Dissension between the guild of the dyers and the wool bosses,
 1380 258
131 The end of the two revolutionary guilds of workmen, February
 1382 259

V: THE CLUSTER NORTH OF THE ALPS, 1378–82 261

Northern France and Flanders 267

132 The first popular uprising [*commocione*] before the crowning
 of King Charles VI 267
133 The king eases the tax burden imposed by his father on the
 people 270
134 Crimes committed by the Parisian insurgents, particularly
 against the Jews 273

135	The lords try in vain to re-impose the subsidies on the *plebes*	274
136	The uprisings at Paris and Rouen because of the subsidies, 1382	275
137	The people of Rouen are punished for their crimes	281
138	The king pardons the Parisians for their offence	281
139	The Parisians refuse the subsidies with a new stubbornness	282
140	Philippe van Artevelde vigorously urges the Flemings to fight valiantly, 1383	285
141	The French pursue the Flemings as they flee	286
142	Tax revolts and attacks on Jews in Paris, 1380	287
143	Tax revolts in Picardy, 1380	288
144	The *Harelle* of Rouen and its ramifications for the commoners of Paris	289
145	The *Harelle*, according to Pierre Cochon	292
146	The hammer men of Paris and the spread of tax revolts through *Langue d'oïl*	294
147	The hammer men according to Pierre Cochon	299
148	The hammer men according to Cousinot le Chancelier	300
149	The hammer men according to Jean Froissart	301
150	The eyewitness account of the Florentine Buonaccorso Pitti	302
151	The 'troubles' in Flanders in 1379 to 1382	303
152	Ordinance of the three estates of *Langue d'oïl*, abolishing all the taxes set since the reign of Philippe le Bel	305
153	Renunciation imposed on the abbey of Saint-Ouën during the uprising of the *Harelle*, 25 February 1381[2]	306
154	Charter of Charles VI granting pardon to those of Rouen for the uprising of the *Harelle*, 5 April 1381[2]	307
155	Charter of Charles VI suppressing the Commune of Rouen	308
156	Remission to a vendor of vinegar for acts of rebellion during the hammer men's revolt	311
157	Remission to a furrier's journeyman for acts of rebellion during the hammer men's revolt	312
158	Remission to a poor man for acts of rebellion during the hammer men's revolt	314
159	An innocent bystander swept up in the crowds of the hammer men	315
160	A wool shearer and the massacre of Jews in the hammer men's revolt	315
161	Remission to a salt merchant for acts of rebellion during the hammer men's revolt	316
162	Hammer men pardoned for crimes of rebellion on 1 March 1382, identified by occupation	317
163	Tax revolts in Laon, 1380	318
164	The troubles in Saint-Quentin, 1380	320
165	Tax evasion in Dieppe, 1382	321
166	A rope-maker stirs up rebellion in Caen, early 1380s	322
167	Collective fine against the bourgeois and commoners of Caen because of their rebellion, early 1380s	323
168	Eustache Deschamps's ballad of the hammer men	324

CONTENTS xiii

Southern France 325

169 Tax revolt sparked in the cathedral at Le Puy when the Virgin was unveiled, 1378 325
170 A notice of the revolt in Béziers, 1381 327
171 Rebellion in Montpellier according to the official chronicler of King Charles V, 1379 327
172 Rebellion in Montpellier according to a local chronicler 328
173 Revolt of Clermont de Lodève, 1379 329
174 Revolt in Alès, 1380 331
175 Rebellions and raids in the region of Toulouse in 1381 and 1382 332
176 The ravages of the companies in the Velay 335
177 Tax revolt in Lyon, 1382 336

EPILOGUE: AFTER THE CLUSTER, 1382–1423 338

France

178 How the University of Paris had a big quarrel with Lord Charles of Savoy, 1404 341
179 A student brawl in Orléans, 13 November 1408 343
180 The revolt of the butchers and the people of the wretched estate [*vil estat*] of Paris, March 1413 344
181 Rebellion of Paris and the imprisonment of the dukes of Bar and of Bavaria, April 1413 345
182 The first revolt of the Parisians, sparked by the most squalid, April 1413 346
183 The laws inspired by the butcher Caboche, May 1413 348
184 Rebellion at Châlons-en-Champagne, 1418 349

Southern France 350

185 Raids and illicit agreements with the enemy in the war-torn mountains above Saint-Flour, 1391 350

Italy 351

186 The Ciompi try to restore their revolutionary guilds, 24 January 1382 351
187 Another failed attempt by the Ciompi and the successful counterrevolution by the old families 352
188 How rioting again erupted in Florence with the Ciompi and those recently recalled from exile arming themselves, March 1382 355
189 How the Ciompi and the exiles re-armed, hoping to bring about a new order [*nuova cosa*], March 1382 355
190 How a conspiracy was planned in Florence solely by those of the lower orders [*gente minuta*], July 1383 356
191 Perugia rioted, March 1383: a contemporary version from Siena 357
192 Perugia rioted: a later version from Perugia 357

xiv CONTENTS

193 A riot in Perugia to change the regime and in support of
 the Church, July 1392 358
194 Art and co-optation of the people's victory, Perugia, 1392 359
195 How the Captain of the Emergency Council [*Balía*] in Florence
 cut off the heads of several artisans and hanged others, 1393 359
196 Peasant revolt in Parma, 1385 360
197 A peasant revolt outside Ferrara, April 1395 361
198 Mountain peasants lay siege to the Florentine stronghold of
 Firenzuola, 1402 362
199 The Florentine state makes major concessions to the mountain
 rebels of the Alpi Fiorentine, 1402–3 367
200 Giovanni di Pagolo Morelli's version of the mountain rebels,
 1402 370
201 Gregorio Dati's version of the same 371
202 Village rivalry near Monte San Savino, 1406 372
203 Village vigilantes seek justice after a monstrous murder of
 a baby in its crib, 1423 374
204 The people of the city and countryside of Siena curse the city rulers,
 1423[4] 374

Suggested reading 376
Index 379

SERIES EDITOR'S FOREWORD

The cluster of revolts which followed the Black Death of the mid-fourteenth century have received surprisingly little attention since the late 1960s when they had an obvious topical attraction for academics. The English Rising of 1381 has been the exception, with continuing interest fuelled by an exemplary volume of sources edited by Barrie Dobson, which first appeared in 1971, and a flurry of scholarly publications to mark the 600th anniversary of the rising. The student who wished to set the English experience in a wider European context remained, however, dependent on two markedly contrasting treatments from the early 1970s, those of Rodney Hilton and of Mollat and Wolff. Professor Sam Cohn has now come to the rescue. The generous selection of source material in the present volume makes available, in most cases for the first time in English, not only material relating to the post-plague 'cluster' but comparative material on earlier and later outbreaks. It is now possible to chart popular protest in France, Italy and the Low Countries across the best part of two centuries. The famous examples – the Jacquerie and the revolt of the Ciompi – take their place not as isolated outbreaks but as peaks on the graph of European disaffection.

But the book does more than provide material for courses on late medieval history, valuable as that is. It points the way towards a new interpretation of medieval popular unrest, which calls into question existing assumptions about its causation and efficacy. Not all those assumptions have been the creation of medievalists. Many have surfaced in the general surveys of popular revolt produced in recent years. Early-modernists and their more modern colleagues have always been inclined to see the medieval as 'other': as something that can be confidently defined as the opposite of whatever is taken to be characteristic of modernity. Professor Cohn here demonstrates that this simply does not work – and nor do the modern taxonomies of revolt or rebellion which some writers have tried to impose on the medieval experience. The result is an important addition to the *Medieval Sources* series which not only embodies the latest research but will prompt more.

Rosemary Horrox
Fitzwilliam College,
Cambridge

ACKNOWLEDGEMENTS

Research for this project began in the Bibliothèque Nationale in Paris. I wish to thank L'École des Hautes Études for inviting me as a 'directeur d'Études for December 2002 and Christiane Klapisch-Zuber for her kind hospitality. Since then I have consulted materials for this work in the Bibliothèque Municipale of Rouen, the Bibliotheca Nationale Centrale and the Biblioteca Berenson in Florence, and especially the Glasgow University Library. I wish to thank Sarah Hamilton for issuing me a private study in the library for the duration of this project.

More than any other project that I have embarked on, this one has forced me to rely on the good will of friends and colleagues. Graeme Small, Jack Warwick, Eileen Millar and Martin MacGregor were ever willing to answer my questions about difficult passages in medieval French, Italian and Latin. Rudolph Binion, Douglas Aiton, Leighton Hodson, Jim Simpson, Fabrizio Nevola, Antonio Fassini, and David Marsh devoted considerable time from their own research to check over various sections of my translations. In addition, William Bowsky, Rudolph Binion, and Debra Strickland read over my introductions. Rosemary Horrox read closely and criticised incisively an earlier version of this work. At MUP, I thank Alison Welsby and Jonathan Bevan for their enthusiasm and patience and to Jinty Nelson for her encouragement at the beginning of this project and her sharp eye at the end of it. Finally, the two external readers of the manuscript read through the texts and notes with great erudition and thoroughness, saved me from embarrassing errors, and made valuable suggestions. The errors in judgement and translation that remain are of course my own. I dedicate this work to my sons, future students of something.

NOTES TO THE READER

- Numbers in brackets indicate document numbers found in this text.
- Different calendars in different kingdoms and city-states began at different times – some at Christmas, some at Easter, and some on 25 March. I have put the years in the original and then added in brackets the year corresponding to our calendar if different from the original. Thus, an event in Florence that occurred on 24 March 1389 would be rendered 24 March 1389[90].
- If I have left out text from the original, I have indicated it with '...'; if text is missing from the original source, I have indicated it with '[...]'.
- In Latin texts from Italy I have translated proper names into Italian; in those from France, into French.
- I have left 'Messer' (meaning lord) in the original for Italian patronymics but translated it as Lord for the first name.
- For certain obscure or problematic place names and phrases I have given the medieval original in brackets.
- For certain key words, for instance, for 'people', 'commoners', 'rabble', 'revolt', 'rebel', 'rebellion', I often provide the original in brackets.
- Most of the place names in these documents appear on one of the six maps; for the others I have specified their location in the notes.
- For currencies and their equivalences I have provided notes, but for further elucidation the reader should consult the tables in Peter Spufford, *Money and its Use in Medieval Europe* (Cambridge, 1988), especially Table 4, pp. 291–3, and graph 3, pp. 296–8.
- For well-known people I have translated Christian names, thus King John II, instead of King Jean, but for others I have left the variants found in the texts, Jean, Jehan, Giovanni, Giano, etc.
- The twenty-four-hour clock of the Middle Ages began at vespers, which at Florence would have been 19:45 at the summer solstices. In translating the summer hours (the vast majority found in these documents) I have rounded the time of vespers to 20:00 and have calculated the others accordingly.

LIST OF MAPS

I	Regions of France and Flanders	*page* xix
II	Towns and villages of the Jacquerie, 1358	xx
III	Towns and villages in Languedoc, 1360–80	xxi
IV	Towns and villages in Central Italy, 1250–1420	xxii
V	Late medieval Paris, *c.* 1380	xxiii
VI	Late medieval Florence, *c.* 1378	xxiv

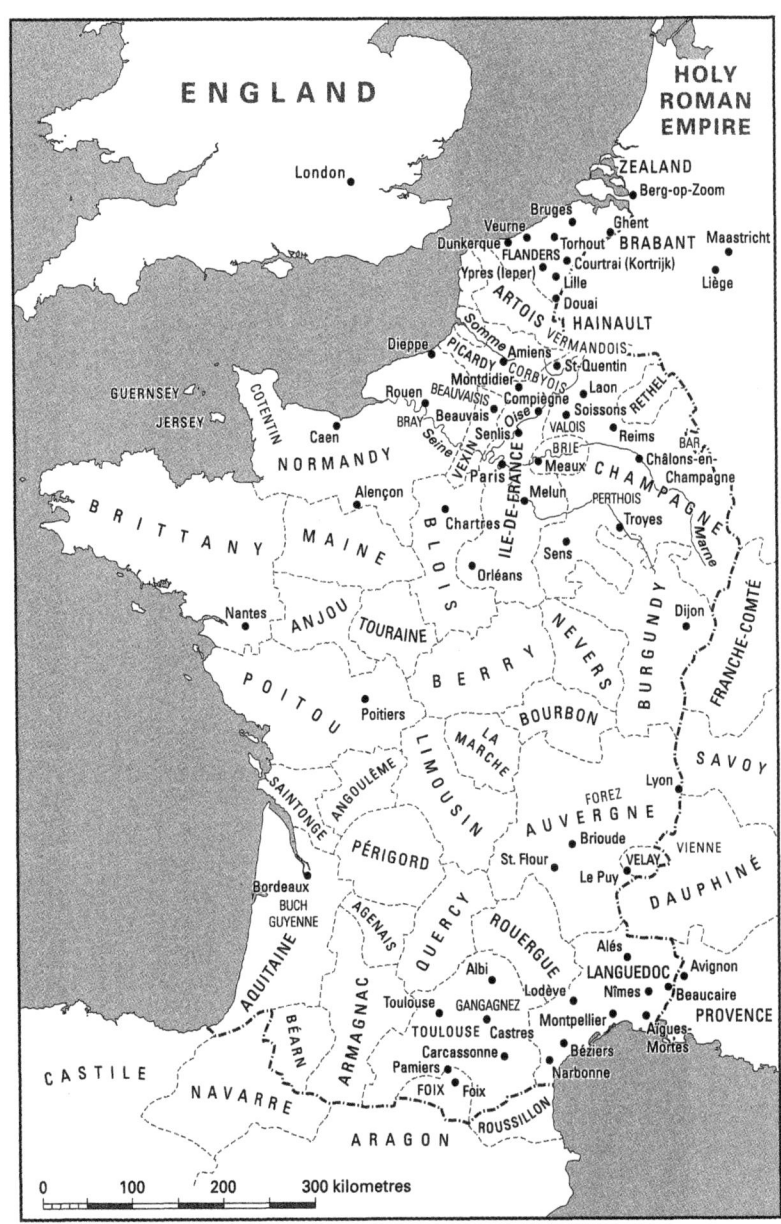

Map I Regions of France and Flanders

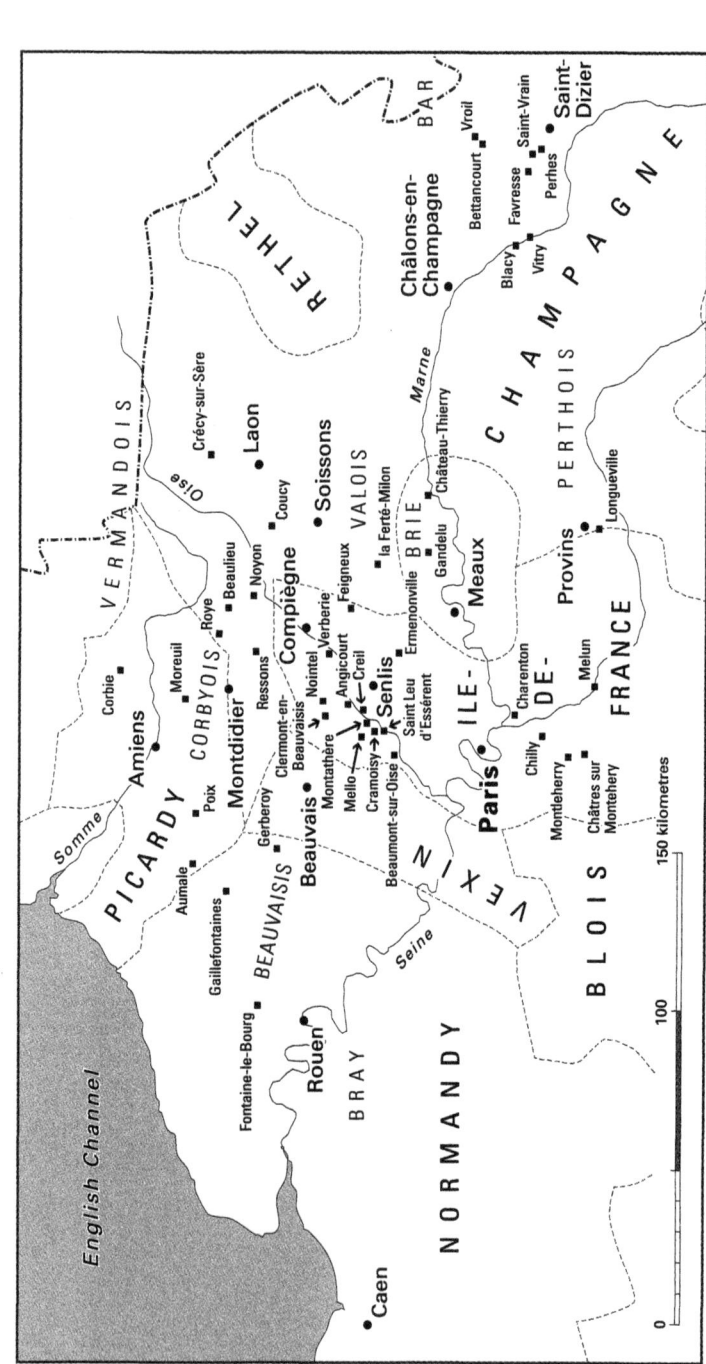

Map II Towns and villages of the Jacquerie, 1358

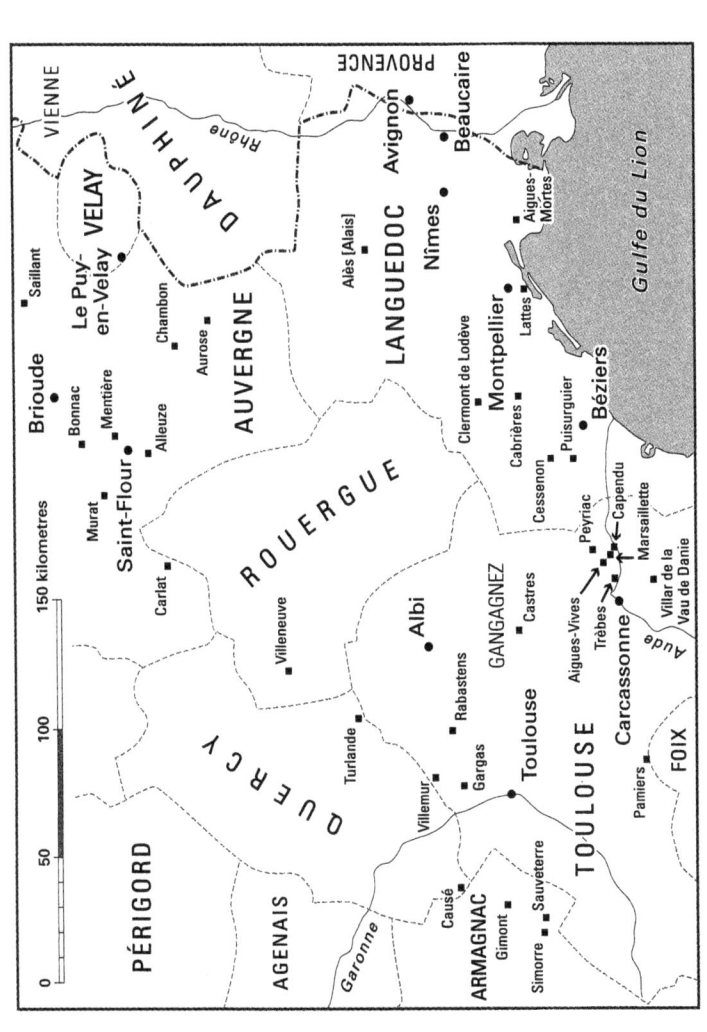

Map III Towns and villages in Languedoc, 1360–80

Map IV Towns and villages in Central Italy, 1250–1420

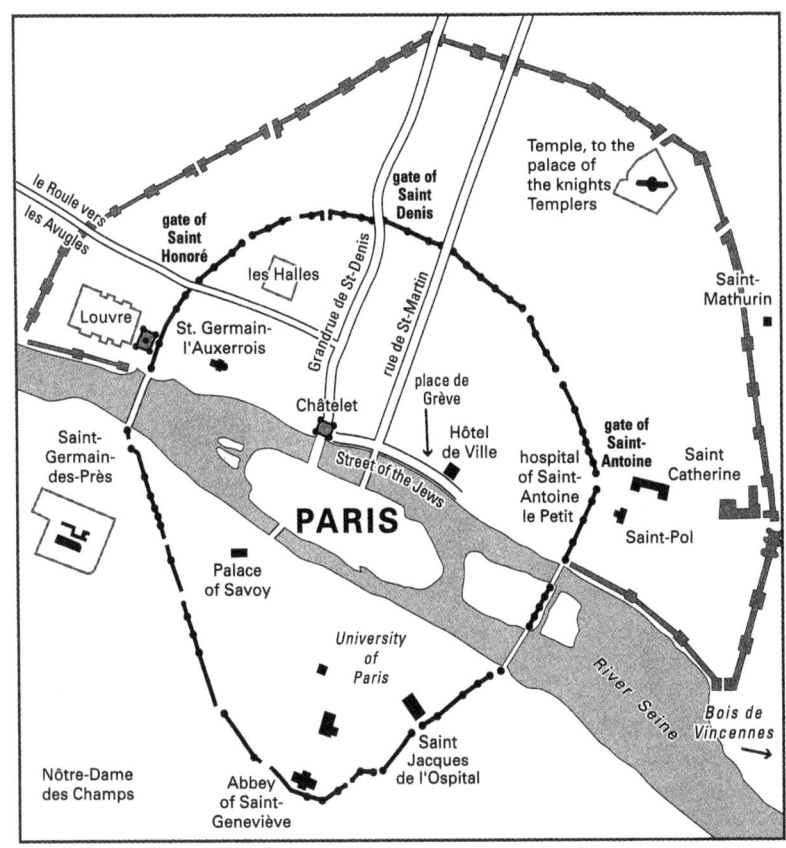

Map V Late medieval Paris, *c.* 1380

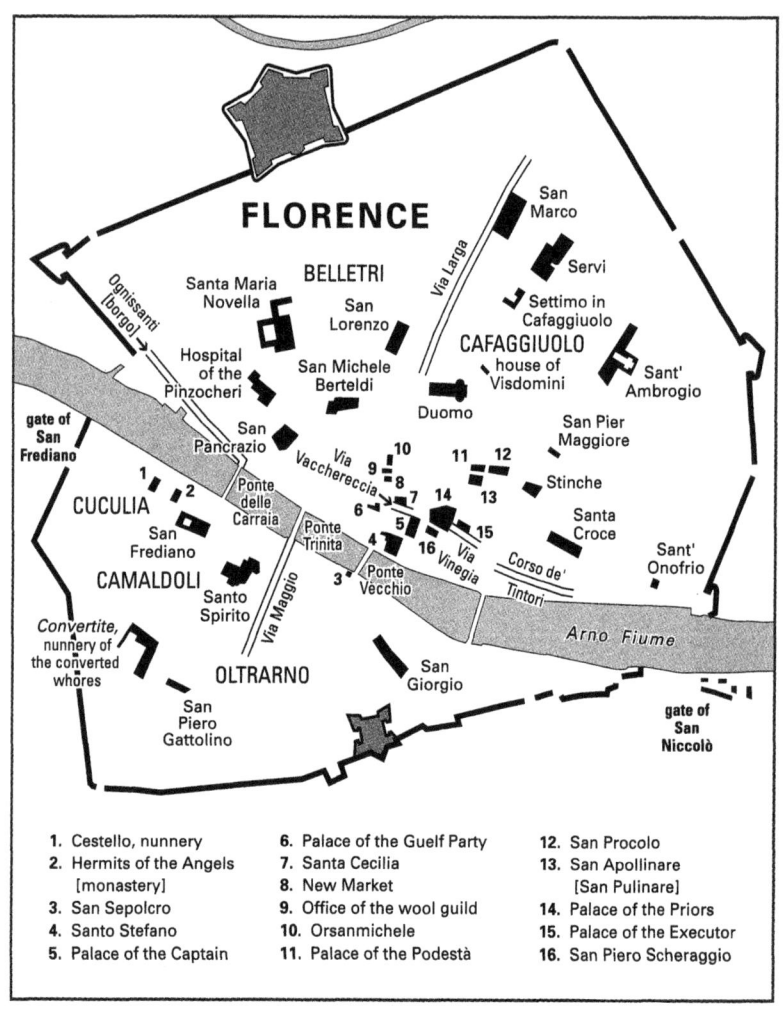

Map VI Late medieval Florence, c. 1378

INTRODUCTION

The documents selected and translated in this volume extend from 1245 to 1424 but concentrate on 'a contagion of revolts' following the Black Death from around 1355 to 1382. They comprise a diversity of sources – chronicles, songs, poems, ordinances, laws, deliberations of city councils, royal remissions of grace, judicial records, family diaries, and even an art commission – and cover a wide variety of popular protest in different social, political, and economic settings. The original purpose behind this project was to pose the question: what difference did the Black Death and its successive waves of pestilence make for the seeming rash of popular protest – a new 'violent tenor of life' to use Johan Huizinga's phrase[1] – and in particular the supposed clustering of revolts between 1378 and 1382?[2]

I have selected and translated these documents with the student in mind. Numerous undergraduate courses turn on the question of comparative revolt in the later Middle Ages, but most students in the Anglophone world can now rely on sources only for one of the many revolts that sprang forth during the 'tumultuous fourteenth century' – the English peasant war or uprising, which lasted for less than a month in all, and for only six days in the capital, as a challenge to royal power (10–15 June). For that revolt, students are well armed with the excellent and thorough collection compiled by R. B. Dobson, *The Peasants' Revolt of 1381*, which has rightly become standard reading for most courses on the social history of the later Middle Ages.[3] For comparison with other uprisings – their forms of revolt, leadership, composition of crowds, symbols, flags, rhetoric, programmes, and ideologies – students have only scattered scraps and pieces, which can be counted on the fingers of one hand – the early fourteenth-century *Annals of Ghent*, the *Chronicle [said to be] of Jean de Venette*, *Chronicles*

---

1 Johan Huizinga, *The Waning of the Middle Ages*, tr. F. Hopman (London, 1924), chapter 1, pp. 9–31.

2 See M. Mollat and P. Wolff, *Ongles bleus, Jacques et Ciompi: les révolutions populaires en Europe aux XIVe et XVe siècles* (Paris, 1970; translated as *Popular Revolutions of the Late Middle Ages*, tr. A. L. Lyttonsells [New York, 1973]).

3 R. B. Dobson, *The Peasants' Revolt of 1381*, 2nd edn (London, 1983).

of the Tumult of the Ciompi, and sections of Froissart's chronicles.[4] Moreover, except for the Froissart selections, these were published in limited editions and are now out of print.[5] Without access to the continental sources how can students gain a comparative view of late medieval social history, much less understand the history of popular protest and the social and political consequences of the Black Death?

With Dobson's collection as my model, I began with the idea of concentrating on the principal sources for the best known of the continental revolts before the Peasants' War in Germany 1524–25 – the French Jacquerie of 1358, the Florentine Revolt of the Ciompi, and the Czech revolt of the Hussites from around 1412 almost to midcentury. It quickly became clear, however, that such an enterprise would be impossible within a single volume. The narrative sources on the Ciompi alone would fill at least three volumes before touching the rich archival records – criminal proceedings, laws, and the day-to-day decision making of the Ciompi government in alliance with the minor guilds during its three and a half years of rule. Moreover, I decided that the Ciompi had to be understood in a broader comparative framework within Florentine history, against the backdrop of earlier revolts, dating to the *Primo Popolo* or 'People's' revolt of 1250, and in comparison with popular insurrection elsewhere in central Italy. Similar comparative contexts would also enrich our understanding of the other well-known revolts. Nor could those protests that endured for forty years – the Hussite rebellions – be easily confined to a single volume, especially given the large number of surviving theological tracts and sermons that must be included alongside the rich chronicle traditions in German, Czech, and Latin.[6]

Thus, my strategy changed. To understand the impact of the Black Death and the explosion of popular protest in its wake, I restricted

---

4 *Annales Gandenses*, ed. and tr. Hilda Johnstone (London, 1951); *The Chronicle of Jean de Venette*, tr. Jean Birdsall, and ed. Richard Newhall (New York: Columbia University Press, 1953); *Chronicles of the Tumult of the Ciompi*, tr. Rosemary Kantor and Louis Green, Monash Publications in History: 7 (Victoria, Australia, 1990); there are numerous translations of selections of Froissart; most readily available is the Penguin edition, *Chronicles of Froissart: Selected, Translated and Edited by Geoffrey Brereton* (Harmondsworth, 1978).

5 According to OCLC, only two university libraries in the UK own copies of *Chronicles of the Tumult of the Ciompi*.

6 For a selection of these sources, see *Geschichtschreiber der Hussitischen Bewegung in Böhmen*, ed. K. Höfler, Fontes Rerum Austriacarum, series II, 2 vols. (Vienna, 1856–65).

my survey geographically and modified it temporally. First, to judge if anything had changed in the character of revolt after 1348 a fair sampling of documents before the Black Death, reaching back to the mid-thirteenth century was required. For instance, were the strike funds and actions of the Florentine Ciuto Brandini on the eve of the Ciompi the first of their kind, as Florentine historians have assumed?[7] Secondly, the revolts of the fifteenth century would be better placed in a separate volume. The Hussite rebellions, the *remensas* in Spain,[8] the revolts of the Swiss cantons, and numerous revolts of the Low Countries of the fifteenth and early sixteenth century fit better as a prelude for understanding the Peasants' War in Germany (1524–25) – the mix of religious expectations and economic aspirations – than they do within the context of the Black Death of 1348 and its immediate aftermath.

As a result of this rethinking, I have concentrated on three geographical areas – Italy, southern France (or more precisely Languedoc), and northern France and Flanders. The three, however, are not given equal attention. Given its revolutionary tradition and the attention given to it by modern historians, Flanders is the most under-represented area in this volume. I have included enough sources, however, to show that this region was indeed what Mollat and Wolff following the late-nineteenth-century Dutch historian Léon Vanderkinde called a 'paradise of social struggles', especially for the latter half of the thirteenth and early fourteenth centuries.[9] Even more than Mollat, Wolff, Vanderkinde, or Henri Pirenne[10] realised, a comparison with that other hotbed of popular insurrection, Tuscany, shows popular

---

7 See Gino Scaramella, 'Ciompi', in *Enciclopedia Italiano* (Rome, 1931), X, p. 385; and Victor Rutenburg, *Popolo e movimenti popolari nell'Italia del '300 e '400* (Bologna, 1971 [Moscow, 1958]), pp. 106–7.

8 These were peasant revolts against *malos usos* or the bad practices of the nobility that culminated in widespread insurrections in the mid-fifteenth century.

9 Mollat and Wolff, *Popular Revolutions of the Late Middle Ages*, p. 272; Léon Vanderkindere, *Le siècle des Artevelde: Études sur la civilisation morale et politique de la Flandre et du Brabant*, 2nd edn (Brussels, 1909).

10 Henri Pirenne, *Histoire de Belgique: des origines à nos jours*, 6th edn, vols. I–II (Brussels, 1948; 1st edn, 1900); *Les Anciennes démocraties des Pays-Bas* (Paris, 1910); and *Recueil des documents rélatifs à l'histoire de l'industrie drapière en Flandre*, ed. Georges Espinas and Henri Pirenne, 4 vols. (Brussels, 1906–24), carried out the greatest in-depth studies of popular revolt in the Low Countries. Pirenne thought (*Les Anciennes démocraties*, p. 168) that the only place where one found 'an equivalent in the richness of their vicissitudes, energy, and duration was in the republican municipalities of Italy'.

revolt in Flanders and parts of northern France about a century ahead of Tuscan cities in the organisation, aims, duration, and repertoires of revolt. On the other hand, I included less on the 'revolts' of the van Arteveldes, both Jacob and Philip, in the 1330s and the early 1380s than some historians might have expected or desired.[11] While these rebellions had the sparks of popular protest, particularly at their origins, they became internecine city-state struggles between Ghent and Bruges and other city-states as well as proto-nationalist rebellions against French overlordship [139, 150]. In this regard, they were closer to the wars between Florence and Milan during the second half of the fourteenth and early fifteenth centuries than to popular uprisings, even if artisan and peasant militias were employed. Secondly, unlike the popular revolts in Paris, Rouen, and other cities of northern France waged against their own bourgeoisie as well as the crown in the early 1380s, the Artevelde struggles against French rule and the imposition of new taxes became a national and linguistic alliance of city-state oligarchies against the French. While these sentiments were certainly present earlier in the Clauwaerts-Leliaerts opposition during the peasant and artisan wars of 1297 to 1302 [11–13] and again in 1323 to 1328 [18–20], class conflict was earlier the directing force. Peasants and artisans had taken the initiative and provided the leadership (not patricians like the van Arteveldes). In the Flemish revolts of 1297 to 1302, it was only after the initial victories of peasants and artisans that the sons of the count of Flanders, Guy of Dampierre, joined in and rallied the commoners' cause into a unified national and linguistic struggle against France.

In this volume I have sought to show the diversity of insurrections in city and countryside. Such 'troubles' range from a dinner-party of armed students who beat up one another, leaving one dead in early-fifteenth-century Orléans, to the six-year armed conflict in the Low Countries, 1323–28, in which thousands of peasants and artisans formed troops, conquered one city-state after another, defied patrician rule, and ultimately challenged the suzerainty of the king of France. Through this diversity, I explore the keywords of this volume, 'popular' and 'protest'. One might argue that the revolts of mid- and late-thirteenth-century Italian city-states – the *primo popolo* or revolts of 'the people' against oligarchic and aristocratic regimes – did not constitute 'popular' uprisings but were more the revolts of merchant

---

11 I believe David Nicholas, *Medieval Flanders* (London, 1992), p. 228, rightly refers to these as civil wars.

classes against entrenched feudal or ecclesiastical oligarchies, who at times came from the very same families. Indeed, for this period, when the survival of criminal records is extremely rare and chroniclers did not list insurgents or their occupations, it is difficult to know exactly who comprised the 'people'. But even if these movements' leaders were not minor guildsmen, small shopkeepers, artisans, or workers, the chronicles reveal that merchants, later to be distinguished as the *popolani*, or *popolo grasso* (the fat cats), were hardly the only ones or even the principal ones in the streets battling against the old oligarchies and their privileges. In 1295, when the Florentine magnate Corso de' Donati challenged the rule and reputation of the people's leader, Giano della Bella, it was the *popolo minuto* (workers and artisans without guild representation in the city) who spoke out and manned the barricades in Giano's defence against aristocratic arrogance and corruption [28]. And in Ancona in 1342, it was the enraged *popolo minuto*, that is, artisans and workers and not established guildsmen or merchants, who 'swept away their magnates from their land' [41].

On what constituted 'protest' or 'revolt' the boundaries again are not crystal-clear, nor should we expect them to be. First, contemporary authors did not use precise terms to distinguish a skirmish from a disturbance, a riot from a revolt, or a revolt from rebellion. Such hierarchies are the constructions of present-day historians and their utility is debatable.[12] The terms rebellion or rebels are used for artisans, workers, and peasants in the north of Europe but are more often reserved in Italy for conflicts in which aristocrats defied the authority of their lords or in which dependent territories 'rebelled' against the lordship of a city-state. For popular rebellion, the phrase was generally 'to rise up'. In France and Flanders insurgents 'moved' and thus were guilty of creating '*commociones*'. In Italy they made noise; thus their revolts or riots were '*rumori*'. In Flanders, France (*Langue d'oïl* and Languedoc), and Italy, nearly all the records, judicial and narrative, accused these 'movements' or 'noises' of hatching 'conspiracies', 'plots', 'plans', illicit assemblies, and disturbances against the 'peace and tranquillity of the state (or status quo)'. On occasion, such 'noises' were in today's terms more the stuff of tabloids than serious threats to

---

12 For such distinctions, see Mollat and Wolff, *Popular Revolutions*, p. 91: 'A revolution is something planned and prepared; it has a programme. A revolt is a spontaneous reaction, a reflex of anger or self-defence, sometimes of both'. Also, see Guy Fourquin, *Les soulèvements populaires au Moyen Age* (Paris, 1972; translated as *The Anatomy of Popular Rebellion in the Middle Ages*, tr. A. Chesters (Amsterdam, 1978), pp. 20–1, 24–5, 83, 101–2, and 109.

political stability. One such case involved villagers outside Siena, outraged at hearing the news of a neighbour's baby snatched from the crib and killed. They assembled and formed a vigilante brigade to apprehend the presumed culprit [**203**]. I included this document not only because of its own intrinsic interest, but also because it is one of only two examples of crowd action reported by Sienese chroniclers after the working-class revolt of the Company or Club of the Caterpillar [*Bruco*] in 1371 [**83**] until at least 1425. In Tuscany, unlike the north of Europe, the near incessant mumblings of post-plague unrest in many urban centres had not ended but had declined sharply by the 1380s if not earlier. For the countryside, however, it was a different story [**196–203**].

I have also selected sources with an eye for diversity within genres. The most important source in reporting these uprisings is the chronicle, which varies in style and character from the single-line yearly entries of the medieval *Annal* to the Florentine diary chronicler, in which hardly a day goes by without detailed reportage.[13] The chronicler of the *Chronicon ms. ecclesiae Rotomagensis* left a mere ten words to report an uprising in Rouen in 1281 [**7**]. By contrast, the longest document in this collection is an anonymous Florentine diary, thought by some to be that of Niccolò Machiavelli's great-great grandfather.[14] Its daily reportage of the events of the revolt of the Ciompi runs to over 12,000 words and would have been nearly twice that length had I not made selections [**121**]. Moreover, by the 1380s the chronicle tradition in northern France began to evolve into the Renaissance history with the *Chronique du Religieux de Saint-Denys*, now known to be the work of the cantor of Saint-Denis, Michel Pintoin (1349–1421).[15] With often over-wrought, self-conscious rhetoric and numerous

---

13 On the transition from the annal to the chronicle, see Denys Hay, *Annalists and Historians: Western Historiography from the VIIIth to the XVIIIth Century* (London, 1977), ch. 3.

14 Robert Davidsohn, 'L'avo di Niccolò Machiavelli, cronista fiorentina', *Archivio Storico Italiano*, 93 (1935): 35–47.

15 On Pintoin's life and work, see most recently, Bernard Guenée, *L'Opinion publique à la fin du Moyen Age d'après la Chronique de Charles VI du Religieux de Saint-Denis* (Paris, 2002), p. 12 seq., and *Un roi et son histoire. Vingt études sur le règne de Charles VI et la Chronique du Religieux de Saint-Denis* (Paris, 1999), esp. pp. 33–78; and Gabrielle M. Spiegel, *The Chronicle Tradition of Saint-Denis: A Survey* (Brookline, MA, 1978), pp. 124–5. He was cantor of the abbey from 1411 to his death and travelled on several occasions to represent the abbey's interests such as in 1381 when he witnessed the revolutionary crowd kicking the head of the Archbishop of Canterbury through the streets of London [**136**].

INTRODUCTION 7

invented speeches – the modern historian Bernard Guenée crowns him as 'the new Sallust' – Pintoin probes the psychology of historical actors, including those in the otherwise faceless revolutionary crowd. His chronicle is the principal source for elaborating on the tax revolts of Paris and Rouen in 1381, the hammer men of Paris, the *Harelle* of Rouen in 1382, the end of the Tuchins in southern France, the town-gown conflict of 1404 which led to the king's demolition of the Palace of Savoy and the exile of his cousin, the count of Savoy, and the butchers' rebellion or Cabochiennes of 1413, which led to an extraordinary set of 258 governmental reforms [61, 132–41, 178, 182]. Despite problems of prejudice that can now readily be seen for instance in Jean le Bel's acid treatment of the Jacques of 1358 and other problems of interpretation that are not as transparent in other chronicles, the chronicle remains the most vivid and essential record for examining popular protest before the survival of large numbers of criminal archives in various regions of Western Europe during the fifteenth century or later.

* * *

This collection of translated documents is divided into six chapters. The first is a prelude to the post-plague rash of revolts. They comprise a wide range in the forms of popular protest before the Black Death, 1245 to 1347, which embrace heretical movements in city and countryside and the most sophisticated industrial revolts found in these documents – strikes, illegal associations of workers [2–4, 6, 9, 12, 13, 47], insurrections led by weavers and fullers [11, 13, 16, 18–20, 46], a general strike of all commoners [12], and a strike of rural labourers to achieve political ends [51].[16] Chapter II extends from 1348 to 1378, or just before the supposed cluster of revolts identified by Mollat and Wolff; it includes the Tuchins in the south of France and a ground-swell of revolts in Italy that reached their peak by the mid-1370s, when over sixty city-states in one year alone and 1,577 fortified villages [*buone castella*] rebelled against papal authority, their legates, and surrogate governments from Naples to Milan with the cry, 'Death to the pastors of the Church and long live the People'.[17]

16 After choosing the documents for this collection, I also found examples of workers' protests involving the breaking of tools and machines.
17 Among other sources, see *Cronaca malatestiana del secolo XIV (AA. 1295–1385)*, ed. Aldo Francesco Massèra, Rerum Italicarum Scriptores [hereafter, RIS], XV/2 (Bologna, 1922–24), p. 38; also, see [86].

Chapter III documents the best-known revolt in France before the French Revolution – the Jacquerie – which spread from the Beauvaisis as far east as Bar on France's frontier with the Holy Roman Empire but which lasted a mere two weeks, 28 May to 10 June 1358. Chapter IV focuses on the best known of the urban revolts of the fourteenth century, the Revolt of the Ciompi, which set off with a constitutional conflict in June 1378, and whose regime in alliance with minor-guild artisans lasted until mid-January 1382. Chapter V views the 'cluster of revolts' of northern France and Flanders, 1378 to 1382, concentrating on the most important of these, the tax revolts of the *Harelle* in Rouen and the *Maillotins* or hammer men in Paris. The chapter includes, however, documents of a less studied cluster of revolts in the cities and countryside of Languedoc – Montpellier, Lodève, Alès, Béziers, and Nîmes – that preceded the cluster of northern France. Chapter VI looks beyond the 'cluster' to the early fifteenth century; it includes a Parisian student conflict against the troops of the duke of Savoy in 1404, the Parisian butchers' revolt and reforms of 1413 (the *Cabochiennes*), a working-class politician, who over a long period of time strove to convince his fellow workers to oust the city councillors at Châlons-en-Champagne, and widespread peasant uprisings in the territories of Parma, Florence and Ferrara, which modern historians have passed over without any notice.

While intended principally for students, this collection also aims to stimulate new research on popular protest in the Middle Ages. During the last quarter of the twentieth century, the comparative study of popular revolt has become an academic growth industry for early-modern, modern, and contemporary European history as well as for the modern histories of Latin America, Asia, and Africa. Curiously, the same cannot be said for the Middle Ages. Our own tumultuous 1960s and 1970s stimulated new studies of the English Uprising of 1381 and the Revolt of the Ciompi, but only two monographs have thus far compared medieval revolt across national boundaries: Mollat and Wolff, *Ongles bleus* [translated as *Popular Revolutions of the Late Middle Ages*] and Hilton's *Bondmen Made Free*. Furthermore, the latter is restricted to peasants' movements and its comparative framework as valuable as it has been is restricted to two chapters and written largely as a prelude for understanding one revolt, the English Uprising of 1381.[18] Both books, moreover, are now over thirty years

---

18 E. B. Fryde: 'The financial policies of the royal governments and popular resistance to them in France and England, c. 1270–c.1420', *Revue belge de philologie et d'histoire*

old, and both were conceived against the backdrop of Marxist debates of the 1960s. Hilton emphasised class struggle and the evolution of class consciousness, even if he considered that class consciousness to have been a negative one nurtured by common hatred of the nobility. He further argued that the revolts of the late Middle Ages had significant and long-term consequences: at least one of them, the English Peasants' Revolt of 1381, resulted in nothing less than hastening the end of feudal servile relations in England.[19] By contrast, Mollat and Wolff saw the revolts of fourteenth-century Europe as the products of misery and desperation. When insurgents expressed any ideology at all, it was conservative, even reactionary, a desire to shore up an idealised status quo or to restore 'lost rights'. As Bernard Guenée, relying on their work, put it: 'When the insurgents did have ideas, these were as unremarkable as their feelings were violent'.[20] By their reckoning, all these movements failed, ending in brutal repression and demographic and economic decline for peasants and artisans over the long term.[21]

To be sure, these debates and other related questions – who comprised the crowds? who were the leaders? what were their ideologies? how did the repertoires of revolt evolve during the Middle Ages? – continue to cry out for new investigation, especially within comparative contexts. But, in the thirty years since these publications, history writing has marched on. Other questions, while not absolutely new, have emerged from the periphery to centre stage and have yet to be framed within comparative contexts for the Middle Ages. These include the methods of communication among insurgents across neighbourhoods, towns, regions, and even countries, the mobilisation of crowds, the ritual, theatres and rhetoric of revolt – insurgents' symbols, leaders' words.[22]

---

57 (1979): 824–60, compares differences between France and England but concentrates more on finance and government than on forms of rebellion. For a useful overview of the Marxist-non-Marxist debates on late medieval and early modern revolt, see Rinaldo Comba, 'Rivolte e ribellioni fra tre e quattrocento', in *La storia: I grandi problemi*, ed. Nicola Trafaglia and Massimo Firpo (Turin, 1988), vol. II, part 2, pp. 673–91.
19 R. Hilton, *Bondmen Made Free: Medieval Peasant Movements and the English Rising of 1381* (London, 1973). Also, see *idem*, *The Decline of Serfdom in Medieval England*, Studies in Economic History (London, 1969), pp. 32–43.
20 Guenée, *States and Rulers in Later Medieval Europe*, tr. Juliet Vale (Oxford, 1985); *L'Occident aux XIVe et XVe siècles* (Paris, 1971, 2nd edn 1981), pp. 194–5. Fourquin, *The Anatomy of Popular Rebellion*, pp. 24–5, has made similar claims.
21 See the conclusion of Mollat and Wolff, *Popular Revolutions*, pp. 271–317.
22 The theme of rituals of violence and revolt has had rich vein of research for the early

New comparative research on popular protest in the Middle Ages should reach beyond its own chronological boundaries and be of use to other scholars, especially historians and sociologists of modern and early-modern Europe, who have built models about crowds and popular protest for the 'pre-industrial' past to understand the distinctiveness of the modern and contemporary world. Thus, for Charles Tilly, 'the form' of popular protest changed from 'communal' to 'associational' in the middle of the nineteenth century. Before this turning point, popular revolts were 'localised, uncoordinated, dependent on the normal rhythms of congregations like marketing, churchgoing, or harvesting ...'[23] For George Rudé, the characteristic form of 'the pre-industrial crowd' was the food riot, which rose and fell with the ebb and flow of grain prices. As a result of this supposed focus on matters of the hearth, women, he claimed, largely composed the pre-industrial crowd; by contrast, modern industrial revolts became the business of men. Further, spontaneity characterised pre-industrial uprisings; their insurgents resorted to direct action, their leaders came, not from the crowd, but from outside it and usually from the upper classes, and their aims were backward-looking; organised strikes were almost unheard of until well into the nineteenth century.[24] While these studies are now several decades old, neither medievalists nor modernists have seriously questioned their suppositions about 'pre-industrial' collective action.[25] More recently, from the perspective

---

modern period; see for example, Natalie Z. Davis, 'The Rites of Violence: Religious Riot in Sixteenth-Century France', *Past & Present* 59 (1973): 51–91; and Yves-Marie Bercé, *Fête et révolte: des mentalités populaires du 16ᵉ au 18ᵉ siècle* (Paris, 1976).

23 C. Tilly, 'How Protest Modernized in France, 1845–1855', in *The Dimension of Quantitative Research*, ed. Aydelotte, Bogue, and Fogel (Princeton, 1972), p. 199. Tilly later developed other categories for social conflict such as 'competitive,' 'reactive,' and 'proactive action'. The third of these was similar to his earlier 'associational forms', characterised by strike action, which again comes about only by the mid-nineteenth century; see 'Hauptformen kollektiver Aktion in Westeuropa, 1500–1975', in *Geschichte und Gesellschaft* (1975): Heft 2: *Sozialer Protest*, ed. Richard Tilly (Göttingen, 1977): 154–63.

24 George Rudé, *Paris and London in the Eighteenth Century: Studies in Popular Protest* (London, 1974), p. 23.

25 William Reddy, 'The Textile Trades and the Language of the Crowd at Rouen, 1752–1871', *Past & Present*, 74 (1977): 62–89, criticised the Rudé-Tilly paradigm by arguing that the food riot was in its socio-economic context a form of strike, but he never questioned that the food riot was the predominant reason for revolt prior to the French Revolution. Also, see my criticisms based on Florentine revolts in *The Laboring Classes in Renaissance Florence* (New York, 1980), pp. 129–54.

of revolt in early-modern Europe, Yves-Marie Bercé has shored up these generalisations. He also has emphasised grain scarcity as the usual spark or precondition of pre-modern uprisings,[26] 'the traditional involvement' of women,[27] and leadership from the outside: clergy, mayors, or lords were the usual rebel rousers.[28] Finally, he has emphasised 'the fleeting character of popular enthusiam, the apparent spontaneity of their gatherings and the ease with which they dispersed'.[29]

These translated documents show a considerable disparity between the modernists' ideal-typical pre-industrial crowd and riot and the realities of popular protest in the Middle Ages. Strikes go back at least to the mid-thirteenth century and seem hardly exceptional in the textile centres or even small towns of Flanders and northern France [2-4, 6, 9, 12, 13]. A century later, on the eve of the Black Death, they arise in city-states of central Italy [46, 47, 51]. On the other hand, food riots are rare in the later Middle Ages, despite periodic shortages and famines before and after the Black Death, comprising the most widespread famines in European history – 1314–18 for the north of Europe and thirteen years later for the Mediterranean. Further, chronicles, letters of remission, and judicial lists of insurgents reveal little trace of women's involvement in popular protest, either as leaders or within the rank and file. While the heroic or incidental actions of women might have set off riots, women were not the backbone of these riots as perhaps they became in the early-modern or modern periods. The scream of a woman hawker of watercress in *Les Halles* at Paris sparked the revolt of the Hammer men, but it came not from any revolutionary plan or because she was a leader (even if by Buonaccorso Pitti's account her scream was 'Death to these taxes' [150]). Instead, she just happened to be the first one the

---

26 Y-M. Bercé, *Revolt and Revolution in Early Modern Europe: An Essay on the History of Political Violence*, tr. Joseph Bergin (Manchester, 1987 [1980]), pp. 100–2.

27 *Ibid.*, p. 107. Also, see his *History of Peasant Revolts: The Social Origins of Rebellion in Early Modern France*, tr. Amanda Whitmore (Cambridge, 1990), pp. 174–5, where he explains the predominance of women in French early-modern bread riots as 'biological' in its nature.

28 Bercé, *Revolt and Revolution in Early Modern Europe*, p. 64. Also, medievalists such as Fourquin, *The Anatomy of Popular Rebellion*, have maintained the same; see chapter 4: 'The Preponderance of Elites in Rebellions'.

29 *Ibid.*, p. 124. Similarly, in *History of Peasant Revolts*, p. 276, Bercé emphasises that 'people [of early-modern France] waited nostalgically for the return of a mythical past. They located this past in the reign of a king with a legendary reputation for justice'. See also Fourquin, *The Anatomy of Popular Rebellion*, pp. 24 and 78.

taxmen seized upon to levy the new subsidies on 1 March 1382 [**136**]. Similarly, a servant woman's scream was the cause of a blood bath of foreign ecclesiastic dignitaries and their servants in Viterbo on 5 September 1367. Outraged at the sight of the cardinal of Carcassonne's retainer washing the cardinal's 'pretty little dog' in the neighbourhood drinking fountain, she screamed and was immediately done in by the retainer's sword. This action then brought the artisan neighbourhood of Scarlano into the streets [**77**]. Further, a woman's scream in Florence's main square, the Piazza della Signoria, set off an abortive riot on 22 December 1379; the reason for her outburst, however, is not reported. Afterwards, the piazza was 'flooded' with men and children to observe the rebels' executions. Who they executed or whether any were women is left unreported, but 'this flood' led to no new insurrection [**121**].

The one exception in these documents may have been the revolt in Bruges against the French in 1302. An eyewitness to these events, the Florentine Giovanni Villani, reported that 'the women did even more than the men', at least when it came to murdering the French, 'slicing [them] to pieces like little tunny fish' [**13**]. Further, a chronicler of Arras reports that women climbed to their sun roofs and threw their chamber pots onto the French.[30] No doubt, sexless terms such as *populares, popolo, pobol, gens, minuti, menu peuple,* and *communeté* included and covered up women's appearances in otherwise near-faceless and sexless crowds;[31] yet to conclude that women were the principal participants would be to disregard the sources entirely. In the hundreds of names provided in these documents in letters of remission to rebels and lists of the condemned, executed, fined, and the absolved, not a single woman insurgent appears.

Further, it is difficult to point to a single riot even in the heat of the Jacquerie that arose spontaneously, that is, without any evidence of prior consultation, assemblies, and election of local leaders. And almost

---

30 *Chronique artésienne (1295–1304) et Chronique Touraisienne (1296–1314),* ed. Frantz Funck-Brentano (Paris, 1899), p. 42.

31 Christopher Dyer, 'The Social and Economic Background to the Rural Revolt of 1381', in *The English Rising of 1381,* ed. R. H. Hilton and T. H. Aston (Cambridge, 1984), pp. 9–42, finds a case during the English Peasants' Uprising of 1381 when a man from Essex had to pay an amercement of 12d., because his wife 'was a rebel and spoke badly of the affeerers' (p. 32). In 1339, after serfs from fifteen villages in the Laonnais 'allied and conspired' against the Dean and Chapter of the Cathedral of Laon, the royal commissioners executed nine men and 'branded many women'; Archives nationales, series JJ 75, f. 186r–187v, n. 316.

invariably these leaders emerged from the same social class as the insurgents; class outsiders, rebel rousers such as the crazed Florentine Lord Andrea degli Strozzi, who led or misled desperate and impoverished *plebes* in Florence 1343 [44, 45], were clearly exceptional and even in this case exaggerated by class-prejudiced chroniclers, covering up the successful actions of the artisan leader.[32]

Nor do these records show the pre-industrial insurrection inevitably failing, ending uniformly in brutal repression, bereft of short- or long-term gains. Instead, against the claims of historians and sociologists, peasant and artisan movements of the later Middle Ages often amounted to much more than 'a will-o'-the wisp, all glow and no substance';[33] 'the power struggle' did not always 'unfold exclusively within the very restricted world of the patriciate'.[34] Nor is it true that 'an uprising only stood a chance of success if it attracted enough of the nobility to ensure its military capacity and of the bourgeoisie to have the support of town walls' as Bercé asserts.[35] Against the claims of modernists, these subaltern forces could influence politics and the contours of state development.[36]

To take only one example: in the early 1380s in Paris and Rouen, ruling elites, even as exalted and powerful as the kings of France, were forced to negotiate with 'the most vile sort', to rethink their tax policies and for a time to abandon them altogether [132, 133, 135, 136, 152]. The documents that follow illustrate many other examples of artisans, workers, and peasants through various forms of protest including armed rebellion successfully challenging and changing their legal, social,

32 After selecting the documents for this collection, I discovered an account from a contemporary chronicler of Pistoia, who reports that after Andrea's embarrassed kinsmen had caught, caged, and dumped him safely beyond the borders of the Florentine state, a dyer named Corazza successfully led a force of 1,300 workers in the wool industry and marched on the Palace of the Priors. The priors allowed them to enter and from fear promised them whatever they wished; *Storie Pistoresi [MCCC-MCCCXLVIII]*, ed. Silvio Adrasto Barbi, RIS, XI/V (Città di Castello, 1907), p. 196. I know of no historian who cites this report.

33 Lauro Martines, *Power and Imagination: City-States in Renaissance Italy* (New York, 1979), p.59.

34 Sergio Bertelli, 'Oligarchies et gouvernement dans la ville de la Renaissance', *Social Science: Information sur les sciences sociales*, 15 (1976): 623.

35 Bercé, *Revolt and Revolution*, p. 126.

36 Charles Tilly, 'Entanglements of European Cities and States', in *Cities and the Rise of States in Europe, A.D. 1000 to 1800*, ed. Charles Tilly and Wim Blockmans (Boulder, Co., 1994), p. 26. For my counter-argument with regard to late-fourteenth- and fifteenth-century Florence, see my *Creating the Florentine State: Peasants and Rebellion, 1348–1434* (Cambridge, 1999), pp. 5–7.

and material conditions. Far from inevitably recording defeat and bloody repression, many of these documents evince that such challenges could topple governments, end with redrafted constitutions, and even overturn social hierarchies: weavers, fullers, carders, and other *minuti*, 'vile plebes' 'those of little wealth' or 'those without underpants' grabbed the reins of power, banished old oligarchs and aristocrats from their cities and territories, and established new governments. The 'three orders' of medieval society were neither so indelible nor so inflexible as medieval ideologues or present-day historians sometimes wish us to believe.

I: BEFORE THE BLACK DEATH, 1245-1348

The social movements and rebellions over the hundred-year period preceding the Black Death show great diversity but few discernible trends. The earliest of these protests were as 'modern' as any on record in the West until the nineteenth century. In northern France and Flanders, abundant evidence of workingmen's associations, assemblies, and strikes appears in city ordinances, court cases, and chronicles by the mid-thirteenth century [2-4, 9, 12], and riots comprised of, organised, and led by textile workers were commonplace here before the Black Death [5, 6, 8, 16, 19]. Nor did such activity emerge only in important textile centres such as Douai, Tournai, Bruges, and Ghent; it was also notable in provincial market towns such as Clermont-en-Beauvaisis and satellite towns such as Poperinge outside Ypres. Moreover, the records of northern France and Flanders show 'those of little wealth' revolting against their city oligarchies and mayors [9-13, 20], against changes in monetary policy and high rents [14], against the privileges and impositions of the French crown [10, 12, 13, 18, 19], and, above all, against the introduction of new taxes [9, 10, 12, 13, 15, 18, 20, 21]. Along with this remarkable array of urban revolts, Flanders witnessed the largest and most widespread peasant revolts before the German Bundschuh at the beginning of the sixteenth century or the German Peasants' War of 1524-25. But in Flanders the revolts of 1297-1302 and 1323-28 [11-13 and 18-20] lasted longer, won more battles, and were better integrated and coordinated with urban insurgency among the lower classes than any revolt seen two hundred years later in German-speaking areas.[1] Curiously, this rich vein of popular protest declined momentarily with the famines of 1314-18.[2]

---

[1] The literature on the German Peasants' War of the sixteenth century is vast; for a good introduction, see Peter Blickle, *The Revolution of 1525: The German Peasants' War from a New Perspective*, tr. Thomas Brady, Jr. and H. C. Erik Midelfort (Baltimore, 1981).

[2] The protests against Philippe le Bel's attempts to raise new taxes to send an army to Flanders in 1314 had no connections with grain shortages or famine and was fought out in assemblies led by the estates general rather than in the streets by the poor; see André Artonne, *Le mouvement de 1314 et les chartes provinciales de 1315*, in *Bibliothèque de la faculté des lettres de l'université de Paris*, XXIX (Paris, 1912).

Against expectations highlighted by modern historical and sociological models of 'the pre-industrial riot', these famines did not spark a single revolt that I have found in northern France or Flanders, even though these were among the worst-hit areas in Europe.[3]

Until the Black Death, no pan-European pattern in the timing and clustering of revolts can be detected. In the second half of the thirteenth and early fourteenth centuries, the revolts in central and northern Italy were different from those of Flanders; nothing akin to the Flemish strikes or revolts led and staffed by textile workers were seen in Italy – not even in places such as Florence with well-developed cloth industries and large numbers of workers without guild recognition or status as citizens. The major contenders of class struggle in the south, the *primo popolo*, pitched the interests of merchants and shopkeepers against landed and mercantile aristocracies including those of local bishops [**23, 25, 28, 29, 35, 40, 41, 50**]. As the documents reveal, these revolts often succeeded in Florence, Pisa, Genoa, Savona, and Ancona. Other examples from Siena, Perugia, Bologna, Rome, and even cities in the south such as Naples can also be readily documented. Their successes, moreover, meant more than simply one elite replacing another; they radically reshaped city-state constitutions and ushered into power new social classes.

Because of the rarity of judicial records listing insurgents by occupation, it is difficult to know exactly who this *popolo* or 'people' was. However, the rebel leaders of the *popolo*, men like the wealthy Florentine major guildsman Giano della Bella, were hardly commoners [**28–9**] and were a world apart from the self-taught Flemish rebel leaders from the ranks of workers and peasants as was Peter the King who in 1301 organised thousands of textile workers and peasants over vast territories to oppose patrician regimes and the king of France. Nonetheless, the establishment of neighbourhood militias with their standards equally distributed [**23**] and the readiness of commoners [*popolo minuto*] to arm themselves and defend the rule of the *popolo* when aristocrats threatened, strongly suggest that shopkeepers and skilled artisans with guild recognition were not the only social forces behind these movements. Instead, textile workers identified their interests with the merchant-artisan governments of the *popolo* at least through the thirteenth century, and outside major industrial centres such as Florence, for longer [**41**].

3 See William C. Jordan, *The Great Famine: Northern Europe in the Early Fourteenth Century* (Princeton, 1996).

In the pre-Black-Death fourteenth century, popular protest in Italy, on the one hand, and northern France and Flanders, on the other, continued to proceed along different tracks. While revolts of textile workers and other commoners began to subside after the massive waves of peasant and artisan revolts 1323 to 1328, they began to rise in the south. Butchers and blacksmiths protested the decisions of the military elites and war policy in Siena, seriously challenging the rule of the oligarchy of the Nine in 1318 [33]. Fistfights and martial arts competitions led to city-wide rioting in Siena in 1324 and again threatened the stability of the Nine [36]. Workers in Florence formed clubs and held street parties in Florence to the great chagrin of their social betters in 1333 [39]. Florentine workers received their own banners and governmental responsibilities in 1342–43 [42, 43]. And in 1343 a member of the Florentine elite ignited discontent among desperate wool workers, rousing them to action [44, 45].

Only in 1343, however, when the fullers of Florence revolted [46], did workers' protests in Florence or Siena begin to approach the sophistication of strikes and worker-led insurrections aimed at toppling governments seen much earlier in northern France and Flanders.[4] Two years later, Ciuto Brandini of Florence organised unions or 'fraternities' of Florentine textile workers with strike funds [47]. In 1346, textile workers and other commoners in Siena united with the aristocratic Tolomei family and seriously threatened the control of Siena's oligarchy – the Nine – which had ruled this city longer than any government of any city-state in Italian history [48, 49]. And a year later, farm workers in the *contado* of Florence[5] staged their own strike – the only rural strike found in these documents. However, again unlike the strikes and workers' revolts of Flanders in the thirteenth century, those of Tuscany took place against a backdrop of scarcity and famine from 1343 to 1347 [43, 45, 46, 48]. Yet none of these Tuscan revolts took the form of a food riot.

---

4 Also see Introduction, note 32, on the protest staged by the dyer Corazza but not reported by any Florentine chronicle or modern historian.

5 The territory beyond the city walls of Florence was divided into the *contado* and *distretto*. The *contado* was for the most part the original countryside around Florence before it began conquering previously independent city-states with their own belts of countryside. The two were subjected to different laws and measures of taxation. For a more detailed discussion of the Florentine territory and its historical development, see Cohn, *Creating the Florentine State*, pp. pp. 7–8, 15–16, 178, and 198–9.

For any inkling of grain riots before the Black Death one has to turn to the Mediterranean years of dearth in the late 1320s. While famines failed to trigger a single riot in the north (that I have so far found), those of central and northern Italy fifteen years later sparked local uprisings in Siena, Rome, and elsewhere [37]. These were not, however, on a large scale; nor do they appear to have spread beyond city walls into the more desperate and destitute zones of the countryside. Further, unlike the earlier industrial revolts in Flanders or the revolts of the *popolo* in Italian cities, they did not topple a single regime (although at Rome it resulted in a senator leaving office [37]). Finally, these riots were not inevitable, as illustrated by their avoidance in Florence because of its enlightened economic policy of grain rationing and subsidies [38].

For Italy the study of late medieval popular protest has focused almost exclusively on Tuscany, especially Florence and Siena. Nonetheless, popular assemblies, tax riots, and armed struggles of commoners to resist and limit the excesses and arrogance of local aristocracies or other ruling elites can be found elsewhere from Venice to the toe of Calabria [24, 27, 52, 54, 55]. Nor were these conflicts inevitable failures, passing episodes that had no bearing on governmental decisions; instead they could result in negotiated settlements that favoured the lower orders and change law and tax policy as in the Kingdom of Naples in the period of the Angevin rule of Robert [the many examples in 52], the tax revolt in Venice of 1266 [24], and the victory of Bologna's 'people without underpants' in 1289 [27] – the prototype of the expression *sans-culottes* five hundred years later.

Finally, clerical-led protests or those clearly inspired by religious belief are more common and easily spotted during the pre-plague period than in the century following the Black Death. For the most part, these heretical movements spread and established their communities outside cities and in opposition to them [1, 17]. But revolts in early-fourteenth-century Carcassonne were exceptional; here a heretical movement led by clerics supported the city's opposition to impositions forced on it by church and the crown [22].

Flanders and Northern France

1 A crusade of shepherds and many children, 1251

Guillaume de Nangis, *Chronique latine de Guillaume de Nangis de 1113 à 1300 avec les continuations de cette de 1300 à 1368*, ed. H. Geraud, *Société de l'histoire de France* [hereafter *SHF*] (Paris, 1843), vol. I, 207–8. Guillaume was a monk at the Abbey of Saint-Denis during the reigns of Saint Louis and Philip III. His chronicle of France from 1113 to 1300 was connected with the great enterprise of chroniclers at the Abbey of Saint-Denis, beginning with Primat in 1274 but relying on manuscripts in the monastery that reached back to the Carolingian period and that to a certain extent was inspired and guided by Abbé Suger (abbot of Saint-Denis from 1122 to 1151).[6] It would become known as the official chronicle of the French kings, the *Grandes Chroniques de France*. Several chroniclers continued and added to Guillaume's work through the fourteenth century such as Richard Lescot and his continuators [96], the Saint-Denis chroniclers of the reigns of John II and Charles V [95], and allegedly the Carmelite friar from the Beauvaisis Jean de Venette, although who exactly this Jean de Venette may have been is now contested [see 97].

[1251] In the kingdom of France, shepherds and many children went on a crusade; some pretended to have visions of angels and to perform miracles, claiming God had sent them to avenge the kingdom of France for Louis [IX].[7] Among them were those who called themselves masters, who like bishops blessed with holy water and made and dissolved marriages as it pleased them even in this city of Paris. They committed many crimes, murdering monks, clerics, and the laity, since no one could stop them. They selected and deselected as crusaders whoever they liked. Indeed, their leader and master, whom they called the master of Hungary, killed a number of clerics while he marched through Orléans with great pomp and committed many evil deeds in Berry, destroying the books of the Jews and unjustly plundering their property. From Berry he entered villages called Morthomiers and Villeneuve above Caro,[8] where the duke of Berry's men killed him. Because of these crusaders' crimes, many were killed and hanged in various places. Then they all scattered, vanishing like smoke.

6 See Spiegel, *The Chronicle Tradition of Saint-Denis*, pp. 39–40.

7 Louis IX (1215–70), son of Louis VIII and Blanche of Castile, canonised in 1297, led two crusades against the Turcomans in 1248–49 and 1270; he died of 'plague' or 'fevers' while encamped at Tunis on the eighth crusade.

8 These villages are several kilometres southwest of Bourges, near the river Cher.

2 Legislation against strikes in Douai, 1245

Recueil des documents relatifs à l'histoire de l'industrie drapière en Flandre, ed. Georges Espinas and Henri Pirenne, vol. II (Brussels, 1909), p. 22: 1245–47: Douai: Document no. 218. Interdiction of the town council prohibiting revolts and coalitions of artisans. [Archives Municipales de Douai, document now lost].

1. It is proclaimed that no one should be so arrogant in this city, whether a bourgeois or not, an officer or a lowly servant girl, as to go on strike [*face takehan*];[9] and whoever should do so, shall be fined 60 pounds and banished from the city for a year and a day. And if no one has gone on strike, the one who made the denunciation shall be fined 60 pounds and be banished from the city for a year and a day.

2. And whoever should organise an assembly against [the laws of] the city, no matter what his trade, shall be subject to these same penalties.

In the year 1245, the month of January.

3 Strikes and disturbances to work in Douai, 1266

Ibid., II, p. 109, document no. 259. Decree of the aldermen [*ban échevinal*] forbidding any complicity with individuals who disrupt work [Archives Municipales de Douai, Reg. AA 94 fol. 21].

And if a bourgeois or anyone else forms an association with, or offers armed force, aid, or counsel to, any people who have gone on strike [*takehan*] or have assembled against the laws of the city or have refused to work or have disrupted the work of any trade whatever, he shall be fined 50 pounds and banished from the city for a year.

1266, Sunday before the feast day of the Magdalene [18 July].

4 Sentences against cloth workers on strike in Douai, 1280

Ibid., II, pp. 141–3. no. 289; Archives Municipales de Douai, FF 88, fols 53–4. The years 1279–80 ushered in a wave of rebellion across much of Flanders, in Tournai, Damme, St. Omer, Douai, Ypres, Poperinge, Ghent, and Bruges. For the most part, artisans and workers in the cloth industry led these revolts.

In 1280, on the Wednesday [4 December] before the feast of Saint

---

9 On the *takehan* and industrial unrest in Douai, see Pirenne, *Histoire de Belgique*, I, p. 229; and idem, *Les Anciennes démocraties*, p. 164.

BEFORE THE BLACK DEATH 21

Nicholas, justice was carried out in this town with the decapitation of Haneton Lauwier, Jehan Boucery, and Collart Caullet, weavers, because of the injuries they inflicted on the aldermen [*eschevins*] and the city council of this city, against the laws of this city, which have been recently passed.

Jehans Posteaux,
Jeans Ermenfrois from Arras

These two cloth-cutters have been banished forever on pain of decapitation, because they prevented and disrupted work in this city, violating the laws and customs of this city. On the feast of Saint Lucy [15 December] 1280.

5 Inquest at Poperinge,[10] after the rebellion of textile workers in Ypres (Ieper), 3 April 1280

Ibid., III, 102–9, no. 626; Ghent, Archives de l'État, Poperinge. Below is one of fifty-one entries of charges brought against several hundred workers. Of those identified by occupation almost all were either weavers or fullers. Before 1302 these workers had no representation in municipal governments in Flanders.

9. Stalins the son of Rikes swore that Jehan Meurins, Crestians Lievins, Pieres Coke, Willaumes Abejois, Hanekins, son of Stasin le Scheppre, Hankens Lievins, weaver, Hanins Wervraeme, Colins Cassekin, Piete Cassekin, Hanins Cassekin, Coppin de Commines were there [at the scene of the revolt]. And he says that Henris Oudewine took up arms and sent men to Ypres and borrowed weapons from his neighbours to give them to Jehan Oudewin, his brother, who dispatched them.

6 The Count of Flanders fines the drapers[11] after the revolt of textile workers known as the Cockeruelle, Ypres, 1281

Ibid., III, 686, no. 851; letter of Guy of Dampierre, count of Flanders,[12] acknowledging receipt of a 2,400 pound fine levied against the drapers;

---

10 According to Nicholas, *Medieval Flanders*, p. 184, 'Virtually the entire population of Poperinge consisted of textile artisans working for employers in Ypres. The insurrection was less a civil struggle within Ypres than a revolt of Poperinge against Ypres'.

11 The drapers were small operators, who gave work to cloth workers but were not members of the merchant oligarchy of Ypres; see Nicholas, *Medieval Flanders*, p. 183.

12 Guy was count of Flanders from the abdication of his mother, the Countess Margaret, in 1278 to his death in 1305. On the period of Guy's rule, see Nicholas, *Medieval Flanders*, ch. 8.

Archives Départementales du Nord, 4e Cartulaire de Flandre, fol. 57v, 11 October 1281.

We, Guy, count of Flanders, make it known to all ... concerning the struggle that has taken place in the city of Ypres between the aldermen and the city council, on the one hand, and the common people of the trades, on the other:[13] the drapers, masters of the Temple,[14] who were involved in the crimes of our city of Ypres and have come before our courts of justice in regard to the conflict mentioned above, and before us have promised to fulfil the conditions set by us and which we have ordered ... the drapers have among other things agreed to pay, and have paid, 2,400 pounds in the money of Flanders. And as they have paid these 2,400 pounds we acknowledge this payment and acquit them of the aforementioned crime ...

As attested in these sealed letters affirmed with our seal at Winendale,[15] in the year of Our Lord 1281, the Saturday after the feast of Saint-Denis [11 October].

7   Revolt against the mayor and city council of Rouen in 1281

A. Giry, *Les etablissements de Rouen: Etudes sur l'histoire des institutions municipales* (Paris, 1883), I, 41, cited from the *Chronicon ms. ecclesiae Rotomagensis*. As the document below attests, the wave of revolts 1279–1281 was not confined to Flanders.

[1281] At the bridge, the *plebes* of this city murdered the city's mayor.

8   Weavers' revolt in Tournai, 1281

Chronica Aegidii li Muisis, in *Corpus Chronicorum Flandriae*, ed. De Smet vol. 2 (Brussels, 1841), p. 170. Poet and chronicler, Gilles Li Muisis (1272–1352) was abbot of the Benedictine abbey of Saint-Martin in Tournai.

The year 1281: most of the weavers of the city conspired against the officials [*rectores*] of Tournai; some were captured, and one Roussian called Li Kos was drawn between horses and hanged.

---

13 A previous letter of Count Guy (1 April 1281, *ibid.*, pp. 679–85, no. 849) indicated the occupations of these condemned workers and craftsmen as 'weavers, fullers, wool beaters, and their adherents'.

14 The name of their guild.

15 The village of the count's palace, near Torhout in the region of Bruges.

9   Legislation against strikes for higher wages; argument for
    the swift repression of revolts; advice against overtaxing
    the poor, Clermont-en-Beauvaisis, c. 1283

The Coutumes de Beauvaisis of Philippe de Beaumanoir, tr. and ed. F. R. P. Akehurst (Philadephia, 1992), p. 314. Philippe de Beaumanoir was the chief royal officer [*bailli*] of the Beauvaisis. His *Coutumes* in seventy chapters and over a thousand pages is one of the chief works of juridical commentary for the late thirteenth century.

Conspiracy against the common good is when some kind of workers promise or agree or contract that they will not work for as low wages as they used to, but they increase the price on their own authority and agree that they will not work for less, and impose threats and punishments [*peine*] on their fellows who will not join their conspiracy. And if they were permitted to do this, it would be against the common law, and good deals for labour would never be struck, for those of each trade would try to obtain greater pay than reason and the common good [*li communs*][16] allow the work to be done for. And for this reason, as soon as the lord or other lords detect such conspiracies, they should arrest all those who have assented to such conspiracies, and keep them in strict confinement for a long term; and when they have suffered a long time in prison, each person can be fined sixty sous.[17]

Argument for the swift repression of revolts by commoners, *ibid.*, pp. 314–15:

Another kind of conspiracy has been seen many times, by which many towns have been destroyed and many lords shamed and despoiled, for example, when the common people of some town or several towns conspire against their lord by using force against him, or by taking his property by force, or by raising their hands wickedly against their lord or his men. Therefore as soon as the lord notices that such a conspiracy has begun, he should arrest them by force ...

Advice against overtaxing the poor, Clermont-en-Beauvaisis, c. 1283; *ibid.*, p. 546:

---

16 Perhaps 'custom' would be a better translation here.
17 A sous was a shilling or soldo.

Many disagreements arise in communes because of their communal tax assessments [*tailles*],[18] for it often happens that the rich who are administrators of the business of the town estimate the taxes of themselves and their relatives lower than they should, and reduce the taxes [*deportent*] of other rich men so that they in turn will have theirs reduced, and thus all of the expense falls on to the mass [*communeté*] of the poor people. And for this reason many crimes have been committed, because the poor did not want to put up with it but they did not know the proper way to pursue their rights except by attacking them [the rich]. And some of these have been killed by the other and the towns damaged [*mal menees*] by these dishonest tax assessors. Therefore when the lord of the town sees a disagreement begin he should intervene and tell the common people that he will set their taxes properly, and for the rich also. And then he should assess the tax in his town by an honest inquiry, the rich as well as the poor, each person according to his estate, and according to the need of the town for the tax to be great or small; and then he should force each person to pay what he has been assessed; and afterwards he should have what was collected by the assessment paid where there is the greatest need, for the benefit of the town; and by doing this the disagreement and the town can be quieted.

10 Revolt of commoners against their masters and the officials of the king, Rouen, 1291

Guillaume de Nangis, *Chronique*, vol. I, p. 282. [1292]

At Rouen the commoners [*minor populus*] rose up against the magistrates of the exchequer and the king's officers because of the evil way they had been squeezed for taxes beyond measure; they waged war against the officers in the city's castle, destroyed the house where the taxes were collected, and threw the money out into the city's squares. But finally the mayor and bourgeois of the city put an end to it, hanging very many of the insurgents and putting many others in various royal prisons.[19]

---

18 Various taxes were called *tailles*; the one described here is clearly a kind of city tax.
19 *Chronicon Girardi de Fracheto et anonyma ejusdem operis continuatio* in *Recueil des historiens de France*, XXI, ed. J. D. Guigniaut and N. De Wailly (Paris, 1855), p. 10, dates this revolt in 1292.

11 Revolt in Flanders of the people of little wealth, 1297

Chronique des Pays-Bas, de France, etc. in *Corpus Chronicorum Flandriae*, ed. J.-J. de Smet, vol. III (Brussels, 1856), pp. 121–2. The recently crowned king of France Philip IV or le Bel, the Fair (1285–1314) desired to bring Flanders under French control, even to annex it. His aggressive politics would culminate in wide-spread insurrections across Flanders from 1302 to 1304, involving major Flemish cities and much of the countryside. By 9 January 1297 the privileges and governance of the count, Guy of Dampierre, had been undermined. He renounced his homage to the king of France and allied himself with Edward I of England. Most of the nobles followed his lead but Philip managed to divide the cities with most of the patricians siding with the French, the party of the Lilies (the fleur-de-lis). Complying with the demands of the king's lieutenant, James of Saint-Pol, they imposed heavy consumption taxes on their commoners in the cities and the surrounding countryside. By May 1300, Philip had absorbed Flanders into the royal domain and had imprisoned Guy and his sons in France.[20]

[1297] While this James [de Saint-Pol,[21] governor of Flanders appointed by the king of France] was in Paris, at least 10,000 men, all of them people of little wealth [*gens de petitte chavanche*], assembled in the city of Bruges and elected a butcher named Jehan Biede [*Bride*][22] as their captain. They went and attacked the castle of Malle. When those inside saw that they could not defend it against such a large force, they handed it over to save their lives. But once the Flemings got inside, they did not keep their word or behave properly; instead, they killed all the French soldiers they found inside and chopped off the heads of the rich bourgeois who sided with James of Saint-Pol. Then they divided up equally the booty found inside the castle and returned to Bruges. They made a weaver named Peter their king. He was clever and skilled in the arts of war, because in his youth he had served in the military. Everyone promised to obey him as their lord until they could bring back Count Guy [of Dampierre] or one of his sons.[23]

20 For the background to the revolt of 1302, see Nicholas, *Medieval Flanders*, pp. 187–92.
21 James de Saint-Pol, appointed by Philip (IV) the Fair, king of France, as his lieutenant in Flanders, was a Flemish nobleman also known as Jacques de Châtillon. The county of St. Pol was then separate from Flanders to the south of Flanders in the region of Pays-de-Calais. His appointment seriously undermined the privileges and authority of the count.
22 Also Jan Breidel.
23 Unlike the *Annales Gandenses*, the chronicle of Giovanni Villani, and other accounts, this chronicler saw the commoners' choice of Peter the King as a temporary leader until the return of the count of Flanders or his sons. After the initial revolt in

12 Revolt in Bruges and Ghent against the patricians and taxes, 1301

Annales Gandenses, ed. Hilda Johnstone (London, 1951), pp. 16–18. [The translation is my own.]

The following winter [1301], while John, count of Namur, his brother Guy, the count's sons, along with William of Jülich, provost of Maestricht, son of their sister, were brooding over the cruel and unjust imprisonment of their father and brothers, they plotted and held secret meetings with some of their Flemish friends and sent secret messengers and letters to some of the rebellious commoners of Flanders, who wished to recover the wealthy lands of their ancestors. Around mid-winter, they advised Peter called the King to return with his followers to Bruges. He made a powerful impression on the weavers, fullers, and other commoners, attracting them by his eloquence, winning them over with smooth and sweet words. As a result, the king's chief officer [*Bailivus*],[24] the aldermen, and the patricians of Bruges dared not to touch him or his associates. Towards the end of winter, when spring was breaking, the envoys from Bruges were unable to conclude their law suit in the king's court against the count of Saint-Pol and his brother; nor could they recover their liberties and privileges; they returned angrily and indignantly to Flanders. Peter the King gained a great hold over the commoners of Bruges, and from the ramparts he threatened and publicly forbade any to obey James of Saint-Pol's orders to destroy the Bruges' fortifications and fill in its ditch. When this became known, the king's chief officer, his judge, the aldermen, and many of the patricians feared for their lives and skipped town, leaving Peter and his friends almost as the town's lords.

While matters stood like this at Bruges, around mid-March rioting [*commotio*] broke out in Ghent, which greatly pleased and encouraged those of Bruges. The aldermen and patricians decided that the debts they had incurred to buy gifts for the king should be paid from the

---

Bruges by Breidel and Coninck, the count's sons who were not imprisoned by Philip soon 'restored a skeletal administration in Flanders around which the anti-French forces could rally'; see Nicholas, *Medieval Flanders*, p. 192.

24 *Bailivus* is not the equivalent of bailiff in English; instead it was the highest royal officer of a region, 'the representative of the king, or better, the king himself (in a region); where *le bailli* is, there is the king'; Guenée, *Tribunaux et gens de justice dans le bailliage de Senlis à la fin du Moyen Age (vers 1380–vers 1550)* (Paris, 1963), p. 144.

above-mentioned taxes.[25] On the first Sunday of Lent [11 March 1302], they announced publicly on behalf of James of Saint-Pol and with the chief officer present, that this tax, which the king had annulled to please the commoners, should continue to be charged at the same rate. When the commoners heard about it, they became furious, protesting and grumbling, especially since it was declared that anyone who opposed the edict would be banished from the town and country or beheaded. Thus the commoners assembled around dusk and agreed that no one would go to work the next day; instead, they would remain idle and discuss how to get rid of this tax. When the king's chief officer, the aldermen, and the patricians heard this, they held a council, and at dawn some eight hundred of them took up arms and marched in troops of thirty, forty, or fifty through the streets and squares, determined to capture or kill any commoners who refused to work. When the commoners saw that the patricians had armed and heard the insults of some, they remained silent for a while, and many went back to work. But about the time of the third bell on the second day, the day after this mid-Lent Sunday, several commoners secretly armed themselves, took their banners and battle standards, and processed in public. By beating [metal] bowls, since they dared not use the belfry, they roused all the commoners; all left work and took up arms. They charged against the patricians, began to fight, and won, forcing the chief officer, the aldermen, and many others, about six hundred of them, to flee to the castle near [the church of] Sainte-Pharaïlde, which had once belonged to the count. The rest [of the patricians] returned home. The commoners, thus enraged, roused, and united, attacked this castle with crossbowmen on every side; by noon they had taken it. Before the patricians had surrendered, two aldermen and eleven others had been killed and about a hundred gravely wounded. They compelled the rest, along with the chief officer, to swear fidelity to them; otherwise they would have killed them all.

13 An Italian's account of the revolt of Bruges, 1299–1302

Giovanni Villani, *Nuova Cronica*, ed. Giuseppe Porta, 3 vols. (Parma, 1990–91), II: Book Nine, chapter LV, pp. 88–90. Giovanni Villani was born around 1276 and died in the Black Death of 1348. He was the major chronicler of medieval

---

25 Excise taxes imposed on commodities, principally beer, first levied by King Philip IV of France on Bruges and Ghent. Those of Ghent called it 'the evil money'; those of Bruges, 'the assize'; see *Annales Gandenses*, p. 12.

Florence and one of the most important and prolific of late medieval Italy. He was a member of the upper-class guild of bankers (*Arte del Cambio*) and in 1300 became a partner of the large and prestigious firm of the Peruzzi – the second largest bank in Florence. From 1302 to 1307 he worked for the firm in Flanders. In 1316, 1317, 1321, 1322, and 1328 he was elected as a prior in the Florentine Signoria – the highest office of the land. He began his chronicle in 1300, which he kept diligently until his death from the plague.[26]

How the lower classes [*popolo minuto*][27] of Bruges rebelled [*si rubellò*] against the king of France and killed the French.

As we left off in the last chapter, the king of France possessed complete control over the government of Flanders, and the count [of Flanders][28] and two of his sons were in the king's prison in 1299. And the king left the country under the control of his men and his officers [*balii*]. They [the king's officers] should have considered a petition that the lower artisans [*artefici minuti*] of Bruges – weavers and fullers of cloth, butchers, cobblers, and others – had sent to the king to adjust their wages to fairer levels and to cut their land taxes, which were intolerable. But the King neither heard their petition nor adjusted the artisans' wages. Instead, because of the pleas of the rich bourgeoisie and their bribes, the king's officers imprisoned the leaders of these artisans and of the lower classes [*popolo minuto*] of Bruges. Prominent among them were Peter the King, a weaver, and Jean Bride, a butcher,[29] along with more than thirty of the most important people from these crafts and guilds. I note that this Peter the King was the leader and rabble-rouser of the commoners. Because of his boldness he had been nicknamed Peter the King, which is Connicheroi in Flemish [Peter van Coninc], that is, Peter the King. This Peter was a poor man, a weaver of cloth, small in stature, lean, blind in one eye, and more than sixty years old. He knew neither French nor Latin but in Flemish spoke better, more ardently and fluently than anyone in Flanders. And by his speeches he moved the entire country towards

---

26 Louis Green, *Chronicle into History: An Essay on the Interpretation of History in Florentine Fourteenth-century Chronicles* (Cambridge, 1972), pp. 9–12.

27 Giovanni Villani saw these artisans and wage-earners through the institutional prism of Florence, where such workers in the cloth industry were banned from possessing their own guilds and thus were not recognized by the commune as citizens; see Cohn, *The Laboring Classes in Renaissance Florence*; and Alessandro Stella, *La révolte des Ciompi: les hommes, les lieux, le travail* (Paris, 1993), and chapter 4 below.

28 Guy of Dampierre.

29 Giambrida in Villani's Italian; Jehan Biede [Bride]; see document [11].

the momentous things that followed. And thus it is right to preserve his memory. The *popolo minuto* of Bruges were won over by him and his comrades; they charged through the country and attacked the *borgo*, that is, the castle where the judges and the rectors of the country resided. The artisans killed some of the bourgeois and forcefully imprisoned their leaders. With this, a truce was reached and the dispute was brought before the king in Paris. The case lasted a good year. In the end, because the rich bourgeois of Flanders spread bribes around the king's court, the sentence went against the lower classes. When the news reached Bruges, armed rioting began all over again. But for fear of the soldiers and the rich bourgeois, they left Bruges and went to the town of Damme, three miles away,[30] where they charged through the streets, killing the chief officer and the king's sergeants. They robbed the rich bourgeois of the city, murdering some of them. Afterwards, desperate and enraged, they went to the town of Assebroek[31] where they did much the same. Then they went to a manor or court called Male, three miles outside Bruges, where the chief officer of Bruges and sixty of the king's sergeants were inside the walls. They seized this fortress by force and without mercy or accepting ransoms slaughtered countless Frenchmen inside. Seeing the force of the *popolo minuto* in action and on the rise, the rich bourgeois of Bruges feared for their lives and their country. Immediately, they sent for help from France. The king responded promptly by sending James of Saint-Pol, the crown's highest officer in Flanders, 1,500 cavalry and a large number of sergeants. On reaching Bruges, they seized and garrisoned the palaces of the main square, which threw Bruges into a state of high alert and tension. With the armed forces and the boldness of the *popolo minuto* on the increase, it pleased God to wash away the rich bourgeois' sins of arrogance and avarice and to crush the pride of the French; the craftsmen and *popolo minuto* who had remained in Bruges swore allegiance [to one another] and recklessly conspired to murder the French and the rich bourgeoisie. They sent for their comrades who had fled to Damme and Asserbroek, along with their leaders and masters, Peter the King and Jean Bride. Once they returned to Bruges, their lust for victory grew bolder, and the murder of the French began. With flags raised, men and women alike came into Bruges on the night of [...] as planned.

30 To the northeast of Bruges, about 8 kilometres [hereafter, km].
31 Andiburgo in Villani's Italian, presently a suburb of Bruges, about 4 km southeast of the city.

They were able to enter, even though the king had dug ditches and had battened down the gates of Bruges. Arriving in the city, these [insurgents] gave those inside [the city walls] the word, yelling out in Flemish, which the French could not understand, 'Long live the Commune and death to the French'.[32] They then barricaded the streets throughout the city. With this began the painful affliction [*pestilenzia*] and death of the French. No Fleming would harbour a Frenchman in his house: either he would kill him or take him captive to the covered market [*Alle*], where the commune was assembled and armed. Once the captives arrived, they were killed, sliced to pieces like little tunny fish. Seeing the rioting, the French armed themselves and united but found that their enemies had taken the bits from their horses and had hidden their saddles. And the women did even more than the men. He who mounted his horse found the streets blocked, and would be showered with stones and would die in the streets. The slaughter lasted an entire day; the French were killed, some by bits of iron, others by stones, and some were thrown from the windows of the towers and the palaces of the market square, where more than 1,200 French cavalry and 2,000 foot soldiers were stationed in the fortresses. Soon their corpses, blood, and carrion filled the streets and squares of Bruges; it took more than three days of hard work to bury them. They were carried in carts outside the city and dumped in ditches dug in the fields. In addition, a good many of the rich bourgeois were killed and all their houses looted. Lord James of Saint-Pol with a few others managed to flee, because he lived near the gate of the city. This plague [*pestilenzia*] took place [...] in the month of [...] in the year of Christ, 1301.[33]

14 Commoners revolt against changes in currency and the rise of rents in Paris, 1307

Les Grandes Chroniques de France, ed. Jules Viard, 10 vols., *SHF*, 423 (Paris, 1924), VIII, pp. 250–2: LXI. How the commoners of Paris revolted [*s'esmut*].[34]

---

32 The cry was instead 'Shield and Friend'.

33 This last bloody stage of the revolt of Bruges was known as 'Matins of Bruges'. It occurred on 18 May 1302.

34 On the *Grandes Chroniques de France*, see [1]; and Spiegel, *The Chronicle Tradition of Saint-Denis*.

In this same year [1307][35] the bourgeois of Paris demanded that the people [*peuple*] of Paris pay their rents for their houses in good and strong money,[36] as it was then called. This caused great dissension, much discord, and rioting. And when many of the commoners [*menu peuple*] rose up, as was to be expected, fullers, weavers, tavern-keepers, and many other workers [*ouvriers*] in other crafts[37] allied together and went after a Parisian bourgeois named Étienne Barbete, who, it was said, had advised that their house rents be paid in good and strong money. This riled and tormented the people. On Thursday before Epiphany [5 January 1307], they invaded and attacked the manor of the bourgeois Étienne, called *La Courtille Barbete*, and set it on fire, which completely destroyed it along with the trees in the garden. They defiled, smashed, and tore everything apart and afterwards left with a great number of his hunting dogs [*alans*], planks of wood, and clubs. They returned to the street of Saint Martin [in Paris], broke down the door, and entered forcefully into the mansion of this bourgeois. And immediately they burst open the casks of wine in the cellar and gave it out in the squares. Several got drunk from drinking too much. Afterwards, they tore apart the fine furnishings of this house, that is, the mattresses, cushions, chests, and other property, and spread them in the mud on the side of the street. And from the mattresses they ripped open the seams and scattered the feathers, throwing them scornfully to the winds. And they unroofed the house in several places and damaged it in many other ways. With this done, they left and returned towards the Temple, to the palace of the knights Templars,[38] where the king of France was with several of his barons. The knights guarded him, so that no one would dare to enter or leave the Temple. And the commoners threw the meat brought

35 According to *Chronique anonyme finissant en M.CCC.LXXXIII* in *Recueil des historiens de France*, XXI, p. 142, the revolt occurred in 1306. It was sparked by an ordinance of 8 June 1306 that established 'strong money' and the consequential rise in commodity prices and especially rents.

36 In the Middle Ages kings and municipalities varied the value of coins by clipping the amount of silver as a ratio of more base metals in the coins' composition. In this instance, the poor of Paris would have had to pay the same nominal rents with better or 'stronger' and therefore more expensive coins. Thus their rents suddenly rose.

37 *Chronique anonyme* also uses the term 'menu peuple' and defines it as 'fullers, weavers, seamstresses, furriers, cobblers, and many others of various types of work'.

38 The Templars were the earliest of the crusading military orders, founded by the knight Hugues de Payens of Champagne in 1118. They took perpetual vows to defend the Christian kingdom from the infidel. Baldwin II assigned them to guard part of his palace in Jerusalem next to the Temple.

here for the king into the mud. Such behaviour finally brought them shame and bodily harm [*à destruiement de corps*]. Afterwards, several barons and the provost of Paris,[39] it was said, appeased the crowds with sweet words and flattery, and the commoners returned peacefully to their homes. On the following day, the king ordered many to be rounded up and put away in various prisons. And on the eve of Epiphany [5 January 1307] by the king's command twenty-eight men[40] who had done these things against Étienne and especially those who had smeared the king's meat in the mud were brought to the four gates of Paris, that is, seven were hanged at the gate leading to the district of Saint-Denis, seven at the entrance to Saint-Antoine, six near the Wheel of Fortune,[41] and eight at the entrance to Notre-Dame des Champs. A little later they were taken down and hanged again from the newly constructed gallows at each of these gates. This greatly tormented the commoners [*menu peuple*] of Paris.

15 Tax revolt in Tournai, 1307

Chronica Aegidii li Muisis, pp. 173–5.

On 10 April 1307 at the second hour of the day, when Lord Gerald bishop of Tournai was holding a synod attended by many prelates and a great crowd of parish priests from the dioceses of Tournai, the governors of the city came forth and decided to raise a new tax [*tallia*], which they would begin collecting that day. However, the commoners [*communitas*], that is, the weavers, the poor, the fullers and others, conspired against these governors. All the commoners, those who were armed and those who were not, joined together, chose captains from their ranks to lead them, and then set out for the market square [*in foro*]. They beat up the tax collectors, then congregated and went to the city gates, where they hanged them and

---

39 According to *Chronique anonyme*, Firmin de Coquerel of Amiens was the provost of Paris, and the consequences were not so dire: Firmin 'appeased them [the insurgents] with sweet words [*doulces paroles*], and 'they returned to their houses'. The provost of the merchants of Paris was the head of the municipal administration of Paris; *Robert dictionnaire historique de la langue française*, ed. Alain Rey (Paris, 1998), III, p. 2935.

40 *La Chronique parisienne anonyme*, ed. Hellot in *Mémoire de la société de l'histoire de Paris* (1884), pp. 1–207, p. 20, names 25 of them.

41 Le Roule vers les Avugles: perhaps this was an inn. I cannot find it in the gazetteers of medieval Paris.

then threw their bodies into the moat. Immediately afterwards, all the other commoners and combatants spurred one another on to greater feats of wickedness and amazingly continued to do so throughout the day. The governors, the powerful, and the rich were rightly stunned by it. And the lords, the bishop, prelates, and parish priests fled as fast as they could. All night the city was in great danger with the commoners enraged coming together in one way or another with more bad than good heard of their scheming. At dawn the next day, they went into the houses of the constables, seized the military standards of the city, and marched with them into the main square, since no one tried to stop them. And they gathered a large number of troops and went to the palaces of the governors and seized them and all those of the law. They locked them up in the city gates and prisons of the city separately from one another, and said to the rich and powerful and those who were close to the rulers: 'Go, arm yourselves and come with us, or else we will take revenge on you'. Like sheep they obediently followed these miserable masters and did as they were told. For certain, if any of them [the insurgents] could have attracted a big enough armed following, they would have killed them [the elites] like animals. But I believe God's vengeance was different, since no one was slain. With a great crowd assembled in the main square, carrying the standards of the city, swords, and clubs, suddenly, out of nowhere, a storm broke with such a flood of rain and thunder that no one stayed in the square. Out of fear they scrambled for refuge into any house that would let them in. Thunder and lightening struck over the parish church of Saint-Piat. And it was said that many saw shapes of demons running about this church and signs in the paintings and on the walls. Because this storm was so sudden and immense it dampened the rage of most of the commoners. After vespers, they spent the night in their parishes consulting among themselves. Moreover, those of the parishes of the Blessed Mary and Saint Nicolas attended meetings and sent for the soldier Matthew de Haudion, who was a wise and faithful man, then staying in our monastery. When he came before them, in unison they pleaded: 'Matthew, you understand and see the state the city is in; for the sake of the Virgin Mary give us your advice'. Resisting their invitation a bit and excusing himself, he then spoke to them elegantly and wisely: 'O esteemed lords, you know that the city of Tournai belongs to the nobles, and it has been justly observed that they are against all the rest; none are spared. Moreover, because of their nobility, the king, his council, and the nobles ought to rejoice when the citizens and the rest are in conflict so that they can show that they can put an end to such things. But, as you can see at present the city is without law and a ruler. Therefore, if you please, I advise you to impose law and order without delay and elect new rectors. As for the old rectors, who are in prison, they should be given a fair trial: if found guilty, they should be punished and if innocent, let go'. Then, immediately and in unison, without a single dissenting voice, they chanted, 'Well said, well said, well said'. After praising him for his advice, they sent messengers to relay it to other parishes. Immediately, all the other parishes agreed with the position taken by the parish of the Blessed Mary. The next morning, they called an assembly of almost the entire city – the magnates, the middling sorts [*mediocribus*], and the little people [*parvis*]; hardly anyone dared not attend. And on that day they chose thirty electors and that night and the following day appointed prefects, judges, and others, who would be so elected every year on the feast day of the Blessed Lucy [13 December]. With this law passed, many who had been exiled for life, for years, or had left because of fines returned timidly, and the commune came forth and received and applauded them. And the governors by common consent chose investigators [*inquisitores*] to examine the old rectors and record in writing everything said. And because new taxes had sparked off this rebellion, they were rescinded, and the order was read out and made known to all the commoners in a public forum. All the commoners there said that these things were wonderful. On hearing this news, the king sent his chief officer of Vermandois, who came secretly with only four horsemen to our monastery. Because of what had happened, he wanted to know what could be done, passed some laws and measures to smooth matters over, and left. Of all the unfortunate and damaging things that occurred during this rebellion [*turbulentia*], the good along with the bad has been written down at length, and I do not wish to revisit much of it. Dijerinus and Pourres[42] and several others did much good and avoided further wickedness. The old rectors openly returned to their homes, one after another, but they were excluded from positions of power and the city council for a long time. I knew of all the above as an eyewitness.

---

42 The editor of this chronicle does not identify these individuals. I imagine they are long-forgotten local heroes.

16 Revolt of fullers, Tournai, 1307

Chronica Aegidii li Muisis, p. 175.

On 3 September [1307] the fullers rioted [*fecerunt routam*] and wanted to murder the provost. But immediately their elected leader was drawn and quartered by horses and [then] hanged for his action. The next day, Peter of Moussein was drawn and hanged for the same crime. A day later, fourth of September, Alard of Bourgella, who had given advice and counsel to the fullers and weavers about the revolt, was beheaded in the main square in front of the House of the Pig[43]; many others were declared guilty and banished.

17 Shepherds' movement, 1320

Guillaume de Nangis, *Chronique*, Vol. II, pp. 25–8.

In that year [1320] suddenly and unexpectedly a violent uprising like a whirlwind [*ad modum turbinis*] erupted in the kingdom of France. A bunch of shepherds and simpletons assembled in great numbers to form an army, saying they wished to cross the sea to fight the infidels and asserting that they had to conquer the Holy Land. In their association, they had leaders of a sort, who had invented these lies; one was a priest, who because of his wickedness had plundered his own church; another was an apostate monk of the Benedictines. These two had so deluded these simpletons that groups of sixteen-year-old boys, against their parents' wishes, followed them, carrying only a bag, a stick, and no money. They abandoned their pigs and sheep and, like the sheep they herded, followed after these two; their numbers swelled into a great magnitude. They were held together more by will and power than by reason or any sense of the community. [But] when the courts tried to punish any of them, they resisted mightily; if imprisoned, the prisons were broken down and they were liberated … None went against them, and thus they were allowed to leave Paris. And from there they hastened towards Aquitaine, having left Paris without any resistance and been allowed to go freely without penalties. Now so emboldened by this experience, they killed indiscriminately all the Jews they could find and plundered their property … Proceeding towards Toulouse and surrounding places, they committed many

---

43 A house with an insigne of a pig on it.

shameful deeds. Here twenty, there thirty-two or so were hanged from gallows and trees ... and like smoke this violent and dispersed movement vanished entirely.

18 Revolt of Flanders, 1323–28

Chronicon comitum Flandrensium in *Corpus Chronicorum Flandriae*, ed. J.-J. De Smet, Vol. I (Brussels, 1837), pp. 34–261. The social and political alliances that led to this six-year revolt that centred on the free peasants from the coastal areas of western Flanders and spread to engage commoners from the principal cities of Flanders against the nobility, patricians, and the French crown were different from those binding the Flemish rebellions of 1297 to 1305. The new count, Louis of Nevers (1323–46), grandson of the Flemish proto-nationalist Guy of Dampierre 'was the most dependent of his dynasty on the French crown'.[44] In 1323 he renounced his grandfather's political resistance to the French crown and sought to enforce the financial penalties owed by Flanders to France under the peace of Athis (1305), even though by 1309 Philip the Fair had agreed not to enforce it with any rigour. Thus the peasantry was suddenly faced again with an enormous indemnity, paying ransoms for nobles imprisoned in France, and welcoming back many banished pro-French nobles, some of whom had been their lords and enemies during the previous rebellion.[45]

p. 187 [1324] Now that the count had returned from Flanders the aldermen and councillors had to make good their promise of a gift to the count. To pay for it, they taxed the commoners [*populares*] at rates that sparked great grumbling [*murmur permaximus*] among them. Because of favouritism and not by law, the aldermen and councillors of the walled towns had taxed the commoners at double the rate promised to the count. And rumour has it that these riots were caused not because of the amount demanded but because the taxes had been imposed unequitably; as is said, it was the duplicity and injustice of the tax that irked them. And the commoners rebelled [*rebellavit*] against the councillors, aldermen, and lords in the territories of Brabant, Bruges, Veurne [Furnensi], Berg-op-Zoom [Bergensi], and elsewhere. They elected captains for their fortresses and against the law formed squadrons. They marched out and captured all the councillors, aldermen, lords, and tax collectors. Once the lords had fled, they destroyed

---

44 Nicholas, *Medieval Flanders*, p. 211.
45 See William H. TeBrake, *A Plague of Insurrection: Popular Politics and Peasant Revolt in Flanders, 1323–1328* (Philadelphia, 1993); and Nicholas, *Medieval Flanders*, pp. 212–16.

their homes. Such a great and dangerous rebellion [*tumultus*] had not been heard of in my lifetime. I saw it and wrote it down faithfully, presenting only what is true. Not even the lord of Asper[46] with help from three Flemish towns could put down the rebellion, no matter how hard they tried.

p. 191. [1324] All who rebelled were commoners [*ignobiles*] and rustics [*rustici*]... On hearing of the commoners' victory in the western provinces ... after a brief period Torhout, Roelers, and Courtrai fell along with their surrounding territories ... At Poperinge they burnt all the mansions of the nobility and of their supporters, and plundered all their possessions in Western Flanders.

p. 195 [1325] While this revolt was gaining strength, Clais Zannekin gathered the people of Veurne and ordered them to advance on Ypres to rouse the people to revolt and take over the city. On hearing this and being afraid of their commoners, the patricians secretly fled the city and left Flanders altogether. Those who remained in Ypres received Clais peacefully, as did those of Bruges; they joined them, opened their gates, and fortified the ditches and gates of their suburbs.

p. 206 [1328] After the victory [of the French troops], the glorious monarch of France did not look on these matters [of the rebels] favourably; rather because of God's omnipotence by which kings rule ... he burnt villages and massacred the rebels' wives and children to leave a lasting memory of his vengeance against their crimes and rebellions ...

p. 208. [1328] But Sigerus, son of John, this felonious rebel,[47] took refuge within the city walls of Oudenburg staying under the bridge next to the monastery of Saint Peter, where he survived for some time with those who had fled from here and there, who had crossed the sea and had come with him from Zeeland. Finally, the chief officer of Bruges captured him unharmed and led him with his son and about twenty others to the prison in Bruges. With the count of Paris present, he was tied to a cart and led naked through all the streets of Bruges. He was burnt little by little with a red-hot poker and then

---

46 There are two places called Asper; both are in eastern Flanders, 20 km from Ghent.
47 Segher Jonssone was a peasant from Bredene, 15 km west of Bruges. In February 1325 Segher and his peasant forces defeated the count's contingent at Gistel west of Bruges, which was a major turning point in this peasant war; see TeBrake, *A Plague of Insurrection*, pp. 72 and 75.

dragged to the scaffold, where his back and limbs were broken. He was then beheaded, put on a wheel, and suspended with this wheel on another hangman's noose, high above for his followers to gaze upon him in awe; thus he received a punishment equal to the crimes he had committed. And thus this plague [*pestis*] of people rebelling against their superiors ended. As with other evil things God protects us from, it did not rise up again. Yet it had lasted and had grown in strength for six years.

19 Revolt of Flanders, 1324–28

Anciennes Chroniques de Flandre in *Recueil des historiens des Gaules et de la France*, XXII (Paris, 1894), pp. 418–19: How one Fleming brought the country of Flanders to revolt [*troubles*].

At this time [1324], the commoners of Flanders began again to stir [*esmouvoir*], because a young man named Clais [*Colin*] Sannequin, a native of the region of Veurne, declared and insisted that the governors of Flanders did not govern the country at all according to ancient customs. In a short space of time, he attracted great numbers of commoners to his side, especially from Bergen-op-Zoom, Veurne, Poperinge, and other towns in West Flanders. They began murdering and putting to death the chief officers and governors of the country, without making any conditions and for no reason. Soon this Colin had brought the people of Bruges over to his cause. And Lord Robert of Flanders, who was then in Dunkerque,[48] rallied the people of the surrounding district against this Sannequin and his accomplices. But Sannequin's men proved so powerful and disciplined against Lord Robert that all those who were with him disbanded and fled. Lord Robert himself, who had retreated to Dunkerque put his wife behind him on a nag that night and rode without stopping until they reached his castle at Nieppe, where he stayed a while. But it was said that he was rather pleased with the uprising and the troubles that ensued, whatever face he put on it, and so it seemed.

When Sannequin saw that he had such a great number of people assembled on his side (he had all of lower Flanders behind him), he went with a large force to Cassel and forced the whole region to swear allegiance to him. Then he went as far as Poperinge, and from

---

48 He was instead in Dixmude.

there asked the people of Bruges to come to his aid, since Ypres had fortified their city against him. The people of Bruges sent word back that they would do so willingly. They assembled a great company, joined Sannequin's army, and together encamped around Ypres.

When those of Ypres felt surrounded on all sides, they sent for Count Louis of Flanders to come to Ypres, for with his aid they would be strong enough to defeat his rebels and enemies. Thus Count Louis ordered all his noblemen to arm and follow him to Ypres without delay. And when they were all assembled in Ypres, Count Louis was advised to go and lay siege to the town of Courtrai, which had just rebelled against him [1325]. On arriving in Courtrai, he first entered the suburbs and set them ablaze; then he entered the city by force and also torched it. Seeing many of their homes on fire and their town beginning to burn down, the residents of Courtrai rushed to arm themselves and launched a passionate attack against the count and his forces on all sides. The lord of Neule was hit by a bolt from a large crossbow and was mortally wounded. Seeing these people's rage, Count Louis tried to escape through a gate, but he met with such great resistance that he lost most of his noblemen. The next day they were lined up before him and beheaded before his eyes. Those of Bruges who knew about these developments went immediately to Courtrai, where they captured Count Louis, their lord and chief justice, led him back to Bruges as a prisoner, and locked him up in the Belfry. Colin Sannequin thereupon went with his great army to Ypres. And when those of his party who were inside the town were alerted, they came out to meet him and led him into the city with great rejoicing. And Lord Robert of Flanders left la Motte au Bois[49] and quickly went to Bruges, where he made an alliance with the inhabitants of Bruges and from there led the commoners against Ghent. But Ghent defended itself so well that neither this Sannequin nor his company gained anything by the siege. And it is said that this is what reopened the war between the kings of France and England.[50]

---

49 15 km southeast of Cassel and 20 km east of St. Omer.
50 The chronicler is referring to the origins of the Hundred Years' War. The young King Edward III had military interests and dynastic claims in Flanders as well as in France. In 1327 he had been married to Philippa, daughter of William I, Count of Hainault.

20 Revolt of Bruges, 1323: an Italian view

G. Villani, *Nuova Cronica*, II, Book Ten, chapter CCXXXII, p. 413: How the commoners [*popolo minuto*] of Flanders rebelled [*rubellarono*] against the nobles and destroyed them.

In November [1323] the commoners of Bruges in Flanders, that is, the peasants around Bruges [*Franco di Bruggia*], rebelled against the nobles of the district. They chose a leader, whom they called Conticino,[51] and charged madly through the countryside, burning and destroying all the manors and fortresses of the nobles, capturing and imprisoning many of them. The reason for this was that the nobles had taxed them too heavily to pay for the peace with the king of France. This conspiracy [*congiura*] grew so large that it contaminated the entire country of Flanders, and they [the commoners] refused to obey their lord, the Count of Flanders. Ultimately, on 22 February, with the help of the commoners of Bruges, they forced their way into the city and rampaged through it, madly killing many of the grand bourgeois. They changed the state and government of the land to their liking.

21 'A general rebellion' against new taxes, Rouen, 1347

Normanniae Nova Chronica ab anno CCCCLXXIII ad annum MCCCLXXVIII e tribus chronicis mss. Sancti Laudi, Sanctae Catharinae et Majoris ecclesiae Rotomagensium, ed. A. Chéruel in *Mémoires de la Société des Antiquaires de Normandie*, 2e Série, VIII (Paris, 1851), pp. 32–3.

The year 1347: around All Saints' Day [2 November], Jean, Duke of Normandy, came to his city of Rouen and with the count of Armagnac and many others in attendance, the duke humbly presented a petition to these counts on behalf of his duchy. The petition was the following: the King of England unjustly and without cause has deceitfully inflicted great damage throughout Normandy, for which the duke has suffered with all his heart. For this reason, he desires to vindicate himself by raising a great army to invade England. For this he asks everyone – prelates, priors, parish priests, clerics, and all the laity – to help according to their abilities, by agreeing to pay a tax on the

---

51 This seems to be the Italianisation of Colin Sannequin, although it is difficult to hear the transliteration; the major chronicle of Siena, *Cronaca Maggiore* di Agnolo di Tura del Grasso in *Cronache senesi*, ed. Alessandro Lisini and Fabio Iacometti, RIS, XV/6 (Bologna, 1931–37), p. 408, also called the leader of the Flemish workers and peasants in 1323 Conticino.

purchase and sale of goods for a period of three months. They benignly conceded this and many other things as a subsidy, [on condition] that the tax would end in three months. But subsequently, the chief officer of Rouen had it proclaimed through the streets and squares of the city that this tax would last [instead] for nine months. On hearing this, a rebellion of all the people [*universalis mutinatio*] erupted through the city with major riots [*magnum monopolium*] in many of the city's neighbourhoods. On the feast day of Saint Martin in summer [4 July], everyone gathered sparking major rioting and horrible violence to defend themselves and root out from their homes all those responsible for bringing about the above-mentioned tax. As things progressed, with the tax imposed throughout all Normandy, the officials decided to withdraw it, and by these means peace was restored.

Southern France

22 Two clerics accused of heresy for leading a revolt in Carcassonne, 1306

Histoire générale de Languedoc, ed. C. Devic, J. Vaissete et al. 2nd edn, 16 vols. (Toulouse 1872–1904), X, cols. 645–6, doc. 235: Letter of remission issued in 1325 for two clerics charged as accomplices of the revolt of Carcassonne in 1306, Archives nationales [hereafter Arch. nat.] series JJ. 67, n. 105.

Charles (IV 1322–28), etc. to Master Jacob, son of Bartholomew, lawyer, and Eustache Fabri, officer of Béziers, our sergeants at arms, warm greetings. The clerics, masters Arnaud Garsie of Albi and Pierre Probi of Castres, were captured and detained some time ago by our esteemed bishops of Saint-Paul and Pamiers, who were authorised for these purposes by the Apostolic See and at the request of our esteemed and loyal [friends] the bishop of Laon at that time and the count of Forez, then in the country of the Occitan, who were responsible for law and order. The two clerics were charged with conspiracy and over a long period of time planning a revolt of the men of Carcassonne to overthrow our royal government; it was said that these men [of Carcassonne] had given the clerics their consent. The officials of the Inquisition responsible for stamping out heresy, whom we defend, were engaged in these cases. The inquisitor had previously brought charges against them and imprisoned them for more than four years. Now to arrange their pardon to release them, we have sent orders through our esteemed and faithful servants of the exchequer in Paris, to whom we have addressed our document concerning this matter ... Issued on 10 June 1325 at Fontenay-le-Comte (Vendée). [With the agreement of the Inquisitor, the two were freed on payment of 2,000 gold florins.[52]]

Central and Northern Italy

From the mid-thirteenth to the early fourteenth century, class conflict in Italy[53] was focused on the rise of the 'primo popolo', or the alliance of workers, artisans, and merchants against the rule of the magnates, an entrenched oligarchy of landed aristocrats. Unlike feudal aristocracies in the north of Europe, however, these aristocrats also had extensive mercantile interests centred on international banking and long-distant trade. As mentioned in the introduction, without lists of rebels or surviving judicial records, it is difficult to know just who these people [*popoli*] were, especially before the 1280s. Indeed, their social composition appears to have changed over the thirteenth century. In mid-century, they cut a wide swath through urban populations from artisans to merchants. By the end of the century and into the next with popular victories in Bologna, Florence, Pisa, Siena, and elsewhere that subjugated magnates to special laws and heavier taxes, new layers and divisions appear in the ranks of the 'people'. Chroniclers and governmental documents continued to refer to the *popolo*, but new terms arose in the chronicles that distinguished *popoli* or *artefici* (craftsmen with guild recognition) from *popolani*, or a more privileged stratum of citizen-merchants often also called *popolani grassi*, the fat cats, on the one hand, and from the *popolo minuto*, or disenfranchised workers principally in the wool industry, on the other.

The documents taken from Giovanni Villani's chronicle show this subtle change in words and social alliances from the mid-thirteenth to the early fourteenth century. Already by 1295, Villani portrays the discord between the *popolani* and the magnates as having become one more of civil war – one group of families or faction or even brothers fighting against one another – than of social class: the temporary peace between the *popolo* and the magnates following Giano della Bella's exile was brought about by 'brothers of good

52 Gold florins were first struck in Florence in 1252. Originally, they were valued at 20 shillings or one pound [*lira*] in silver or a money of account; however, its value against the *lira* rose steadily so that by the mid-fourteenth century, it was worth three-and-a-half *lire*.

53 Historians generally conceive of the 'rise of the *popolo*' as a movement that was exclusive to the city-states of northern and central Italy, but at least Naples and probably other southern mercantile centres experienced the same urban tensions and social developments during the mid-thirteenth century; see Carlo de Frede, 'Da Carlo I D'Angiò a Giovanna I, 1263–1382', in *Storia di Napoli*, vol. III (Naples, 1979), pp. 1–334, esp. p. 120.

families' mediating between themselves [29]. By the early fourteenth century, at least in Florence, the most significant division in society was no longer that between the people and the magnates, but rather a new rift had arisen within the 'people'; now, the most serious civil division was the cleavage between disenfranchised workers [the *popolo minuto*], those denied the offices and other rights of citizenship, and citizens. To avoid harsh laws and taxes, magnates increasingly petitioned for and acquired *popolani* or commoner status, while merchants of popular status married into magnate families or took on the airs and violent life-style of magnates.[54] Yet on the eve of the Black Death, magnates were still able to exploit the divisions within the people, between the *popolo minuto* and the *popolani* for their own ends [44, 45].

The rise of the *popolo* and in particular the people's crowning achievement – the promulgation of anti-magnate legislation in the last decades of the thirteenth and opening years of the fourteenth century – have been most intensively studied for Florence. The extent to which this conflict was a 'class conflict' has been one of the principal debates of late medieval Italian history in the twentieth century.[55] The documents below give us an insight into the nature of this conflict, what was at stake politically, who was involved, what coalitions emerged in different city-states, and how the conflict differed from place to place and changed over time. We begin with Florence [23, 26, 28, 29] but present documents on armed conflict between the people and magnates and the rise of popular power in less well studied places – Viterbo [25], Pisa [35],[56] Genoa and Savona [40], Ancona [41], and Rome [50].

At the same time, the documents below show a wide spectrum of other forms of popular protest flourishing in Italy before the Black Death – tax revolts

---

54 On the character of magnate culture, violence, and masculinity, see Carol Lansing, *The Florentine Magnates: Lineage and Faction in a Medieval Commune* (Princeton, 1991).

55 Gaetano Salvemini, *Magnati e popolani in Firenze dal 1280 al 1295* (Florence, 1899), argued that economic differences defined the political struggles between the *popolo* and the magnates. Although the Florentine magnates had urban palaces, lived part or even most of the year in the city, and were merchants, their economic interests focused more on their landed properties in the countryside and their politics turned to securing the highest prices for grain and other foodstuffs. The *popolo* even when they were wealthy bankers were by contrast more tied to the interests of the local urban economy of Florence than were the magnates, whose business interests tended to be international and focused across the Alps. A generation later Nicola Ottokar, *Il Comune di Firenze alla fine del Ducento* (Florence, 1926), argued that economic interests did not separate the magnates from the *popolo*; rather the two were political factions bearing very similar social and economic profiles; anti-magnate legislation was a tool for branding and penalising political rivals. More recently, with new research outside of Tuscany, the pendulum has swung back to favour Salvemini; see John Koenig, *Il popolo dell'Italia del Nord* (Bologna, 1986); and Paolo Grillo, *Milano in età comunale (1183–1276): Istituzioni, società, economia*, Centro italiano di studi sull'alto medioevo (Spoleto, 2001).

56 For Pisa, see Emilio Cristiani, *Nobiltà e popolo del comune di Pisa: Dalle origini del podestariato alla Signoria del Donoratico* (Naples, 1962).

[24], protests against law enforcers [27], a student revolt at Bologna against a miscarriage of justice and their mass migration to Imola [34], internecine struggles between craftsmen [36], protests over food shortages [37, 38], the frustrations and revolts of youth kept out of government [30], heretical movements in the Alps [31, 32], popular protest against war policy and foreign diplomacy [33], associations of workers for boisterous entertainment [39], and even a peace march by small children [55]. But it is not until the 1340s and only in Florence and Siena (as far as research presently reveals) that industrial strikes and organised political action on the part of artisans and disenfranchised workers finally approached the sophistication of workers' struggles witnessed in northern France and Flanders even for towns as small as Clermont-en-Beauvaisis a good hundred years earlier.

23 The rise of the *Primo Popolo*: the people's victory over the aristocracy, Florence, 1250

G. Villani, *Nuova Cronica*, I, Book Seven, chapter XXXIX, pp. 326–9: How the first government of the people [*il primo popolo*] arose in Florence to redress the violence and injuries inflicted by the Ghibellines [1250].[57]

With the return of the enemy troops into Florence, the citizens of Florence were greatly impoverished, because the Ghibelline rulers burdened the people with intolerable land and excise taxes. But these taxes yielded little, because the Guelfs were dispersed through the Florentine *contado* and held many castles and made war within the city. Moreover, the Uberti clan [*casa*] and all the other Ghibelline nobles tyrannised the people, inflicting on them severe stress and pain. For this reason the good men[58] of Florence assembled to rebel. They made

57 The Guelfs and Ghibellines were two inter-regional, even international, associations of aristocrats from the Italian city-states. The factions (at least in name) came into being with rival claims over the Holy Roman Empire in the time of Frederick II Hofenstaufen (1220–50). The Guelfs (derived from the German *Welf*) supported the Papacy's candidate, the Saxon Otto IV, against Frederick II. On the other hand, the word Ghibelline derived from the Hofenstaufen castle *Waiblingen* and became a battle-cry of Frederick's forces. Although these factions determined much of the internal strife within city-states, by the late thirteenth century certain cities became consistent strongholds of one party or the other. While Florence, Lucca, and Bologna were usually Guelf cities, their opponents Pisa, Siena, Pistoia, Arezzo were Ghibelline. Their alliances to the Papacy or the Holy Roman Emperor were, however, anything but stable over the thirteenth and fourteenth centuries as the history of Florence well attests; see Daniel Waley, *The Italian City-Republics*, 3rd edn (London, 1988), pp. 145–56.

58 Later, in fact, as a result of this revolt of the *primo popolo*, the *Buoni uomini* would mean the governmental council of the Twelve Elders but here it means simply the citizens.

the church of San Firenze their headquarters. But because of the strength of the Uberti, they did not dare stay there and instead went to the church of the Friars Minor at Santa Croce. Here they remained armed without daring to return home. They feared if they laid down their arms, the Uberti and the other nobles would smash them, and they would be condemned by the Signoria. They went armed to the house of the anchorites in San Lorenzo,[59] who were very tough, and where they remained armed. They elected thirty-six leaders of the people to add to their forces, took the government away from the podestà[60] who was then in office, and dismissed all the officials. And having done this, without delay they formed a government of the people with new decrees and statutes and elected Lord Uberto from Lucca as the first captain of the people. They created [a council] of twelve elders, two from each sixth of the city.[61] They guided the people and advised this captain, meeting in the houses of the Badia[62] beyond the gate that led to [the church of] Santa Margherita but returned to their houses to eat and sleep.[63] And this took place on 20 October 1250. On that day the people authorised this captain to distribute twenty banners to the leaders of the citizen militias [*compagnie d'arme*] and neighbourhoods, which comprised several parishes each. Thus, when the need arose, each was to take up arms behind the banner of his company and then with those banners to follow the captain of the people. And they made a bell, which this captain put in his tower of the Lion. The captain also kept there the most important banner of the people; it was half white and half vermilion. The insignia on these banners were as follows: [Villani then describes in great detail the insignia on each of the twenty neighbourhood banners.] And as the people arranged insignia and banners for the city, they did the same in the *contado* for all of its

59 The parish of San Lorenzo in the quarter of San Giovanni was the largest parish in Florence. I do not know the precise location of the anchorite house. It is not listed as such in Walter Paatz, *Kirchen von Florenz: ein kunstgeschichtliches Handbuch*, 6 vols. (Frankfurt am Main, 1940–52). Perhaps it was the hospice just north of the church of San Lorenzo.

60 A chief executive officer, head of the judiciary and the police, who was a lord from another city-state and usually served a single term of six months.

61 Until 1343, when the quarters were created, the city was divided into six districts with twenty neighbourhood districts called *gonfaloni*.

62 The monastery of the Badia di Firenze.

63 Later, to avoid corruption and internecine family fighting, the priors ate and slept in the Palazzo Signoria. Their rooms were cells like the dormitory of a monastery, and they took their meals in the Sala di Gigli; see Nicolai Rubinstein, *The Palazzo Vecchio, 1298–1532: Government, Architecture, and Imagery in the Civic Palace of the Florentine Republic* (Oxford, 1995), p. 36

parishes [*pivieri*] which numbered ninety-six; and they organised these into leagues, with one linked to another, so they could come into the city as an armed force if the need arose. By these means the ancient people of Florence were organised to defend themselves well. They began to build their palace behind the Badia in the square of Sant' Apollinare [Pulinare], the one with the ornamented stone tower. At first the government did not possess a communal palace in Florence; instead, it moved from one part of the city to another. And as the people had taken over the government and state, it was ordered for their greater safety that all the towers of Florence[64] over 120 arms [300 feet][65] in height be cut down to 50 arms [125 feet] and no more. And this was done, and from these stones the city walls south of the Arno[66] were built.

24 Tax revolt in Venice, 1266

Marino Sanuto, *Vitæ Ducum Venetorum italice scriptæ ab origine urbis, sive anno CCCXXI usque MCCCCXCIII*, in Ludovico Muratori, *Rerum Italicarum Scriptores* [hereafter, Muratori], XXII (1733), col. 564. Marino Sanuto (or Sanudo) the younger, Venetian patrician (1466–1536) continued writing his lives of the doges until 1530.[67] Although he was not an eye-witness to the events of the thirteenth and fourteenth centuries, his *Lives of the Doges*, based often on direct citation from earlier chroniclers that have now disappeared, is a principal chronicle for late medieval Venetian history. He is perhaps best known for his fifty volumes of political 'diaries' that register the daily discussions and decisions of the Venetian councils as well as news gathered throughout the city from 1496 to 1533.

In Venice [1266],[68] the gabelle[69] on milled grain [*la Macina*] was increased, doubling its payment in order to come up with the money

---

64 These were family towers owned by the old families of Florence and used to lord over their neighbourhood enclaves.

65 A *braccia* was about 2.5 feet.

66 The river that runs through Florence and Pisa.

67 The Doge was the chief magistrate of the Venetian state.

68 By Sanuto's account, the year could be either 1265 or 1266; however, chroniclers, who were eye-witnesses, the fourteenth-century Doge, Andrea Dondolo (Andrea Danduli, Dux Venetiarum, *Chronica per extensium descripta*, aa. 46–1280, ed. Ester Pastorello, RIS, 12/1 [Bologna, 1938–58], p. 314) and *Venetiarum Historia vulgo Petro Iustiniano Iustiniani filio adiudicata* (ed. Roberto Cessi e Fanny Bennato, Monumenti Storici, Deputazione di Storia Patria per le Venezie, 17 [Venice, 1964], p. 176), date it as 1266. These sources give only a few lines to the 'tumultus in populo' and say nothing about the way the revolt was mediated by the

BEFORE THE BLACK DEATH 47

for war. The taxes were hard to collect, and the people, impatient with such unaccustomed abuse, rose up and revolted [*facendo sedizione*]. Some ran to the Palace of the Doge to confront those who had supported the increase in the gabelle. The Doge chose judicious words and for the most part appeased those who had wanted to raid the country, destroying property, etc. But once the riot [*tumulto*] had ended through the mediation by the heads of the neighbourhoods [*contrade*], the Doge with the council ordered the arrest of several leaders on charges of sedition; they were hanged at the columns near the church of San Marco. These were Niccolò Bocco, Giovanni di Candia, and a few others. And to placate the people, the increase in the gabelle was revoked.

25 *Gran tumulto* in Viterbo, 1282: the people chase the nobility out of the city

Niccola della Tuccia, *Cronache di Viterbo e di altre città* in *Cronache e Statuti della Città di Viterbo*, ed. Ignazio Ciampi, Documenti di storia italiana, V (Florence, 1872), p. 32. Niccola della Tuccia was born in 1400 and died in 1473. He is the principal chronicler of late medieval Viterbo, who held various offices in communal government and travelled to Rome on official business on several occasions and was an ambassador of Viterbo to Pius II in 1461.

At this time [1282], a great dispute erupted between the nobility [*gentilomini*] and the people [*popolari*], because the noblemen had snuffed out [*soffogati*] most of the villages [*castelli*] of Viterbo and continually insulted the people. A knight named Lord Pietro di Valle, but of popular status [*omo popolari*], who was brave and wise, was made standard-bearer of the people.[70] He called a meeting attended by all the nobility and the people, where he rose to his feet and declared that he thought the villages occupied by the nobles should be turned over to the commune. The meeting decided that it should be done. From fear the nobles consented. Then they returned to their houses

---

neighbourhoods; nor do these sources of the nobility, in the first instance of the Doge himself, give any hint that the revolt was ultimately a success, resulting in the revocation of the tax. They only note that the 'principal authors of these wicked deeds were hanged once the revolt had ended'. Andrea Dondolo adds that the revolt took place against a backdrop of famine in Venice.

69 *Gabelles* were indirect taxes or sales taxes on a wide range of commodities and often in Italy on services such as the drawing up of contracts. They were not just salt taxes as English readers sometimes suppose.

70 The highest office within Italian city-state republics.

in the parishes of San Tomé, San Salvatore, and elsewhere, and afterwards all came out together armed in the church of San Salvatore, conspiring to kill this knight. The following morning, filled with great agitation and all armed, they went to the Palace of the Commune. Thereupon, the said Lord Pietro had all the gates of the city locked and with his guards at the palace defended themselves as best they could [*da loro gran pezzo*]. The rioting spread throughout the city with cries of: 'Long live the people and death to the wolves'. Gathering their men in the main square, they chased the nobles back to San Salvatore, killing two of their servants. When the people returned to the square, Lord Pietro chose two hundred young men from their [neighbourhood militia] ranks and stationed them behind the palace at the foot of the square. He allowed all the others to go home to eat without disarming, but if they heard rioting, they were to return to the square. And so they did. With matters now quietened, the nobles sent some of their men into the square of the commune. Finding no one there, they rushed with all their force into the square to take over the Palace. As soon as the racket was heard, however, all the people ran into the square and according to plan took over all the streets around it. Then Lord Pietro came forward with his two hundred brave and well-armed youngsters, whom he had trained well, and attacked the noblemen, killing some and chasing the others away: twenty-three were killed; the others fled from Viterbo. Lord Pietro followed up his defence by going out with the banner of the people to the occupied castles in the countryside, where his troops from Viterbo encamped for fourteen months, thus liberating eighteen of these castles [from the nobility's control].[71] And his troops stripped away the property from as many nobles as they could get their hands on. Those who surrendered peacefully and gave up their castles were allowed to remain in Viterbo without further harassment: these were called the Bertoni, that is, those of the Gattechi, Tignosini, Monaldeschi, and Alessandrini clans. Lord Pietro held a council and issued a statute that no nobleman could hold office in the commune or go down the paved section [*selciata*] of the piazza to go to the town hall.[72] This occurred in 1281[2], in the time of Pope Martin IV, who was made pope in Viterbo the year before, and who gave the people absolution for their misdeeds.

71 According to another source 48 castles were liberated.
72 I do not understand why this restriction was imposed; nor does the editor of the chronicle give any clues.

26 Magnates versus merchants and the 'weak': the first anti-magnate laws in Florence, 1293

G. Villani, *Nuova Cronica*, II, Book Nine, chapter I, pp. 9–12.

In February 1292[3] Florence was great, powerful, and self-satisfied: its citizens were fat and rich. From this excessive tranquillity, which naturally breeds arrogance and novelties [*novità*], citizens became envious and snooty towards one another, and many murders, assaults, and insults occurred between one citizen and another and especially among the nobles, called the magnates and the powerful [*grandi e possenti*], who attacked the merchant class [*popolani*] and the powerless both in the *contado* and the city. They used force and violence against the people and seized the property of others. Because of this, certain good men, merchants and artisans of Florence who wanted to live well, thought of trying to remedy and cure this pestilence. Among the leaders there was one valiant man named Giano della Bella from an old and noble family but of popular status, who was rich and powerful, from the parish of San Martino. He had the support and advice of other wise and powerful citizens. In the council of magistrates, they decided to reform our laws and statutes. Just as in earlier times our governments made reforms, they now made certain laws and statutes with severe consequences for the magnates and powerful, who used force and violence against citizens [*popolani*]. They doubled the common penalties [on magnates] otherwise charged [if the condemned had been a commoner], held a kinsman of a magnate responsible for the crimes of another, and deemed that the testimony of two witnesses made before officers of a tribunal [*di pubblica voce e fama*] was sufficient to establish a magnate's crime. Thus, their privileges within the commune were overturned. And these laws they called the Ordinances of Justice. And to preserve and put them into effect, they added to the six priors, who governed the city, a standard-bearer of justice for each of the six [districts of the city], whose term of office would change every two months as with the priors. With the ringing of the bells and assembling of the People, the banner of justice was put in the church of San Piero Scheraggio,[73] which had not been done before. And they decreed that no prior could be from a family [*casa*] of nobles called magnates unless the family previously had had many

---

73 An important medieval church of Florence, located at the present entrance to the Uffizi Galleries; Giorgio Vasari ordered it to be demolished in the sixteenth century to build the Uffizi.

good merchants in it, even if they had all been magnates. And they decreed that the banner of this people and the neighbourhoods should be a vermilion cross on a white field. And a thousand citizens were appointed [to the citizen militia], divided among the six districts of the city with banners for each neighbourhood [*contrade*] and fifty foot soldiers under each banner. They were to be armed each with a coat of mail and a shield bearing the insignia of the cross, and, if there were a disturbance, they were to come out. And on request from their local standard-bearer they were to go to the house or Palace of the Priors[74] and defend it against the magnates. Then these militiamen grew to two-thousand foot soldiers and later to three thousand. The army of the people were given similar orders, and militias were established in the *contado* and district of Florence with the same insignia and were named the league of the people. The first of these standard-bearers was Baldo de' Ruffoli from the gate of the Duomo.[75] And in his time, armed with the banner he went and destroyed the property of the Galli clan [*casato*] of the gate of Santa Maria, because one of their members had murdered a citizen of popular status [*popolare*] in the kingdom of France. This novelty of the people and transformation of the state had a great effect on the city of Florence with various consequences for our commune, some bad, some good, as we shall mention later. And this change and rebirth of the people would not have happened, given the power of the magnates, had they not been in such conflict and disarray at the time. On top of this, the Guelfs returned to Florence, which set off a great war between the Aldimari and the Tosinghi families, the Rossi, and the Tornaquinci ...

27 The revolt of the 'people without underpants' [*popolo senza brache*], Bologna, 1289

Corpus Chronicorum Bononiensium [hereafter *CCB*], ed. Albano Sorbelli in RIS, 18/1, Vol. II (Città di Castello, 1910–38), *Cronaca A* [called *Rampona*], *Cronica di Villola*, and *Bolognetto*, II, pp. 232–3; also see the shorter version of Matteo Griffoni, *Memoriale Historicum de rebus Bononiensium*, ed. Lodovico Frati and Sorbelli, RIS, XVIII/2, p. 25. [I have put together various pieces of information from all these sources, which in fact borrowed from one another.]

---

74 The town hall of Florence was called by various names, the Palazzo Signoria, Palace of the Priors, Palace of the People, the Communal Palace, or Palace of the Commune.

75 The cathedral of Florence, at that time called Santa Reparata, later to be called Santa Maria della Fiore.

And in this year [1289] great discord erupted in the city of Bologna, because the said Lord Antonio [podestà]⁷⁶ did not want to remain in office as required by the statutes of Bologna. Some of the craftsmen did not want him to stay on. These people were called 'the people without underpants',⁷⁷ and they led him into the town square and threw two stones at him, putting his life in danger. Immediately, all his officers were detained, who stayed on in office and were acquitted of wrongdoing. These commoners accompanied him to the bridge of Reni; among them were Zanobi, the servant of Jacobo from Panico, Michele of Vado, who stayed with Michele of Panico, and many others of still lower condition [*de villiori condicione*].

28 Aristocratic backlash in Florence, 1295

G. Villani, *Nuova Cronica*, II, Book Nine, chapter VIII, pp. 22–5: How the great citizen of the people, Giano della Bella, was chased from Florence.

In January 1294[5], Lord Giovanni from Luccino in Como had just assumed the office of podestà in Florence and had before him a court case, in which Lord Corso de' Donati, a nobleman and one of the most powerful citizens of Florence, was accused of murdering a man of popular status, the servant of Lord Simone Galastrone, Corso's kinsman. A brawl between the two had resulted in wounds to both, and the servant died. Lord Corso Donati went before this podestà with the assurance [that he would be absolved] because of having friends in high places and in the government. But the people [*popolo*] of Florence expected the podestà to condemn him. He had already been tried before the court of the standard-bearer of justice and had been absolved. When the declaration of innocence was read out from the Palace of the Podestà and in addition Lord Simone Galastrone was condemned for assault, the *popolo minuto* shouted: 'Death to the podestà!' They then ran out of the palace, chanting: 'To arms, to arms, long live the People!' A large part of the people, especially the *popolo minuto*, took up arms and rushed to the house of Giano della Bella, their leader. And it is said that they sent him with his brother to the Palace of the Priors to seek out the standard-bearer of justice. But they did not do this; instead they went straight to the Palace of the

---

76 Lord Antonio from Fossarogo was podestà for the first six months of 1289.
77 Not everyone could afford to wear underclothes; see D. J. Herlihy, *Pisa in the Early Renaissance: A Study of Urban Growth* (New Haven, 1958), pp. 145–52.

Podestà, which the enraged people attacked with crossbows and other weapons. After setting fire to its gates and burning them down, they went inside. They seized and robbed the podestà and his men [*famiglia*] shamefully. But Lord Corso, fearing for his life, fled the palace from roof to roof, which had yet to be walled off. The priors, who were quite near the Palace of the Podestà, did not like the agitation but could not pacify the infuriated people. Several days later, after the rioting had died down, the magnates could not sleep for scheming how to do in Giano della Bella, since he had been among the leaders and spokesmen of the Ordinances of Justice and wanted to take the seal and the funds from the captains of the Guelf Party, which were considerable, and hand them over to the commune to beat down further the magnates. Giano had done this not because he was not a Guelf or of the Guelf league [*nazione*] but to reduce the power of the magnates. Seeing themselves treated so, the magnates formed an alliance with the college of notaries and judges, who also held a grudge against him, as we have mentioned, and with other rich citizens [*popolani grassi*], friends, and kinsmen of the magnates, who did not like Giano della Bella controlling the majority in the commune. They thus endeavoured to make a strong office out of the priors and accomplished it. As a consequence, they were able to force Giano to leave office before his term ended. At that point, as they [Giano's enemies] were still in office, they colluded with the captain of the people to press charges against Giano della Bella and his associates and followers and against those leaders who had set fire to the Palace [of the Podestà]. They alleged that these ones had instigated the rioting in the city, disturbed the peace, and assaulted the podestà in violation of the Ordinances of Justice. With this, the *popolo minuto* were greatly upset. They went to the house of Giano della Bella and offered to be with him in arms, to protect and defend him, and to fight for their country. His brother took a banner with the arms of the people into [the church of] Orsanmichele, but Giano, who was a wise man even if a bit arrogant, saw himself being cheated and deceived by the very ones who had backed him to improve the lot of the people. Seeing that allied with the magnates they were very powerful and that they had already assembled and were armed in the Palace of the Priors, he did not wish to risk a civil war [*battaglia cittadinesca*] and bring his country to ruin. Also, fearing for his life, he preferred to yield rather than press on. He left Florence on 5 March, hoping that the people would bring him back to power. But with the charges brought against him he was condemned in his absence and made an outlaw. He died in exile in France (where he was a business partner of the Pazzi[78]). All his property was destroyed and several other citizens [*popolani*] were accused with him. Thus, great damage was done by him to our city and especially to the people [*popolo*], even though he was the most faithful and righteous of citizens [*popolani*] of Florence and the greatest lover of the commune's well-being. Nonetheless, those he put into office did not benefit from it. He was arrogant and vindictive: he used the power of the commune to carry out a vendetta against his neighbours the Abati. And perhaps because of these sins, he was treated unfairly and condemned with an unjust verdict that defeated him with the very laws he had created. And note that this serves as an important example for citizens in the future: they should guard against lording over fellow citizens and being too arrogant. Instead, they should remain content with a commune of citizens. For the same ones who had helped in making him [Giano] great, out of envy betrayed and plotted to bring him down. And such has been indeed the experience of Florence in the past and at the present: whoever has been made leader of the people or of a society[79] has been knocked down; the ingratitude of the people never allows for any other recompense. Thus, this revolution [*novitade*][80] caused great upheaval and change for the people and city of Florence, and from then on the craftsmen and commoners [*popolani minuti*] were left with little power in the commune, which instead remained in the hands of the fat cats [*popolani grassi*] and the magnates.

29 'How the magnates of Florence instigated a revolt to break the People', 1295

G. Villani, *Nuova Cronica*, II, Book Nine, chapter XII, pp. 29–31:

By 6 July 1295, the magnates and powerful of the city of Florence had become fed up with the heavy penalties levied against them by the Ordinances of Justice, which the people had devised, and especially those laws holding one kinsmen responsible for another and that proof of guilt could come from only two witnesses. With friends in the priorate they endeavoured to break these ordinances of the people.

78 An important magnate family of Florence.
79 A guild militia or confraternity.
80 A meaning of *novità* is 'sedizione, ribellione, mutazione di governo'; *Dizionario della lingua italiana nuovamente compilato*, ed. Niccolò Tommaseo and Bernardo Bellini (Turin, 1869), III, pt. 1, p. 524.

First, they settled the great enmities among themselves, especially between the Adimari and Tosinghi and the Bardi and Mozzi.[81] This done, they called a meeting on a certain day and asked the priors to change these two laws. This brought the entire city into armed rioting with the magnates on armoured horseback supported by a great number of peasants and other armed foot soldiers. Wishing to charge through the city, they lined up their forces, some in the square of San Giovanni under the regal standard of Lord Forese degli Adimari, others in the square of the bridge [Ponte Vecchio] under the standard of Lord Vanni Mozzi, others in the New Market under the standard of Geri Spini. The upper guildsmen [*popolani*] came out armed in great numbers, arranged in order by their insignia and banners. They barricaded the streets in many parts of the city to block the cavalry and prevent them from breaking into the Palace of the Podestà and that of the Priors, who at that time resided in the house of the Cerchi behind [the church of] San Procolo. The people were powerful and well organised in their armed forces. Because the priors were suspect, the people guarded them with a militia, comprised of the wealthiest, most powerful, and wisest citizens [*popolani*] of Florence, one from each sixth [of the city]. The magnates were no match for them; the people could have won, but they thought it better not to start a civil war. After mediation by brothers of good families, each side disarmed, and with other initiatives the city quietened down. The people kept control of the government. The only change was the law requiring proof from two witnesses; it was increased to three, but the priors passed it through against the will of the people. The ruling was revoked, and the law returned to its earlier position. But this rebellion sowed the seeds of change and the beginning of a shameful and bad state for the city of Florence that would soon ensue; from here on, the magnates would not cease searching for ways to remove the people from power. At the same time, the leaders of the people sought every means to strengthen the people and bring down the magnates by fortifying the Ordinances of Justice. They confiscated the large bows [*balestra grosse*] from the magnates and gave them to the commune. Many clans [*casati*] that were not tyrannical or so powerful withdrew from the ranks of the magnates and came over to the people, thus diminishing the magnates' numbers and increasing those of the people. When these priors left office, their ankles were struck from behind and rocks thrown at them, because they had been seen as

81 Old and powerful magnate families.

BEFORE THE BLACK DEATH 55

favouring the magnates. And with this rioting and change, the people changed their stripes, bringing into power the Mancini, Magalotti, Altoviti, Peruzzi, Acciaiuoli, Cerretani, and many others.

30 Revolt of disenfranchised gentlemen, Venice, 1299

Sanuto, *Vitæ Ducum*, col. 582:

In 1299 Marino Bocco, Giovanni Baldovino, Michele Juda, and their followers, seeing that they were not included on the government's ruling council [*Consiglio*], conspired to riot in the piazza [of San Marco] and to kill the Doge and any nobles [*gentiluomini*] they could get their hands on, that is, those who remained on the Council. But God did not wish that such evil should transpire. Once this matter was discovered, immediately the Doge with the Council seized these criminals, and Marino Bocco and the above-mentioned were quickly hanged between the two columns near the church of San Marco.

31 Fra Dolcino's heretical kingdom, 1305–7

Historia Fratris Dulcini Heresiarche di Anonimo Sincrono, ed. Arnaldo Segarizzi in RIS, IX/5 (Città di Castello, 1907), pp. 9–10 and 13. In horror, chroniclers across Italy and France told the story of Fra Dolcino, the brutality of his heretical communities in the hills of Novara and of their brutal suppression. Dante condemned the friar to Hell alongside Mohammad. The anonymous chronicle below, from the area of Biella, is the only narrative source that survives from the region and shows the most precise knowledge of local mountains and villages.

After having narrated the errors of this most wicked sect along with their many other crimes, I still have to expose many other of their evil ways, those perpetrated by the most wicked of these heretics, the Cathars [*Gazzaros*].[82] Indeed, while these Cathars were at Monte Trivero, they hanged many of the faithful of Christ from the gallows, including a little innocent boy age ten or so. Item. They hanged many other men with their wives and relatives looking on. They did not wish to ransom them, since they possessed the judgement of dogs. They killed others, starving them to death in prison. They cut off the

---

82 The chronicler and others used the word 'Cathar' as a slur without any sense of a set of specific doctrines or beliefs. In the next document, the Sienese chronicler used another slur 'fraticello' instead of 'Cathar'.

lips and noses of some women, from others, their breasts, and others, their feet. With one pregnant woman, they cut off her hand and arm. The next day, she gave birth on this mountain, and her son perished without baptism. They totally destroyed and burnt the villages of Mosso, Trivero, Còggiola, Fléccia, many cantons in the Crevacuore, and many homes in Mortigliengo and Curino.[83] They set fire to the church of Trivero; they disfigured sacred images and paintings; they stole the altar tables [*lapides sacros*] from the altars; they tore off an arm from a wooden statue of the Blessed Virgin enthroned [*maiestati*]. They stole the books, chalices, and ornaments of this church. Then they destroyed the bell-tower of Trivero and smashed its bells. They stole all the plates from a confraternity and all the property of the priests. And they brought these stolen goods to the mountain named above, Mount Rubello, now called the mountain of the Cathars.

[p. 13] On Holy Thursday, 10 March 1306[7], the aforesaid brother Dolcino the heretic, along with his perfidious followers numbering 1,300 or so went up to Mount Rubello, which is above the mountains of Trivero, and in the following year on Holy Thursday, 23 March, he was captured and imprisoned with his followers, those pestilential dogs.

It is to be noted that after the expulsion of Fra Dolcino and his followers from Monte Rubello, as narrated above, the rectors of the churches of Ionginqui and other priests, who used to swear oaths to demons and evil spirits because of the hailstorms, used to put these evil spirits on Monte Rubello, as had been commonplace since antiquity, believing this place to be uninhabitable, and near here no-one could live nor cultivate its lands.

32 A Sienese account of Fra Dolcino's movement

Cronaca Maggiore di Agnolo di Tura del Grasso in *Cronache senesi*, ed. Alessandro Lisini and Fabio Iacometti, RIS, XV/6 (Bologna, 1931–37), p. 293 [A. 1305]. Agnolo di Tura called Fatso was the principal medieval chronicler of Siena, a stolid member of the merchant class and supporter of the oligarchy of the Nine. Like the Villani of Florence and other major chroniclers of Italian city-states, his reportage relied on an extensive web of merchant correspondence and as a consequence his coverage went far beyond the territory of his city-state.

83 Localities in the Province of Vercelli in the region of Biella, above Trivero and near Monte Rubello in the lower Alps. They extended northeast of Biella from about 10 to 55 km.

Fra Dolcino, who was not a friar of an ordained order but a *fraticello*[84] without an order, wrongly rounded up a great company of heretics in the countryside of Novara in Lombardy.[85] His followers were men and women from the countryside and the mountains as well as small proprietors [*di picolo affare*]. Fra Dolcino preached and spread the word that he was the true apostle of Christ, that all goods should be held in common, similarly that women were common property and could be used without sin, and many other disgusting articles of heresy. He claimed that the pope, cardinals, and other leaders of the Holy Church did not observe what the Gospels taught and that he was worthy of being pope. With a following of more than three thousand men and women, they stayed in the mountains, living in common alongside the animals. And when they lacked provisions, they took and robbed wherever they could. And he reigned like this for two years. In the end, those who followed this dissolute life began to regret it, and many left his sect because of the hardships of living in the snow. He was captured by the people of Novara and with his companion Margherita, and many other men and women living with him in these erroneous ways were burnt at the stake.[86]

33 A riot of butchers and blacksmiths, Siena, 1318

Agnolo di Tura del Grasso, in *Cronache senesi*, pp. 371–3 [A.1318].[87]

On 20 July a part of the army returned to Siena,[88] that is the foot soldiers from the neighbourhood militias along with the butchers and the blacksmiths. When they reached the [square of] Postierla they began to chant: 'Death to the traitors and death to Viviano d'Uliva de'

---

84 A term of abuse attached to the heretical branch of the extreme Franciscan Spirituals, who wished to follow St. Francis's strict rules on property and poverty.

85 The vast region surrounding Milan.

86 See G. Villani, *Nuova Cronica*, II, Book Nine, chapter LXXXIV, pp. 169–70.

87 For an analysis of a similar coalition of classes and another failed attempt to topple the Nine in 1311, see W. M. Bowsky, 'The Anatomy of Rebellion in Fourteenth-Century Siena: From Commune to Signory?', in *Violence and Disorder in Italian Cities, 1200–1500* (Berkeley, 1972), pp. 229–72. Also, see my criticisms of his analysis in 'Rivolte popolari e classi sociali in Toscana nel Rinascimento', *Studi Storici* (1979): 748–9.

88 They were returning after a secret treaty had been signed to topple the current regime at Massa in the Maremma of Siena, about 70 km southwest of Siena. Once the treaty had been revealed (by a cobbler in the pay of the Nine) a portion of the Sienese troops were called back to Siena.

Forteguerri',[89] who was a knight. To insult him, they called for Viviano to come out, and they continued chanting when they reached the Campo[90] and also screamed: 'Death to the captain of the people and death to the traitors', which they chanted as an enraged people. They [the army] had returned because they had been ordered to do so by the [government of the] Nine,[91] without having achieved a victory and without knowing the reason for the truce. They believed that the captain of the people and the government of the Nine ordered the retreat, because they thought they would not be victorious over Massa.[92] Thus the people of Siena were astonished to see these troops returning without a victory, and, not knowing the reason for the retreat, they derided and jeered at those who had returned.

On Friday, 21 July, the captain of the people with his knights returned to Siena. When they arrived in the Campo, all the butchers, blacksmiths, and others who had been encamped at Massa, along with many from the lower classes [*popolari minuti*] were even more astonished to see the captain and his knights returning without a victory at Massa. The entire Campo was filled with people, and they began to rebuke and mock the said captain and the other knights. And as well as swearing at them, they began to hurl rocks and seized and barred all the streets that led into the Campo with chains. Observing these matters with fear, the captain entered the Palace of the Nine, and the other knights, with good cheer [*buone parole*] but great fear, left by the alleyway of Saint Paul in the midst of the popular uproar, who were chanting: 'Death to the traitors, the captain, and Viviano d'Uliva de' Forteguerri'. Out of hatred, [these knights] refused to speak to the knight Lord Viviano. But, as we have said, none of these soldiers knew anything of the pact, since the Nine had signed it in secret. And in secret, [the captain and his men] sought out the truth. The said captain of the people, that is Lord Pavolo de' Baglioni, who was still confused and did not know what was happening, went into the Campo to make himself available to the Nine and was met by the rioting, as you have heard.

89 A military commander from one of Siena's most powerful magnate families; see W. M. Bowsky, *A Medieval Italian Commune: Siena under the Nine 1287–1355* (Berkeley, 1981), pp. 16 and 66.
90 The main square of Siena with the Palazzo Pubblico at its base.
91 A regime of wealthy merchants, bankers, and some noblemen, which ruled Siena from 1287 to 1355; see Bowsky, *A Medieval Italian Commune*.
92 Massa Marittima: a major military outpost and market town in the Senese Maremma.

The judges and notaries of Siena went into the palace to the office of the Nine and presented a petition, demanding that the Nine give them and other good men[93] of the city a role in the government.[94] Beyond this demand, they said much more, provoking the lords of the Nine to curse them; with scorn, they threw out their petition and abolished their lordships, that is, their posts in the countryside and other offices. And in this conspiracy, the notaries and judges joined the ranks of certain other magnates of Siena along with the butchers. The leaders of this revolt were the notaries – Ser Feo Gratia, Ser Pino Beneincasa from Asciano, Ser Antonio of Asciano, Ser Tura Forte, plus many other notaries. Among the judges, Lord Antonio di Love Ricovaro of Asciano was a leader; among the butchers, Cione di Vitaluccio; and among the magnates from the Tolomei clan were Lord Sozo Dei de' Tolomei, Lord Deo di misser Cuccio Guelfo de' Tolomei, Lord [...] de l'Incontro, and Gabriello di Speranza de' Fortegueri.

The judges, notaries, butchers, and others allied with them along with many followers from the commoners [*popolari minuti*], and other conspirators of Siena staged an armed rebellion [*romore*], wearing armour, suits of mail, and other weapons; indeed they had many weapons. They went to the entrance of the *Casato*,[95] chanting: 'Let's break the chains and storm the gate of the Palace of the Nine, destroy their houses, shops, and those of certain other rich ones'.

And this was on Thursday, 26 October, the feast day of Saints Simon and Jude. They chanted: 'Death to the Nine and Long live the People'.

And the office of the Nine, which knew of this conspiracy and the impending revolt, made preparations, arming all their soldiers, all their police [*birivieri*], and at least three hundred foot soldiers called the *balzanelli* [the palace guard], who should have gone to Genoa in the service of King Robert.[96] Thus, when the judges, notaries, butchers, and their followers came rioting from the entrance of the *Casato* to the Campo, they met the Nine's troops at the foot of the palace and entrance of the *Casato*. A great battle ensued and lasted almost to the first ringing of the bells. The notaries and butchers waited for the

---

93 Citizens and not the *popolo minuto*.
94 As with disenfranchised workers, the Nine barred those belonging to the guilds of the judges and notaries from holding major governmental posts in the city. As this document shows, they could hold posts in the countryside.
95 A street that led into the Campo from the south west of the city.
96 The Angevin king of Naples; see [52].

nobles, their co-conspirators, to come to their aid with their troops, that is, those of the Tolomei and Forteguerri families with their followers. But because of Lord Deo de' Tolomei's advice, many did not show up. Instead, they remained armed in the square of the Tolomei, leaving the notaries and butchers to fight alone without any help. The bells of the commune rang calling citizens to arms, which drew many into the fray from one part of the city or another, and this battle began at night at the second ringing. A bitter fight developed with many killed on both sides, especially among the notaries, many of whom were killed by missiles shot from the commune's big crossbows. The Nine restored order and captured the insurgents' weapons. The notaries and butchers along with many of the Forteguerri and Tolomei families were defeated and forced to flee; many others were arrested; at least four of the leaders of the butchers were handed over to the podestà of Siena; almost all the rest escaped.

The governing lords ordered the podestà to record the names of all the leaders of this conspiracy and many of their followers; all who were captured were to be beheaded and those who were not were condemned as rebels ... Certainly, had the Tolomei not stayed in their piazza and instead come in time to assist the other conspirators, they would have been victorious; the rule of the Nine would have been broken, their regime ended.

34 Student solidarity, Bologna, 1321

Cronaca Gestorum ac factorum memorabilium civitatis Bononie a Fratre Hyeronimo de Bursellis [ab urbe condita ad a. 1497], ed. Albano Sorbelli, RIS, XXIII/2 (Città di Castello, 1911–29), pp. 37–8.

1321. A student [*scolarius*] at [the University of] Bologna was condemned to death for an affair with a woman related to Lord Giovanni d'Andrea.[97] Agitated by this decision, they all withdrew [from Bologna]

---

[97] The student, Iacopo da Valenza, was decapitated by the podestà of Bologna for running off with a young girl, the daughter of the notary Michelino Zagnoni and niece of the famous canon lawyer and professor at the University of Bologna, Giovanni d'Andrea (1270–1348), friend of Cino da Pistoia, Francesco Petrarca, and legal advisor to Pope John XXII. Among his many published law tracts and commentaries, he wrote a summa on engagement and marriage; see G. Tamba, 'Giovanni d'Andrea', *Dizionario Biografico degli Italiani*, 55 (Rome, 2000), pp. 667–72

and left for Imola. Because of this, the city [of Bologna] was in great turmoil.[98]

35 'Of the riots and great turmoil that occurred in the city of Pisa', 1322

'Of the riots and great turmoil that occurred in the city of Pisa because of factions among its citizens';[99] G. Villani, *Nuova Cronica*, II, Book Ten, chapter CLIII, pp. 351–2.

In May 1322, the city of Pisa rioted because of the factions among its citizens. Lord Corbino of the Lanfranchi clan [*casa*] killed Lord Guido from Caprona, one of the most important citizens of Pisa. The people [*popolo*] revolted, captured this one of the Lanfranchi, and cut off his and his brother's heads. Because of this, the rioting did not die down but heated up: Count Nieri de' Gherardeschi,[100] commander of German soldiers [*masnade*][101] and other magnate families from the countryside rushed into the city to join the fray. Abetting the rage of the magnate families – the Lanfranchi, Gualandi, Sismondi, and Capornesi – other factions came out against the people. They killed three powerful burghers [*popolani*] and hunted down all those who belonged to the faction of Coscetto of Colle, claiming that they were the ones who had ordered the murder of Guido. And they summoned Coscetto of Colle to appear before them.

Because of these murders and injustices, the [people] despised this Count Nieri and went after him and the magnates. On the second day, they took up arms and rioted through the streets to carry out their own justice: they condemned as rebels fifteen leaders from these magnate clans and destroyed their property. Had it not been for the strength of his knights, the people of Pisa would have also hunted down the count himself. He claimed not to have been involved in these killings; instead, he had entered the city to protect it from

---

98 The students also went to Siena and other places in Central Italy. The matter was not resolved until the end of April, 1322, when the students were enticed to return to Bologna.

99 This incident and change of government receives far less attention from the local chronicler of Pisa, *Cronaca di Pisa di Ranieri*, ed. Ottavio Banti (Rome, 1963), 75–6, than it does from Villani.

100 An old noble family of Pisa with vast cattle-grazing lands in the Maremma south of the city.

101 These would have been brigands or soldiers of fortune.

Castruccio,[102] who with all his forces had twice penetrated as far as Monte San Giuliano.[103] The Pisans now feared that [Castruccio] would rampage through the city and sack it; they mobilised to block him. They remained armed and on maximum alert for many days because of these divisions and factional strife. Coscetto dal Colle, a burgher and man of great standing and courage, who had been head of the people of Pisa when Uguiccione da la Faggiuola[104] was chased out of town and afterwards had killed those members of the Lanfranchi clan, as we have mentioned, was now outside Pisa, condemned as a rebel. From messages sent by his friends inside the city, he heard of these divisions in Pisa and planned to enter the city, to overturn the state, and to kill and chase out the count and his followers. He stayed just outside the city walls in a peasant's hut in order to enter Pisa at a precise moment the next morning. But his comrade and confidant betrayed him. With great rage, the count captured Coscetto, led him into Pisa, and without a trial, had him dragged, which tore him to pieces; his body parts were then thrown into the Arno. Afterwards, the city settled down and a great festival and procession were held. Many nobles and burghers of the Coscetto faction were sent into exile to distant parts of the world. And on 13 June 1322 this Count Nieri became lord and defender of the people of Pisa. Thus, within a few days Count Nieri's fortune had spun from one side [of the wheel] to the other.[105]

36 A match of fisticuffs explodes into city-wide riots in Siena, 1324

Autore Anonimo, in *Cronache Senesi*, pp. 127–8: How in the Campo on Sunday of the Carnival in 1324, a great game of hand-to-hand combat was held that resulted in a riot [*romore*] in Siena.[106]

102 Castruccio Castracani was the great military leader of Lucca, who made inroads into the territories of Pisa and Florence in the early fourteenth century. A century and a half later, he was Niccolò Machiavelli's model of a military captain and strategist.

103 Today, San Giuliano Terme, 6 km northeast of Pisa.

104 He had been lord of Pisa and head of the Ghibelline Whites at the beginning of the fourteenth century, when the Ghibellines were divided into two factions – the Whites and Blacks. He was one of the most powerful lords in Italy, featuring in Machiavelli's *Istoria fiorentina* and condemned to Hell by Dante, *Inferno*, XXXIII, line 89.

105 Villani here employs one of the most popular images of the later Middle Ages, the wheel of fortune.

106 *Cronaca di Agnolo di Tura*, in *Cronache Senesi*, pp. 416–17, describes this same insurrection that resulted from this game of combat.

In the period of this government [of the Nine] and of Lord Gherardo degli Abruciati of Parma,[107] those of San Martino[108] and of Camollia[109] staged a big match of fisticuffs[110] and hand-to-hand combat against the third city district called la Città.[111] The competition began with the throwing of stones and then went on to fights with sticks, and from sticks to combat with large and small shields and then to daggers [*collate?*]. From there they continued with lances, swords, and spears. And such was the riot [*rumore*] in the Campo that it seemed the whole world had gone topsy-turvy. And all the soldiers of the commune took up their arms and came out into the square along with the lord podestà and his troops under the command of the government of the Nine. But by no means could they break up the battle. Men were knocked off their horses; horses were killed and even several men, among them, some soldiers. Because many left [the Campo] from the streets with long lances, crossbows, breastplates, and daggers [*falcioni*], the fighting renewed with greater force. And it seemed no one by any means could remedy the situation or stop the destruction. However, the priests and friars of the orders of Siena went out into the fray. The bishop walked into the square carrying the cross in front of him right to where the battle was most fierce, and they let him pass through. The numbers of priests and friars then multiplied and began to quell the battle. Because they saw the Holy Cross in front of them and also because of the great prayers of the holy clergy and the bishop, who prayed continuously, the battle ended, but not before four had been killed. And a man named Sano di Tonio, a cloth vendor [*ligritiere*], set fire to the church of Saint Paul on the side towards the Campo. The first time he set the fire, it failed to light, so he tried again; this time with results. He did it to encourage the crowds to leave the battle without considering the damage he was causing. It was very difficult to put the fire out. After the battle had been quelled and the fire put out, the Nine held a council meeting and made proposals to deal with the consequences of this game – the fire that was started and the four who had been killed. Quickly, it was

---

107 According to *Cronaca di Agnolo di Tura*, Misser Gherardo di misser Arighetto de li Abruciati was from Brescia, not Parma. He was podestà of Siena at the time of this riot and then elected for another six-month term in March 1325.

108 The southeastern 'Third' of the city.

109 The northwestern 'Third' of the city.

110 Despite its name – giucho di pugnia – this was more a battle of weapons than of fists as this document attests.

111 The western 'Third' of the city.

advised that from now on these 'games of fists' would not be tolerated. And this was done to lessen the scandal. And a price was put on the heads of those who had murdered the four and the one who had started the fire, if anyone knew who it was. And as soon as the decision was made public, anyone who thought he might be found guilty bolted as fast and far as he could [*andarsi chon Dio*]. And in this way order was restored. As we have said, had it not been for those men of God, that is, the clergy who intervened in the thick of battle at the moment when Siena was in revolt and in danger, the state would have been overturned and the Nine sent crashing to the ground.

37 The political consequences of food shortages in Rome, 1328

G. Villani, Book Eleven, chapter CXVIII, pp. 669–70: How because of the food crisis the Romans took the government of Rome from the hands of King Robert.[112]

In these times, 3 February [1329], Lord William of Eboli,[113] King Robert's baron and senator in Rome guarded the city with three hundred cavalrymen. Because of a great food shortage created by the high prices all over Italy, the Romans complained that King Robert had not supplied them from his kingdom [Regno].[114] The people [*popolo*] began to riot, chanting: 'Death to the Senator', and ran him down, assaulting him fiercely in the Campidoglio;[115] his troops were unable to resist them. He surrendered and left his office with great injury and shame. The Romans placed in power their own senators, Lord Stefano de la Colonna and Lord Poncello Orsini,[116] who from their own supplies of grain and those of other powerful Romans ordered shipments for the city market, and this quietened down the people.

---

112 On famine and riots at Siena in 1328 see Dean, *The Towns of Italy in the Later Middle Ages*, ed. Trevor Dean (Manchester, 2000), doc. no. 69. On this Angevin king of Naples, see [52].

113 A town about 35 km southeast of Salerno.

114 The grain exporting regions of Sicily and southern Italy.

115 On the Capitoline hill, the seat of government during the Roman Republic and of the medieval commune.

116 The Colonna and Orsini families were two of the oldest and most powerful noble families of medieval Rome; at least three popes came from these families.

38 How the Florentines avoided food riots, 1328–30

G. Villani, *Nuova Cronica*, II, Book Eleven, chapter CXIX, pp. 670–2: How in this year and the following one, the prices for foodstuff soared in Florence and almost everywhere in Italy.

In 1328 and lasting until 1330, prices of grain and other provisions in Florence soared. At harvest time in 1328 grain cost 18 shillings [*soldi*] a bushel [*staio*][117]; suddenly, in a few days, it jumped to 30 shillings. Then, at the beginning of the next year [25 March], the price mounted every day so that by Easter[118] it had reached 42 shillings. Afterwards, and perhaps for the first time, it climbed to one gold florin[119] a bushel in many parts of the *contado*, making it impossible to purchase grain, except by the rich as opposed to those with the greatest need, causing great misery and suffering for the poor. And this not only happened in Florence but all over Tuscany and a large part of Italy. The shortages were so cruel that those in Perugia, Siena, Lucca, Pistoia, and many other city-states of Tuscany could not sustain themselves and kicked out all the poor beggars [from their cities]. But with wise counsel and good preparation, the commune of Florence, being pious and desiring to alleviate suffering, supported a large part of the poor beggars of Tuscany by spending a great sum of money to supply the grain stores; they ordered grain from Sicily, having it shipped by sea to Talamone in the Maremma.[120] From there it was brought to Florence at great risk and expense. It was also brought from the Romagna and the *contado* of Arezzo without concern over the high costs and with severe shortages still growing. The price of a bushel of grain was fixed at half a gold florin in Florence's central market [Orsanmichele],[121] even though the grain was mixed with a fourth-part of barley. And because of this, the rage of the people mounted so that armed officials of the government needed to stay on guard at Orsanmichele with the block and henchman's axe to render justice: they had to cut off the limbs of violators. Over these two years, the

---

117 The measure varied slightly from one city-state to the next but was approximately one bushel.
118 Easter fell on 23 April in 1329; see A. Cappelli, *Cronologia*, 7th edn (Milan, 1998), p. 100.
119 In 1329 the florin would have been worth around 60 Florentine shillings.
120 The port for Siena.
121 Florentine law required all grain to be distributed from one central market; it remained at the church of Orsanmichele until 1367, when it was moved about sixty metres to the new Mercato del Grano, now called the Mercato Nuovo.

commune of Florence lost over 60,000 gold florins to sustain the people. And all these measures would have come to naught had the officials of the commune decided not to sell grain in the central market and make bread for the commune from all of its ovens and then to sell it every morning at three or four shops in each city district [*sesto*] at a weight of 6 ounces a loaf of mixed grain for 4 pennies a piece. This policy sustained the people and the poor and contained their rage, so that everyone could have enough bread at least to live on and thus could survive spending between 8 to 12 pennies a day. No one was allowed to profit by buying a bushel [of grain]. At this time, I, the author, though not worthy of such high office, served as an official along with others in these bitter times, and with the grace of God we discovered a remedy and policy that pacified the people, cooled their rage, and left the poor content without any scandals or rioting of the people of the city. And by this testimony, it is true that in no other country did the powerful and merciful citizens give so much charity to the poor as did the Florentines during this extreme famine. Therefore, without bragging, I believe that by this charity and provisioning of the poor people and by God's providence our city was saved from great adversities. We have spoken at such length about this matter to provide a lesson for our citizens for making policy in the future, when our city might again face such a dangerous famine. With God's will and reverence to Him the people can be saved and the city can avoid the danger of rage and revolution [*rubellazione*]. [Villani then continues with an explanation of thirty-year cycles of famines, based on the conjunction of the stars.]

39 Florentine craftsmen start up clubs and have parties, 1333

Marchionne di Coppo Stefani, *Cronica fiorentina*, ed. Niccolò Rodolico in RIS, XXX/1 (Città di Castello, 1903), r. 495, p. 173. Stefani (or Bonaiuti as some argue he should be called) was born in 1336 and was the major Florentine chronicler from the death of Matteo Villani in 1363 to his own death in 1386. He was involved in politics in the 1360s but gained his first major office in 1372. He was elected as a prior in the government of the Minor Guilds in the tumultuous year 1379 and probably because of this involvement was unable to participate after the return of oligarchic rule in 1382. Although he relied heavily on the Villani chroniclers for materials before 1363, he provides some new material and insights of his own.[122]

122 On Stefani's break from the providential and astrological frameworks of the Villani, see Green, *Chronicle into History*, pp. 86–105.

When things change it always seems that what follows is neither useful nor decent. In Florence, the craftsmen's arrogance mounted, such that every day they invented new sorts of festivals, games, and other forms of entertainment, much more than they deserved. And they held many street parties [*brigate*]. We will recount two of them. One took place in the via Ghibellina[123]: 477 men dressed all in yellow, elected lords from among themselves and celebrated with dinners and lunches and at great expense. And this was in May and lasted a month. Another one took place in Sant'Onofrio in the avenue of the Dyers [Corso de' Tintori][124], with another 520 men dressed in white, who jousted and partied. On the feast day of Sant'Onofrio they ran a horse race [*palio*], competing for a white banner. And they still celebrate that feast day in the same fashion but not on such a grand scale. There then followed a flood, which damaged that neighbourhood [*contrada*] more than any other [3 November 1333].[125]

40 The people topple the Doges in Genoa and Savona, 1339

Giovanni Villani, *Nuova Cronica*, III, Book Twelve, chapter CII, pp. 213–14: How the cities of Genoa and Savona formed governments of the People [*Popolo*] and called their heads of state doges.[126]

On 19 September 1339, those of the city of Savona[127] created the government of the People [*Popolo*] by taking over the two castles of that

---

123 A major street of the northeastern part of the city that runs along what had been part of the second ring of city-walls; it runs from the Badia fiorentina into what was then countryside.

124 This was the meeting place of the dyers from around 1280; see Robert Davidsohn, *Storia di Firenze*, tr. G. Klein (Florence, 1972), VI, p. 136; Paatz, *Kirchen von Florenz*, IV, pp. 458–62, describes a church of Sant'Onofrio in the via Malcontenti, founded in 1280 that later became a church of the Cappuccins.

125 See G. Villani, *Nuova Cronica*, II, Book Eleven, chapter CCXVIII, pp. 784–5

126 See also Georgii and Iohannis Stellai, *Annales Genuenses*, ed. Giovanna Petti Balbi in RIS, XVII/2 (Bologna, 1975), p. 129, but the Florentine source is more detailed. There is a serious lacuna in the rich chronicle tradition of Genoa from the *Annales Ianvenses* of Caffaro and his continuators, which ends in 1294, to after the Black Death, when the Stella brothers resume the story from ample documentation and by the end of the century from eye-witness accounts. For Genoa's first successful revolt of the *popolo* led by Guglielmo Boccanegra in 1257, see *Annali Genovesi*, ed. Cesare Imperiale di Sant'Angelo, IV (Rome, 1926), p. 25; and Steven A. Epstein, *Genoa and the Genoese 958–1528* (Chapel Hill, N.C., 1996), pp. 135–8 and 146–7.

127 On the sea of Liguria, 46 km southwest of Genoa.

land and throwing out the ruling families; one was held by the house of the Doria of Genoa, the other by the Spinoli of Genoa. And then, three days later, the citizens of Genoa revolted [*si levaro a romore*] and deposed their leaders, who were, on the one hand, the Spinoli and, on the other, the Doria. They chased them out of the country, along with their relatives and other magnates. They created a government of the people, and called upon Simone di Boccanegra of the middling sort [*de' mediani*] to be doge in the manner of the Venetians. He was a bold and valiant man. The following year certain magnates conspired against him. He captured and cut off the heads of two from the Spinoli family and many of their followers. His justice was severe, and he cleared Genoa and its coastal regions of pirates. His government always remained Ghibelline, and he increased the number of armed galleys to protect the commune from coastal threats from pirates.

41 The people of Ancona hound out their magnates, 1342

G. Villani, *Nuova Cronica*, III, Book Twelve, chapter CXLII, p. 287.

At the beginning of June of this year [1342], because of offences suffered from the hands of certain magnates, the commoners [*popolo minuto*] of Ancona rose up in rage, revolted, and assailed the nobles and magnates of their city. Killing many and wounding others, they chased them out of the land and robbed their houses. But this was a cruel operation, with some paying for the deeds of others: thus all the nobles, the innocent along with the guilty, were punished severely.

42 A revolution from above: the Duke of Athens sides with the lowliest artisans and workers of Florence, 1342–43

G. Villani, *Nuova Cronica*, III, Book Thirteen, ch. III, p. 295: How the duke [of Athens][128] deceived the priors and took over the government of Florence [1342–43].

To carry out the previously mentioned judicial decisions made by the duke in person, he appointed wealthy citizens [*popolani*] from the major families of Florence – the Medici, Altoviti, Ricci, and Rucellai.

128 To resolve their factional strife, the Florentines invited the French lord, Walter of Brienne, duke of Athens, to become the head of their state in 1342; see Gene Brucker, *Florentine Politics and Society 1343–1378* (Princeton, 1962), p. 7

The duke was greatly feared and held in terror by all the citizens. But, on the other hand, the magnates took great assurance from him, and the *popolo minuto*, great delight, because they now could put their hands on the reins of power. Thus they praised the duke, and when he rode through the city they shouted: 'Long Live this Lord!' And from fear and to gain his good graces citizens painted his coats of arms on almost every street corner and palace of Florence.

[Chapter viii, p. 308] What the duke did in Florence while he was lord ... On 15 October the duke appointed new priors, mostly lowly artisans [*artefici minuti*] and the most wretched of the old Ghibelline families. And he gave them a banner of justice with three arms, one with a diagonally-slanted spear with the arms of the commune against a white field and the red lily; on the second, a golden lion in the middle of a field of blue dots and on the lion's neck a shield bearing the arms of the people; on the third, the arms of the people against a white field and a brilliant red cross with royal crenellations above it. And the priors were put away in the little palace previously occupied by the executor [of the Ordinances of Justice] with few duties and even less authority attached. To inaugurate their office, there was no ringing of the bells or congregating of the people as had been the custom ... [p. 309] And thus the duke pimped [*puttaneggiava*] the Florentines: he gave the citizens false promises, took away all assurances from the magnates, who had made him lord, and robbed the people of their liberty and all their power and authority, except for [the title of] priors and the people. He closed down the offices of the standard-bearers of the militia, took away their banners, and rubbed out all the laws and officials of the people. Yet, by his consent, he retained the good graces of butchers, vintners, wool carders, and other minor artisans and gave them committees and rectors at their will. He violated the ancient laws of the guilds and allowed their workers [*sottoposti*] higher wages for their labour as they saw fit. For these reasons and other deeds of the duke, as you will find on reading ahead, conspiracies against him cropped up among the magnates and the upper guildsmen [*popolani*]. Therefore he confiscated all the large crossbows from the citizens, built an outer door to the Palace of the People, and barred the lower windows of his palace with iron grates out of hatred and suspicion of the citizens. He further built an outer wall surrounding his palace that also enclosed the palaces of the sons of Petri family and the towers and houses of the Manieri, the Mancini, and those of Bello Alberti, including their ancient gardens and squares ...

[p. 310] And he took away from the citizens certain palaces and fortifications and beautiful houses around his palace, where he lodged his barons and soldiers, who paid no rent ...

[p. 312] Three new judges were ordained, called those of Summary Justice, who held court in our houses, and in the courtyards and *loggia* of the Villani sons of the parish of San Pancrazio. These judges rendered their justice according to the size of the bribes.

43 The Duke of Athens flies the banner of the people in a last-ditch attempt to placate them

Stefani, *Cronica fiorentina*, r. 579, p. 206 [1343].

How the terrified duke [of Athens] asked for advice and flew the banner of the people and of the commune from his tower.

It happened on Sunday morning: sensing that the citizens were united against him, the duke called on the priors, who gathered in the communal palace with him. From fear, however, he called only for those he liked and trusted, to be advised by his friends, and he took their advice. They advised him to release immediately all those he had imprisoned and to make Antonio di Baldinaccio a knight. He said that he did not wish to perform the act with his own hands, but the priors wanted him to suffer the indignity, and he did it. And at the prison gate Antonio and the other prisoners walked free and went to their homes. Believing he had pacified the people, the duke flew the banner of the people and of the commune from his tower. But this was not enough for the people; they barricaded the piazza [della Signoria] at every point and guarded it well so that no one could enter or leave the Palace of the Commune.

44 A mad lord rouses wool carders to revolt against taxes and the fat cats, Florence, 1343

G. Villani, *Nuova Cronica*, III, Book Thirteen, chapter XX, pp. 350–3.

The magnates continued to be pressured by the foul disposition of the priors and would have gladly sought revenge and threatened to do so continually. On the other hand, they feared the force and rage of an angered and rebellious people, who might attack them with arms and cavalry. Thus, they sent out men to befriend them. But the people were not appeased and erected barricades through the city that were bigger and stronger than those constructed when they booted out the duke [of Athens]. They mounted a large number of guards throughout the city, who stood there night and day, fearing that the magnates might try some new tricks, and they sent calls for friendship to the Sienese and others. With the city at this boiling point, a crazed and mad knight of the upper guilds [*popolani*], Lord Andrea degli Strozzi, rose up against the will of his relatives, mounted his horse covered in armour, and assembled a following of troublemakers – carders in the wool industry and other similar sorts who wished to steal. They numbered in the many thousands. He promised to make them all rich, to give them abundant grain, and make them lords. On Tuesday 23 September he led them through the city with them yelling: 'Long live the *popolo minuto*, death to the gabelles and the fat cats [*popolo grasso*]'. They arrived in the square of the priors without any opposition, ready to besiege the Palace, proclaiming that they wanted to make Lord Andrea lord of the people. But Lord Andrea's kinsmen and other good citizens had forewarned the priors, and they made the enraged crowd and Lord Andrea disperse, but it did not happen until rocks had been thrown and crossbow bolts [*verrettoni*] shot against them, killing some and wounding many. The undisciplined and unarmed rabble [*popolazzo*] with their mad leader then left and went to the Palace of the Podestà to take it over, but in a similar way, arrows from the troops of the Marchese of Valiano, the podestà, were fired, and with the help of good citizens in the neighbourhood, they were sent away and began to disperse, going from one part of the city to another. And the beast Lord Andrea returned home, was captured by his kinsmen and neighbours, and against his will sent into exile, condemned to death as a rebel and agitator of the rebellion and conspiracy against the republic and peaceful state of Florence, and his property was confiscated. With this riot of the lower classes [*popolo minuto*], the magnates, who wished the worst for the people, were delighted, believing they could now divide the people and thereby unite with the *popolo minuto*. Calling for the downfall of the citizens, they all yelled the same chants from fortresses and barricades alike: 'Long live the Popolo Minuto and death to the fat cats and the gabelles!' And they continued to reinforce their ranks and waited on troops to help them.[129]

---

129 For this document and the next, see my comments in the introduction, note 32, based on the anonymous chronicle from neighbouring Pistoia, the *Storie Pistoresi*.

45 A street-corner revolt, Florence, 1343

Niccolò Rodolico, *Il Popolo Minuto: Note di Storia Fiorentina (1343–1378)* (Florence, 1899; new ed., 1968): Doc. 9, pp. 93–4: Archivio di Stato, Firenze [hereafter, ASF], Capitano del Popolo, Libro delle inquisizioni: Criminal inquest of Pagnotto degli Strozzi, accused of having incited the people against the condemnation of Andrea degli Strozzi, March, 1342[3].[130]

The magnificent and powerful knight Lord Raynaldus [the Captain of the People] brings this inquest against:

Pagnotto, son of the former Lord Andrea degli Strozzi, of whom the lord captain and his court have heard and been informed ... Instigated by the spirit of the devil and neglectful of the fear of God and love for the republic, this Lord Pagnotto incited a large body of people to riot [*in seditionem*], disturbing the peace and tranquillity of the city of Florence, while people and men of the city of Florence were standing around the corner of [the house of] Celle, former son of Ciardo, the boundaries of which are described below. Said Pagnotto contributed to the disturbances, rebellion, and detriment of the present peaceful and tranquil state of the city of Florence and incited sedition among these people and men who were standing, listening to, and taking in his speech, which he delivered to them by shouting in a loud voice: 'You dogs, dogs, dogs; you who die of starvation; you who have scraped for what ought to be given to you for ten shillings a bushel;[131] even I can make only a morsel out of you, you vile bunch'. And he said very many other disrespectful and vituperative words to them, which inspired many of those standing around to riot [*insurrexit*]. Pagnotto perpetrated these crimes in March of this year at the corner of Ciaro's [house] in the parish of San Lorenzo, next to the street and the houses of Domenico and Nuto, the sons of the former Ciardi ... [Pagnotto denied the charges, was fined 1000 pounds, and sent to Siena in exile.]

---

130 This is one of the earliest surviving documents from the judicial archives of Florence, which begin in 1343. This archive was badly damaged in the flood of 1966. Slowly, registers ruined in the flood are coming back to life.

131 This was the price of grain in good years but in the famine of 1328–29, it had reached three times that amount. Unfortunately, the records of Domenico Lenzi's *Baidaiuolo* are missing for the 1340s and 1350s; see Richard Goldthwaite, 'I prezzi del grano a Firenze dal XIV al XVI secolo', *Quaderni Storici*, 28 (1975): 15–36.

46 A riot of wool carders and the lower classes [*gente minuta*] explodes in Florence, 1343

Stefani, *Cronica fiorentina*, r. 593, pp. 215–16.

How a crowd [*brigata*] of the *gente minuta*, having been accused of robbing and seen themselves robbed, also wanted to rob.

In this year on the following day [25 September 1343] the wool carders and others of the *gente minuta*, perhaps 1,300 men, gathered together at the Servi.[132] They did not know what they wanted to do or what to ask for; they did not have a clue. On hearing this, the rectors took command. They mounted their horses and led foot soldiers from the neighbourhood militias [*Gonfalonieri*] and other good men, who were well armed. With the henchman's axes, blocks, and nooses, they proceeded in an orderly formation to the Palace of the Podestà to seek out the henchmen. When they arrived at the *loggia* of the Pazzi,[133] they heard the uproar and saw the rush of people. They were moving from the house of the Visdomini,[134] where they had just been. Already, they had begun to defend themselves against their assailants. The podestà, a wise man, wished to know the reason [for their insurrection]: they said that lord Ciritieri[135] had ruined and robbed Florence. And since they were poor, all they wanted was the belongings of the duke [of Athens] that had been stashed away in the house of the Visdomini. With words and not threats, the podestà tried to placate them but was unable to do so. The podestà sprung on [*gli sprona addosso*] one of them, who spoke more arrogantly than the rest, and arrested him. A scuffle then ensued, and the crowd was broken up. To be sure, the good men won. And the podestà's men arrested one, the first to have joined in, and cut his hand off; another was led up front and his foot was cut off. The frightened gang ran, some here, some there; none of them dared to gather again. One was captured and led back to the Palace [of the Podestà], who said that they had decided to rob the Visdomini, since they had robbed everyone else, and the

---

132 The friary of the Servites, better known as SS. Annunziata, located at the end of via de' Servi, northeast of the Duomo.

133 A prominent noble family of Florence; their palace was located on the northeast corner of the piazza of San Pier Maggiore, northwest of Santa Croce.

134 An old noble family of Florence; their enclave was around the church of San Michele Visdomini, located northeast of the Duomo.

135 The editor does not identify this lord; nor have I found him in any of the histories of the period.

rabble said: 'Our numbers will increase so, and we'll gain great wealth; the poor in turn will become the rich'. Having seen these events, the priors and others punished some, pardoned others, and brought law and order to keep the country from ruin.

47 A union of wool workers with a strike fund, Florence, 1345

Rodolico, *Il Popolo Minuto*, doc. n. 14, pp. 102–4: ASF, Capitano del Popolo, 17, Inquisizioni: The trial against Ciuto Brandini, carder, accused of trying to form a union of the disenfranchised workers of the Wool Guild, 30 May 1345.

30th May

This is the inquest which the above-mentioned lord captain and judge and all those [officials] in their courts and offices have made and have intended to make against Ciuto Brandini of the parish of San Pier Maggiore of Florence,[136] a man of evil ways, contacts, life, and reputation ... Led by the spirit of the devil, without God in mind, and acting as the enemy of human kind, this Ciuto wished to injure, act deceitfully, fraudulently, and maliciously. Under the pretext of the law, this man of evil ways, contacts, life, and reputation committed illegal acts. He is odious and hateful to Florentine citizens because of his calls to form an assembly [*conventiculas*] and for other offensive changes for the city and commune of Florence. By commanding and wishing to deceive good and honest men, he negotiated and made decisions together with many, many others, whom he seduced and subjugated to his own plans. He was able to gather great numbers of carders, combers, and other workers in the manufacturing of wool and to form a certain fraternity [*fraternitas*] with as many workers as he could get to join from many parts of the city of Florence. For this purpose, they had the resources [*materia*] in turn to meet and to elect committee members and leaders to organise gatherings and meetings to bring about easily the worst possible outcome. He subjected, procured, solicited, and called together meetings on many occasions and on various days, which assembled a multitude of these said men of unruly and evil ways. And among other things taking place in these gatherings and meetings, this Ciuto proposed, arranged, negotiated, and ordered a collection to be taken among these members in these

---

136 An artisan neighbourhood in the northeast of the city.

gatherings and meetings. Everyone who had assembled was to pay a certain sum of money to strengthen and sustain this iniquitous society and organisation ... In order to achieve this illegal act and many other such deeds and to resist with words, assaults, and other deeds, they enacted that this payment [should be paid], thus imposing this tax on themselves, against each and everyone of good habits to remove and withdraw [money] from those present and others called to these iniquitous meetings and organisations conceived to carry out their plans.

Adding further mischief to these evilest of deeds, he supported similar actions with heedless daring and wished to attempt even worse deeds and foster even more poisonous novelties to damage, harm, and waste the property of the men and persons of the city of Florence and their peaceful state. These illegal acts, schemes, and commands might have worked, had the office and troops of the captain [of the people] and his courts not apprehended and detained him. Because of this, the revolt, sedition, and disturbance that Ciuto planned could not come to fruition among the commoners [*popolares*] and craftsmen of the city of Florence. Ciuto committed and perpetrated these deeds in May of this year in the city of Florence, that is, in the church of Santa Croce...and in the church of the Servites ... against the laws, statutes, and ordinances of the city of Florence and against the good and pacific state of this city ... [The inquest goes on to say that Ciuto di Brandino confessed to all the charges.]

48 The *popolo minuto* of Siena organise secret meetings and revolt

Agnolo di Tura del Grasso, in *Cronache senesi*, p. 549 [A.1346]

In Siena rioting flared up on Sunday, 13 August, at 9 in the morning: the lower classes [*popolo minuto*] of Siena had organised a secret meeting and a conspiracy; their leader was Spinelloccio, the son of Lord Jacomo di misser Meo Tavena de' Tolomei. A part of these conspirators rioted and attacked the house of Berto Lotti, which was near the gate of the Friars Minor. They held a mid-day lunch with certain foreigners and citizens of Siena, among them, Giovanni di Ghezo Foscherani. Another part of the rioters, that is Simone from Volterra and two comrades, went armed and attacked this Giovanni and wounded him badly. They then left chanting on their way back to [the neighbourhood of] Ovile:[137] 'Long live the People and death to those who are making us starve', because there was a severe famine. On seeing Giovanni so badly beaten up, his son, named Meio, ran home for his sword and shield and went to confront this Simone and avenge his father. But Simone murdered Meio. While he was fleeing down the road, Minuccio Scotti and Benedetto nicknamed Meio, yelled after him. Simone turned back against them, wounding both of them and ran off again, shouting: 'Long live the People and the Guilds, and death to those who make us starve'. And thus he left Siena, safe and sound.

The city thus remained extremely tense, and the governing Nine was in great fear; they outlawed any who had assisted Simone and his comrades by placing a thousand gold florins on their heads, but no one was captured. Tensions in Siena grew steadily worse. Thus the Nine sent for help to many places, and numerous soldiers gathered in Siena from Florence, Pistoia, San Gimignano, Colle, Montepulciano, Montalcino, and places in the Sienese *contado*. They stayed on guard night and day especially around the Palace.

Siena's war captain[138] conducted investigations and brought to trial those suspected of rioting; several were found guilty, and a number from the lower classes [*popolari minuti*] were seized. On 23 August three commoners [*popolari minuti*] were beheaded: Pietro, a tailor, who was poor and old, aged 80; Robuccio, the bastard son of the parish priest of the Renaldini at Larniano;[139] and a young wool carder from San Gimignano. Then on 30 August the captain banished Biagio and Spinelloccio the son of Lord Jacomo di misser Meo Tavena de' Talomei and several commoners [*popolari minuti*] found guilty of this conspiracy. The commune destroyed part of the Tolomei's palaces and their rural estates at Campriano and Maciareto [Macereto]. It took

---

137 It was the epicentre of the revolt in 1371 and home to the Company of the Caterpillar.

138 Although the war captain had no legal officials comparable to the judges and notaries of the podestà and the captain of the people, he could make condemnations. Like the other chief officers of Siena, his term was for six months, but unlike the podestà and captain of the people, his term could be renewed. As a result, captains such as Guidoriccio di Messer Niccolò dei Fogliani of Reggio, Siena's most famous captain, immortalised by Simone Martini's fresco in the Palazzo Pubblico, served for six-and-a-half years and became the most important official in the Sienese government; see Bowsky, *A Medieval Italian Commune*, pp. 48–9.

139 There is a Larniano in the district of San Gimignano; see *Repertorio dei toponimi della provincia di Siena*, ed. Vincenzo Passeri (Siena, 1983), p. 189.

fifty master builders to wreck these properties as commanded by the captain. Also Pietro di misser Jacomo Attagrifi de' Talomei was banished, his palace knocked down, and his rural properties destroyed; it took thirty-eight master builders to carry out this demolition. Then on 2 September, Buono, a tailor, was beheaded.

49 The Podestà of Florence condemns the insurgents of Siena, 1346

Rodolico, *Il Popolo Minuto*, Doc. 10, pp. 94–7: ASF, Podestà, sentenze, 27 January, 1346 [7]: Death sentence against several members of the Tolomei family, accused with many workers of having revolted in Siena in January 1347.

In the name of God. Amen. These are the condemnations and sentences given, laid down, and pronounced by the magnificent and powerful knight Lord Guido de Fortebracchis of Montone, the honourable podestà of the commune and people of the city of Florence, its *contado*, and district against the men listed below ... in the year of our Lord 1346, the 15th indiction, in the time of Pope Clement the Sixth ... [27 January 1347]

Spinelloccio di messer Iacobi
Piero di messer Iacobi di Mactagufi } of the Tolomei family of Siena
Biago di messer Jacobi
Fransesco of Sambuca from Citeno
Chierobino, the servant of Spinelloccio
Bandino di Gabrielle, tailor, parish of S. Cristoforo
Pascuto di Ser Sani, parish of S. Pietro Ovile
Pagolo d'Andrea, parish of S. Stefano
Andrea, carder
Cecco di Pucci, cobbler
Francesco, son of the woman Nonna
Giannozzo, needle worker
Toma di Martino, cobbler, parish of S. Giusto
Cecco, cobbler, parish of the Mansione
Cambio, carder
Cecco, servant of Spinelloccio de'Tolomei
Guido di Meo called Guido the Scumbag [*del feccioso*]
Francesco, son of master Vanni of Opino
Francesco Vannini, locksmith
Niccolò di Goro, scabbard maker

Bandino di Calvello, tailor from Arezzo
Francesco di Chele di Baroccio, a wool manufacturer
Lodovico di Guccino or the son of Lady Catelina
Ser Tecco, master carpenter
Francesco di Guccino cobbler, parish of Mansione
Lippo, carder, son of the woman Angela, formerly from Florence, now living in the parish of Mansione
Iacopo di Narduccio, cobbler
Piero di Lippo, called Rossello, son of the woman Barda, parish of S. Martino
Giovvani di ser Dote, a carder, parish of S. Martino
Noccio, saddle maker, son of Anne, called Capecchio, parish of S. Cristoforo
Grano, cobbler and brother of this Noccio, the sons of this Vanni, parish of S. Cristofo
Simone di Lottino, carder from Volterra, now living in Siena, parish of S. Cristoforo
Giovani di Ballarino, tanner, parish of S. Stefano in the Third of Camollia

Against these and each one of them, whom we have examined by our inquest in our court ... and who have been denounced by [...] the lord captain of war in the city of Siena and its commune and have been denounced and called to appear by the priors of the guilds and the standard-bearer of justice of the city of Florence. Instigated by the spirit of the Devil, not having God before their eyes, and to the harm, abuse, scandal, diminution, disturbance, and subversion of the said city and people of Siena and its peaceful state, [those sentenced] planned, carried out, and committed the following, that is: this Spinelloccio commanded and schemed with Simon, a carder from Volterra, Giovannozzo di Ballarino, Pagolo d'Andrea, and many others from the city of Siena and foreigners; that the above listed Simone, Giovannozzo, Pagolo, and others should cry out and riot in the city of Siena, and should arm themselves, and run through this city shouting and calling out loudly for others living here to arm themselves and once armed to charge through the city devastating and overthrowing its peaceful state. And that this Spinelloccio with those listed above should go and ask them for help, and they should give him help, advice, and favours. Then Simon, Giannozzo, and Pagolo, armed with offensive weapons, knives, and other weapons, as had been ordered and planned by the said Spinelloccio, gathered together and with their knives unsheathed rampaged through the city and especially from the gate of Ovile to the house of Spinelloccio, shouting and chanting: 'Long live the People and death to the dogs who make us starve'. But this violence towards the people of this city did not succeed; nor did this outrage and revolt overthrow the city or devastate its peaceful state. [The same accusations were repeated for all the conspirators collectively 'who had also assaulted and killed many of popular status in this city ...' The accusations further singled out Simone di Lottoccio and Giovani di Ballarino 'who had planned the aforesaid revolt armed with steel knives; they yelled and cried out to others of the city and those who were staying in the city, running through the city and especially from the gate of Ovile to the house of the said Spinelloccio and with these knives thus unsheathed in their hands, they killed and murdered Meo di Giovanni Ghezzo of this city and assaulted many others of popular status of this city'. In their absence, they were condemned to death.]

50 Cola di Rienzo's revolt of Rome and his rise as champion [*tribuno*][140] of the People, 1347

G. Villani, *Nuova Cronica*, III, Book Thirteen, ch. XC, pp. 495–8.

Of the great transformations [*novitadi*] happening in Rome and how the Romans created a champion of the People.[141]

On the feast of Pentecost, 20 May 1347, Niccolò[142] di [Renzo] returned to Rome from the papal court [then at Avignon] on behalf of the people of Rome to request that the pope return with his court to the seat at Saint Peter's, as he should. Having received from the pope a good reception, even if all hope was in vain, he held a public meeting [*parlamento*] in Rome attended by many of the people [*popolo*]. Here, he described his embassy with clever and ornate words as if he were

---

140 Certainly, the ancient Roman associations of a magistrate or leader of the *plebes* is intended here.

141 The fullest account of Cola's rise to power comes from Anonimo romano, *Cronica*, ed. Giuseppe Porta (Milan, 1979); see Dean, *The Towns of Italy*, doc. no. 68. Villani's less often cited account provides additional insights, especially, the perspective from a contemporary outside Rome and on the relations of Cola's revolutionary Rome within the wider world of Italian and German diplomacy.

142 Today, he is better known by the shortened form of Niccolò, 'Cola' di Rienzo, but most contemporary chroniclers referred to him as Niccolò.

a master of rhetoric. He arranged with certain captains of the lower classes [*popolo minuto*] to announce that he had been made the leader [*tribuno*] of the people and had been installed on the Campidoglio to govern. From now on, the government would be rid of every lord and degree of the nobility in Rome and its environs. After capturing the old leaders, who had robbed Rome and its environs, he began to impose severe degrees of justice, sending into exile certain members of the Orsini and Colonna families[143] and other nobles of Rome. And most of the other nobles left Rome for their country villas and castles to escape the rage of this demagogue and the people [*popolo*]. And he took from them all their fortifications in the Roman countryside. He sent troops against the prefect and city of Viterbo, which refused to obey him. Soon, his summary justice in Rome and its environs had established considerable safety; one could now walk the streets safely day and night. He sent letters to all the heads of cities in Italy, one of which came to our commune [Florence] and was written with great eloquence. He then sent five solemn ambassadors to praise him and then [one to] our commune, [extolling] how our city was the daughter of Rome, founded and built by the people of Rome. Then they requested help for his army. We received these ambassadors with great honour and sent a hundred cavalry to the new leader of Rome and promised more help when it was needed. And the Perugini sent 150.

And then on the feast day of Saint Peter in Vincolis, the first of August, as announced earlier by his letters and ambassadors, he had himself appointed as supreme head [*cavaliere al sindaco*] of the people of Rome at the altar of Saint Peter. First to signify his grandeur, he was bathed in the basin of black marble [*conca del paragone*] in the Lateran, that is, where Emperor Constantine had been bathed when Pope Saint Sylvester cured him of leprosy. And to celebrate his new dignity, he held a great festival and feast, where he assembled the people, and he gave a great speech, saying how he wished to govern all of Italy under the rule of Rome as in antiquity. Yet the cities would maintain their liberty and justice. He paraded several new insignia, which he had commissioned. One of these, he gave to the mayor [*sindaco*] of the commune of Perugia, which bore the arms of Julius Caesar on a vermilion field and with a golden eagle. Another was entirely a new creation with an old woman seated as the figure of Rome and in front of her a young woman standing erect with a map of the world in her hand. She represented Florence offering Rome the

[143] See note 116.

world. He called the mayor [*sindaco*] of Florence to receive it. But in his absence, it was hoisted on a pole and he [Niccolò] said: 'He will surely come and take it at the right time and place'. He gave many other standards to the mayors of other towns near Rome. And on that day he hanged the lord of Corneto,[144] who had robbed the countryside around Rome. And having done this, his crier proclaimed at this meeting that he had been made emperor, and he followed up this with letters summoning the electors of the empire of Germany, Ludwig of Bavaria, called the Bavarian, and Charles of Bohemia, who had recently been made emperor, to come to Rome and on the feast of Pentecost to demonstrate their titles and authority to elect emperors and cast their votes. He also extracted and made public certain privileges from the pope, which [Niccolò] had commanded him to make. But we will leave aside for the time being those new and grand enterprises of the new leader of Rome. Even if his lordship and government could have achieved all that wise and discerning men had claimed [he would], the undertaking of this leader was a work of fantasy and short-lived.

51 Farm workers in the *contado* of Florence go on strike, 1347

Rodolico, *Il Popolo Minuto*; doc. n. 25, pp. 114–15, ASF, Provvisioni, n. 35, 22 January 1347[8]: Petition brought by landowners to the priors to impose severe penalties against rural communes, parishes, and farm labourers accused of going on strike and conspiring against Florentine citizens.

In the presence of the lord priors of the guilds and the standard-bearer of justice, the following petition is reverently presented for the common good. Certain communities, baptismal districts [*plebatus*], and parishes [*populi*][145] in the *contado* and district of Florence and their officials in these communities have tried through illegal means and deceitful plots to harass, oppress, and prevent commoners [*personas populares*] from cultivating landowners' fields, remaining in their homes, and grinding and milling their grain in the landowners' mills. They have ordered that no one should do business with these landowners or their labourers and tenants, thus bringing about the devas-

---

144 Today, Tarquinia.
145 The *Plebatus* was a parish church with a baptismal font; within its jurisdiction were dependent churches and parochial communities called *populi*. Unfortunately, this petition does not name these communities or the landowners who petitioned the government.

tation of the landowners' goods and produce. [These communities] have imposed taxes and other burdens on the landowners' rustics [*colonos*] and tenants, and have imposed and collected their own gabelles on the landowners' products and profits. Moreover, they have made iniquitous decrees and statutes against the landowners and have conspired, plotted, and performed many other unjust acts against them by various devious means and machinations. These wicked actions are in violation of the statutes and decrees of the commune of Florence, especially since so much of their evil has yet to come to light or provided an occasion to be prosecuted. In order that these commoners [*populares*] may live in peace and unity, defend the commune of Florence, end these scandals and conflicts between these people, and end these iniquities, your lordship ... is petitioned to see to it and confirm that these communes, baptismal districts, and parishes mentioned above, and any of them in the future, which might commit such acts, should be punished and condemned to pay 500 pounds each, and that each of their officers now and in the future or whoever presides or will preside there should be fined 300 pounds, and each person belonging to these baptismal districts, communes, and parishes committing these deeds should be fined 200 pounds ... [The landlords' petition was voted through and approved.]

Southern Italy

52 Rural and small-town insurrections in southern Italy, 1310–28

In 1943 the German army set a fire that destroyed entirely the *Cancelliera Angionia*, the rich collection of documents from the Angevin kings of Naples. This archive contained 375 registers in parchment and over a hundred volumes in paper, comprised largely of petitions from the king's subjects – nobles, townspeople, and rustics. Since 1949, Riccardo Filangieri and his successors at the Archivio di Stato in Naples have reconstructed fragments of these registers from earlier transcriptions and microfilms. Over forty volumes have now appeared but thus far none covering the reign of Robert of Anjou, 1309–43,[146] when, according to Romolo Caggese [*Roberto d'Angiò ed i*

---

146 Robert was the second son of Charles II, king of Naples, and of the French house of the Angevins; he was head of the Guelf forces against the imperial aspirations of Henry VII to unify Italy; he ultimately failed in his life-long ambitions to regain Sicily for the Kingdom of Naples; he has been immortalised in the third tale, book six of Giovanni Boccaccio, *Decameron*, and in Simone Martini's wood panel, *St. Louis of Toulouse Crowning Robert of Anjou* (1317), now in the Museo di

suoi tempi 2 vols. (Florence, 1922–30), I, p. 333], the violence between nobles and commoners became 'monstrous and intolerable'. Caggese's descriptions from the Angevin registers of the social conflict during the reign of Robert, unfortunately, do not contain full transcriptions of documents, and only occasionally did he transcribe fragments from the originals. Until fragments from these registers reappear for Robert's reign (if ever), Caggese's summaries must be relied on as though they were primary sources. Relying on Caggese's descriptions, Rodney Hilton, Britain's most prominent recent historian of the peasantry in the late Middle Ages, described southern Italy in the Middle Ages as 'a continuous Jacquerie' of peasant insurrection. Closer inspection, however, suggests that many of these revolts were championed by townsmen [*popolani*] and in some cases would have been citizens of high social standing. Further, these activities appear to cluster in the years of Robert's kingship (1309–43). [The passages in quotation marks are Caggese's citations from the now destroyed originals.] Caggese, *Roberto d'Angiò*, I, pp. 319–32.

At Angri,[147] we are in full battle. The people [*popolani*][148] succeeded in 'redoing and revising their tax assessments'. They threw off their heavy burden of taxes imposed on them by the nobility of this small town (p. 319). The nobles of Monticello in Abruzzo were dispossessed of all their lands, and in a real battle, four of them lost their lives [31 December 1321]. Guglielmo di Sabrano compiled for the duke of Calabria a very long list of the lands [of the nobility], which were violently taken from them and occupied by the peasants [23 April 1322]. At Montevarano[149] [25 March 1310] the lords were denied payment of their annual tax [*colletta*] and payment of numerous services [the peasants] owed them. At Montepagano the people [*popolani*] grew tried of fighting the nobility on legal grounds to induce them to pay taxes to the commune. Thus one day in the early autumn of 1320 they armed themselves, arrested those who resisted, and threatened to kill the nobles. They forced them to sign an act, in which they agreed to abide by the laws of the commune from then on [20 December 1321] (p. 324). At Crotone [Cotrone][150] ... it was the

---

Capodimonte (Naples). For a recent view of the state of preservation of the chancellery records produced during the reigns of Charles and Robert, see Andreas Kiesewetter, 'La cancelleria angioina', in *L'État Angevin: pouvoir, culture et société entre XIIIe et XIVe Siècle: Actes du colloque international* ... (*Rome-Naples, 7– 11 November 1995*) (Rome, 1998), pp. 361–415.

147 A town 27 km southeast of Naples.

148 *Popolani* means here more vaguely 'people' and not what it meant in fourteenth-century Florence, merchant-citizen or upper guildsmen, but it certainly would have encompassed more than ordinary workers and artisans.

149 Near Castellammare di Stábia or about 25 km southeast of Naples.

150 A major coastal town of Calabria on the Ionian sea.

people [*popolani*] who succeeded in occupying the lands of the nobility, reducing them to considerable poverty [7 December 1321] (p. 325). The anger of the people of Castroprignano[151] rose to great fury against their lord. After having refused to perform and pay the customary services and tribute, they assaulted the son of the baron along with other kinsmen and servants. They beat them brutally and killed the bailiff of this land. Not content with this, they deliberated amongst themselves and imposed on themselves a special tax [*colletta*], which they forced even the resistant clergy to pay. And having collected a small sum, they went to the royal court and began legal proceedings against this odious lord [3 February 1318]. Another lord, Guglielmo of Corsano,[152] was just as unfortunate. While he was inspecting his lands one day, his peasants [*vassalli*], armed and in great number, attacked him. Just in time, he managed to lock himself in his castle in the village, where he remained locked up with his wife. Meanwhile, the forces of the rebels grew and they attacked the castle, wounding mortally a poor servant woman of the lord who tried to placate the angry crowd. They threw rocks and spears against the tower and yelled menacingly: 'burn down the castle!' [22 March 1318, p. 330]. A few days after the revolt of Corsano, in the spring of 1328 a great crowd of armed peasants attacked the nobility and their servants at Scurcola, forcing them to abandon their lands. The conquerors seized possession of the property of the vanquished and 'set up their own rule', promulgating laws and 'creating their own elite [*archipopulares*] and party leaders'. The people of Tagliacozzo, Rocco di Cerro [Roccacerro], and neighbouring places rebelled using the same methods and reaped the same fruits. In the small region of Biyani in Basilicata[153]... the people prevented the bishop of Strongoli[154] from enjoying his ancient rights and injured him gravely. Finally, the fury of the people drove him from his residence; his only recourse was to call for the king's justice (p. 331). At Cotrone in the spring of 1339, a real battle exploded: with spears, knives, and pick-axes, the people attacked the nobility; they destroyed the nobles' houses and harassed their followers. But it was the captain of the city and the chief justice [*Giustiziere*] of Calabria – the true symbols of public power – whom they wished most to overthrow and who received the brunt of the

---

151 20 km northwest of Campobasso.
152 Near the tip of the heel of Puglia, 10 km north of Santa Maria di Leuca.
153 A region of high plateaus about 100 km east of Naples.
154 A hill town about 10 km from the Ionian sea, about 25 km north of Cotrone.

crowd's anger. They shut the gates of the city, provisioned the towers and fortresses, and for a long time succeeded in preventing the chief justice from entering his city. Only after resorting to unheard-of force did this official succeed in breaking the resistance of the rebels (p. 332).

53 The villagers of Lauria, Basilicata, overthrow their governor, 1317

Registri d'Angioni, no. 212, c. 78, 13 November 1317. Below is one of the few passages that Caggese transcribed at any length, Caggese, *Roberto d'Angiò*, I, p. 330.

The men of the walled village of Lauria [Basilicata][155] gathered illegally and incited the people to rebel [*fecerunt seditionem et tumultum*]. With the call of the village crier, the entire village congregated; they broke into the house where the *vicarius*[156] [Ugo di Clairmont] of this district resided. Enraged and with a great uproar they shouted: 'Death to the *vicarius*, death to the *vicarius*'.

54 Tax revolt in Ascoli-Piceno, Marche, in 1269

I Registri della Cancelleria Angioina ricostruiti da Riccardo Filangieri, II: (1265–81) (Naples, 1951), p. 63: collecting taxes in Ascoli-Piceno [*Esculo*] and depositing them at the royal court.

Charles etc. the castellan at the fort of Sant' Agata, etc. The under-secretaries of the district [*Capitanate*] recently reported to our Excellency [...] that while collecting the tax money totalling 59 gold ounces and 15 *tarcenos* from the commune of this land, the men of this commune rose up against these tax collectors, taunting and assaulting them with rocks and nails [*clavis*] [...] wishing to wound them. As far as possible, we intend to collect this money fully from this commune and bring it back to our court. Thus at the request of the under-secretaries we ask you to appoint soldiers in this walled village, together with the tax collectors [...] to use any means to coerce this commune into paying these taxes... Issued at Foggia on 13 April [1269] [Reg. 4, f. 33].

155 A mountain village about 35 km southeast of Potenza.
156 The king's local official.

55 A peace march by small children in Naples, 1347

Cronicon Siculum incertis authoris ab a. 340 ad a. 1396, ed. Joseph de Blasiis, *Monumenti storici*, 1st series: *Cronache* (Naples, 1887), p. 8. This extraordinary protest for peace and unity of the then divided two Sicilies takes place with ships of Sicily in the Bay of Naples poised to attack the city. Who orchestrated it, what results it may have achieved, what were the reactions of the ruling elite – the Angevin queen, Joanna I (1343–82), her court, and officials – are left unanswered in the brief report of this anonymous Neapolitan chronicler of the late fourteenth century.

In that year [1347] with banners of the Sicilies[157] [*banderiis siculorum*] raised and chanting 'Peace, Peace', small children [*pueri parvuli*] of Naples marched through the streets of the city until they reached the royal castle.

[157] The Sicilian Vespers (Easter, 1282) was a rebellion sparked by a French soldier sexually harassing a woman of Palermo at a festival outside the city. The rebellion spread across the island and led to the massacre of French soldiers and any others who spoke French and against Charles of Anjou's domination of Sicily from Naples. Eventually, in 1302 it led to Sicily's independence with the crown granted to Peter III of Aragon. Strife and armed attempts by both the Aragonese and Angevin crowns to regain the former unity of the Sicilies continued through the fourteenth and early fifteenth centuries until Alfonso the Magnanimous (1435–58) succeeded in reuniting the crowns of Naples and Sicily (1435) with Naples as the centre of his Aragonese Empire.

II: FROM THE BLACK DEATH TO 1378

Revolts involving or spearheaded by commoners in Rome, Siena, and Florence were on the rise in the years immediately preceding the Black Death of 1348. But the catastrophe of 1348 put a temporary end to these developments. Until the toppling of Siena's government of the Nine in 1355 [**71, 72**], social and political protests with concrete aims are difficult to find. In the market town of Barberino Valdelsa south of Florence, tempers rose at the end of the summer of 1348, leading to a bar-room brawl and then rioting [**68**]. But the cause of the conflict predated the plague and stemmed from attempts to redress corrupt election results of the previous year when a much larger riot had engulfed this walled village.[1] Two years after the plague, city chroniclers reported a conspiracy to topple the government of the Bentivoglio in Bologna [**69**]. It amounted, however, to little, was immediately repressed, and has left no trace in Bologna's rich judicial archives that survive from the thirteenth century on. In 1353, the Roman *popolo* chased the ruling senator, Luca Savelli, out of town. But the ex-senator and nobleman, Rainaldo Orsini, lead them and pulled the strings and the governor of Rome (Giovanni Cerroni), not the people, benefited in the end [**70**].[2]

Similarly, in France and Flanders, revolts or even minor skirmishes involving commoners with economic or political objectives find few traces in the chroniclers from 1348 until the revolt of the Parisians and the Jacquerie in the spring of 1358. A tax revolt in Rouen is an exception. Although merchants began it, workers paid the price with thirty-six from the cloth industry left swinging from the gallows [**56**].[3]

---

1 Unfortunately, the sentences for this case, which would have appeared in Podestà, n. 204, do not survive; nor have I been able to find the case in the surviving inquisitions for 1347.

2 The late-sixteenth-century historian Padre Pompeo Pellini, *Dell'Historia di Perugia*, I (Venice, 1664), pp. 909–10, mentions 'un poco di tumulto' in front of the town hall, whose participants chant 'Long live the People', but Pellini gives no source for the incident, and I can find no mention of it in the published chronicles.

3 In 1349 Louis de Male instituted regimes throughout Flanders that systematically excluded the weavers from city governments in favour of the fullers. At Bruges in 1351 and Ghent in 1349 and 1353, weavers and millers battled against the fullers,

Beyond the geographic borders of this study, such revolts are equally difficult to spot in the plague's immediate aftermath. In 1348, the smiths of Nuremberg revolted against the oligarchy to gain guild recognition,[4] but the first wave of plague had failed to reach Nuremberg. In 1348, the cities of Aragon continued their resistance to King Pere III and were brutally repressed in the year of the Black Death, but the Union of the six principal cities of Aragon and the brief success of their revolt for independence had begun in 1347, well before the plague arrived.[5]

To be sure, the Black Death and its immediate aftermath did give rise to social violence. But this violence differed markedly from the organised social protests with assemblies, elected leaders, and concrete political and economic objectives that spread with increasing frequency from the late 1350s through the early 1380s and across wide swathes of Europe. The violence 1348 to 1352 appears as spontaneous as any to be found in medieval chronicles. With little or no evidence of prior planning, assemblies, or election of leaders, flagellant movements, opposed by local governments and the church,[6] and the burning of Jews swept across large German-speaking areas, Spain, France, and the Low Countries. Rather than struggling for concrete goals or redressing specific political, economic, or social grievances, these social movements looked to forces outside society – the scapegoat and the heavens – to resolve their fears, anger, and insecurity.[7]

---

but the weavers and Flemish towns did not effectively attack the count or redress their grievances against the impositions of the king of France until 1359, when weavers, fullers, and drapers reunited along with many other tradesmen against urban patriciates and the count; see Henri Pirenne, *Histoire de Belgique*, 3rd edn (Brussels, 1922), II, p. 135; Nicholas, *Medieval Flanders*, pp. 225 and 308; idem, *The Metamorphosis of a Medieval City: Ghent in the Age of the Arteveldes, 1302–1390* (Amsterdam, 1987), pp. 5 and 155; and idem, *The van Arteveldes of Ghent: The Varieties of Vendetta and the Hero in History* (Ithaca, NY, 1988), pp. 109–11.

4 Mollat and Wolff, *Popular Revolutions*, pp. 72–3.

5 Pere III of Catalonia (Pedro IV of Aragon), *Chronicle*, tr. Mary Hillgarth and ed. J. N. Hillgarth, Medieval Sources in Translation (Toronto, 1980), pp. 400–49.

6 In the Low Countries, the flagellant movement appears at least initially to have been more carefully organised, even orchestrated, by leaders from the nobility; see Kervyn de Lettenhove, *Histoire de Flandre*, III (Brussels, 1847), pp. 354–8.

7 For examples of these immediate post-plague acts of violence, see Rosemary Horrox, *The Black Death* (Manchester, 1994), doc. nos. 68–75; S. Simonsohn, *The Apostolic See and the Jews*, vol. I. *Documents: 492–1404* (Toronto, 1988), nos. 373–4 and 399–400; and *The Jew in the Medieval World: A Source Book, 315–1791*, ed. Jacob Rader Marcus, 2nd edn (Cincinnati, 1999), pp. 49–55. In addition, W. M. Bowsky, 'The Medieval Commune and Internal Violence: Police, Power and Public Safety in

With the second wave of plague, which infected the north of France, Flanders, and northern Germany in 1357–58, the number of social protests and revolts began to rise. I devote an entire chapter to the most famous of these, the Jacquerie that spread through the Beauvaisis, Picardy, the Île de France, and as far as the region of Bar on the northeastern frontiers of France in late May of 1358 [111]. Its revolutionary zeal along with that of the merchants of Paris influenced revolts in other cities, such as in Caen [113], and the seizure of the royal castle at Rouen [57]. In 1359–60, the internecine conflicts between fullers and weavers quietened; artisans reunited and led a tax revolt against merchants and the count that seriously challenged Louis de Male's urban policies and even his life [58, 59].[8] In the early 1360s similar revolts by artisans, who refused to pay new taxes are seen in Tournai [60].

Behind these revolts of Flanders and northern France were certainly the realities of increased warfare and the difficulties of finance that resulted from the plague and the consequential halving of the tax base. The combination of political instability, roaming brigands, war, and above all new taxes to be divided amongst many fewer also weighed heavily on the mountainous areas of southern France. Soldiers, peasants, and townsmen formed bands to redress personal grievances and pursue economic advantage in this milieu of hardship, war, and half-hearted truces between the French and English. Evidence of these bands called the Tuchins (which have been compared to the Mafia of nineteenth-century Italy[9]) date from 1363 and continued to 1384, when the duke of Berry, Charles VI's uncle and his lieutenant for Languedoc, crushed them.[10] Similar bands, however, continued to pillage and organise cattle raids in the Massif Central and other parts

---

Siena, 1287–1355', *American Historical Review*, 73 (1967): 16, has shown that the Sienese city council believed that in 1350 crime had increased greatly and that in the year of the plague and immediately afterwards 'criminals now acted with ever-growing impunity'. Yet the breakdown in law and order led to no known incidents of popular rebellion in the city until 1355.

8 In addition to the secondary literature, principally Pirenne and Nicholas (note 3), see *Recueil de documents relatifs à l'histoire de l'industrie drapière en Flandre*, III, pp. 781–90; and *Cartulaire historique et généologique des Artevelde*, ed. Napoléon de Pauw (Brussels, 1920), 711–18.

9 Marcellin Boudet, *La Jacquerie des Tuchins 1363–1384* (Riom, 1895), pp. 111–12.

10 John of France, duke of Berry (1340–1416), the son of John II and Bona of Luxemburg, is known better for his art patronage and collections of Books of Hours than for his savage repression and over-taxation of peasants and townsmen in the south of France.

of Languedoc well into the fifteenth century. I begin the presentation of documents on the Tuchins at their end in 1384 with the only chronicle description of them that I have found – tales from the cantor of Saint-Denis of their brutality, especially against churchmen [61]. On the other hand, the social dynamics of this movement, the web of personal rivalries, masculine bravado and insults, and the efforts of townsmen to defend themselves, can be plotted from rich archival materials – royal letters of remission preserved in the Trésor des Chartes[11] [62–5]. These letters of grace were extended to bandits as well as to those who took the law into their own hands, defending themselves and their communities against Tuchinate attacks. In these years, similar forms of social conflict also mounted in other areas of southern France [66–7].

The battlefields of the Hundred Years War were not the only areas of Europe to see increased warfare, political instability, and tax increases demanded from greatly reduced populations because of the plagues' incursions. In 1355 a combination of social forces from the richest magnate families in Siena to the *popolo minuto*[12] successfully ended Italy's longest-lasting city-state regime [71, 72]. Afterwards, governments fell even more frequently than those of post-World-War-II Italy. In five months alone, 1368–69, no fewer than five governments were toppled and replaced with new regimes [79]. In all of these permutations, artisans and workers – the *popolo minuto* – played a significant role and secured governmental offices and privileges for themselves. Revolts in Siena culminated in 1371 with the uprising of the wool workers organised around their neighbourhood association, the club of the Caterpillar [83]. After this failure, rioting and serious threats to political stability from the lower classes died down or disappeared altogether, at least as far as can be seen from city chroniclers.[13]

11 On letters of remission as a source, particularly for criminal behaviour, see Claude Gauvard, *'De Grace Especial': Crime, état et société en France à la fin du Moyen Age*, 2 vols. (Paris, 1991).

12 On the *popolo minuto* outside the Florentine context, see Jean-Claude Maire Vigueur, 'Comuni e signorie in Umbria, Marche e Lazio', in *Storia d'Italia*, ed. Giuseppe Galasso, VII/2 (Turin, 1987), pp. 321–606, esp. p. 466. In contrast to Florence, where the term applied to those workers who could not form guilds, in Siena and elsewhere the term was vaguer, encompassing two distinct groups or classes – manual labourers and artisans without guild recognition, who were mostly immigrants, on the one hand, and small shopkeepers and skilled craftsmen, on the other.

13 Because of their destruction in large part by insurgents, the fourteenth-century judicial records of Siena are extremely fragmentary.

Because of the Revolt of the Ciompi, historians have paid greater attention to popular revolt in Florence than anywhere else in Italy. Insurrections, however, were as numerous if not more so in other regions of central Italy during the last years of the 1350s to the 1370s. These included tax revolts [73, 74], insurrections of artisans and workers in the wool industry [79–83], and various attempts by artisans and underlings [*sottoposti*] to change the political control of their city-states in Pisa, Lucca, Cortona, Perugia, and Siena [75, 80–82, 84]. In addition, subject towns or walled villages struggled to regain independence and throw off the yoke of their dominant cities as with Montalcino's struggle against Siena and Galliano's against Lucca [76, 85].

The most important sweep of revolt, however, came in the 1370s. This wave has received scant notice from modern historians of social movements. In sheer numbers, revolts in the Marche, Tuscany, Umbria, Emilia Romagna, and the Papal States dwarf those of Florence as well as the supposed cluster of revolts Europe-wide in the years 1378–82 tabulated by Mollat and Wolff. Thus, in one year alone, 1375, according to the contemporary chronicler Giovanni de'Mussis of Piacenza, sixty cities revolted and were 'liberated from the yoke of church rule', that is, a third more than Mollat and Wolff list for all of Europe during the four or five years, 1378–82. These revolts, moreover, continued for the next two years with a count of 1,577 villages rising up against the 'pastors of the church'.[14] I have translated several brief chronicle reports of these central Italian uprisings and in one case a long and heretofore unpublished judicial record found in the Bolognese archives [86–90].

By contrast, other than the Florentine Ciompi, treated in chapter IV I know of only a handful of riots in Italy recorded in the chronicles for 1378 to 1382 – a 1378 revolt of the *popolo* in Genoa, which in fact may not have involved artisans and workers;[15] crowd pressure in Rome

---

14 *Chronicon Placentinum ab Anno CCXXII usque ad Annum MCCCCII auctore Johanne de Mussis Cive Placentino*, ed. L. Muratori, *RIS*, XVI (Milan, 1730), col. 521. Pellini, *Dell'Historia di Perugia*, p. 1041, lists 25 places that revolted against papal rule and taxation in 1375 in addition to 'many places and cities in the Romagna and the Marca of Ancona', which he does not name, and a poem by the anonymous diarist of Florence lists thirty-four cities; see [86]. By contrast, Mollat and Wolff, *Popular Revolutions*, pp. 139–41, find only 42 across Europe for the years 1378–82, and some of these, such as the wars led by Philippe d'Artevelde, I, along with David Nicholas, would not classify as popular revolts.

15 Stella, *Annales Genuenses*, pp. 171–2.

that convinced the college of cardinals to elect an Italian pope in April 1378;[16] a small tax revolt against the imposition of a land tax [*aestimum*] in the city of Parma in 1380;[17] a revolt of wool workers in Perugia in March 1383 (actually slightly beyond the cluster) [**191, 192**]; and an insurrection of 'the people' to overthrow the ruling Carriger family in Treviso around 1380 (the date is not clear from the chronicler). According to Treviso's town chronicler, however, they singled out and killed only one man, an officer named Pirinzolus, 'who was alleged during the last war to have captured Trevigan women and pulled up their slips to their groins to ruminate on their private parts [*remandere ad propria*]'.[18] But, as in many Italian conflicts of the later Middle Ages, it is difficult to know without judicial records who exactly these people were, whether they were workers and artisans or simply members of one ruling faction fighting another.

Throughout this period, c. 1355 to 1378, in marked contrast to the pre-plague period and with the flagellant and anti-Semitic movements of the plague's immediate aftermath, 1348–51, there is a striking absence of clerics as leaders or as members of the rank and file in these revolts. Nor do the sources reveal religious fervour or heresy as a driving force behind these insurrections as can be spotted in a number of revolts before the Black Death. The one exception of clerical involvement in these post-plague revolts proves the rule: in 1360 clerics and friars led and supported Pisan artisans who plotted to remove the pro-Florentine government from power in Pisa. Their reasons, however, had nothing to do with religion as far as the documents reveal. Instead, they sought to lift the Florentine embargo on their port, because it was causing artisan incomes to decline [**75**]. Unfortunately, the chronicler does not explain these clerics' motivation.

---

16 Numerous chroniclers across Italy and France report this revolt of the Roman crowd and the beginnings of the 'Great Schism of the West' initially between Urban VI and the anti-pope, Clement VII.

17 *Chronica abreviata, Fr. Johannis de Cornazano O.P* in *Chronica Parmensia a sec. XI. ad exitum sec. XIV.* ed. L. Barbieri, Monumenta Historica (Parma, 1858), p. 397.

18 Ser Andrea de Redusiis de Quero, Cancellario Communis Tarvisii, *Chronicon Tarvisinum, a. 1368–1428*, in Muratori, XIX (Milan, 1731), col. 789.

Northern France and Flanders

56 The merchants' revolt against new royal taxes, Rouen, 1351

Chronique Normande de Pierre Cochon notaire apostolique à Rouen, ed. Charles de Robillard de Beaurepaire, Société de l'histoire de Normandie (Rouen, 1870), pp. 75–6. Little is known of this chronicler. He was born after 1360, was an official of Rouen in 1406, began his chronicle in 1409, and became the notary of the Episcopal court in Rouen in 1425. He lived perhaps into his nineties, dying in 1456.

And in his time [Philip VI][19] began the imposition of taxes the people called the gabelles. And when they came to Rouen [1351], the merchants staged a sort of revolt by throwing the cabinets [*les buffés*] in which the taxes were collected into the Seine under the bridge of the Seine.[20] And on account of this rebellion, Sir Simon de Bucy, first president of the Parlement,[21] came to Rouen and ordered on behalf of the king that no one should leave his house until the king's justice was executed, which was done on the eve of Saint Lawrence [9 August 1351]. Thirty-six from the cloth industry in this city were hanged from the gallows.

57 Seizure of the royal castle at Rouen, 1358

A. Chéruel, *Histoire de Rouen pendant l'époque communale 1150–1382* (Rouen, 1843–44), I, p. 203: Charles's pardon to the bourgeois of Rouen for excesses committed in 1358, Archives Municipales de Rouen, reg. U/1 47r. This letter makes no specific mention of the Jacquerie and revolts in Paris but the '*troubles*' which had stirred up the surrounding regions' no doubt alluded to them. Certainly, the Norman *Chronique des quatre premiers Valois* reported it in this vein: 'once the news [of the massacre of the Jacques] had reached Rouen, the people began to riot and the bourgeois became deeply suspicious of Lord Jehan Sonnain, then the captain of the castle of this town'.[22] On the other hand, those appealing to the king for his grace and forgiveness wished to put

---

19 In 1342 Philip established the salt gabelle in many places in the kingdom to pay for the costs of war; now these sales taxes were being extended to other commodities.

20 The riot occurred in August 1351, sparked by the Estates of Normandy's agreement with the king to impose a tax [*aide*] on the purchase and sale of commodities.

21 One of John II's chief advisors in exile; the Estates General on the eve of the Jacquerie saw him along with Pierre de la Forêt and Robert de Lorris as a corrupting influence on the crown; see Jonathan Sumption, *The Hundred Years War*, Vol. II: *Trial by Fire* (London, 1999), p. 282.

22 *Chronique des quatre premiers Valois*, ed. S. Luce, SHF (Paris, 1862), p. 77.

the best possible light on their previous misdeeds to gain as much remission from former and future reprisals as possible. Similarly, the king and his councillors in granting remission did not wish to appear to be insouciant in rewarding criminal or insurrectionary behaviour. Thus the bourgeois, the mayor, and the king might choose not to state the underlying reasons for a revolt in a letter of remission or admit that they had been inspired by the example of Paris to extend their rights as a city-state.

By letters recently sent to our loyal friend Jean Sonnain, chief officer for Caux, and guard of our castle at Rouen we have appointed him as the captain in our name in charge of this castle. But during his absence, the mayor, the bourgeois, and commoners of this town of Rouen, fearing the revolts [*troubles*] which had stirred up the surrounding regions, seized this fortress in order to keep it from being delivered by treachery to our enemies, who were overrunning the country, and to keep the town from being sacked and devastated. However, some were frightened at the consequences that might result from the occupation of the castle; they feared being fined or sentenced to corporal punishment. Knowing as we did that they were acting faithfully towards us in taking this citadel, we agreed to pardon and grant remission to the mayor, bourgeois, and commoners of the town of Rouen, to all, individually and collectively, for the above-mentioned deed ...

Issued in Paris, 4 September 1358.

58 Internecine artisan conflict in Bruges and its resolution, 1359

Matteo Villani, *Cronica con la continuazione di Filippo Villani*, ed. Porta (Parma, 1995), 2 vols., II, Book Nine, chapter XXXVIII, pp. 338–40 [1359]. Matteo, the brother of Giovanni, took over the city chronicle immediately after his brother's death in the plague of 1348 and continued it until his own death with the second plague in Florence of 1363. Like his brother, he relied on a vast web of international merchant correspondence. Although less famous than his brother's account, Matteo's chronicle was more detailed and intellectually more pretentious.

Before the revolution of 1302 [see 11–13], the weavers and fullers in Flemish cities had generally been united in their efforts to overthrow ruling patrician governments. Afterwards, now having gained a stake in these governments, they became hated rivals. The weavers tended to be the more radical and revolutionary of the two guilds, even though they earned more and often employed the fullers. Unlike Florence and most other Italian city-states, the weavers after 1302 represented a wide spectrum of artisans and small entrepreneurs in Flanders, sometimes being little different from drapers in the structure of the cloth industry.

Concerning a scuffle between the artisans of Bruges.

We have said many times that because of their sins, people throughout the world do not know how to remain at peace with themselves, and the woes of which we shall relate corroborate this. One can truly say that our work is a book of tribulations and strife. In these days, around 17 July, the count of Flanders called together the commune of Bruges to sentence someone for some crime. Arrogantly, a cobbler rose up in the assembly and spoke out against the count's actions. Because two from other trades then rebutted the cobbler and spoke out against him, the cobbler drew his sword and said that whoever wished to follow him with their arms should go to the covered market [*alla*] of Bruges. Whereupon many tradesmen followed him. Gathered at the market with their arms and padded coats [*transegne*] they stood ready, waiting to respond to whoever might try to run them off. Other tradesmen, with the fullers and weavers at their head, who were unhappy about the town being taken over in that way, took up arms. Soon, a crowd had assembled in the market. Suddenly, without any further consultation, these craftsmen went straightway into the square where they were grouped into squads and then punched and beat up one another, leaving fifty-seven dead and many others covered in wounds. Afterwards, they came to an agreement with their adversaries, selecting from their ranks three leaders – a weaver, a carpenter, and a cobbler – on whose shoulders was placed the whole burden of government. They did not harm the count, nor misbehave in any way. In the blink of an eye, the boiling rage of the people suddenly subsided. The three leaders announced that everyone must return to the business of his trade and put down his weapons, which was done. Who would have thought that such an unbelievable and astonishing thing could have happened, that a revolt [*tumulto*] with so many people, with such outrage and passion, could have subsided so easily, leaving no memory of the bloody injuries that had been mixed in with the peace! What can be said is that at one moment there was a bitter and cruel war; at the next, peace.

59 The weavers and fullers of Flanders unite, 1360

M. Villani, *Cronica*, II, Book Ten, chapter LXVI, pp. 536–7.

Of the upheavals [*rivolture*] in Flanders during the summer. In July [1360], for some trivial reason, a great battle in the city of Bruges suddenly erupted, pitting the weavers and fullers on one side against the burghers on the other, and not without a considerable number of deaths and injuries for both sides. Shortly afterwards, the fullers and weavers of Ypres overthrew the authority of the count's chief officer [*balio*] without paying the consequences for this act of treason. At this time, the count of Oudenaarde [Louis de Male][23] was preparing the wedding celebrations for his daughter, whom he had given in marriage to the duke of Burgundy.[24] In these circumstances, the count sent to the aldermen and others asking them [in Ypres] to wait until his festivities were provided for, saying that he would then bring his chief officer to justice, and if he found him guilty they could be assured that he would deliver justice and revenge to their satisfaction. The beastly and arrogant ones among these tradesmen, however, dismissed the count's plea contemptuously and with shame and spite suspended him [in effigy?] from the window of his palace, which greatly upset him and his followers, but he was resigned to show that it did not faze him.[25]

60 Tax revolt in Tournai, 1365

Chronique des Pays-Bas, de France, etc, in *Corpus Chronicorum Flandriae*, ed. J.-J. de Smet, vol. III (Brussels, 1856), pp. 207–9.

On Sunday, 2 February, Candlemas [1365], the people [*gens*] [of Tournai] went into the market place [*halle*] to see the gabelles collected. They were so many that they could not all fit into the hall,

---

[23] Louis of Male [not of Oudenaarde (*Audinarda*)] was count of Flanders from 1346–84.

[24] In 1356 Louis had pledged his only legitimate daughter, Margaret, to marry Philip of Rouvre, the last Capetian duke of Burgundy, who died in 1361. In 1369 she married the first Valois duke of Burgundy, Philip the Bold.

[25] Pirenne, *Histoire de Belgique*, II, pp. 200–1, and Nicholas, *Medieval Flanders*, pp. 225–6, refer briefly to the revolt in Ypres but mention only that Louis de Male suffered a humiliation; neither gives the detail found in the Florentine chronicle; nor do they cite a Flemish chronicler that does so.

and many had to stand outside. One said to another: they might well levy us, but we'll pay nothing. When the tax collectors were about to begin, Sire Jehan Floquet, the sovereign provost, came down from the hall to go to the market [*marquiet*]. But there were so many people at the back of the hall that the provost could not press forward. And some said to him: 'Sir, they are wasting their time taxing us, because we'll pay none of it'. And all day he struggled to advance without saying a word until an old man beside him said: 'Sire, sire, this is pointless, since we'll pay nothing'. And with this he said loudly: 'Good people, make way, let the provost pass, since he has worked so hard'. When the provost heard himself mocked in this way, he was peeved and grabbed the old man by the head as though to strangle him, and he ordered his sergeants to take him away to the prison in the moat. As the sergeants were trying to lead him away, the old man began yelling: 'Good people, will you let them take me away? What I said I said for you as much as for myself'. With that, many ran forward and freed him from the sergeants, in spite of the provost's order. Then, they began shouting: 'Riot, riot!' And from here they rushed to the mansion of Master Pierre d'Orgimont, who had initiated the order to impose this gabelle at the request of some of the most powerful of the city. But they could not find him; with great speed he had left the city and had gone to Paris. From there, burning with anger, they returned to the belfry to ring the bells calling the commoners to assemble and arm themselves, but they found the cord cut. Some then climbed to the top of the bells and rang the emergency bell [*bancloqque*] and the curfew bells for closing the taverns [*Wingeron*] which never stopped [*joquèrent*] ringing until mid-morning the next day.

When the governor and those who were in the hall heard the hullabaloo, each scampered away as best he could. The governor went into hiding in the church of Nôtre-Dame and stayed there overnight. Other bourgeois of this city also went into hiding, each to the place he thought he would be safest. From the belfry, the people went towards the bishop's court to break down the prison doors and free the prisoners. Also, they thought that they might find there this Pierre d'Orgimont. The bishop came out to try to restrain them, saying: 'Good lord [of the city], be you at peace, and I promise you, at the risk of losing my bishopric that the governor and I shall approach the king to make sure that these gabelles are annulled. For you know that it was not the governor's doing; he is a good and loyal knight. But he must obey the king's orders, which no one can contravene'. After these words, the people left the bishop's men. But, because the night was dark, they lit many torches as they were leaving, and they said that they would go through the city to find those who levied these taxes. And from there they went to the gate of the Mauls and broke into the prison, freeing a Fleming who had broken the peace, and he went with them all night long. And from there they went to the mansion of Sir Jehan Floquet, the sovereign provost, broke down his door and windows and searched everywhere, in the haylofts and the granaries, but could not find him. On leaving, they took all the torches and candles large and small that they could find and went to get those who kept the keys to the gates and guard-posts of the city. And they were able to get all the keys to the gates and handed them over to one of their comrades to guard in order not to let anyone leave the city without their knowledge. Afterwards, they went all night through the mansions of the rich bourgeois, such as those of Sire Watier Wettin, Sire Finart Mouton, Sire Vinchant Dare, Jehan Maquet, and many others. They broke down the doors and windows of the houses they found locked and searched through the rooms and lofts. Then some took food and drink and torches and candles to light their way, for it was very dark. And in these mansions, all the rooms, lofts, coffers, and whatever they wanted open, were opened to them. And they were shown very great respect, and they did nothing beyond searching for those they sought; afterwards they left without committing any crimes. Thus they went all night long from house to house, crying out: 'Get the tax collectors [*censiseurs*], the tax collectors! the gabelles! the gabelles! We'll have none of it'. And they made up a rhyme, which they sang as a song in the streets:

The gabelle is levied in Lille and Douai;

Killing [*moroit*] a hundred men there, it then ran to Tournai.

And all day the emergency and curfew bells rang out without pause.

Many children and servants of the bourgeois joined the insurgents, disguising themselves by blackening their faces and wearing strange clothes. And they went yelling and carrying on like the others...

Southern France

61 The Tuchins: a retrospective view from the north

Chronique du Religieux de Saint-Denys, ed. M. L. Bellaguet, Collection de documents inédits (Paris, 1839–42), VI/1, Book 5, pp. 306–13. The principal sources for our knowledge of the Tuchins are archival letters of remission. Local chronicles of fourteenth-century Languedoc were few and of the published ones none mentions the Tuchins. The fullest narrative account of them comes instead from the north, the official chronicler of Charles VI (Michel Pintoin), who resided a safe distance away at the abbey of Saint-Denis, north of Paris.[26] Although this narrative portrayal was far removed from the struggles within the mountains of the Auvergne and comes at the Tuchins' end, it provides the most vivid image of them, and the one that has most coloured historians' perceptions ever since. For this reason, I begin with their end.

Of the nefarious crimes and revolts of the Tuchins of the Auvergne and Poitou.

The confirmation of the truce between the kings of France and England ensured a rest for the French on land and sea during this year [1384]. Among the few memorable events that took place, I shall mention the voyage of the duke of Berry. At the pope's request, he took a leave from the king of France and went to Avignon in May via Auvergne and Poitou. He decided to stop for some time in these provinces to repress the fury of the commoners [*popularium furorem*], then oppressing the country. Indeed, a large multitude of the most impoverished men, who because of their disorderly habits were called the Tuchins,[27] had unexpectedly burst forth everywhere in these parts like restless worms. They abandoned their work in menial crafts and agriculture and banded together. Spurred on by terrible speeches they were moved to submit no longer to shouldering the yoke of the subsidies and instead were inspired to preserve their ancient liberties, to try to throw off this harmful yoke placed on men. Soon, seeing their numbers increase, they committed ever-greater crimes. By diabolical instinct and spurred on by savage madness, they declared themselves to be the enemies of churchmen, nobles, and merchants. Here, in the open, there, by ambush, they rose up and robbed their victims of all

---

26 For more on this chronicle, see the introduction, pp. 6–7, and the introduction to chapter V.

27 According to Boudet, *La Jacquerie des Tuchins*, p. 2, the etymology of *Tuchin* or *Tochis* derives from *Tue-chiens*, killer of dogs. 'The dog-killer was a man reduced to such poverty that he killed and ate dogs'.

their goods, blinding some, dismembering others, and hanging many without mercy. Then they dispersed into bands here and there and in a blind rage torched the houses in the country, reducing them to ashes, if one refused to redeem them in cash. Everywhere, people frightened of being killed extended to them a warm welcome, but often, the Tuchins went against civil custom, even the manners observed by barbarians. Violating the laws of hospitality, they robbed those who had treated them so generously.

News of their monstrous crimes and horror spread through neighbouring regions. Thus a merchant on business would seek to avoid them by taking a less travelled route to reach his destination. Travelling by the most remote roads, he would dress as a rustic in rough clothing to conform to their ways in the hope of escaping death. Wishing to avoid any tricks, however, the Tuchins gave themselves an uncouth leader named Pierre de la Bruyère. This brutal man was immediately the choice of their detestable deputies [*detestabilibus ministris*]. Thus, he ordered the Tuchins not to receive any into their bands, except those with rough and callous hands, and if any mixed with them or passed among them who appeared too sophisticated in their gestures, manners, or speech, they were to be killed immediately.

All of them swore to practise this cruel rule. Thus they butchered many whose names are not remembered, but from witnesses worthy of trust I can attest that an illustrious soldier named John Patrick from Scotland, sent to meet the king of Aragon, was captured. And in their madness, they murdered him savagely by crowning him with a trivet of red-hot iron. One day they seized a monk of the order of the Holy Trinity,[28] and discovering a cross, the sign of his profession, was hidden under his peasant cloak, they tied him to a tree and ran him through with a roasting spit. On another day, they stopped a priest on his way to the papal curia in Rome, and out of hatred and distrust for his ecclesiastical dignity, they cut off the ends of his fingers, peeled the skin from his body with shears, and then burnt him alive. They committed other, even more revolting atrocities. No one thought these brigands deserved to live or that they should not be stopped. But instead of forming a single corps, the Tuchins marched in bands, one separated from the other and thus were left to practise their cruelty with their gnawed bows, dull swords entirely covered in rust,

---

28 The Order of Trinitarians was founded in Spain in the late eleventh century for the redemption of those captured by the infidel in the crusades. It became an officially recognised order with Innocent III's bull of 17 December 1198.

and batons of oak. Fear of their numbers prevented anyone from opposing them, that is, until the duke of Berry arrived. Having learnt with horror of the abhorrent crimes committed by these most vile men, this prince took on any soldiers he could enlist and ordered them to charge against these hideous murderers, whose transgressions against the laws of men and God made them worthy of all the wrath from the heavens. They were to be exterminated without mercy; none were to be spared. When the Tuchins heard the duke's edict, their foolish arrogance soon vanished; their boldness and courage evaporated. Although they numbered in the many thousands, they had no tactics and could not withstand the first attack of their assailants. When they saw their adversaries approach with swords unsheathed and lances lowered, it was as if they had been hit by a plague from the stars [*pestifero sydere*] and could regain their senses only by flight. With total wrath and an almost beastly rage that resulted in maximum carnage, the army pursued them relentlessly for many days. The French did not wish for any of these criminals to have mercy: all were hanged, drowned, or sliced through with swords. This is how this band of brigands was annihilated and received just punishment for their crimes. As usual, a bad ending finishes off those enterprises that begin with such evil.

62 Locals try to rid their region of a band of Tuchins, 1367

Marcellin Boudet, *La Jacquerie des Tuchins, 1363–1384* (Riom, 1895), pp. 125–7: Arch. nat. JJ. 112, no. 177: The Company of the Tuchins in the Gireuge and the Bonnac, Jean and Pierre from Luzers, its captains. Pardon granted to Pierre Sarament, squire (April 1367). For a general discussion of letters of remission as a source, see the introduction to the next chapter and my comments before documents 103 to 120.

Charles, the king, etc. [...] let it be known to all men present and future that the case on behalf of Pierre Sarament, esquire, has been put before us. As has been known already for a long time, for about ten years or so, under the shadow of the war then being fought between us and our enemies in the region of Auvergne, there arose in that country a company of robbers and thieves, who were commonly called by the good people of this land 'Touchis'. In the woods and in other parts, these *touchins* spied on, robbed, destroyed, and murdered worthy people [*bonnes genz*], oftentimes committing many monstrous, horrible, and villainous deeds to destroy this country as best they could. As was commonly known in these parts, the leaders and captains of this company were the brothers Jehan and Pierre from Luzers.[29] This esquire [Sarament] along with many others in this region who had been abused and hurt by this company had come to realise that these captains were being lodged in a manor house called Girigo in this region. This esquire along with the priest of the parish of Bonnac, called Jehan Bossecha, and many other good people of this region, gathered together and one dark night went to this manor house. And when they were very near it, they stopped, and the parish priest left them to spy on the manor house to see if these criminals were there so that the priest's comrades could capture and bring them to justice. When the priest returned to his comrades, he thought that some of these so-called *touchis* were approaching him. He showed signs of resistance and stopped with his sword unsheathed. At that moment, one of his comrades, not realising that it was the priest, for he had not called out his name or said a word, promptly pierced him through with a lance. And from this blow he immediately died. All his comrades including this esquire, not realising [what they had done], were then terribly stunned and incensed [*courociez*] once they recognised the priest in the darkness. And that is why the friends of the deceased have never brought the case to justice or brought charges against the supplicant as has been said. However, in order not to be charged later for this incident, the supplicant has petitioned and begged us to consider that he has always been a man of good behaviour and reputation, whom no one could accuse of being involved in any villainous deed apart from the case described above, for which he hardly could be blamed. On this matter, we should therefore desire to be merciful and forgiving. Thus, considering and understanding the things said above, we are inclined to grant our pardon to this esquire. With our full royal power, authority, and special grace, we have remitted, forgiven, and granted pardon ... in the case before us ...

Issued at Paris in April, 1367.

63 The Tuchins and personal antagonisms in a village outside Saint-Flour

Boudet, *La Jacquerie des Tuchins*, pp. 127–9: Arch. nat. 122, no. 207: The Tuchins of Aurouze and the company of Étienne Boutefeu, 1381–2.

---

[29] Luzers, commune of Saint-Mary-le-Plain, contiguous with Bonnac.

Charles, etc. let it be known to all present and future that the close friends of Girart de Vens, recently the gatekeeper of the castle of Aurose[30] in the diocese of Saint-Flour, have informed us that a year ago or thereabouts, the late Étienne Boutefeu, who while alive was a thieving tuchin and habitually carried out many crimes and wicked deeds, endeavoured on many occasions to murder and maim Durand de Vens, the brother of Girart, who had done him no harm. Later, Boutefeu, armed with his breastplate and protective cloak [*jaque*], sword, and other weapons attacked these brothers, crying out, 'to your death' and tried to threaten and injure them, saying to Durand that he would cut his flesh up into tiny pieces like meat at a butcher's if he would not give him a doublet worth two francs. Because of this and fearing the danger and rage of Boutefeu, who was a criminal and a man of evil ways, as has been said, this Girart went to the lord of the castle of Aurose and informed him of what had been said and that he wished to redress these matters for himself and his brother. In Boutefeu's presence, the lord told Girart that he should watch out for himself as best he could, that he could do nothing for him. On hearing this, Girart then very amicably beseeched Boutefeu for God's sake to come to peace with his brother and that if he had done anything bad against him, he would set it straight. To which Boutefeu responded that he would kill his brother if he did not give him a doublet worth two francs and would have sex with Giraut's wife, who was young and beautiful, whether she liked it or not, and then would hand her over [*huteroit*] to his mates.

One day a little while later, when Boutefeu was coming down from the castle into the town of Auroux and Giraut was going up to the castle, they happened to meet. Boutefeu was carrying a big club and tried to wound Giraut. Giraut blocked the blow with a lance he happened to be carrying. And perhaps in defending himself with the lance and repelling force with force, he wounded Boutefeu, who died almost instantly. As a consequence, Giraut left the region fearing severe punishment. He beseeches us to consider what has happened, the great outrages and villainous acts Boutefeu committed against him and his brother, and Boutefeu's evil and wicked life, for he is a criminal as has been said, whereas Giraut and his brother are and have been all their lives people of good reputation and worthy behaviour and thus [we should] consent to confer our grace on this Giraut ...

Issued at Paris, in April 1383 ...

30 Above the town of Auroux about 100 km southeast of St.-Flour.

64 Tuchins, cattle raids, and the gang of Guillaume Gracia

Boudet, *Jacquerie des Tuchins*, pp. 129–31: Arch. St.-Flour, chap. IV, art. 6, no.8.

Letters of grace from the duke of Berry to the inhabitants of Saint-Flour, because of their seizure and razing of the castle of Brossadol and their killing off the whole gang of Guillaume Gracia.

John, son of the king of France, duke of Berry and Auvergne, count of Poitou, lieutenant of my lord the king in this region, the duchy of Guyenne, and all the territories of Languedoc, let it be known on behalf of the consuls and inhabitants of the town of Saint-Flour that we have been informed that the castle of Brossadol, situated half a league from this town, was in a strong place and could greatly endanger this town and the region of Auvergne if our enemies should occupy it. And since the lord of this castle does not have the means to protect it securely, our chief officer of the Mountains of the Auvergne and commissioner responsible for issuing [tax?] exemptions in this our region, after consultation with good men who are expert in these matters, ordered this castle to be demolished and entrusted it to a certain royal sergeant to demolish it if no trouble would arise. The sergeant failed to execute this command. And for the security of this castle at the request of the lord of the castle long before and after this order had been given, these supplicants sent and supplied [...] certain men to guard and defend the castle. One day last May, this lord sent these men outside the castle [...]. And on that day two or three thieves from the band of Guillaume Gracia entered and occupied the castle. Soon six others of their gang arrived at the castle. Then Guillaume Gracia and his company of many armed men and plunderers came to the village of Murat, three leagues outside Saint-Flour, and planned to come to the castle. Guillaume boasted by means of it [the castle] that he could hold the whole surrounding countryside at ransom. These matters came to the attention of the vicar of the bishop of Saint-Flour and to the good people of this town. Fearing the rage of this Guillaume Gracia and his accomplices, who had committed many murders, robberies, raids, and other crimes in this region, they assembled and went armed to the castle, which was held in subfeudation [*arrièrefié*] by the bishop. They attacked it, broke into the stockade, and set it ablaze. During the assault, the said thieves, who were in the castle, wished to negotiate with the vicar and allowed him to enter with certain persons. The vicar commanded the townsmen to offer a cease-fire, saying that Guillaume was handing over the castle to the bishop in return for safe passage for his men. But the townsmen did not comply and instead persevered: they entered the castle, burnt it, knocked it down, demolished it, and killed those who had taken it and their comrades inside. Further, they took and carried off all the weapons and other property that they found in this castle, which belonged to the lord, valued at no more than sixty francs. Much of it he [the lord] later recovered along with the thieves' belongings. Having committed these deeds at the instigation of some of the most unpleasant comrades, the supplicants feared they would be punished. Thus, given the things said above and that this castle in the wrong hands could have caused great harm to this town and all the surrounding countryside, may it please us to apply and impart our grace to these inhabitants, to each and everyone of them. Considering what has been said along with the great, good, and wise obedience that these town consuls and inhabitants have always shown and continue to show my lord and to us, and for the public good of our country ... we have forgiven, dismissed the charges, and pardoned the consuls and inhabitants of this town of Saint-Flour ...

Issued at Paris in July 1384.

65 Village assassins and the early training of a Tuchin

Histoire générale de Languedoc, col. 1867–8, no. 758: Arch. nat. JJ. 149, no. 1: Letters of remission for a former partisan of the Tuchins.

Charles, etc. Let it be known, etc. that we have heard the humble supplication for Jean de Corneilles, esquire, son of the late Raimond de Cornillan, former knight of the village of Puisserguier in the diocese of Narbonne. It reports that in 1381 or thereabouts, this supplicant, then about fifteen years old, had been with the cavalry under the command of his late father, who was allied with the rebels from the three districts of Languedoc. And he was present when his late father had four squires [*varlez*] killed, named Simonnet de Reclanes, Adenet, Hugo, and Jennequin. Three were dumped in a ditch or stream called Fichaux; the other in the moor of Croissant. But this supplicant did not strike or injure any of the four; nor did he consent to their murder. Moreover, the supplicant should be acquitted of these deeds, since he is covered by the general remission made and granted by us to these rebels in return for a payment of 800,000 francs. He contributed and paid his share with the inhabitants of the villages of Puisserguier and Cessenon [-sur-Orb]. Further, a while back, he was taken and imprisoned in the prison of our city of Montpellier and later at Lattes, where he was locked up for two and a half years or so. Out of fear of the rigours of the law, he broke out of the prison of Lattes. Nonetheless, while the supplicant was in Paris on his own business, some of his enemies denounced him to our friends and faithful councillors, the men who held the petitions in our palace in Paris. They captured and imprisoned him in the Conciergerie of our palace,[31] where he stayed for three weeks or so. Then, by an ordinance of our councillors he was put into the prison of our Châtelet of Paris,[32] where he has been for some time and remains in great poverty, misery, and at risk of ending his days here before long, grievously punished by the law, if our grace and mercy is not imparted to him ...

Issued in Paris in November, 1395.

66 Conflict between aristocrats and commoners in the region of Toulouse, 1364

Histoire générale de Languedoc, cols. 1818–20, no. 732: Letters reporting the uprisings in the towns of Gimont and Simorre in 1364, remission to Bertran d'Asterach: Arch. nat. JJ. 140, n. 100. As the next two documents illustrate, marauding bands of thieves and murderers were not the only form of social protest to be found in the south of France during the 1360s.

Charles etc. Let it be known ... on behalf of Bertran of Rabastens [d'Asterach], knight, that about twenty-six years ago he served our Holy Father the pope, making a crusade against the military companies then in our realm, and when the commoners and plebeians of the towns [*villes*][33] of Gimont and Simorre in the district of Toulouse, by their evil spirit or otherwise, tried to pursue their evil and iniquitous plans without just cause. Like mad men, they assembled to battle against the now deceased Pierre Raimond of Rabastens,[34] then knight and lord of Sauveterre[35] and the lands of Gangagnez, went to the

---

31 La Conciergerie is on the Île de la Cité; it was the first prison of Paris.

32 Louis VI built it around 1130 to protect the Île de la Cité. It served as both a fortification and a prison until it was razed between 1802 and 1806.

33 *Ville* in medieval French can mean either town or village. I have chosen town because the inhabitants are called *les communs et plebeians* and later *populaires* and not *paisans, rustici,* or villeins.

34 Captain for the king of France in the Agenais in March 1370.

35 There are many villages named Sauveterre, but most likely this is the one just south of Toulouse.

village and castle, where this lord and his lady lived, and entered it by force. They sacked and burnt [the castle] and took this lady with three of their children, their servant, and moveable goods and led them to the village of Simorre, where they burnt some of their servants [*familiers*], hanged the others from the trees, and committed many other very great, inhumane, and detestable acts of evil, outrage, and injury to this couple and their family. Because of these crimes and after complaints about them made to our now deceased, very dear, and much loved uncle, the duke of Anjou, who was then our lieutenant in the region of Languedoc, our uncle and his council in favour of the lord of Sauveterre and his aides in this lawsuit sentenced these communes and commoners [*populaires*] to a fine of 25,000 pounds or thereabout. Then these commoners did not wish to pay; they remained steadfast, delaying and refusing continuously to pay, disobeying this ordinance and the sentence of our uncle. And for this, the supplicant, his son and heir, and those of the former lord of Sauveterre, seeing that they were not going to get any satisfaction from the law courts, with some of their relatives and friends began a war against these commoners and communes of Gimont and Simorre to avenge the injuries that had been committed, as is said, to their father and mother. Thus they stole and looted many animals and other goods from these commoners, killing some of them or having someone do it for them. Because of these murders and pillaging, the supplicant feared the rigours of the law, that sooner or later, he would be summoned and prosecuted. Thus he humbly beseeched us to impart our grace and mercy. Considering these matters and that this Bertran of Rabastens, his relatives, friends, and especially the count of Asterac, his cousin, have performed many valuable and worthy services in our wars and in other matters, we have acquitted this Bertran ...

Issued in Paris, February 1390[1]

67 The people of Carcassonne attack a royal castle, 1364

Histoire générale de Languedoc, col. 1329–31, no. 511: Arch. nat. JJ. 98, no. 74: Letters of remission for the people of Carcassonne.

Charles, etc. Let it be known etc. that we have heard the supplication of our dear and loyal council of the town of Carcassonne: that at the instigation of some odious members of the council and others in office ... in this year [1364] around the feast of John the Baptist [24 June] about 300 men of the town of Carcassonne, armed with various weapons of war, after negotiations and with the consent of the town councillors of Carcassonne, went to the village of Trèbes, a league outside Carcassonne, and made war on our castle, set fire to the gates, and were able to enter this castle. Seven men from the village of Peyriac in the district of Carcassonne and of this large and cursed company were detained in the castle under the charge of our dear and loyal commissioner Arnoul, Lord of Audenehan, marshal of France and now lieutenant of our father for the region of Occitanie.[36] A few days afterwards, more than two thousand men of this town armed with various weapons left this town and went towards our city of Carcassonne, approaching its city walls to make war and to kill those who have arrested these seven men of this city and afterwards had led them back here. They wished to set them free. It was understood and made public in the town that some townsmen wished to set the seven free...and to lead them out of this city so that justice could not be done. By their consent and negotiations those who were then on the town council gave their support, approval, and assistance. On these matters undertaken by these councilmen and the people of this town, they neither asked nor received permission from this marshal and the lieutenant of our father, who was then in this city, or from any of our other commissioners in Carcassonne for making war, disturbances, sedition, and rioting [*tumultum & seditionem ac rumorem*] in this place and in our country. By bearing arms and in various other ways, [these townsmen] violated our embassies, thus offending and doing violence to us, the lieutenant of our father, and our court. For these matters, these councillors and individuals of these places could incur criminal and civil penalties to their persons and property. Thus these councillors and individuals of this place humbly beseeched us to grant them forgiveness for all the injuries committed against us, our lieutenant, court, and our commissioners in Carcassonne, for the murders, advice, and approval they gave in carrying out these crimes. Thus, having heard this marshal's report on these matters and so as not to bring injury to us, this marshal, or our court at Carcassonne ... we should hand over this matter to the charge of the inquisitor of depraved heretics in the district of Carcassonne, who is in residence, or to his lieutenant, because of allegations that the leaders were heretics, considering their principles and ideas. For this, we have relied on the voluntary and praiseworthy services of the present council members,

36 He was appointed captain general of Languedoc in September 1361.

FROM THE BLACK DEATH TO 1378

the commune, and inhabitants of this town, and the previous kings of France, whose faithful support, aid, and assistance has constantly prevented our enemies from destroying this town by fire and other forms of destruction, etc. We wish to confirm and obtain this pardon for all those inhabitants of Carcassonne, who committed murder or gave advice or help. Each one of them is to be individually named and given this pardon ...

Issued in Paris, October 1369

Italy

68 A tavern riot over earlier election results, 1348

ASF, Atti di Podestà, n. 334: This riot and brawl harks back to and briefly summarises a more serious political disturbance over the disputed election of the communal officials for the market town of Barberino Valdelsa, south of Florence, that took place in July or August 1347, whose records no longer survive. The below is an unpublished document.

Amundo and and Griffo } brothers and sons of the former Griffo
Antonio, son of the former Gualteri
Simone, son of the former Chele } all from Barberino Valdesa
Buonacorso di Chiano
Ridolfo di Giovanni and
Francesco di Vanni

Each and everyone of them has been charged before our court and by Giovanni di Puccio of the Commune of Barberino[37] ... The above-mentioned Francesco di Vanni and Francesco di Giuntino, officials of this commune and Raineri di Francesco, treasurer of the commune, all of this walled town [*castro*] of Barberino, came into the church of Saint Stephen of Barberino to seal the letters of election with the official seal of the Commune of Barberino, which the notary of the commune had notarised. Armundo, Griffo, Antonio, Simone, Buonacorso, and Ridolfo, armed with offensive and defensive weapons, attacked these officials and took the seal of the commune from them, thus preventing them from sealing the elections. They said: 'these officials

---

37 Most likely he was the local lay rector of the town, responsible for making charges against criminal activity within the town's jurisdiction. On this office, see my *Laboring Classes*, pp. 198–200.

are not good officials, and we want to see that the officers for the commune are put right; we want other officials elected'. Because of this, a big riot [*maximus rumor*] exploded in this town, with many men joining in.

A year and a month afterwards ... at night time, after the ringing of the bells for the night and before the ringing for the next day, which meant that penalties are doubled according to Florentine law, these men [the old elected officials] were having supper together in a certain inn described in the inquest. In a street in front of the inn described in the inquest, this Ridolfo threw a rock through the window of this inn and onto the table where these men were eating; he then threw another rock into the inn. He also said many, many offensive words to the noble lady, the widow of Nuccio, the former innkeeper. Immediately afterwards, the said Francesco di Vanni, who was eating at the inn, got up and walked out, saying to Ridolfo, 'What an outrage you've inflicted on us!' Then, with a naked blade he stabbed Ridolfo in the shoulder, causing blood to spurt out. Next, said Ridolfo yelled out loudly, 'to the streets, men, to the streets, riot, riot!' And many men came out into the streets and joined the riot and went after this Francesco, trying to apprehend him; with the town bells ringing out, a serious riot erupted in this town. Soon afterwards, Ridolfo, armed with a sword, knife, and other weapons and accompanied by his mate, whose name we do not know, went to Francesco's house, which he rented ... With a knife in his hand, he barged in, demanding and yelling: 'Where is this thief? Where is the thief?' and 'Set the place on fire'. With this, many men entered the fray and a big riot and clamour ensued in this walled town ... which could have overturned the peaceful state of this walled town and brought damage to it and to the Commune and People of Florence... [The accused failed to appear in court but were sentenced to be led to the place of justice in Florence and beheaded; all their property was to be destroyed as an example to others. The sentence was declared on 13 September 1348.]

69 A riot of the 'people' cut down to size by the Bentivoglio of Bologna, 1350

CCB: Cronaca A and the *Cronaca of Villola*, pp. 603 and 607. [1350]

There was a great riot in Bologna, that is, the people [*puovolo*] wished to take up arms, but it appeared to me that God did not want their efforts to succeed since it would have been for the worse. And this happened on 20 October [1350]. The Bentivoglio[38] made it very clear that the city was not about to be handed over to the people, and so they cut them down to size [*ritaglio*].

They rebelled so fiercely and ardently, because those with money could get out of paying the hearth tax [*fumante*], and enough of them escaped payment and even received the right not to pay, with or without an official immunity [*carta de paxe?*]. For those who were taxed things remained the same.

70 The Roman people [*popolo*] kick Luca Savelli out of town, 1353

M. Villani, *Cronica*, I, Book Three, chapter XXXIII, pp. 365–6: Uprising [*novità*] in Rome.

At the beginning of September [1353], the rector of the Roman people[39] was outraged by Luca Savelli[40] and was scarcely listened to by the people. He wished to hold a public meeting [*parlamento*] to resign from office. Divisions hardened within the people: some wished him to resign; others, to stay on. In this conflict, Lord Rainaldo Orsini,[41] who was senator, took up arms and, with a following from the people, chased Luca Savelli and his supporters out of Rome. But they did not stay out for long and drifted back into the city. The rector wanted to strengthen the people with new laws to prevent the princes from ruling over them so harshly. Thus he called the people to assemble by their neighbourhoods [*rioni*] with the ringing of church bells. Anyone who did not show up was arrested as a suspect. And

---

38 A ruling family of Bologna of popular origins, who were in power at various times during the fourteenth and fifteenth centuries, but their great period of city domination came at the end, with the last of the Bentivoglio rulers, Sante, who controlled the city for sixty years until the entry of Pope Julius II in 1506; see Cecilia M. Ady, *The Bentivoglio of Bologna: A Study in Despotism* (London, 1937), pp. 1–4.

39 The rector or governor of Rome was Giovanni Cerroni. On this episode, see Eugenio Duprè Theseider, *Roma dal comune di popolo alla Signoria pontificia (1252–1377)* (Bologna, 1952), pp. 628–9.

40 The Roman senator; medieval Rome vacillated between having one or two senators. The Savelli were an old senatorial family. In fact, in the thirteenth century, there had been two Luca Savelli who were senators.

41 The Colonna and Orsini were the two most prestigious and powerful families of medieval Rome.

112   POPULAR PROTEST IN LATE MEDIEVAL EUROPE

finding that he had control over six thousand gold florins, which the Church had given the people to help maintain their government[42] and other money, which they had collected, the rector left Rome for Abruzzo[43] and bought a castle in the countryside, and thus abandoned the weakened republic. For their fickleness, the people got what they deserved.

71   The *popolo minuto*, magnates, and the emperor boot the Nine out of Siena, 1355

Donato di Neri e di suo figlio Neri, *Cronaca senese* [A.A. 1354–5], in *Cronache senesi*, pp. 577–9. Donato di Neri, the continuator of Agnolo di Tura's grand chronicle of Siena was of a different social class than the Noveschi merchant Agnolo. He came from a family of middling condition, vendors of linen, wool, and silk cloth (*ligrittieri*), who before the fall of the government of the Nine were barred from holding positions in the government's councils. After the revolt, they were enrolled as members of the 'Ordine' or 'Monte' of the Twelve, which governed Siena along with the nobility until the revolt of 1368 (see [79]). Little more is known of Donato's background. He was born in the early part of the fourteenth century and died in either 1371 or 1372. His chronicle often takes the form of the day-to-day recounting characteristic of the diary-chronicle.

The said emperor Charles[44] sent his marshal with 150 horsemen, handsome soldiers, who were well equipped, to Siena. They entered Siena on 5 March [1355], and on the very same day the marshal swore loyalty to the priors of the government of the Nine in the town council [*concestoro*], agreeing to defend them at all costs and to follow their command in the honour of the emperor and according to mutual agreement. A day or so later, the coats of arms of the emperor were placed on all the gates of Siena and especially on the Palace where the

---

42 To sustain the government of Cerroni the pope had given the commune two large sums of money, first 14,000 and then 6,000 florins; see Duprè Theseider, *Roma dal comune*, p. 628.

43 The mountainous region west of the Roman territory (Lazio). It is not known exactly where Cerroni's castle was; see Duprè Theseider, *Roma dal Comune*, p. 629.

44 Charles IV of Bohemia was born in Luxembourg and was Holy Roman Emperor, 1347–78; he founded the University of Prague in 1348 and made the city into a cultural capital of Europe. In 1353 the league of city-states (Florence, Siena, and Perugia) invited Charles into Italy as a bulwark against the Milanese Visconti's efforts to expand territorially and influence Italian politics. Charles came into Italy in 1355 to challenge Louis of Bavaria's claims to Empire and to legitimate his own; see Bowsky, *A Medieval Italian Commune*, pp. 169–70 and 299–302.

governors of the Nine resided. The tops of the windows were also rimmed in fine gold. Beautiful.

The emperor Charles left Pisa on [23 March] and reached Siena the same day. He went about to meet many citizens, those of magnate and merchant families and the Nine, who greeted him honourably with flags waving and men jousting with lances. Decked out in silk headdresses, with shouts of praise, the ringing of bells, and with various liveries, they all celebrated with great delight. It was a festival the likes of which no one had seen before. A horse race was run for a *palio*[45] made of fine gold that served as a baldachin for the emperor and another was made for the empress. His troops dismounted at the palace of the Salimbeni,[46] and in the middle of this great palace he had with him about a thousand barons and knights. Once they had dismounted, they ripped up all their flags.[47] Then a riot broke out with the chants: 'Long live the Emperor and death to the Nine'. The magnates of the Piccolomini family[48] started it, having been ordered to do so by all the other magnates, except for the Giovanni. And thus on the next day, the *popolo minuto* took up arms and followed suit. On the night of the 24th, [the *popolo minuto*] ordered all the chains of the city to be cut including those guarding the palaces of the nobility of Siena. They started fires and broke through all the gates of Siena. The rioting then spread to the house of Lord Grifolo of Montepulciano[49] and to the son of Lord Tancredi. Scuffles began and their houses were set on fire, along with many others belonging to the Nine. It was left to the emperor to decide what to do. Assembled in their palace, the Nine were greatly frightened; late that night, they ordered all the keys to the chains of the city to be brought to them and they handed them over in a basket to the emperor. But the emperor replied: 'I want more than just these keys'. The Nine became very suspicious and that night did nothing more.

1355. At noon the next day, 25 March,[50] the *popolo minuto* rioted

---

45 A painted banner usually made of silk

46 A powerful noble family of Siena with rich land holdings in the Sienese countryside.

47 Often in such processions and festivals, flags were ceremonially ripped up. I wish to thank Fabrizio Nevola for this note.

48 One of Siena's most powerful noble families; the family of the mid-fifteenth-century pope, Pius II.

49 A market town on the southeastern corner of the Florentine territory, contested by Perugia and Siena.

50 The Sienese calendar year began on 25 March.

throughout Siena; the whole city was armed and all the chains of the city locked, that is, those that could be locked. As we said, many of them had been cut during the previous days. Thus the whole city was in great fear and trouble. The governors of the Nine then sent for the emperor, who came to the palace by horseback at 7 at night, followed by a great crowd of the people, who almost bodily swept him into the palace. The rioting then spread to the Campo with shouts of: 'Long live the Emperor and death to the Nine'. And all chanted the same thing, from the magnates and noblemen to the *popolo minuto*. And thus with the emperor in the palace at the table of the governors of the Nine, he rescinded his agreement with them, annulled every oath he had taken on their behalf, and tore up and burnt every document and privilege he had granted them. During this revolt, many noblemen charged through the streets with the *popolo minuto* to storm the palace of the counsellors of the Merchants' Court [*Mercanzia*],[51] where they seized and stole the books, charters, and other items of the court, tearing them up or carting them away. Then, they ran to the Biccherna,[52] taking all their books of judicial sentences and the treasury account books and brought them to the Campo. And there in the presence of the emperor, they tore them up and burnt them. And they burnt the houses of wool workers. Some of the rioters ran to the prison and broke it open; they burnt what they could and liberated all the prisoners.

They then ran to the church of Camporegi[53] where a box containing the urns filled with the names of those eligible for office [*bossoli*] in the government of the Nine were kept in a large chest [*cassone*] in the sacristy. They broke open this cabinet, grabbed the box containing the names of those eligible for all the offices in the government of the Nine, and carried it off to the palace, where it was given to the emperor. The emperor ordered the box to be thrown out the window, which stirred up further rioting in the Campo: they took the battered box and tied it to the tail of a donkey, which dragged it, spewing the ballots out all over the city. Sweeping them up, the insurgents cried: 'Death to the Nine'.

---

51 The highest merchant court, a sort of super-guild of the wealthiest merchants; see Maureen Mazzaoui, *The Italian Cotton Industry in the Later Middle Ages 1100–1600* (Cambridge, 1981), pp. 120–5.

52 The treasury of the Commune of Siena, see W. M. Bowsky, *The Finance of the Commune of Siena, 1287–1355* (Oxford, 1970).

53 The church and cloister of the Dominicans.

They also went charging to the house of the podestà, that is Lord Ciappo de' Ciappi from Narni, robbing him and chasing him away. They went to the house of the Captain of War, that is, Neri from Monte Carullo, robbed and chased him away; weakened by the ordeal he died in a few days.

The Captain of the People of Siena, Befanuccio from Rocca di Malencone, was also chased out of town.

And thus the government of the Nine and its prior at this time, Lorenzo di Toro Baraglia, were disposed of.

The insurgents continued their chanting, demanding that the emperor then in the palace chase the Nine out of office. And if the emperor chose not to do it, there were others in the palace, whom the people [*popolo*] could rely on to cut the Nine to pieces.

Once the people and the magnates realised they could not get their hands on the members of the Nine, they ran in a rage to many of the houses of the Nine, robbing and burning them; everyone let off steam and avenged his injuries; old memories created new injuries. And thus many were injured or killed here and there throughout the city, and no one said a word; anyone who was around just shrugged his shoulders. And thus all the members of the Nine, along with their brothers, children, and kinsmen fled and hid; all were robbed. No one wished to take them in or even see or hear them, neither the clergy, nor anyone else. And the foreigners who followed in the emperor's train were put up and given the houses of the Nine. Many nasty things were now said about the Nine, that they were thieves and traitors; that they embezzled money belonging to the commune and divided it up among themselves. He, who could say worse, did so. Their workers, servants, maidservants, and wet nurses left them; and thus the clergy and everyone else shouted abuse at them; no one wished to talk or be seen with them.

Also during the rebellion, with lances and spears the insurgents destroyed all the coats of arms of the People, which had been painted on the houses of the Nine. They did this because they now saw themselves as the regime of the people and did not wish for the Nine to retain these accolades, now that they had been deprived of governing. Also, the riot had spread to robbing the custom house of the salt tax, but the troops of the emperor went there and chased them away. Later that same day the insurgents returned to the custom house to rob it, and again the emperor's troops saw them off; but two of them were captured and their right hands cut off, and it was ordered that everyone should lay down his weapons.

Lord Giovanni Bisdomini of Arezzo was made podestà of Siena.

On this very day, 25 March, with the will of the people who were assembled in the Campo, the Emperor Charles elected several syndics [to govern the city]. With delight and festivities, these citizen syndics of Siena swore fealty to the emperor. Later that day the emperor elected twelve citizens from magnate families and eighteen from the lower classes [*popolari minuti*] of the city of Siena to set up a new government [*riformare*] for the well being of the city. And thus the people who were then in the Campo confirmed that these citizens should form a new government for the well-being of the city in which all good citizens should be able to enter government, except those of the Nine and their children.

The emperor left Siena for Rome and was crowned emperor and [his wife] empress on Easter Sunday, 9 April, in Saint Peter's ...

Those citizens elected to reform the government of Siena were thrown out. The noblemen, with their characteristic arrogance wished to place these matters [under the control] of their own committeemen [*collegio*], who were in the town hall. And by the will of Giovanni d'Agnolino and other noblemen, it was established that the said eighteen citizens [*popolari*][54] should be placed in the government of the city and *contado* of Siena in this way: there would be twelve *popolari* for each ballot [*pallotta*], that is four for each Third [of the city] with terms of office of two months, one of whom would be the captain of the people, that is, one of these so-called Twelve [*Dodici*],[55] who would live in the town hall. And with each election, six noblemen would be chosen for their college, but they would not reside in the town hall. However, these twelve governors would not be allowed to do anything of importance, not even open letters without the permission of the six noblemen. And these six were called the college. And the so-called eighteen citizens who were to set up the new government, as it had been laid down, made the ballot with eighteen positions and were to begin that May.[56]

54 Previously, they had been called *popolari minuti*.
55 Later, a principal faction of Siena or 'monte' would be called after them, the Dodici.
56 For a modern analysis of the revolt against the Nine, which tempers earlier views of the revolt as one against tyranny (Pietro Rossi) or as a democratic movement (Giuliano Luchaire), see Bowsky, *A Medieval Italian Commune*, pp. 299–301.

72 The organisation of the guilds in the new regime of the Twelve, Siena, 1355

Documenti ... del Comune di Siena dal 1354 al 1369, ed. Giuliano Luchaire (Lyon, 1906), no. 12, 1–9 December 1355: Statuto 31, Riforma delle Arti, pp. 43–6. The lists below show that with the fall of the Nine even those who performed menial tasks in the wool industry, leather manufacturing, and hardware gained guild recognition and thereby citizenship and the right to elect the highest officers of the state, the priors. It was harbinger of the changes to come twenty-three years later in Florence as a consequence of the Revolt of the Ciompi. In addition, the upper-class guild of bankers, the principal profession of the previous members of the Nine, was diluted with artisans, goldsmiths and polishers.

Names of the principal twelve guilds and those crafts arranged under them.

In the name of the Lord amen ... and for the peaceful and tranquil state of the honourable government of the Twelve lord governors and administrators of the republic of the city of Siena ... regarding the composition of the laws and statutes ... the wise men of the Twelve governors ... have agreed unanimously, declared, and arranged that the below mentioned guilds and crafts [*artifices*] are arranged into twelve principal guilds as contained below. And they will meet in these principal guilds, where they are to elect and call forth one prior for each of them, so that there should be twelve priors, according to the form of these laws, in the year 1355, the ninth indiction, 29 December, in the presence of Simone di Pietro [...].

The guilds and their crafts that have been arranged and declared as members of these principal guilds mentioned above are the following, that is:

I. *The wool guild:* dyers, leather dressers, slipper makers [*Ciarbolactarii*], purse makers, cloth cutters, finishers, stretchers of woollen cloth, sewers, wool combers, and rug makers;

II. *The guild of fire:* blacksmiths of large things, other blacksmiths, knife and sword makers, pan and helmet makers, shield makers, harness makers. *Users of fire for smaller objects* [*Fuoco minuta*]: saddle makers, bakers, keysmiths, buckle and nail makers;

III. *The Guild of Cobblers:* cobblers and tanners;

IV. *The Guild of Notaries:* notaries, judges, scholars and masters of the various arts of letters;

V. *The Butchers' Guild:* butchers, vintners, innkeepers, animal merchants, excluding bankers, poultry butchers, and greengrocers;

VI. *The Grocers' Guild:* grocers, sellers of iron goods and peddlers, grain and flour dealers;

VII. *The Guild of Master Carpenters:* Masters of wood, of stone, crossbow makers, painters, joiners, barrel makers, and table makers;

VIII. *The Silk Guild:* silk merchants, furriers, veil makers, belt makers, glove makers;

IX. *The Bankers' Guild:* bankers, goldsmiths, and polishers [*Sbraghieri*];

X. *The Linen Guild:* Vendors of linen, wool and silk cloth [*Ligrictieri*],[57] doublet makers, workers in linen cloth, linen merchants;

XI. *Cloth Cutters' Guild:* cloth cutters and stocking makers, tailors and shearers;

XII. *The Druggist Guild:* druggists, barbers, and doctors.

73 Tax revolt in Ravenna, 1357

M. Villani, *Cronica*, II, Book Seven, chapter LXX, pp. 94–5: Uprising [*novità*] in Ravenna.

When the news raced through Ravenna that the army of the legate [Cardinal Albornoz][58] had stormed the city walls of Cesena by force, the lord [of Ravenna] who owed allegiance to the legate, commanded his citizens not to celebrate the victory with bonfires and fireworks. However, on Sunday, 28 May, the citizens assembled in their streets [*contrade*] and squares and celebrated. In these gatherings they began

---

57 Ludovico Muratori, the great scholar of the early eighteenth century, thought this profession was the same as the *rigattieri* – dealers in used clothes – and modern historians often follow this mistake. Unfortunately, the word does not appear in the *Vocabolario degli accademici della Crusca* (1612 and later editions) or the most complete historical dictionary of Italian, *Grande Dizionario della lingua italiana*, (Turin, 1961–2002), or any other dictionary I know; on the correct meaning of this occupation and guild, see Paolo Viti, *Dizionario Biografico degli Italiani*, 41 (Rome, 1992), pp. 75–7.

58 In 1353 Innocent IV appointed Cardinal Alvarez Carillo Gil de Albornoz (1310–67) as legate and vicar general of the Papal States with extraordinary powers to restore the papal territories lost during the papacy's residency in Avignon; see E. Duprè Theseider, 'Il cardinale Albornoz in Umbria', in *Storia e arte in Umbria nell'età comunale: Atti del VI Convegno di studi umbri* (Perugia, 1971), II, pp. 610–40.

to speak out against Lord Bernardino da Polenta, their lord,[59] because of his taxes. Within a short space of time they had been forced to pay their *estimo*[60] three times at seven pounds and ten shillings per pound assessed.[61] Thus the citizens were all upset. And their blood began to boil when heated up by the fires of the celebration. They elected several leaders and began to chant: 'Long live the People; death to the *estimo* and the gabelles!' With their voices rising and the numbers who joined the riot multiplying, the people took up arms and began to fill the squares, which further amplified their cries. Hearing the shouts, the lord sent two of his retinue [*famigli*], into the main square, who were killed one after the other by the People as soon as they arrived. Realising that the situation was deteriorating, the tyrant armed himself and with his soldiers mounted his horse and rode into the main square. Armed, the People turned against him, but he managed to save his skin and return to his castle. Gathering more help, he returned again to the square hoping to quell the People. But their fury had increased, and he was forced again to retreat by another street at the rear gate of his castle. These vile servants of the rabble, now having liberty in their own hands, did not, however, know how to use it; following on from their own laziness [*proprio pigrizia*], they behaved as if they were all lords. Thus, as night fell, they began to leave the square without any order or leader, and they returned home as though leaving a sporting match, few remaining there and [those that did were] poorly defended. And for this reason, in the middle of the night, the bastard brother of the lord with twenty-five of his knights [*masinadieri*] suddenly fell upon this stunned people. And the lord with a few on horseback stood at the gate of his castle to get back his own. But the vile *plebes*, still being in great numbers and without much resistance, could strike, kill, and chase off this small number of assailants. The *plebes* then left the square and returned home. The following morning, the lord sent for several citizens, who as if recovering from a drunken stupor and feeling safe came to him. With these first ones caught, he sent for others, rounding up 120 or more, whom he imprisoned; he then routed the city. By various means, most of the captured were put to death and others fined. And as a result, he governed his people thereafter more severely. They remained obedient, fearful, and defeated.

59 The da Polenta dynasty began ruling Ravenna from the late thirteenth century. After a civil war against his brothers, Bernardino da Polenta (1318–59) took control over Ravenna shortly after his father's death (Ostasio) in 1346.

60 A tax assessed on real property.

61 This rate makes no sense to me.

74 Taxes beyond measure, Bologna, 1357

M. Villani, *Cronica*, II, Book Seven, chapter LXXXI, pp. 107–8.

Concerning the taxes the tyrant imposed on the Bolognese [1357].

When the troops [*la compagna*] – the cavalry of two thousand, which Lord Bernabò[62] held in the territory of Modena and near Sassuolo in the territory of Bologna – had crossed the region of Romagna, he made no new manoeuvres in order to keep his allies, even the papal legate, guessing. However, the Lombards in the league assembled their troops, and the Bolognese tyrant[63] strengthened his forces by taxing the Bolognese indecently beyond all measure. Every month he imposed on his subjects a salt tax of five shillings [*soldi*] per mouth and four shillings for the grinding of a bushel [*cobra*] of grain,[64] in addition to other charges for the milling, and for every *tornature*[65] of land, 20 shillings of Bolognese money per annum, plus the other gabelles, the gate tax, those on wine, and on other things that enter the city by pack animals and carts; all were taxed. And in this way he was able to bleed them of[66] 15,000 Bolognesi pounds [*libbre*] a year. Beyond this, the citizens were stripped of their weapons; anyone wishing to possess them had to join the army. Under this heavy yoke, the people rose up with sticks and short lances [*lanciotti*], since they lacked other weapons. They went to where the tyrant was in charge of his troops and stayed encamped for two days without provisions and at great risk to their lives, but they did not dare speak a word to anyone. The forces of the league left with increased numbers in order to fight the cavalry of Lord Bernabò, who was at Sassuolo. On 21 July, part of one army clashed with the other, and the troops of Lord Bernabò were broken. Sensing defeat, his other cavalrymen left, returning safe and sound to Milan. After they had left, a treaty was discovered that they were to be handed over at the gate to the castle of Bologna; the soldiers [who remained] were arrested for treason and sentenced accordingly.

---

62 Bernabò Visconti (1319–84) was lord [despot] of Milan.
63 Bolognia's ruler was then Messer Giovanni da Oleggio, who maintained his control by an alliance with Papacy.
64 A Bolognese measure equal to 79 litres.
65 A measure of agrarian land in Emilia Romagna that varied between 2,000 and 3,000 square metres.
66 In Italian, 'take from their ribs and flanks'.

75 Conspiracy of artisans, workers, priests, and friars, Pisa, 1360

M. Villani, *Cronica*, II, Book Nine, chapter LXXVIII, pp. 398–9.

Of a conspiracy that was uncovered in Pisa.

The artisans of the city of Pisa, and especially those from the minor guilds [*arte minuta*],[67] were seeing their incomes fall because of Florence's embargo of their port. They complained, grumbled, and cursed [the Florentines]. With this conflict brewing, a large number of them met, made oaths in great secrecy, and drew up ordinances between them. They swore that on the third of April, Good Friday,[68] they would kill a large part of the big shots [*maggiorenti*] who controlled the city government wherever and however they could be found, either alone or together. With this done, they sent for the Gambacorti,[69] who had gone to Florence to bring in new legislation, negotiate a peace, and reopen the port. Among the conspirators were a number of clergymen – priests and other clerics. One of these, a priest, was seen talking quite obscenely and in an abusive manner with certain of the lay conspirators. Either because of what was being agreed or the manner in which he was speaking, he came under suspicion; the police were called and he was apprehended. He confessed to the whole plan. Soon afterwards, four priests and seven friars were arrested, followed by a hundred artisans from the minor guilds.[70] The governors of Pisa proceeded further in this affair, discovering that many others had been involved in the conspiracy, which for the best had been stopped. There were no more arrests, but of those arrested, twelve were hanged – those found most guilty and the leaders. The others were fined and paid up quickly to be released. This revolt [*novità*] disturbed and frightened the city greatly, toppling the government of the Seven, which then ruled. The city remained greatly divided, and the lower classes [*popolo minuto*] were discontented and worse off than before.

---

67 Florence and some other cities divided the guilds into major and minor ones. The major guildsmen tended to be merchants and entrepreneurs, while the minor ones were for the most part master-craftsmen or shopkeepers.
68 In 1360, Good Friday fell on 3 April.
69 A ruling family of Pisa.
70 I am not certain what professions these would have included in the Pisan context.

76 Independence and resistance of a subject town, Montalcino, 1359

Donato di Neri e di suo figlio Neri, *Cronaca senese*, p. 592.

Montalcino. Fifty men were made exiles, hunted out of Montalcino. The fifty were followers of Giovanni d'Agnolino Salimbeni.[71] These fifty went and pleaded with this Giovanni, saying that they wanted to return to Montalcino. On 15 October these exiles returned to Montalcino and burnt and destroyed whatever they could. On hearing this, the Sienese sent their ambassador to Montalcino, saying that the commune of Siena had allowed all of them to enter Montalcino, that any partiality must end, and all past injuries committed against the commune of Siena would be pardoned. It did not appear [just] to the rulers of Siena that such men should be kept out of Montalcino. The governors of Montalcino responded that they wished to be free. The faction then in power [*la parte dentro*] sided with the Tolomei,[72] and [said] they did not wish to hand Montalcino over to the commune of Siena. And thus factional conflict continued, and the faction that was kept out created great havoc by setting fires and destroying property. And the ambassadors returned to Siena to report what was happening. Then the Sienese sent their ambassadors again to Montalcino, who said that they wanted Montalcino to be under the control of the commune of Siena and have the city as their lords, and if they chose not to, Siena would send many troops there.

Within a few days the Sienese assembled their troops, the crossbowmen of Siena and other soldiers of the city and the Masse of the *contado*,[73] who encamped in Montalcino, so that within a few days the Montalcinesi had surrendered to the commune of Siena with the following principal agreements: that twenty-four of the leaders of Montalcino would go to Siena as hostages and would remain there as long as it took to carry out the necessary reforms for Montalcino. Afterwards, they could return to Montalcino at the will of the governing

---

71 See [71].

72 Another important noble family of Siena, often in factional conflict with the Salimbeni.

73 Massa or Masse et Cortine: the zone immediately adjacent to the city comprising between forty and fifty-one villages; they were taxed separately from both the city and the *contado*; see W. M. Bowsky, 'Medieval Citizenship: The Individual and the State in the Commune of Siena, 1287–1355', *Studies in Medieval and Renaissance History*, 4 (1967): 228.

Twelve [of Siena]. Secondly, the Sienese would send a podestà and other officials, who were Sienese citizens, to [govern] Montalcino. Thirdly, the Montalcinesi would be exempted from taxes for two years, but then would pay all gabelles [indirect taxes] and other payments as did other citizens [of Siena] and they would become citizens of Siena.[74] And, when the troops of Siena returned to Montalcino, men and women, the rich and poor [*i piccoli e grandi*] of Montalcino, greeted them with olive branches in their hands and around their heads, chanting; 'Long live the commune of Siena'.

77 Riot over the cardinal's pretty little dog, Viterbo, 1367

P. Pompeo Pellini, *Dell'Historia di Perugia*, (Venice, 1664), I, pp. 1031. Chroniclers in Viterbo and beyond, reaching even as far as the official chronicle of the kings of France, have reported this revolt, especially the diplomacy afterwards to convince the pope not to enact the measures of savage repression he initially announced.[75] I have chosen the brief description from the sixteenth-century historian of Perugia, because he has assembled points found collectively in the other accounts but not found in any one contemporary chronicle.

In 1257 the papacy began construction of a papal palace in Viterbo, where popes frequently spent long periods to escape the often more tumultuous Rome.[76] Along with the pope, cardinals built palaces and set up their households with their retainers in Viterbo. In the second half of the thirteenth

---

[74] Such a treaty of territorial incorporation was much more generous and egalitarian than what Florence usually offered its new subject towns; see Cohn, *Creating the Florentine State*.

[75] For other accounts see *Le croniche di Viterbo scritte da Frate Francesco d'Andrea* in *Archivio di R. società Romana di storia patria*, XXIV (1901), pp. 335–7; Niccola della Tuccia, *Cronache di Viterbo e di altre città* in *Cronache e statuti della città di Viterbo*, ed. Ignazio Ciampi, *Documenti di Storia Italiana*, V (Florence, 1872), p. 35; *Cronaca Senese di Donato di Neri*, p. 616; *Cronaca di Ser Guerriero da Gubbio dall'anno MCCCL all'anno MCCCCLXXII*, ed. Giuseppe Mazzatinti, *RIS*, XXI/4 (Città di Castello, 1902), p. 16; *Istoria della città di Viterbo di Feliciano Bussi* (Rome, 1742), pp. 204–5; *La chronique romane*, in *Le Petit Thalamus de Montpellier*, Société archéologique de Montpellier (Montpellier, 1840), pp. 380–1; *Chronique des règnes de Jean II et de Charles V*, ed. R. Delachenal, *SHF*, 348, (Paris, 1910–20), II, p. 32. These focused more on the pope's indignation, the harsh punishments he wished to impose, and the diplomatic pressures that led him eventually to soften the penalties he imposed on the people of Viterbo.

[76] For instance, after a popular revolt against the papacy in Rome in 1405, the pope threatened to move his entire court with all the cardinals from Rome to Viterbo. Because of the economic consequences of such a move, the Roman people humbly had to beg Innocent VII not to leave. Among other places, see *Cronaca Volgare di Anonimo Fiorentino dall'anno 1385 al 1409 già attribuita a Piero di Giovanni Minerbetti*, ed. Elina Bellondi, RIS, XXVII/2 (Città di Castello, 1915–8), p. 328.

century, the cardinals held their conclaves here to elect four popes – Urban IV (1261), Gregory X (1271), John XXI (1276), and Martin IV (1281).

1367 September [5]: A member [*famiglio*] of the cardinal[77] [of Carcassonne]'s retinue, whom others might call master of the pope's household [in Viterbo], was washing the cardinal's pretty little dog [*cagnolino*] in the Fountain of Scarlano.[78] A servant woman of a citizen of Viterbo, who had arrived there just at that moment to fetch water shouted at him. Insulted by her enraged indignation, he killed her, which sparked others of the neighbourhood [*contrada*] to take up arms and seek revenge. Whereupon, others of the papal court came out into the fray, which in turn increased still further the numbers of the Viterbesi [who came out into the streets]. In great numbers[79] they chanted, 'Long live the Pope and death to the foreigners'. With great rioting [*con gran tumulto*] they stormed the castle where the pope was in residence and there in front of his door killed many soldiers and servants of the cardinals.

78 A grain riot in Florence because of the high price of bread, 1368

Rodolico, *Popolo Minuto*: Doc. 11, pp. 97–9; ASF, Podestà, 19 August 1368: Sentence against certain citizens accused of provoking a riot because of the high price of grain.

Massario di Bertini, parish of San Pier Maggiore

---

77 *La chronique romane*, p. 380, identified him as the servant of the marescal.
78 An artisan neighbourhood of Viterbo. In 1353 it had been the scene of an uprising against Viterbo's ruling prefect. It failed and many heads rolled including members of the church; see Niccola della Tuccia, *Cronache di Viterbo*, p. 34.
79 *La chronique romane*, p. 380, estimated their number at three thousand – probably an exaggeration but possible. This was before the plague of 1369, in which according to a letter of Coluccio Salutati, three thousand died counting only the papal and cardinal courtiers [*curiales*] and the foreigners (*Epistolario di Coluccio Salutati*, ed. Francesco Novati, Fonti per la storia d'Italia (1891–1911), vol. II, p. 91). Furthermore, the chroniclers of Viterbo report that 6,667 perished in the plague of 1400 among inhabitants and foreigners, the rich and the poor. (See for instance, *Le croniche di Viterbo scritte da Frate Francesco d'Andrea*, ed. P. Egidi in *Archivio della R. Società Romana di Storia Patria*, XXIV (1901), p. 362.) This figure was not a numerical invention. With the plague of 1400, which hit Viterbo particularly severely, the bishop began keeping tallies of the numbers who died in plague.

Betto di Stefano, parish of San Piero of Monticello [outside of the city of Florence]
Frogino di Tano, parish of S. Quirico, *contado* of Florence; also called Figno
Piero di Berto, parish of San Pier Maggiore
Berto di Puccio, parish of San Piero Scherraggio

Against these and each one of them, who have been brought to court by the magnificent and powerful knight, Lord Ungaro di messer Giovanni of Actis of Sassoferrato, podestà of Florence at that time ...

[the indicted] together with many others, amounting to more than five hundred, whose names for the better are at present kept silent in this inquest, were of a subversive spirit and were intent on disturbing the good and peaceful state of the city of Florence. It is said that they approached the loggia[80] where grain and wheat are sold and here with many who had gathered began shouting and rioting, grabbing many sacks of grain, which were here on sale. They threw them open on the ground chanting: 'Long live the People'. Not content with this, they took a certain quantity of grain, beyond twenty bushels [*staia*], also on sale here in this loggia, and along with this congregation of people went with this grain to the Palace of the lord Priors. Here they shouted, 'Long live the People'. And they took this grain to the door of the lord priors and dumped it on the ground. Having done it, they returned to the loggia, chanting along the way, 'Long live the People'. They took a certain quantity of flour beyond twenty bushels on sale in this loggia and with this flour went off shouting to the Palace of the lord Priors, threw it on the ground in front of the door of the lord priors, and threw rocks at the guards of the lord priors and those of the podestà of the city of Florence in serious breach of and prejudice to the present peace of the city of Florence. Each and every one of these acts might have overturned the peaceful state of the commune of Florence. But they did not succeed in overthrowing this state ...
[The sentence against Berto di Puccio, who was absent, follows]: 'that he should be led to the customary place of justice with the hangman's noose of hemp around his neck and with this hemp be suspended from the scaffold by the throat until dead and his soul separated from his body'. [The others were absolved.]

---

80 It would have been the newly built Mercato del Grano; see [37].

79 Regime change in Siena, six governments in five months, 1368-69

Donato di Neri e di suo figlio Neri [A. 1368], in *Cronache senesi*, p. 618.

Because of their sins, those who governed Siena were divided into two factions [*sette*], the Canischi and the Grasselli, as I said above. The part of the Twelve called the Grasselli told those of the Salimbeni family, who supported them: 'Arm yourselves and be on guard, because the Canischi are holding an assembly and are plotting against us'. And in turn the Canischi told the Tolomei, who supported them, 'Fortify yourselves, because we have heard that the Grasselli have plotted against us and that they have gathered great numbers'. And because of this the nobility [the *Gentiluomini*] gathered in Siena and along with the [faction of the] Nine assembled eight thousand soldiers. And seeing the iniquity of the Twelve and what they would do to cut the nobility to pieces, the nobility of Siena agreed to unite by taking a general oath amongst themselves and promised the *popolo minuto* and the Nine to reform the government according to their wishes.

Then, on 2 September, they said to the Twelve that they wanted the palace and to change the government of the city; in short, without raising a sword, the Twelve gave the nobles the town hall and free rein over the government. As a consequence, the nobles entered the town hall, took over the governmental benches, the official seals, the bells, and all the fortifications of Siena. They had overturned the city's government and counsellors...

p. 619. And the Salimbeni immediately used their money to begin plotting with certain members of the Twelve. They were given the government's official seals and secretly sent envoys to the emperor ... The emperor accepted them and immediately sent Lord Malatesta Unghero de' Malatesti of Rimini with a cavalry of eight hundred. They were put up at Fontebecci just outside the city gates, where they stayed without doing or saying anything.

The nobles' ambassadors discovered Lord Malatesta and his troops en route. Not knowing the outcome of these plots, they made their own way to the emperor. The emperor received and listened to them willingly, and they came to an agreement. With these plans laid down and with the most beautiful words in the world and the strongest oaths of allegiance and pledges of faith the Salimbeni were forced into a garden on Saturday, 23 [September]. [The faction of the noblemen] then left the garden, yelling 'Long live the People and the Emperor'. With many armed men and with the Twelve they began to tear down the gate of San Prospero and another gate and gave the sign to Lord Malatesta, who rushed in with his men and began a fight at Sant' Andrea. And there they held Lord Andrea Barattucci and his brigade, and the Marzi[81] and their brigade along with troops from the Massa of Camollia.[82] They entered the city and valiantly battled for three hours. Donadolio of the Massa, the constable, and two foreign soldiers were killed, and many from every party, and two from the Salimbeni, and many more were wounded and beaten up. By the end, all the magnates from every clan [*casata*] along with the counsellors who were in the town hall had come out into the streets, and a great and bitter battle ensued. In the end, the Salimbeni allowed Lord Malatesta and his troops to enter [the city], and Francesco di Paolo from Calvoli, the defender of Siena, went through [the neighbourhood of] Camollia with 200 'barbute'[83] soldiers of the commune, who divided, captured, and robbed all the nobles. In more than ten places the people [*popolo*] battled for Siena against the nobles and defeated them. Immediately, the people signed a pact with lord Malatesta, who gave them the day, the town hall, and entire control over the government of the city; many came into power, as we will see below. The people entered the town hall with Lord Malatesta and robbed those gentlemen, who had been the counsellors, leaving them only in their undershirts. They also stole everything they could find from the treasury, and three of the Nine remained in the town hall. The people and Lord Malatesta changed the constitution, [giving offices] to the Nine, the Twelve, and the People,[84] that is, three to the Nine, four to the Twelve, and five to the *Popolo Minuto*. All the noblemen fled, clearing out with their families and possessions ... And the Salimbeni were in the majority and gave the commands as if they were enthroned; in a matter of days, they took possession of the castles, keeps, everything. And by their orders they called on those [the others in government] to change the government and to refashion the city according to their desires.

---

81 Another patrician family of Siena.
82 The zone of countryside just beyond the gate of Camollia to the north of the city.
83 A type of helmet.
84 Here the term *Popolo* and the faction or 'monte' of the *Popolo Minuto* appear to be used interchangeably.

[p. 622] On Monday, 11 December, a riot broke out in Siena, because it had been thought that a pact had been made between Lord Malatesta, the Twelve, the Salimbeni, and several from the lower classes [*popolo minuto*] to chase and kick out the Nine [from the government]; as a result, throughout the city the *popolo minuto* armed themselves. And in the end, the people set fire to the gate of the town hall, burnt it down, and entered the palace, where they chased out the three members of the Nine and the four of the Twelve, leaving only the five of the People [in government]. And thus the agreements with the Nine and the Twelve to govern were broken. And these five of the People, who remained in the government, called on ten of the *popolo minuto* [to join them], creating a government of fifteen. And these stayed in office until January. And these governors created a great council of 858 counsellors. And names were to be drawn [*bossolo*] to elect fifteen governors, that is, three from the Nine, four from the Twelve, and eight from the *popolo minuto*. And from these eight, the captain of the people and the standard-bearer of justice were chosen and called 'Defenders'.

[A. 1368], p. 624: At the third hour on 18 January 1368[9] a riot broke out with the cry 'Long live the People'. And Lord Niccolò Salimbeni, Nuccio da Bigozo, Jacomo Boccacci, and many others of their class with a large armed troop screamed with rage and rioted throughout the city. And at the house of Lord Marsilio, they found Iscotto di Minuccio, who was of the people and captain of his neighbourhood company: he got up and addressed Niccolò, asking him to have a seat. Niccolò took him by the breast and gave it to him in the throat, killing him instantly. They then went through the neighbourhood of the *Casato* to the houses of Renaldo del Peccia, the Ruffaldi, and all the Nine there, killing and robbing all of them as they passed through. Lord Bartalo Fonda and Ser Francesco Bartali with many others of their band went armed, shouted with rage, and rioted in the neighbourhood of Camollia. Squeezing down the alley of the Cock, they entered the street and suddenly were at the house of the Marzi, which they attacked, giving them many blows. But they were well armed and defended themselves ... In the end, they [the insurgents] fled, breaking into all the houses and shouting: 'Set'em a blaze! Death to the traitors, who want the noblemen [to return to office]!' And they sacked all the houses down to the ladies' bonnets and killed all the beasts of burden found in their stables ... [p. 625] ... Lords Piero and Cione Salimbeni, armed and on horseback, went to the palace of the governing 'Defenders'. They entered with many troops, negotiated

FROM THE BLACK DEATH TO 1378 129

courteously and left as the lords [of the city]. This plot made the Twelve governors again; they entered relations with the emperor and Lord Malatesta, to whom they had promised much money.

80 A failed conspiracy of artisans, Lucca, 1369: a chronicler's view

Le Croniche di Giovanni Sercambi, Lucchese, ed. Salvatore Bongi (Lucca, 1892), 3 vols., I, pp. 204–5. Sercambi (1348–1424) was from the middling ranks of Lucchese society, the son of a druggist or spice merchant [*speziale*], who continued in the trade of his father. He was a loyal supporter of the ruling Guinigi family (first Lazzaro, then his son, Paolo, who ruled Lucca until 1430) and supplied the government with its stationery and medicines.

CCXXVIII: How conflict originated from changing the government's name from 'the People' to 'the Commune', and for this several got their heads cut off.

In 1371 [2] in February conflict broke out among various citizens, who had no respect for our traditions. Since it is not nice to name them, I'll keep quiet. But let it be said that many wished Lucca to be ruled under the auspices of the People and wished to have the coats of arms of the People painted everywhere. And many others said they would only live in a Commune, where those of the People were not elected [to governmental posts]. And the conflict became great and lasted a good while, each holding fast to his position. And with matters clearly growing worse, a council was held one Sunday, attended by many notable citizens. When they were deliberating whether to live under a government of the People, an armed riot broke out with flags and pennants of the neighbourhoods [*gonfaloni*]. The podestà of Lucca, Lord Ugolino Galuzzi from Bologna, entered the fray and captured some of the insurgents [*romori*], among them, Nicolao Lippi, a needle worker, and Nuccino Sornachi, citizens of Lucca, members of the Guelf Party and friends, along with Pieretto, a weaver. In the town square of Lucca, the podestà beheaded Nuccino and Nicolao and cut off the right hand of Pieretto. After a few days, a Stefano called Trombante [loud mouth] from Quarto, a gold beater, was caught and similarly his head was cut off in the square. And all this happened in Lucca simply from a desire to change the name [of the city] from People to Commune. And thus hatred sprouted forth among citizens in such a way that it continues to today.

81 A failed conspiracy of artisans, Lucca, 1369: the judicial records

Archivio di Stato, Lucca, Sentenze e Bandi, n. 43, np, 1370.vii.20; Sentence of the podestà and captain of war of Lucca against artisans who conspired to overthrow the government of Lucca. This document has not been previously published.

In the name of God Amen. These are the corporal punishments and sentences of those condemned, imposed and similarly pronounced and promulgated in these documents by the magnificent and powerful knight Lord Ugolino, son of the former Lord Guidiccario de' Galluti of Bologna, the honourable podestà, captain of war, and guardian of the city of Lucca, its *contado*, fortresses, and districts on behalf of the magnificent and powerful men, the lord elders and the standard bearer of justice ...

Nuccino, son of the former Bettucco Sornachi, citizen of Lucca of the parish [*contrata*] of San Cristofano and

Pieretto, son of the former Giovanni, weaver and citizen of Lucca, of the *contrata* of San Piero Cigoli

men of evil ways, deeds, and reputation; each has been condemned corporally ... through our inquest by the office of our captain ... Not from evil or suspicious testimony but by trustworthy, loyal, and honourable persons, it has often been brought to our attention that this Nuccino together with Master Lorenzo, a cobbler, and Bindinello di Tadicione instigated by the spirit of the devil, not having God in their sight but instead looking to the enemy of humankind, deceitfully and knowingly, often held discussions and made plans with this Master Lorenzo, Bindinello, and certain other citizens of the city of Lucca which disturbed the peace and tranquillity of this city of Lucca. To execute the promises, plans, and orders given on Thursday, 25 July, this Nuccino, together with Master Lorenzo, Bindinello, and others of their accomplices and associates, were supposed to meet in the church of Saint George and from there lead all their friends, who were armed, and come together at the Palace of the lord Elders of the city of Lucca, where they were to expel these lord elders, the imperial vicars,[85] and

---

85 These were elected citizens of Lucca, preferably knights, who resided over the court of the Vicariates, which had civil and criminal jurisdiction; see Christine Meek, *Lucca, 1369–1400: Politics and Society in an Early Renaissance City-state* (Oxford, 1978), p. 15.

to chose and summon other new ones to take their place. After accomplishing this, they were to make their way to the houses of those of the Guinigi family,[86] the Bucciolli family, of Lord Simone of Barga, Orlandino di Volpello, and many other citizens of the city of Lucca and to set them on fire, rob them, and kill any who might resist, thus subverting the present state, peace, and tranquillity of the city of Lucca. These actions were ordered to take place on Thursday, 25 July, but several of these citizens, the said Nuccino, Master Lorenzo, and Bindinello, reconsidered who ought to be with them in this plan. They said that [there were those] who did not want to be with them on that day to foment this conspiracy, and so they made a [new] plan and gave commands in the church of San Cristofano ... And since this Nuccino and his aforementioned associates saw that they could not carry out and execute their iniquitous and depraved plan on this Thursday, they decided to meet together again to execute this plan at another place and time. To achieve these deeds, this Nuccino with Bindinello and their other associates came together on Saturday, 27 July, during the night after the third ringing of the bells by the guards of the city. They came into the city through the gate of San Cervagio, seeing and passing a guard who was stationed there. Once in the city of Lucca, he [Nuccino] went to the house of the Guinigi to see if there were any guards. And at the time they planned to attack these properties, the [Guinigi] houses were in the hands of soldiers [*gientibus*], defended by their kinsmen and good men; thus he retreated and returned home. And Nuccino, Master Lorenzo, Bindinello, and their associates were unable to accomplish their mission, because their plan had been revealed to the lord elders of the commune of Lucca.

Concerning Pieretto: on the morning of 25 July the entire city of Lucca and the men of the city were agitated, because this conspiracy had recently been revealed to the lord elders. Therefore, the lord elders called their members to assemble in their palace. The said Pieretto knowingly charged into this council meeting with his knife unsheathed under his cloak. When he was discovered with the knife, he fled, sparking off a major riot throughout the entire city of Lucca with shouts of 'Long live the People'.

And each and everything contained in this inquest was declared to us and in our court and verified by the lawful and spontaneous confessions of the said Nuccino, Pieretto, and each of the others in our court

---

86 The leading family of Lucca's ruling elite; see *ibid.*, pp. 180–3.

... And to punish this Nuccino, Pieretto and each of the others for these crimes ... they are to be made examples and led into the square of the commune, commonly called the square of San Michele in Foro, and here, the head of this Nuccino should be completely and fully severed from his shoulders until his soul is separated from his body, and all his goods shall be confiscated...
And the right hand of this Pieretto should be amputated, entirely separated from the arm.
Dated and carried out on 28 July 1370.

[A day later, in another trial, two other citizens of Lucca were sentenced for the same conspiracy and rebellion in the city. Neither bore a family name nor was identified by an occupation, but they collaborated with another leader named Lotto di Taldo, who was a weaver. Further, this case reveals that when Nuccino Sornachi was being apprehended by the captain and his police, Niccolò, a citizen indicted in this case, was addressing an armed crowd in the square of San Michele in Foro, where 'the majority of the people of Lucca' were assembled. He harangued the crowd, 'shouting loudly, many, many times: "Do not leave us, you must lead the citizens of Lucca".' The two were also brought out as examples, beheaded in the square of San Michele in Foro, and their property confiscated. In short, the criminal case, in which artisans plotted against the most powerful oligarchic family of the city – the Guinigi – suggests that more was at stake than simply a frivolous change in the name of the government from 'the People' to 'the Commune' as the apologist for the Guinigi regime, Sercambi, sarcastically concluded.]

82 Revolt of the wool workers in Perugia, 1371

Donato di Neri e di suo figlio Neri [A. 1371] *Cronaca Senese*, p. 639. The Sienese chronicle gives the fullest account of this revolt; moreover, it is the only one that is contemporaneous with the event.

On 16 May a riot suddenly broke out in Perugia: it began in the [main] square when workers [*gente lavorante*] in the wool industry and foreign[87] gangs of thieves [*forestieri masnaderotti*] provoked it, shouting: 'Long live the Church and the People'. Fourteen people are known to have

---

[87] In other words, those born outside the territory of Perugia.

been killed; houses were burnt and robbed, and the Raspanti[88] were all kicked out of town. Great damage was done, with deaths, robberies, and houses burnt and then sacked. Thus, with this the Church took over Perugia. The Sienese and Florentines showed their discontent with this state of affairs, and all good citizens lamented over it. The Salimbeni, the Twelve, and their followers, however, were happy about it, and many others [in Siena] discussed these affairs and showed their emotions.[89]

83 Wool workers and carders of Siena clash with their bosses over wages: the revolt of the Club of the Caterpillar, 1371

Donato di Neri e di suo figlio Neri [A. 1371], in *Cronache senesi*, p. 639–40.[90]

The workers and carders of the wool guild of Siena clashed with their bosses over their wages, demanding that the commune and not the wool guild should set them. They went to the town hall but were not let in and began to riot, threatening to kill their bosses and others. With this, Cecco from le Fornacci,[91] Giovanni, the son of the woman Tessa, and Francesco d'Agnolo, called Burbicone – all wool carders and members of the Club of the Caterpillar [*Compagnia di Bruco*] – were apprehended. The chief justice [*senatore*] interrogated and tortured them with ropes around their necks [*collati*]; they confessed what could have cost them their lives. Because of this, all those of the Club of the Caterpillar and others came together and swore allegiance [to support one another].

On Monday 14 July, these men took up arms, charged the Palace of the Chief Justice, demanding the release of the three: if they were not handed over, they threatened to send his palace up in smoke. Hearing

---

88 The ruling oligarchic faction at this time, comprised of merchants and nobles.
89 The principal chronicler of Perugia, the late-fifteenth-century Graziani, [192], pp. 215–16, presents this conflict as one between the *popolo* and the Raspanti, which exploded over a controversy on whether the legate of Pope Gregory XI should come to Perugia. The people took up arms and cried: 'Long live the People' and burnt and sacked a number of houses. Maire Vigueur, 'Comuni e signorie' pp. 543–4, argues that this was essentially a struggle between wool workers and their bosses in the wool guild.
90 Also, see Dean, *The Towns of Italy*, doc. no. 71, which concentrates on the economic and social context running up to this riot. I have included parts of this chronicle's description, which Dean left highly abridged and fragmented.
91 A village in the Masse, 3 km southwest of Siena.

this and with the whole city up in arms, the captain of the people at that time, Francesco di Maestro Naddo, left his palace with his banner and trumpeters leading the way. He went to the palace of the chief justice, where a big battle ensued; many of the chief justice's men were killed and others injured. And the captain worked hard to get the three released and then returned to his palace. The Club of the Caterpillar, with these three back in their hands, went to the Palace of the Commune, rioting and chanting 'Siena has been deceived by the Twelve and the Nine'. And this was done with the three rulers of the Nine and the four of the Twelve inside the Palace of the Commune. And thus rioting spread throughout the city with shouts of 'Death to the Twelve and long live the People'. The insurgents went to the houses of Ser Cecco Andrea del Fonda, Meo d'Agnolo, and many others, whom they tried to kill. They met Pellicciaria Nannuccio di Francesco, who had been captain of the people in November and December, rioted and killed him, because when he was captain he had done many nasty things at the beck and call of the Twelve and the Salimbeni. Feraccio, captain of the Club of the Caterpillar, killed him. Then they went to the house of the Salimbeni and took away the banner of the people, which the Salimbeni held as associates of the people, and wounded the prior of the Salimbeni.[92] Further, they grabbed the banners from the standard-bearers and hung them from the windows of the Palace of the Commune. This Feraccio also wounded Bartalo del Forniere, who makes armour. Afterwards, with the sound of trumpets they returned the banners to their standard-bearers along with the trumpets. On their return, these brigands pushed their way into the neighbourhood of Porione[93] and began a scuffle with [the city rulers] at the foot of the palace; they [those of the Catepillar] then left and headed for the house of the Salimbeni, where fighting broke out between them [the Salimbeni] and the Club of the Caterpillar. This drew out those of the Malavolti, Montanini, and Tolomei families,[94] who robbed [those of the Catepillar] of their weapons but nothing else.

92 The Salimbeni family as a faction in the government had its own elected prior.
93 To the southeast of the Campo.
94 All were noble families of Siena.

84 Domestic servants of the Governor of Cortona attempt to kill him and overthrow the government, 1371

Donato di Neri e di suo figlio Neri, *Cronaca Senese*, p. 639.

Cortona: certain citizens of Cortona, mostly the household servants [*domestici*] of the town's governor, plotted and swore an oath to murder their lord and tear him to pieces. On 13 June they had lunch and spent the day with him. One who was by his side ran his knife through his shoulder and quickly ran outside along with other armed men, shouting 'Death to the tyrant and long live the People'. But the lord escaped from their hands, fled to his keep, armed himself, and quickly came out against them. The townsmen failed to back the insurgents, and thus the servants were beaten and fled. With support from the people, the lord searched through the land, captured and brought eight of them to justice; others were killed by the governor's troops or by landowners in the countryside [*terrieri*]. Clearly, the lord remained victorious and the sole ruler over Cortona. But he immediately sent for help and support from Siena. In response, the Sienese sent him many armed men, city guards [*centorini*] with three hundred crossbowmen, and an honourable embassy comprised of many [Sienese] citizens to protect this country and its ruler, called Lord Francesco.

85 A subject town rebels, Gallicano, Lucchesia, 1372

Sercambi, *Le Croniche*, I, r. CCXXXIX, pp. 205–6.

And while they were rioting in [the city of] Lucca, those of Gallicano rebelled [against Lucchese rule] and gave themselves over to Alderigo[95] and his followers. The [Lucchese] official at Gallicano at the time of its loss from Lucca's jurisdiction was Giovanni di Dino Honesti. Many people think that he had instigated it, but I did not agree: Oh, let them believe what they want. When the [council of the] elders heard the news, they immediately called a council and decided to send help to Gallicano. The captain of the field, Lord Giovanni degli Opizi, podestà of Lucca, rode out with the entire army

---

[95] Alderigo degli Antelminelli with Milanese support threatened the Garfagnana region. The Antelminelli family had been exiled from Lucca in the Black and White conflict in 1300. In 1372, they were barred from office as elders in the town council of Lucca; see Meek, *Lucca, 1369–1400*, pp. 1, 4, 131, and 184.

of Lucca along with some from Barga,[96] who had been given to us by the commune of Florence. They moved against the enemy, fighting vigorously, killing many with many wounded on both sides. In the end the castle town was retaken and agreements were negotiated similar to those of another place to be mentioned later.[97]

86 Overthrow of Papal authority in Cento, 1375

CCB; Vol. III, pp. 304–12: *Cronaca A* and *Cronaca di Pietro and Floriano da Villola* [1375]. The Bolognese chronicles briefly mention rebellions that toppled governments supported by the Papacy at Urbino, Perugia, Viterbo, Montefiascone, Forlì, Città di Castello, Rontana and Calavello in the Romagna 'and many other castle towns in Tuscany, the Marche, and the Papal States (lo Patrimonio)' in 1375 (pp. 299–301) and at Fermo, Assisi, Gubbio, Camerino, and Ascoli in 1376 (pp. 305–6). In a long poem, the anonymous diary-chronicler of Florence, now believed to be the great-great grandfather of Niccolò Machiavelli [121], lists over thirty-five cities for 1375 alone, some of which he says had up to twenty cities in their regions, which 'turned against the Church' and 'yelled out for liberty'.[98] Others claimed that sixty cities revolted against 'the pastors' rule' along with 1,577 walled villages.[99] Below are several examples of the feverous spread of insurrection against church rule; the first comes from a market town in the plains north of Bologna. Similar to revolts in France and Flanders, this is one of the very few cases I have found in the Italian chronicles or archival documents, where the report describes one town's revolt as inspired by another.

In these days [1375], because of rumours that there had been a change [in government in Bologna], the men of the castle town of Cento, who were under the jurisdiction of the bishop, took up arms and charged through their town, yelling: 'Long live the Commune of Bologna and the Church'. And they said that they wanted to do what the Bolognese had done. And they ran to the house of the officials of the bishop, who were citizens. And they attacked all their houses, creating great damage. Immediately, the news spread to Bologna, and

---

96 A small town up the Serchio river, 37 km north of Lucca, at that time within Florence's dominion.

97 Sercambi makes no future reference to agreements between Lucca and its subject towns and villages.

98 *Diario d'anonimo fiorentino dall'anno 1358 al 1389*, ed. Alessandro Gherardi, in *Cronache dei secoli XIII e XIV*. Documenti di storia italiana, IV (Florence, 1876), pp. 319–21.

99 See introduction, note 17.

many there became frightened; citizens were sent immediately to reconcile those of Cento [with the Church] and put them back on good terms. And this happened because of the bishop's bad rule.[100] It is said that he had been good and loyal to the Holy Church and to the commune of Bologna, but they no longer wanted this bishop or to obey him.

87 The city of Fermo rebels against the Papacy and creates a government of the People, 1375

Cronache della città di Fermo, ed. Gaetano de Minicis, Documenti di Storia Italiana, I (Florence, 1870), p. 4.

1375: in the time of the Lord Pope Gregory XI, the last day of December, the city of Fermo rebelled [*rebellavit*] against Church rule [*Pastorem Ecclesie*] and created [a government of] the people [*Popolo*]. They killed Gregory of Mirte, the podestà of Fermo at the time, and the son of Ser Cecchino of Ripa Transonum.

88 Revolt of mountain men against the cardinal legate of Bologna, 1376: the story from the judicial records

Archivio di Stato, Bologna, Curia del Podestà: Guidici ad Maleficia: Sententiae, n.22, 98r-9r, 11–16 April 1376: Sentence against twenty-three men, mostly rustics from the mountains near or on the border dividing the territories of Bologna and Florence. (This is an unpublished document.)

11 April, 1376:

Bargatino di Domdollo
Pietro called Bad arm
Bruscallino di Giannoli
Luigi di Giuto
Compagnino di Petracchio
} from Bruscoli, the *contado* of Bologna[101]

Gremaldino called Bad Hand from Ligliano, the *contado* of Bologna
Zeminniano from Polticinillo
Zambonnio called Spolterra from Valdereno, the *contado* of Bologna

---

100 Bernardo Bonavalle, bishop of Bologna, formerly bishop of Spoleto.
101 At 765 meters in altitude, Bruscoli was on the border between these two city-states. It became part of the Florentine territory in 1402; see Cohn, *Creating the Florentine State*, pp. 38, 185–6.

Feta di Giubinerio from Ligliano
Grissante called Barnarossa from Ligliano, the *contado* of Bologna
Melchiore di Alberto
Ricciardino di Nigro
Beldono di Jacobo } from Pianoro, the *contado* of Bologna
Francesco called Red
Michele di Bartolo
Dino di Liberto } from Valdereno, the *contado* of Bologna
Francesco di Tonio
Francesco di Berto called the Giant
Roso di Guillelmo from Tirli[102]
Lapo di Domenico called the Head from Firenzola[103]
Ligo di Giovannello called Half Saint } from Podere[104]
Pieroncino di Ditudolo
Antonio called the Abbot from Florence

and many other foreigners [*forenses*] and those of the *contado* of Bologna whose names are not known at present and against whom this inquest and public proceeding has been given legal authority by the lord elders ... against those named in this inquest ... rebellious men of sedition, authors of the worst agreements, associations, and of the worst reputation...it has been heard and recorded by us and in our court often and consistently that the indicted, each and every one of them, acted under the influence of the devil, out of contempt for the sanctity of the Holy Roman Church, with reckless abandon and a sacrilegious mind. They treated violently the Most Reverent Father in Christ, the renowned Lord William of Sant'Angelo, the compassionate divine deacon and cardinal, the vicar general in the city of Bologna and other provinces and lands of the said sacred Roman Church for the said Most Holy Roman Church, Christ, and Our Father, Lord Gregory XI, Pope of divine Providence. Armed with offensive and defensive weapons, that is, lances, swords, knives, catapults [*balistis*], missiles, projectiles, armour, helmets, shields, and other arms, these men went against him, this most reverent Father, with rage and passion and the force of their weapons, and savagely and furiously

---

102 A highland border village that Florence incorporated in 1373; see Cohn, *Creating the Florentine State*, pp. 164–5.

103 The regional centre of the Alpi Fiorentine; created as a new town in 1332 to control the northern passes leading to Florence.

104 A mountainous region of the northeastern corner of the Florentine territory, which borders the lands of the Romagna.

expelled and forced him from his palace, his usual place of residence, whose location is indicated in this inquest. And from this aggression, this most Reverend Father was wounded and bled from a blow with an iron weapon held by one of the indicted ... and then the indicted robbed him, stealing his horse, tools, rings, yokes, and other things, against the will of this most reverend Father, and they took them away for their own use, and because of this sedition and scandal they were able to take them out of the city of Bologna. And this most reverend Father left this city. In committing this crime, each and every one of the indicted received help, advice, and favours [from others]. And the aforesaid crimes were committed and perpetrated by each and every one of the indicted in the city of Bologna and in this said palace in the present year and month of March, against the customs, statutes, and ordinances of the commune of Bologna and against and contrary to the will of the good men of the city of Bologna, the Commune, and People of the city of Bologna, and with serious injury and offence to his most Holy Father [i.e. the pope] and to the lords of this most Holy Pontificate [i.e. the rulers of the Papal States] and in disturbance of the city, the Commune, the People, and the Church.

[On] 12 April

Tono di Girardo of Bologna and the parish of San Barbaziano, town crier of the city of Bologna, in front of the Discus of the Bear in the council chambers of the Old Palace of Bologna, located in the town square ... and in the presence of the general council of the eight hundred good men of the commune and city of this city of Bologna,[105] at the ringing of the bells and after the sound of the trumpet, commanded by the said lord podestà customarily gathered here ... shouted loudly and proclaimed that the above-mentioned indicted [each name is then read out in full] is outlawed from the city, *contado*, and district of Bologna ... [Condemned in their absence, each of the indicted was 'to be led to the customary place of justice and suspended from the gallows until dead, their souls separated from their bodies'; further, all their property, houses, real estate, and goods were to be confiscated and destroyed. The sentence was given on 16 April, 1376.]

---

105 A legislative council of the Bolognese commune also called the council of the *popolo*. It was not, however, the broadest or largest council of Bologna at least in 1288, when according to the statutes there was a council of Two Thousand; see *Statuti di Bologna dell'anno 1288*, ed. Gina Fasoli and Pietro Sella, 2 vols. Studi e testi, nos. 73 and 85 (Città del Vaticano, 1937–39).

89 The same: the chroniclers' view

CCB, Vol. III, pp. 306–8: *Cronaca B* [called *Varignana*] and *Cronica Bolognetti* [1376]. Were the mountain men who carried out the insurrection simply pawns of Bologna's country counts? Did the former have grievances of their own against the Church? Why did the mountain men from Monzuno not join their comrades? Who were 'the bad ones' blocked by 'the good citizens' from carrying the revolt further? What was their agenda?

On 19 March several magnates of Bologna organised a large gathering of men from the city with many nobles from the *contado* of Bologna. They entered Bologna at 2 in the morning under the walls, through the portcullis [*sarasinescha*] that had been cut for water to spill through. And those of the Miralsole, the *contrata* of Castiglione [dei Pepoli][106] along with Domenico from Vizano,[107] who was inside the walls, tore open this sluice gate. The leaders inside the walls with the count of Bruscolo were Guilielmo from Loiano, Ugolino from Pianora, and Zampolo from Vizano. And with them were all the mountain men, except for those from Monzuno, who decided not to go against the Church. That night, before the people came out into the square, these men had taken the castle of San Felice and its insignia. In the morning before sunrise they went into the square, yelling: 'Long live the People'. These are the magnates, who chased the Church out: Lord Taddeo degli Azziguidi, Lord Ugolino Malavolti, the Bentivoglio family, the Galluzzi, Ugolino and Baldoino of the Bianchi, the Ghixelieri, the Gozzadini, those of the Salexedo, and many other powerful ones. And they called themselves the Party of the Scachese. And with ease they took over the Palace [of the cardinal legate] without any resistance from the soldiers, and they robbed all the foreigners. And the cardinal was very badly treated as he was led out [of his palace]; at that point Count Antonio of Bruscolo forced off the cardinal's rings from his finger and treated him vilely. The cardinal was led into the church of the Hermit friars, who later took him to Ferrara.

According to *Cronaca A*, pp. 312–13:

The cardinal was led out very roughly by a peasant and his hand was a little scratched from having his rings forced off, and it was Count Antonio of Bruscoli who did this. Had it not been for the good

---

106 Castiglione dei Pepoli, in the mountains near the border of Pistoia, 55 km south of Bologna, the stronghold of the Pepoli family, previous rulers of Bologna.
107 On the border of the Alpi Fiorentine and the Podere.

citizens, the bad ones would have treated him worse. Two hermit friars took him off to San Jacomo. And it is said that they took the clothes from his back. But all this was against the will of the men of Bologna. Had he[108] given up the keys to the gates immediately when this gang was ordered into action, these magnates would have simply put him away honourably into some monastery. There would have been no revolt; neither the cardinal nor any from his staff, not even the foreigners, would have been robbed. But perhaps it is better that this robbery did take place; otherwise, the shops of the citizens and even their houses might have been destroyed. With events like these, it is impossible for everyone to escape unscathed. But thank God with such a big event so little was damaged.

Even though more orders were given, no one chanted: 'Death' or 'Long live'; only 'the People, the People' was shouted, but this was a chant for everyone. No one said 'Death to the Church' or 'Death to its pastors'; and only one banner was raised, the one with the arms of the people.

And also [in this riot] the podestà from Ascoli was wounded and robbed, not because he wasn't such a good man, but because the government would not let him control his officers, who acted up: one did in another and he was held accountable without any reason.

With this event over, the government at once elected sixteen elders, that is, four for each quarter; they were a cultured bunch, comprised of magnates and the middling sort [*mezani*], and were placed in the palace, where the cardinal once stayed.

90 Ascoli creates a government of the People and rebels against the Church, 1377

Cronache della città di Fermo, p. 4.

27 February 1376, the city of Ascoli created [a government of] the People and rebelled [*rebellavit*] against Lord Gomesio[109]; and indeed, this city would have been completely destroyed had men from the city

---

108 An unpopular podestà from Ascoli, who served during the first six months of 1376.
109 Nephew of Cardinal Albornoz, created Marchese of the Marches after Gentile da Mogliano was chased out. He gave possession of the city of Fermo to Giovanni Visconti of Oleggio (*Cronache della città di Fermo*, p. 121).

and *contado* of Fermo, foot soldiers and cavalry, numbering well over ten thousand, not invaded [in support of the insurgents] on the day following the insurrection [*novitatem*]. They did so because of their affection and compassion for Ascoli. ... Next, the horrible Lord Raynaldus of Monteverdi returned because of the revolt [*novitatem*] of those of Fermo against the rule of the Church... Lord Gomesio, his wife, children, and his officers stayed for ten months camped out above the citadel of the city of Ascoli. In December of this year, this citadel came back into the hands of those of Ascoli with a peace treaty.

III: THE JACQUERIE

The revolts and social movements of chapter I spanned a hundred years, those of chapter II, a generation. The documents of this chapter describe an event, or rather two interconnecting events, that of the mainly rural uprisings in the Beauvaisis, Picardy, and the Île de France, along with the Parisian charge against the king's stronghold at Meaux. These lasted a mere two weeks, from the peasant attacks against nobles at Saint-Leu d'Esserent near Chantilly on 28 May to the king of Navarre's slaughter of the rustics between Mello and Clermont on 10 June 1358.[1] Yet the Jacquerie is probably the best-known revolt in France before the French Revolution. Historians and the public alike now use the term 'Jacquerie' to characterise any revolt that manifests excessive and gratuitous violence, appears to be spontaneous and leaderless, is usually comprised of peasants and arises from desperation and poverty. This view of the original Jacquerie comes largely from one source, Jean Froissart's chivalric chronicle [92], which by the early-modern period had become required reading for gentlemen across Europe. Much of what Froissart said about the Jacquerie, especially his most memorable tales of peasants roasting their lords on spits with their ladies looking on and the rape and murder of fair maidens, he lifted almost verbatim from the aristocratic chronicler and canon of Liège, Jean le Bel [91].

Unlike contemporary chronicles and diaries of the revolt of Ciompi, no descriptions survive from the insurgents themselves. Instead, the chronicles fall into four categories: those of the lay nobility [91–2, 94]; the official chronicles of the king, composed by the monks of the abbey at Saint-Denis, just north of Paris, where the kings of France were buried [95, 96]; those of other clergymen more sympathetic to

---

1 There are many summaries of the events of the Jacquerie: the best are Sumption, *The Hundred Years War*, II, pp. 327–36; Raymond Cazelles, 'The Jacquerie', in *The English Rising of 1381*, ed. R. H. Hilton and T. H. Aston (Cambridge, 1984), pp. 74–84; Guy Fourquin, *Les Campagnes de la région parisienne à la fin du Moyen Âge* (Paris, 1964), pp. 229–40; R. Delachenal, *Histoire de Charles V*, I. (1338–58) (Paris, 1909), pp. 394–410; and Siméon Luce, *Histoire de la Jacquerie d'après des documents inédits*, 2nd edn (Paris, 1894), pp. 45–55.

the Jacques, most importantly, that of the Carmelite Jean de Venette[2] [93, 97]; and views from outside France [98, 99].[3] The outsiders show their removal from the events in northern France. The *Anonimalle Chronicle*, written in Anglo-Norman French by a monk at St. Mary's Abbey, York, numbers the peasant rebels at 190,000 as opposed to the more reasonable number estimated by local chroniclers of between seven and ten thousand [93 and 97], even when they gloated over the numbers slaughtered [102].[4] Further, the Yorkshire monk's tales of peasant excess go beyond even the horror stories of the deeply incensed Jean le Bel (whose tales can find approximate parallels in the letters of remission[5]). According to *The Anonimalle Chronicle*, 'this Jak Bonehomme uprooted babies from their mothers' wombs and with these babies' blood quenched their thirst and anointed their bodies in contempt of God and his saints' [98]. On the other hand, the Florentine Matteo Villani saw the Jacquerie exclusively in terms that he was familiar with; under his pen, it became a struggle between the urban *popolo minuto* and bourgeoisie against the Dauphin and the aristocracy. Rustics are not even mentioned [99].

While all the narratives condemned the peasants for their excesses and for violating the hierarchy of the feudal orders, they did not all see the uprisings as springing forth without leaders or without any organisation. Indeed, even by the end of Jean le Bel's account, he felt obliged to admit that the Jacquerie could not have happened in places as far apart as villages south of Paris and others in Normandy had there been no guidance. His suspicions, however, turned to outside agitators, tax collectors, the bishop of Laon, the provost of Paris, and the king of Navarre, even though the last led the brutal massacre against the Jacques. Other chronicles, however, never hinted that the Jacques were leaderless and pointed to prior assemblies of peasants [94, 95, 97], in which they elected their own captains, most prominently Guillaume Charles, Carle, Calle, or Cale, a rich peasant from the village of Mello, south of Clermont-en-Beauvaisis.[6] Nor did they cloak

---

2 On questions of this author's identity, see [97].

3 For an excellent analysis of these chronicles, see Marie-Thérèse de Medeiros, *Jacques et Chroniqueurs: Une étude comparée de récits contemporains relatant la Jacquerie de 1358* (Paris, 1979).

4 Froissart, who was also a non-eyewitness outsider from Valenciennes put the Jacques' numbers at 100,000 [92].

5 Medeiros, *Jacques et Chroniqueurs*, p. 35; and Sumption, *The Hundred Years War*, II, p. 328.

6 Sumption, *The Hundred Years War*, II, pp. 328–9.

this Cale entirely in demonic garb. The Carmelite de Venette saw him as 'astute' [97], and the provincial cleric of Normandy, author of the *Chronicle of the four Valois kings*, described him as 'a knowledgeable man, well spoken, handsome, and well formed'. Further, this chronicler saw him as exercising restraint on his followers, and instead of being corralled by outside forces, especially the provost of Paris, Cale is pictured as the initiator of negotiations with the provost of Paris, which resulted in their joint forces, those of the villagers and the bourgeois ['the third estate'], defeating the nobles as far away as Gaillefontaines [93].

Nor did all the accounts portray these revolts as bereft of all reason. Even the continuator of Richard Lescot, a monk at Saint-Denis and close to the king, gave the peasants a reasonable voice: 'We charge against these noble traitors, who have shirked on their duties to defend the kingdom, who desire to do nothing but devour the sustenance of the commoners' [96]. Similarly, Jean de Venette begins his treatment of the Jacquerie by claiming that Paris was 'ill-treated and little defended' and 'that peasants living near Saint-Leu-d'Essérent', where the Jacquerie was born, were threatened 'on every side'; 'the nobles gave them no protection but rather oppressed them as heavily as did the enemy' [97].

With the systematic study of royal letters of remission by Siméon Luce during the second half of the nineteenth century[7] and with quantitative studies of the economy of France in the 1960s, views of the Jacquerie changed. First, Luce read the documents with a sympathetic eye towards the peasantry, emphasising the contexts of war, terror, and destruction to the countryside by the English *routiers*, gangs of brigands, and above all else, 'the decadence of French chivalry'. The nobles' loss of military prestige, their failure to protect the peasantry, and their need to burden them with new exactions to provision and repair their castles were the Jacquerie's pre-conditions. In short, as the contemporary Carmelite friar Jean de Venette put it: 'the wolf becomes the intimate friend of the dog, which kills the sheep'.[8]

Secondly, instead of a revolt arising from economic desperation and misery (which not even the most hostile aristocratic chroniclers in fact ever claimed), Georges Duby, Robert Fossier, Guy Fourquin, and

---

7 Luce, *Histoire de la Jacquerie*.
8 *Ibid.*, pp. 31–44.

Raymond Cazelles have emphasised the opposite: the Jacquerie arose among the most privileged peasants in the wealthiest agricultural regions of France – the Île de France, the Beauvaisis, and Picardy.[9] Moreover, the prime battlefields and places peasant unrest would erupt were the richest lands within these zones, where in 1358 the spoils and plunder of the Hundred Years War had only recently touched.[10] Indeed, when the letters of remission point to poverty, it was after the revolt and as a consequence of its bloody repression, after villagers had been forced into hiding and stripped of their lands [110]. In one letter, Colart du Four called Melin complained to the king of his 'poverty and misery', but before the nobles had stolen or burnt his property he had possessed landed property, not only substantial enough for his family's subsistence, but large enough to be farmed out to others [109].

Thirdly, in addition to Guillaume Cale, the letters reveal the names of a myriad of other locally elected leaders throughout the Beauvaisis and the Île de France, who organised village assemblies throughout the lands of the uprisings [108, 109, 112-5]. Fourthly, instead of uncontrolled spontaneous violence, the letters argued that village insurgents often acted with restraint and urged caution. On occasion, the peasants assembled but after their deliberations refused to rise up against their lords, to burn or pillage property [108, 111, 114]. In contrast to the disclaimers of Étienne Marcel,[11] who in a letter to the

---

9 Ibid., 22–3; Georges Duby, *L'économie rurale et la vie des campagnes dans l'Occident médiéval* (Paris, 1962), II, p. 602; Robert Fossier, *Histoire sociale de l'Occident médiéval* (Paris, 1970), p. 343; and Fourquin, *Les campagnes de la région parisienne*, pp. 191–215. However, Fourquin (p. 233) insists that it was 'a revolt of poverty (une révolte de misère)', that 'the disparity between cereal and industrial prices, born from the crisis of 1315, continued to persist. The Jacquerie was a revolt against the consequences of the grain crisis from the beginning of the century'. But he never shows any evidence from the contemporary sources of food or grain revolts during the Jacquerie, or of any protests about grain prices. Nor does he explain why it took forty-three years for the peasants to rebel against a crisis that erupted in 1315 or why it should have later occurred only in the richest regions of the Île de France, the Beauvaisis, and Picardy. By contrast, chronicles and letters of remission point to the rich booty that nobles gained from their later repression of the Jacques; as *La Chronique normande du XIVe siècle* [94] put it: '[the nobles] carried off their [the Jacques'] wealth, of which much was to be had'.

10 Sumption, *The Hundred Years War*, II, p. 327.

11 Étienne Marcel was a cloth dealer and provost of the merchants of Paris from the mid-1350s to his assassination in 1358. There are numerous biographies and studies of him; see Jacques Avout, *Le meutre d'Étienne Marcel: 31 Juillet 1358* (Paris, 1961).

city councillors in Picardy and Flanders later tried to distance himself and the bourgeois of Paris from the peasants and their excesses [101], the peasants can be seen refusing to obey Marcel's military commands to attack their own lords [110].

Following on from these letters, Raymond Cazelles has concluded that the Jacquerie was not a peasant revolt (or for that matter, a revolt at all[12]). Indeed, those from Paris and provincial towns such as Amiens, Senlis, and Montdidier[13] joined villagers in attacks on noble strongholds in the surrounding countryside, and towns such as Senlis successfully resisted the aristocrats' counter offensive [93]. Further, letters of remission show that those from some provincial cities wished to join the peasants (as did those ordered by its radical mayor in Amiens [94, 119]). The same places, however, could also turn their backs on the Jacques as did the bourgeois of Senlis[14] and Compiègne, who refused to let the Jacques enter their city walls [95] or the Amiens magistrates, who called back their citizen militia [119][15] or at Beauvais, where the town government acquiesced in butchering hundreds of peasants [94], and ultimately at Paris, where Étienne Marcel disassociated himself and Paris's cause from that of the Jacques [101]. The official chronicle of Saint-Denis even saw the Jacquerie not wholly as a peasant-noble conflict but in part as one between rural society and its surrounding towns [96].

Even if townsmen on occasion joined the Jacques against noblemen, should we go along with Cazelles, concluding that it was not rustics or those who worked the soil but 'country artisans, well-to-do proprietors, petty officials, and some members of the clergy' who comprised the ranks of the Jacques?[16] First, his thesis that the Jacquerie occurred at the least likely moment for farm labourers to revolt, given

---

12 The logic here is strange: supposedly because the Jacques did not attack the crown, it was not a revolt; Cazelles, *Société politique, noblesse et couronne sous Jean le Bon et Charles V*, ch. xxxiii: 'La guerre sociale', pp. 318–37: 'La Jacquerie n'est pas une insurrection; à aucun moment l'autorité royale n'a été mise en cause par les Jacques' (p. 323).

13 See Sumption, *The Hundred Years War*, II, pp. 329–31.

14 Guenée, *Tribunaux et Gens*, pp. 48–51; Cazelles, *Société politique*, p. 322; J. Flammeront, 'La Jacquerie en Beauvaisis', *Revue Historique*, 4 (1879): 135.

15 Sumption, *The Hundred Years War*, II, p. 331.

16 Cazelles, 'Les mouvements révolutionnaires du milieu du XIVe siècle et le cycle de l'action politique', *Revue Historique*, 228 (1962): 279–337; 'La Jaquerie fut-elle un mouvement paysan?', *Academie des inscriptions et belles lettres* (1978): 654–66; and 'The Jacquerie', esp. p. 82.

the pre-harvest seasonal intensity of work in June, does not stand up to comparative history across time and place. One only has to look across the channel to see a peasant revolt spreading at almost exactly the same moment – early June[17] – or even closer to home, southern France, where the Tuchins regularly set about their raids and revolts in May [65]. Indeed, as the mountain peasant revolts above Florence in 1402 make clear, it was at this time of year, before the harvest had been gathered and shipped off to the cities, that peasants could exercise the greatest stronghold over their cities and rulers [198–201]. Second, he has not tallied the occupations of the insurgents found in the letters of remission. Nor do one or two examples prove that the rank and file of the Jacques were filled with 'priests, law officers, and petty officers of the crown'.[18]

For instance, unlike the English Uprising of 1381, when priests such as John Ball, John Wrawe, and at least twenty other clerics can be counted as filling key leadership roles, [19] I know of no rural clergyman mentioned in the chronicles and only one in a letter of remission – the curate of Blacy – who was even suspected of being a Jacque follower, much less a leader.[20] Moreover, the curate of Blacy was hardly a willing participant. Instead, his peasant parishioners forced him to follow, compelling him to carry a big stick, which they used to make him dance and do their bidding. Far from being a leader, he was the object of the peasants' mockery and abuse, and they stole his goods and grain for their own profit. Further, there is no reason to suppose that this nameless crowd in this small parish in the plains of Perthois was composed of artisans and notables [112] as Cazelles would ask us to believe. As with most of the seven thousand or so Jacques, these received no royal letters of remission and a week later may have well been among the numbers ruthlessly massacred by the king of Navarre's troops and the nobles' counter-offensive.

Finally, should we assume, as Cazelles does, that a 'laboureur' was not

---

17 Also, Cade's revolt in 1450, Kett's in Norfolk in 1549, rural revolts in Forez, 1422–31, the Croquants in southwest France in 1636, and the revolts of mountain peasants in Florence of 1402 began in late May or early June.
18 Cazelles, *Société politique*, p. 323.
19 Wrawe was the leader of the peasants in Suffolk. For other local leaders who were clergymen, see Hilton, *Bondmen Made Free*, p. 207–10.
20 The only urban clergyman to arise from the letters of remission was a priest and canon of Meaux, who was pardoned; see [106].

an agricultural worker?[21] Instead, specialists in agricultural history and the historical dictionaries define the term as a substantial peasant, who possessed a plough and might have had enough property to supplement his labour by employing others[22] as indeed seems to have been the case with the peasant Colart du Four called Melin [109]. At any rate, *laboureur* was not the word chronicles or the letters used to label the Jacques. Instead, the chroniclers called them peasants [*paisans*], rustics [*rustici*], and villeins [*villains*] [91–4, 96–8], and the letters of remission simply referred to them as 'men from the plains' [*les genz du plat païs*] [101, 108, 111, 112, 115]. Finally, as has been charged,[23] these letters cost money to write, to be heard favourably, and to obtain concessions from the king; they thus would represent a skewed sample of privileged rebels, even if impoverished supplicants occasionally could receive them.

At present, there is no consensus among historians on the character of the Jacquerie. After Luce's efforts to soften the hard edges of Jean le Bel's and Froissart's condemnations, Jean Flammeront wrote a strong rebuttal, challenging Luce's dates of several key documents, the revolt's origins, and the character of the peasant insurgents. Flammeront held that the Jacquerie arose out of fights with soldiers, not from grievances arising from Article 5 of the Ordinances of Compiègne, which had placed a blockade on the major rivers supplying food to Paris and had prompted Étienne Marcel to enlist peasant support, as Luce had surmised. Further, Flammeront moved the historiography back to a prejudicial and emotionally-charged position not so distant from where it had been in the passionate hands of contemporaries of elite society such as Jean le Bel and Jean Froissart, who momentarily saw their world turned upside down. In Flammeront's words, the peasants were 'brutes, drunk on wine and blood ... We find nothing similar in the Jacquerie [equal to the revolt of Étienne Marcel]; these insurgents were stupid peasants, without education, training, brutalised by poverty and their own drunkenness'.[24] Surprisingly, this view has persisted among major historians into the twentieth century with

---

21 Cazelles, *Société politique*, p. 323.
22 Pierre Goubert, *The Ancien Régime: French Society 1600–1750*, tr. Steve Cox (New York, 1969), p. 110. *Robert dictionnaire historique*, II, pp. 1954–5, gives a similar definition for 'labeur' and 'labourer', indicating that it pertained to strenuous agricultural labour or labour associated with ploughing.
23 Fourquin, *Les campagnes de la région parisienne*, p. 234.
24 Flammeront, 'La Jacquerie en Beauvaisis', p. 123–43 and esp. pp. 127 and 131.

Flammeront's article used as a corrective to Luce's exhaustive research into the sources.[25]

Finally, historians now stress long-term economic causes for the Jacquerie's rising, going back as far as the grain crisis and famine of 1315.[26] Whether or not one accepts the argument that 'the price scissors' between industrial goods and grain created by that crisis explains why forty-three years later the Beauvaisis and the Île de France happened to become the principal battlefields of Jacquerie discontent, the shorter-term political setting for the revolts cannot be underestimated. In addition to the changes of fortune in the Hundred Years War that tilted towards England's way with France's defeat at Poitiers (19 September 1356) and the capture and ransom of King John II, northern France became deeply divided between the forces of Charles the Bad, king of Navarre, and of John's eldest son, the Dauphin Charles, later King Charles V in the years immediately leading up to the Jacquerie. This civil war widened the space for conspiracies and political ambition among the nobility, merchant elites, and the clergy, while it heightened instability and created the conditions for the nobility's social treason of its dependents as so many of the documents that follow reveal.

91 A view from the church elite: Jean le Bel

Chronique de Jean le Bel, ed. J. Viard and Eugène Déprez, *SHF*, 317 (Paris, 1904–5), 2 vols., I, pp. 255–62.

Chapter 100: How certain leaderless people revolted; intending to murder gentlemen, ladies, and maidens, they inhumanely committed evil deeds.

As soon as news arrived in France that the two kings [of France and Navarre] had drawn up an agreement between them and were allied against all others, the provost of the merchants [of Paris] was in greater fear than before, for he knew well that the duke of Normandy[27]

---

25 See Delachenal, *Histoire de Charles V*, I, pp. 394–410; Mollat and Wolff, *Popular Revolutions*, pp. 125–31; and David Bessen, 'The Jacquerie: Class war and Co-opted Rebellion?' *Journal of Medieval History*, 11 (1985): 44–5. Despite abundant evidence of meetings and locally elected leaders, Fourquin, *Les campagnes de la région parisienne*, p. 234, also claims that 'the revolt had been everywhere spontaneous'.

26 See note 9. In addition, Mollat and Wolff, *Popular Revolutions*, p. 128, repeat Fourquin's view in their interpretation of the rise of Jacquerie.

27 King John II's eldest son, the regent or dauphin, soon to be King Charles V.

THE JACQUERIE

loathed him; everywhere he complained about him because of the humiliation he had endured at the Palace of Paris.[28] So many details of the agreement were questionable [*si quist*?] that the King of Navarre was sent for, and when he arrived, the provost and the bourgeois of Paris made such a fuss over him that he swore and promised them that he would stick with them against everyone, without exception, including the king, which greatly surprised many.

Soon afterwards, around Pentecost [20 May], a mysterious affliction [*tribulation*] broke out in many parts of the realm of France, in the regions of Beauvais, Amiens, Brie, Perthois,[29] [Île de] France, and Valois as far as Soissons. Some rural people had assembled in their villages but nowhere with a leader. At first there were not a hundred of them, saying that the nobles, knights, and squires were ruining and disgracing the kingdom, and it would be good if they were all destroyed. Each one said: 'He speaks the truth; he speaks the truth. Shame on him who allows them to live!'

Thus, without further advice and without weapons other than iron bats and knives, they first went to the house of a knight, broke down his door, killed him, his wife, and children, and then burnt the house. Next, they went to a strong castle and did much worse: they captured the knight, tied him up with a strong rope, and raped his lady and daughter before his eyes. Then they killed the lady, who was pregnant, the daughter, and then the knight and all his children, and then burnt the castle. They did the same with many other castles and good houses. And their numbers multiplied, reaching more than six thousand. Everywhere they went, their numbers increased, because anyone with the same views followed them. As a consequence, knights, ladies, esquires, and maidens fled anywhere they could. They left their manors and castles, often carrying their little children on their shoulders for ten, even twenty leagues.[30] Thus these leaderless people gathered together, burnt, and robbed everything and murdered gentlemen, noble ladies, and their children; they raped ladies and virgins without any mercy whatsoever.

---

28 On 22 February 1358 Étienne Marcel summoned his men to break into the dauphin's private rooms on the second floor of the Louvre, where before his eyes they butchered his two marshals and chief advisors, Jean de Conflans and Robert of Clermont; see Sumption, *The Hundred Years' War*, II, p. 312.

29 Region around Perthes, Seine-et-Marne, near Melun; see Luce, *Histoire de la Jacquerie*, p. 209.

30 A league was about three miles, although it varied from place to place.

Certainly, among Christians, even Saracens, there has never been such uncontrolled, diabolical madness. He who dared commit the greatest evil and the vilest deeds – such evil a human creature could not even think of without shame and disgust – was deemed the greatest master. I would not dare write or tell of their atrocious deeds or of the indecorous things they did to ladies. But, among other indecent acts, they killed a knight, put him on a spit, and roasted him with his wife and children looking on. After ten or twelve of them raped the lady, they wished to force feed them the roasted flesh of their father and husband and made them then die by a miserable death. They destroyed and burnt more than sixty beautiful homes and strong castles in the Beauvaisis.[31] So much had the mischief multiplied that had God not remedied matters by His grace, the commoners would have destroyed all the nobility, the Holy Church, and all the rich throughout the entire country, because these people did the same in the regions of Brie, Perthois, and along the banks of the Marne. It behoved all the noblemen, knights, and esquires, who could escape, [along with] their ladies and maidens, to flee to Meaux in Brie; one after another other, they fled, wearing only their nightshirts.

They did the same in Normandy, between Paris and Noyon, Paris and Soissons towards the lands of the lord of Coucy. And in these two regions, they devastated more than eighty castles, beautiful homes, and worthy manors of knights and esquires. They would have killed and destroyed everything had God by his grace not sent help, for which each good man must give thanks, as you will hear later.

One must marvel at how such boldness came to these wicked people all at the same moment, separated from one another and scattered in various places, if it had not been instigated and advised by some of those governors and tax collectors, who did not wish for peace in the kingdom because they would lose their offices.

Some suspected the bishop of Laon,[32] who was and has always been spiteful, and the provost of the merchants,[33] since they were of the same party,[34] shared the same ideas and received aid from the king of

---

31 The region of Beauvais, the Beauvosin or Beauvaisis.

32 Robert Le Coq.

33 Étienne Marcel. On Le Coq and Marcel and their political alliance, see Arthur Layton Funk, 'Robert le Coq and Étienne Marcel', *Speculum*, 19 (1944): 470–87.

34 Perhaps the author is referring to their membership in the radical group of the Council of Eighty, which before the Jacquerie had pushed for radical reforms for the liberties of *les bonnes villes* and to the king's administration.

Navarre. I do not know if they were guilty and will not dwell on it; instead, I will speak about the remedy God sent us.

You realise that when these lords of the Beauvaisis and the Corbyois[35] saw their homes destroyed and their friends killed so wickedly, they sent for help to their friends in Flanders, Poitou, and elsewhere. They mowed down these wicked people on all sides, killing them by hanging them from the first trees they found. And when asked why they [the insurgents] had behaved so, they answered that they had only followed what they had seen the others doing; so they did it also, thus thinking it was all right in this way to destroy all the gentlemen. There were even those who confessed to have helped in raping the ladies; some claiming six ladies; others, seven; still others, eight, nine, ten, and twelve, and they killed them as well, even if pregnant.

As soon as these foreign troops arrived in the Beauvaisis and had inflicted the first defeat, these wicked people felt so lost and dizzy that they did not know what had hit them. The men-at-arms went from village to village within the region as far as Creil, wherever they thought these wicked people might be. They burnt and robbed all of them alike, having no time to make an inquest.

How can anyone think that such people could have dared to begin to perform such diabolic acts without support from others? Can one believe it, that such help could have even come from within the kingdom of France? In a similar way, the lord of Coucy sent his soldiers everywhere he could; they attacked their neighbours, destroyed them, hanged them, and had them killed by such miserable means that would be unimaginable to record. And these wicked men had a captain called Jacques Bonhomme, who was nothing but a lout [*un parfait villain*], who let on that the bishop of Laon encouraged him to do this, since he was one of his men, and also the lord of Coucy did not like this bishop.

Chapter 101: How certain knights and esquires, who had retreated to Meaux in Brie, killed many of these commoners.

Now I wish to return to those who had fled to the city of Meaux as you have heard. There were the count of Foix, the duke of Orléans and well over two hundred men-at-arms, knights, and esquires, and at least three hundred ladies with all their children. And they were kept

---

35 The area around the same town of Corbie, about 10 km northeast of Amiens.

in the castle of the Marché.[36] Having seen their homes destroyed and villages burnt throughout the region, they did not dare go out to defend themselves.

When news reached Paris that these great ladies and gentlemen were at Meaux and did not dare to leave, people left Paris with malicious motives and gathered at a certain place until at least six thousand of them had arrived. Then they went to Meaux and stopped just outside its gate. Seeing such a great number of people, these lords, gentlemen, ladies, and maidens became unimaginably frightened; they did not know what to do or what advice to follow. Some advised fleeing by the other gate; others said they did not know where to flee and that it would be better to die sooner rather than later. So, some ran to arm themselves to man the barricades. The wicked people of the town did not want to block the entrance to those of Paris, so they opened the gates and let these wicked people enter freely, who like crazed men charged the Marché to kill all in sight. But when they came to the barricades and found the soldiers equipped for defence, they were not quite as bold as before. Some ran ahead and began to charge but not for long. Before anyone could say 'Ave Marie', they had retreated, running so hard that they fell on top of one another. These men-at-arms then charged and killed them like swine, one on top of the other. With so many to kill and the streets so narrow it was difficult for the troops to advance; as a result, a great many of the Parisians were able to break through and escape into the fields. When the soldiers had killed all those they could find, they pulled back and then set the town on fire, burning it as far as the Marché, and they took everything they could find. They saw the townsmen as their adversaries, since they had let those from Paris enter.

These lords, ladies, and maidens had lived long enough in this Marché in great discomfort before this good fortune arrived, which was not only very sweet for them but for all Christianity. Had it gone the other way, these people would have never been stopped; instead they would have continued multiplying in pride and in their diabolic acts, and day after day they would have become stronger against the nobility. And many others [like them] would have arisen everywhere had God not remedied matters through his divine mercy. Certainly France would have been defeated. When the provost of the merchants

36 The king's fortifications on an island in the Marne, divided from Meaux by a canal. Its outer walls were two kilometres in circumference.

THE JACQUERIE 155

and his cronies heard the news, they made a show of being enraged,[37] but no one who had supported [the Jacques] was reprimanded or punished by them.

92 An aristocrat's view: Froissart

Les Chroniques de Froissart, ed. S. Luce, *SHF,* 147 (Paris, 1874), V, pp. 99–106.

Soon after the deliverance of the king of Navarre, strange and great afflictions broke out in many places in the kingdom of France ... [the next six paragraph are lifted almost verbatim from Jean le Bel; that which follows shows some variations on his principal source.]

§414. When the gentlemen of the regions of Beauvais, Corbie, Vermandois,[38] Valois,[39] and in other lands, where these people cavorted and carried out their madness, saw their homes destroyed and their friends killed, they called for help from their friends in Flanders, Hainaut, Brabant, and the plain west of Liège [*Hesbain*]. Many came at once from all over. The foreigners assembled together and the gentlemen led them into the region, where they began to kill and behead these wicked people without pity or mercy; they hanged them from the branches of beech trees, wherever they found them. Similarly, the king of Navarre seized more than three thousand of them in a day near Clermont-en-Beauvaisis. But, they had by now so multiplied that all together they numbered a hundred thousand men. And when you asked why they had done what they did, they responded that they did not know, but that they had seen others doing it, so they did the same. They thought in this way they could destroy all the genteel and noblemen of the world; none would survive.

At this time, the duke of Normandy [the future Charles V] left Paris without knowing about those of Paris and all their troops [the followers of Étienne Marcel]. And he was afraid of the king of Navarre, the provost of the merchants, and those of his party, since they were all united. He went to the bridge at Charenton on the Marne[40] and there called for a great number of noblemen to come and be at his command

---

37 No doubt a reference to the letters that Marcel sent out to city councils across Picardy and Flanders.
38 A region on the eastern border of Picardy.
39 A region just to the northeast of the Île de France.
40 On the southeastern outskirts of Paris.

to defy the provost of the merchants and those who aided him. When the provost of the merchants heard that the duke of Normandy was at the bridge of Charenton with his men-at-arms, and that knights and esquires wished to harass the Parisians, he feared that a great evil was upon them and that the duke would come during the night and overrun Paris, which was then entirely open. He put labourers to work, as many as he could get, to build defences everywhere, to dig big ditches all around Paris, and then to build buttresses, walls, and gates. They worked day and night, over three thousand workers for a year. It was a great feat to have enclosed with walls and defences all around it within a year, a city as large as Paris with such a circumference. And you can be sure that this was the greatest good any provost of the merchants had ever done in his life. Otherwise, the city would have been invaded, robbed, and attacked many times and by various means as you will hear about later. Now, I wish to return to those who had fled to Meaux in Brie for their safety.

§415. At this time when these wicked people were rampaging through the countryside, the count of Foix[41] and his cousin, the captal[42] of Buch,[43] returned from Prussia.[44] On the way, they heard that they must return to France because of this pestilence and the horrors that had swept over the nobility, and these two lords had great pity on them. They rode for several days until they came to Châlons in Champagne, where they could progress no further because of these rustics' deeds; nor could they enter Châlons. Here, they were told that the duchesses of Normandy and of Orléans [the wife and sister of the dauphin] along with at least three hundred ladies and maidens and the duke of Orléans were at Meaux in Brie and were at great risk of harm from this Jacquerie [*jakerie*].

---

41 Gaston Phoebus, famous antagonist of the Valois.

42 Captal was a southern French title meaning chief officer.

43 Jean de Grilly, one of the heroes of the Anglo-Gascon army at the Battle of Poitiers, 1356: 'Rarely had political divisions been so completely closed by the common interest of caste' (Sumption, *The Hundred Years War*, II, p. 334).

44 Between 1300 and 1413 the Teutonic knights organised annual raids and full-scale campaigns into Lithuania, which relied on the crusading zeal of aristocratic volunteers from Western Europe. The count of Foix and the captal were returning from one of these *Preussenreisen*; see Norman Housley, *Religious Warfare in Europe 1400–1536* (Oxford, 2002), p. 18; and Eric Christiansen, *The Northern Crusades* (London, 1997), pp. 135–76.

THE JACQUERIE

These two good knights agreed to go help these ladies to restore their power, even thought this captal was English.[45] But now there was a truce between the kingdoms of France and England, so the captal was free to ride anywhere, and he wished to display his chivalry [*gentillèce*] while in the company of the count of Foix. The two of them could call up around forty lances from their troops but no more since they had been on a pilgrimage,[46] at least, that is what I was told. They rode until they reached Meaux and went immediately to the duchess and the other ladies, who were very happy to see them, since for days the Jacques and rustics of Brie as well as those of the city had harassed them, as had become apparent. When these wicked people began to hear that there was such a great gathering of ladies and maidens with their young children, they gathered and with those from the county of Valois made their way to Meaux.

From the other direction, those of Paris, well aware of this assembly, left Paris in herds and flocks to join the others. All together, at least nine thousand were acting violently and with mischief. All day, their numbers increased with people from various places coming along many roads to converge on Meaux, and they came as far as the city's gates. And the wicked people in the town did not try to block them but opened their gates to them. They entered in a horde so great that all the streets were filled up to the Marché.

Now, God's great grace was seen to be bestowed on these ladies and maidens. They would have been violated, raped, and killed as nobles, which they were, if these gentlemen and especially the count of Foix and the captal of Buch had not been there. These two knights devised the plans to defeat the rustics.

§416. When those noble women who were lodged in the Marché of Meaux, which is just outside the city walls but well guarded and defended because it is encircled by the river Marne, saw such a great crowd of people running towards them, they were very startled and frightened. But the count of Foix, the captal, and their troops, which were well armed, lined up at the Marché and went to its gates, which they opened from the back; they then faced these peasants [*villains*], who were dark, short, and poorly armed. And with the flags of the count of Foix, the one of the duke of Orléans, and the pennant of the

---

45 At this time Buch (in Gascony) was under the suzerainty of the English crown.
46 Actually, a crusade to northeastern Europe, see note 44.

captal, their lances and swords in their hands, they were equipped to the nines for the defence and protection of the Marché.

When these wicked people saw them so well ordered and that they [the wicked people] were not such a great number to face them, they were no longer so bold as before. The first ones then began to retreat, and the gentlemen pursued them, throwing their lances at them and cutting them down with their swords. Thus, those in front, now feeling the blows they had dreaded, retreated in horror, all at once, one falling on top of the other.

Thus all sorts of men-at-arms then came out from the barricades and quickly won over the square, striking down these wicked people. And they beat them senseless, butchering them like animals. And they attacked them again once they had escaped outside the town, so that they could not regroup. And the gentlemen had killed so many they became completely exhausted and worn out. They dumped the bodies in heaps into the river Marne. In short, they killed more than seven thousand that day. None escaped; if they fled, they were caught before long.

And when the gentlemen returned, they set fire to the toppled town of Meaux, burning everything including all the rustics of the borough they could lock in. After this defeat at Meaux, they [the peasants] did not reassemble anywhere. For the young knight of Coucy,[47] called Lord Enguerrand [VII],[48] had a great multitude of nobles, who put an end to any they found anywhere without pity or mercy.

93 A view from the Norman clergy

Chronique des quatre premiers Valois, ed. S. Luce, *SHF*, 109 (Paris, 1862), pp. 69–77. This chronicle of an anonymous cleric from Rouen, written around 1397–99, runs from 1327 to 1393 but shows originality from the reign of John II on, with eye-witness detail particularly for Rouen and parts of Normandy.

Charles, duke of Normandy and dauphin of Vienne, the eldest son of the king of France, could not tolerate, suffer, or abide the governors of the three estates ruling or administering the kingdom of France. And because of this and also in fear for his safety, he left Paris to the

---

47 Today, Couchy-le-Château, 18 km north of Soissons.

48 Lord Enguerrand (1342–98) married Isabel, the daughter of Edward III and Philippa of Hainault in 1365.

THE JACQUERIE

harm and discontent of the principal officers of the three estates and those of Paris. He went straight to the Marché of Meaux, a heavily fortified place, where he summoned the duchess and assembled his nobles in this place. The people of Meaux wished to take the Marché and endeavoured to do so by attacking it, but nothing came of it. Some of the duke's men came out, captured some of the townsmen and put them to death. The duke then entrusted the count of Foix to protect the duchess.

After the duke had left Paris, the provost of the merchants and the men of Paris took over the Louvre[49] and placed a captain there. Then Pierre Troussac,[50] Pierre Gilles,[51] Pierres Guiffart,[52] Jossien de Mascon,[53] and many other armed men, all from Paris, left Paris for Meaux, desiring to capture the fortress of the Marché of Meaux. But the count of Foix, who guarded it for the duke, came out against the Parisians and fought them on the bridge of Meaux. Here Pierre Gilles levelled insults at the lady duchess, which were false and wicked. And when the Parisians realised that they had failed to take the Marché of Meaux, they returned to Paris. They then became frightened of the elites [*les generaulx*] of the three estates and made a sort of alliance at Paris, forced the powerful of Paris to wear buckles of silver, and swore an oath of allegiance to these elites of the three estates ...

At this time, the Jacques of the Beauvaisis rose up and began to move towards Saint Leu de Cerens[54] and towards Clermont in the Beauvaisis. Among them was a knowledgeable man, well spoken, handsome, and in good shape, named Guillaume Charles. The Jacques made him their leader. But he saw that these were people of little worth and for this reason refused to lead them. Nonetheless, the Jacques seized him and made him their governor along with a man who was a knight

---

49 The king's palace and principal residence.
50 Should be Charles Toussac, an alderman of Paris, known as a great orator, who directed the commune of Paris with Marcel from 1355 to 1358; he was decapitated in the *place de Grève* on 2 August 1358.
51 A rich grocer and chief commander of Parisian troops, who attacked the nobility in the countryside around Paris before marching on Meaux. As early as February 1358 he had commanded the armed forces of the Parisian guilds.
52 Philippe Giffart, alderman of Paris, killed alongside Étienne Marcel on 31 July 1358.
53 Joceran de Mâcon, alderman of Paris, decapitated with Charles Toussac on 2 August 1358.
54 de Serans, Cerans, or d'Essérent, near Creil.

hospitaller [*hospitalier*],[55] who had fought in wars. Guillaume Charles also knew a thing or two about war and told the peasants that they were to stick together. And when the Jacques saw what a great crowd they were, they charged against the nobility, killing many. Worse, they became deranged, mad people of little sense, often putting to death noble women and children. Many times Guillaume Charles told them that they had gone way too far, but nothing could make them stop.

After a while Guillaume Charles saw that things could not continue as they were; once they had left a place, the noblemen hunted them down. Thus, he sent some of his wisest and most notable men to see the provost of the merchants of Paris and wrote to him that he was at his service and would aid and help him if the need arose. This filled the leaders of the three estates with joy, and they wrote to Guillaume Charles that they were all ready to give him help. These Jacques went as far as Gaillefontaines. The countess of Valois who was there mistrusted them but put on a good face and gave them provisions. For they had become accustomed in the villages and places they passed through to have the people, men and women, put tables out into the streets [for them]. The Jacques ate and then went on their way, burning the homes of the nobility.

Then the gentlemen approached the king of Navarre at his retreat and asked if he would like to remedy matters by having these Jacques knocked down, beaten, and put to death. They said to him: 'Sir, you are the noblest man in the world. Can you just stand by seeing the nobility being reduced to ashes. If these people they call Jacques last much longer and the principal towns give them support, they will reduce the nobility to ashes and destroy them all'. Thus Charles, king of Navarre, agreed to help them defeat the Jacques. And the gentlemen promised him that they would never go against him, and he took them at their word.

When the king of Navarre had taken on good faith that the noblemen would never betray him or go against his affairs, he left for Longueville with noblemen and Englishmen[56] numbering around four hundred fighters, and they went riding out after the Jacques near Clermont in

---

55 A military order that may have antedated the Crusades, known as the Hospitallers of Jerusalem until 1309, then the Knights of Rhodes from 1309 to 1522, and since 1530 as the Knights of Malta.

56 The king of Navarre had been the commander of English troops in Normandy against the French crown.

THE JACQUERIE

the Beauvaisis. Here, the gentlemen of France divided into two battalions with the King of Navarre leading one and the knight of Piquegny and the Viscount of Kesnes, the other. Robert Sercot led the English.

The Jacques knew well that the king of Navarre and the noblemen were coming after them. Then Guillaume Charles said to them: 'Handsome lords, you know that the gentlemen are about to confront us, and they are powerful people fit for war. If you trust me, we will go towards Paris and take up a position there, since we will have the support and aid of those of the city'. Then the Jacques cried that they would never flee and that they were strong enough to fight the gentlemen. Because they saw that they were in great numbers, they were overly confident in themselves. Guillaume Charles and the hospitaller lined up the Jacques in two battalions, putting two thousand men in each. They placed those with bows and crossbows in front and then in front of them they put their carts. They formed another battalion of their horsemen, fully six hundred men, who were mostly armed. They were lined up there for two days.

[He then lists thirty-six monsignors, barons, 'proud' knights, and seneschals mainly from the north of France.] All these nobles and many others whose names are not recorded here, at least a thousand men-at-arms, joined the king of Navarre's company to face the Jacques, who with a fierce demeanour held their ranks, tooting their horns and trumpets and crying haughtily 'Mont Joye',[57] and they carried many insignia painted with the *Fleur de lis*.

The king of Navarre sent for the leader of those who wished to negotiate with him. Guillaume Charles went alone; he did not ask for any hostages [from Navarre's side]. And as he came to the king of Navarre, leaving the Jacques without their leader, Robert Sercot with his entire battalion attacked the Jacques on all sides and with their swordsmen broke one of their battalions. Then, their cavalry charge violently broke and destroyed all the Jacques before them. The Jacques were now completely lost since their leader was no longer with them; they were entirely defeated. And the English put many of them to death. Then another battalion of gentlemen attacked another battalion of the Jacques, defeating them with their swordsmen and cavalry. And the barons and lords named above with great anger took to killing the Jacques. When they saw those on their side return in defeat, those Jacques on horseback fled and most survived. But Monsignor Friquet

---

57 The traditional battle cry of the king of France.

of Friquans and Monsignor Regnault of Braquemont pursued them with a hundred swordsmen and killed well over one hundred.

Charles, king of Navarre and all of his battalion, which was very large, attacked the Jacques who were on foot, killing all of them, except a few, who lay low in a wheat field and at night fled. Many were killed in this field but the field was very large. After the Jacques were defeated, the king of Navarre went to Clermont-in-Beauvaisis, where he beheaded the captain of the Jacques. In a troop of gentlemen were Le Baudrain de la Heuse, Monsignor Guillaume Martel, Monsignor Jehan Sonnain, Monsignor Jehan le Bigot, and the chief officers of Caux, along with three hundred swordsmen, who had aided the king of Navarre against the Jacques. When they heard the news that the Jacques had been defeated, they came down to the border of the Beauvaisis, where they found several troops of Jacques. These Norman gentlemen of the regions of Amiens and Bray assembled and found a troop of Jacques near Poix[-de-Picardie], who were headed for the great army ruled by Guillaume Charles. Without mercy, these gentlemen put them all to death, more than thirteen hundred of them. Then they rode out to Gerberoy with monsignor de Beausaut, monsignor the castellan of Beauvais, and monsignor of Boulainvilliers, who added well over seven hundred swordsmen and ninety archers to their troops. Once assembled, they fought another troop of Jacques between Roye and Gerberoy and killed over eight hundred of them. And made a spectacle of burning [alive] at least three hundred of them. Then they went to Gaillefontaines, where Madame de Valois was, and caused her great distress, because she had given the Jacques provisions, as they said, and here they killed a good thousand peasants [*paisans*]. Thus the Jacques had been defeated and destroyed in the Beauvaisis and in the borderlands around it. In Brie, the count of Roucy[58] killed a great many and hanged them on their own doors. Thus they were entirely destroyed.

I am told that after the defeat of the Jacques, a troop of gentlemen sought to take the city of Senlis, took one of it gates, and entered inside. But the townsmen fought them with such force that they poured boiling water on top of the gentlemen. The fittest and best equipped of the town courageously met them with carts, which they rolled onto the gentlemen with such force and power that they were chased out of the town.

---

58 Robert, count of Roucy.

94 A view of a provincial knight

La Chronique normande du XIVe siècle, ed. A. and E. Molinier, SHF (Paris, 1882), pp. 127–32. This chronicle, which runs from 1294 to 1372, concentrates on Flanders as much as northern France before 1328. Unlike the previous Norman chronicler, this one was certainly not a cleric; he wrote in particular detail about matters of war, especially between 1356 and 1369.[59] H. Moranvillé has seriously questioned the originality of this chronicler and calls it a compilation. Indeed, for the Jacquerie little distinguishes it from the Flemish account found in *Istore et Cronique de Flandre*, ed. J. Kervyn de Lettenhove.[60]

At that time when Charles the regent was at Meaux, he assembled some of his loyal knights and complained to them of the cruelties that were being carried out against him and his friends. Then the regent was advised to order those of his knights in [the Île de] France and the Beauvaisis who had fortresses to stock their garrisons quickly with plenty of provisions and to blockade Paris from receiving food and merchandise. Those knights with fortresses gathered together to decide how to implement the regent's order; some did not have the means to supply the provisions for their castles. So they were advised to take the provisions from their own men [*leurs hommes*][61]. They followed this counsel and outrageously took the goods from their own men. Thus these peasants [*paisans*] were mortified that the knights who were supposed to protect them had decided to seize their property. For this reason, the peasants rose up with prodigious force and charged against the knights and all the nobles, even their own lords. They gathered and with great cruelty killed many noble women and children, and demolished their fortresses and homes. When the provost of the merchants [of Paris] knew of this ruthless rebellion of the peasants, he sent his troops beyond the borders of the commune of Paris to destroy the tower of Gornay, the forts of Palesuel, Trappes, and Chevreuse [...] and many other villages and fortresses surrounding Paris.

At that time the peasants [*paisans*] went into the Beauvaisis around Compiègne and ordered that all the nobles be sent and handed over to

---

59 See *Dictionnaire des lettres françaises: Le Moyen Âge*, ed. Geneviève Haenohr and Michel Zink (Paris, 1992), pp. 288–9.
60 'Version non normande', ed. J. Kervyn de Lettenhove in *Istore et Croniques de Flandres* (Brussels, 1879–80), II, pp. 85–8.
61 In the 'Version non normande', 'paisans' is the word.

them, but the bourgeois refused and gave guarantees to the noblemen, who stayed in the town of Compiègne. At that time, all noblemen of [the Île de] France and Beauvais fled the region, because many of them greatly feared the cruelty of the peasants [*paysans*], who without pity and without [asking for] ransom killed men, women, and children of noble lineage. And these peasants went and laid siege to a castle named le Plaissie, which belonged to Mathieu Raoul of Coucy[62] and was defended by several noblemen. But Raoul of Coucy and many other knights gathered together, went against these peasants, and defeated them, killing a great many of them. Then other peasants reassembled in many other places in the Beauvaisis and [the Île de] France, including even some of the [town of] Beauvais, who [also] were against the nobles. They sent many to Beauvais, where they [the Jacques] were killed with the consent of the town's commune. And the mayor of Amiens also sent forth a hundred men of the commune,[63] but the town council disapproved and recalled them. They returned without doing more or less any harm to the nobles. Thus the nobles of the Île de France sent out to many parts of Christendom for help and made many merciful pleas in their letters. As a result, they assembled the nobles from many countries. At least three thousand of these Jacques went to burn and destroy the castle of Poix, and they destroyed whatever they could find belonging to the nobles and in their homes. And they went to Aumale and as far as Lignères and here found over 120 men-at-arms, Normans and Picards. And the Jacques fought in good order but were defeated with over 2,210 killed. And also a knight named Testart of Pinquigny died, killed by the Jacques when they were discussing with him their safe passage and before the fighting had begun. These nobles passed from here [Lignères] as far as Poix and towards the Beauvaisis, and a great number of them were killed.

And at that time the king of Navarre assembled a great army, consisting of men-at-arms from England, Normandy, and Navarre. They marched to the castle of Clermont, and sent for one of the captains of rustics to talk with him, promising that he [the king of Navarre] wanted to be on their side. Thus, he [Cale] went there, but as soon as he arrived, the king chopped off his head. Then with all his men he attacked the villains, who thought that they were coming to aid them as had been promised, but they were mistaken. The king's men killed more than eight hundred of them.

62 Coucy-le-Château, about 25 km southwest of Laon.
63 The 'Version non normand' adds 'to aid these rustics [*villains*]'.

THE JACQUERIE 165

At that time, those of Paris went to Ermenonville[64] and attacked the castle, taking it by storm. Here Robert de Lorris because of fear rejected his nobility, swearing that he loved the bourgeoisie of Paris, where he was born, better than the nobles. For this he and his wife, who was from Paris, and also his child were spared, but his goods inside the castle were looted and taken away. These men then repaired to Paris.

And then the regent, leaving the queen behind at Meaux, went to Compiègne to assemble his knights and noblemen with the Bègue of Villaines[65] and Heron de Mail, le Borgne of Chambeli, and many other noble men. And they stocked the garrisons of the fortress of the Marché greatly with provisions, putting there all they had along with what they had confiscated in many places from the defeated and dead peasants. Because the men of Meaux became frightened, they sent for help to the Parisians, and the provost of merchants sent them thirteen hundred armed men of the Commune of Paris, whom they received joyously. Thus they went to the bridge to attack the fortress of the Marché, but the nobles put up a strong defence. The Borgne of Chambelli, a brave knight, was killed. But the nobles steadily held on to the fortress of the Marché and forced the Parisians to retreat. Soon afterwards the nobles entered the town, raging through it, they looted and set the town on fire and killed a great many people with most of the town going up in flames.

When the provost of the merchants found out that the noblemen had reinforced their troops and that they had been assembled by the regent, he and the commune of Paris agreed to make the King of Navarre leader and governor of the city. They summoned him, and he came, leading a great number of English troops and other men-at-arms. And with his advice, thirteen thousand men of the commune went with him to lay siege to the regent at Compiègne. They went as far as Senlis and heard that a great number of nobles summoned by the regent of France were coming; so they returned from Senlis to Paris.

64 The castle of Robert de Lorris, chamberlain to King John, one of his most unpopular councillors.
65 He was a minor nobleman and friend of Robert of Clermont, one of the king's marshals killed in the Dauphin's private apartment by the forces of Étienne Marcel on 22 February 1358. As a result, the Bègue organised an aristocratic reaction in favour of the dauphin in the Île de France, capturing the vital port on the Seine of Corbeil; see Sumption, *The Hundred Years War*, p. 316. As sénèchal de Béziers in 1360 the Bègue appears again leading 'a bloody and humiliating repression of rebels of the *viguerie* of Gignac, who protested against losing their administrative district and being absorbed into the *viguerie* of Béziers; Arch. nat. JJ 91, f.155r, n. 302, 1362.viii.

At that time the nobility assembled from many regions to march on the Beauvaisis, where they burned everything in many places, killing and hunting down the people and carrying off their wealth, of which much was to be had.

95 The official view of the king's chronicler

La Chronique de règnes de Jean II et Charles V, ed. Delachenal, *SHF* (Paris, 1910–20), I, pp. 177–88.

On the beginnings and the first gathering of the evil Jacquerie of the Beauvaisis.

On Monday 28 May many people of little worth [*menus gens*] in the Beauvaisis, from the villages of Saint-Leu d'Esserent, Nointel, Cramoisy, and the surroundings, assembled to stage an evil uprising [*mouvement mauvais*]. They charged against many gentlemen, who were in Saint-Leu, killing nine – four knights and five grooms. With this done and emboldened full of evil intent, they marched through the countryside of the Beauvaisis, increasing every day in number and killing all the gentlemen and gentle ladies they found and even many children. They tore down or burnt the homes of all the gentlemen they found, including fortresses and other houses. They elected a captain called Guillaume Cale and went to Compiègne, but the townsmen would not let them enter. Then they went to Senlis and forced many of the town to flee into the countryside. They knocked down all the fortresses of the region, Ermenonville, Château-Thierry, and a part of the castle of Beaumont-sur-Oise, where they flushed out the duchess of Orléans, who escaped to Paris [...]

Of the cruelty of those from the Beauvaisis and how the regent left Meaux for Sens.

At this time, the ranks of the people of the Beauvaisis multiplied greatly; they re-united and brought in many others in various throngs in the region of Morency,[66] and they knocked down and burnt all the homes and castles of the lord of Morency and other gentlemen of the region. Moreover, they assembled others, such as the people in Mucien[67]

---

66 I cannot find this district or castle on modern maps or in the topographical appendix of Luce, *Histoire de la Jacquerie.*

67 I cannot find this district on modern maps or in the topographical appendix of Luce, *Histoire de la Jacquerie.*

THE JACQUERIE

and in other nearby places. These assemblies were comprised mostly of labourers [*gens de labour*], but rich men, bourgeois, and others filled their ranks. And they killed all the gentlemen they could find and did the same to gentle ladies and many of the children with madness beyond measure.

At this time, the regent, who was at the Marché at Meaux, which he had reinforced day by day, left for the castle of Montereil or the fort of Yonne; soon afterwards, he left for the city of Sens, where he arrived in the morning on Saturday 11 June. The people of that city received him honourably, as they were obliged to do, since he possessed the rights as their lord [*leur droit seigneur*], which his father, king of France, had established.

And everywhere, there was hardly a village, town, or other place in the Langue d'Oil[68] that had not revolted against the gentlemen either out of sympathy with the Parisians, who despised the nobles so much, or because of the uprising [*mouvement*] of the people. Nonetheless, the regent was received in Sens with great peace and honour. And here the regent enlisted a great number of men-at-arms.

How those of Paris and Cilly[69] were defeated at Meaux and of the death of the mayor of Meaux, Jehan Soulaz.

On the same, Saturday 11 June 1358, many left Paris and went to Meaux, about three hundred, under the command of Pierre Gilles, a grocer, and around five hundred, who gathered at Cilly-en-Meucien under the command of one named Jehan Vaillant, the provost of the royal mint. And it was said that Jehan Soulaz, then mayor of Meaux, and several others of this town swore to the regent that they would be good and loyal and not allow anything to be done against him or his honour; nevertheless, they opened the gates of this city to those of Paris and Cilly and lined the streets with tables covered with tablecloths and provisioned with bread, wine, and meat. And these men drank and ate as much as they wished, refreshing themselves. Afterwards, they went into battle, going straight for the Marché of Meaux, where the duchess of Normandy and her daughter [the wife and daughter of the dauphin] were, along with the regent's sister, Madame Isabel of France, who was then wife of the son of the lord of Milan and was countess of Virtù; her father, King John, had arranged

---

68 The north of France, distinguished from Languedoc.
69 Chilly-Mazarin, near Longjumeau, south of Paris, now on the outskirts of Orly airport.

this marriage.[70] With them were the count of Foix, the lord of Hangest[71] and many other gentlemen, whom the regent had left to protect the duchess, his wife, daughter, sister, and the Marché.

The count of Foix, lord of Hangest, and several others, about twenty-five men or so, left the Marché and sallied forth against the aforementioned Pierre Gilles and his company and fought them. A bolt from a crossbow struck a knight of the Marché, called Monsignor Loys de Chamby, near his eye and killed him. Eventually, those of the said Marché edged towards victory. And those of Paris, Cilly, and many from Meaux, who fought along aside them, were defeated. And for this those of the Marché set fire to the city and burnt several houses.

Later they were informed that many of this city had been armed against them and had sought to betray them; for this, those of the Marché sacked and burnt part of the city. But the great church was not burnt; nor were the houses of the canons, but for all that, everything was taken; the king's castle was also burnt. And the fire was so great in the city and castle that it lasted for more than fifteen days. And those of the Marché captured Jehan Soulaz, their mayor of Meaux, and many other men and women, who were imprisoned in the Marché. Afterwards, they executed the mayor, as was just.

Of Guillaume Cale's death at the hands of the king of Navarre and how this king went from the Beauvaisis to Saint-Ouen[72] to negotiate with the provost of the merchants.

At this time, the king of Navarre rode through the Beauvaisis putting to death many commoners, and, most importantly, cutting off the head of the said Guillaume Cale at Clermont-en-Beauvaisis. And because the men of Paris requested that he should meet them in Paris, he went to Saint-Ouen, to the king's palace, called the Noble-House, where the provost of the merchants came to negotiate with this king. Then on 14 June the king of Navarre went to Paris [... Developments of the King of Navarre's affairs in Paris follow.]

70 Her father-in-law was the duke of Milan, Galeazzo II Visconti (1320–78). In 1360, at age eleven she was sold to him to help pay John's 300,000 écu ransom and arranged to be married to the duke's eight-year-old heir.
71 John, lord of Hangest, commanded the French cavalry against Walter Bentley and the English archers in a campaign of 1352. At the battle of Meaux he would lead the first offensive of the men-at-arms in the Marché against the Parisian troops commanded by the grocer, Pierre Gilles.
72 Luce identifies this place as La Croix-Saint-Ouen, near Compiègne. I cannot find it on a modern map.

On that Friday (15 June) the regent, who for the past week had stayed at Sens, left and went to Provins, then towards Château-Thierry, then towards Gandelu, where it is said he held a large meeting with those commoners called Jacques Bonhommes. And the gentlemen kept streaming in from all around. And Queen Joanne was in Paris, who with great diligence tried to keep in touch with the regent and often sent messages to him and to the Parisians. For this reason, the queen left Paris on Saturday 24 June to see the regent, who was staying near Meaux, waiting for his soldiers to arrive.

And still the gentlemen were burning the houses they found belonging to inhabitants of Paris, unless they belonged to officials of the king or the regent. And they seized and carried off all the goods they found that belonged to these inhabitants. No one passing through the countryside dared admit that he was from Paris. The gentlemen also killed all those they could find who had been of the company of the Jacques, that is to say, the commoners who had killed the gentlemen, their wives, and children and had knocked down their homes. So many were killed that certainly one could hold that by John the Baptist's day [24 June] twenty thousand or more had been killed [... The chronicle then returns to speak again about the king of Navarre.]

Monsignor the regent first went in the direction of Château-Thierry, la Ferté-Milon, and nearby to smash many gatherings of the Jacques there. But after the nobles accompanying him had put to death many of these Jacques and burnt and destroyed all the countryside between the Marne and the Seine rivers, he turned around and went towards Paris, taking up lodgings at Chele-Sainte-Bautheut in the last week of June, that is, on Tuesday, 26 June ...

96 Another view close to the royal councillors: the chronicler of the abbey of Saint-Denis

La Chronique du continuateur de Richard Lescot, ed. J. Lemoine, *SHF* (Paris, 1896), pp. 126–7.

Concerning the Jacquerie: Since the plundering was happening everywhere and no one was around to oppose the brigands and enemy troops, the fields now lay barren.[73] As a result, on 27 May [1358] the

---

73 The area had only recently suffered from attacks by the English, who were allied with the forces of the king of Navarre against the French crown.

peasants rose up [*insurrexerunt*] against the nobles around the villages of Saint Leu d'Essérent, Moreuil, Cramoisy, and also around Clermont and in the diocese of Beauvais. They were led by a certain rustic [*quodam rustico*] called Guillaume Cale. From these places, their numbers mounted; in the Beauvaisis to Compiègne and as far as Senlis, the traces of their wickedness swelled; they put to death any noblemen they found, even noble children. Nor did they spare those being sweetly suckled and brought up by them. And even many noble ladies and maidens were rounded up to be inhumanely murdered, even those they saw who were pregnant. Then they set their homes on fire to be greedily devoured in flames. As this pack of rabid dogs went about, coming and going, they single-mindedly devoted themselves to destroying Senlis, Ermenonville, Thierry and razing the castles nearby to the ground and attacking the castle of Beaumont-sur-Oise.[74] They forced the duchess of Orléans, the daughter of the king of France, to flee Paris, and, as is known, they destroyed a great part of the village [of Beaumont-sur-Oise]. Similarly, they incited the men of the valley of Moreuil to perpetrate even more nefarious and wicked deeds. And many bourgeois flocked together in troops to join them and engaged in vicious acts on the side: [To justify their actions they said:] 'We charge against these noble traitors, who have shirked on their duties to defend the kingdom, who desire to do nothing but devour the sustenance of the commoners'.

97 The view of a Carmelite: the chronicle of the supposed Jean de Venette

The Chronicle of Jean de Venette, tr. Jean Birdsall, ed. Richard Newhall (New York: Columbia University Press, 1953), pp. 76–7. Recently, historians and linguists have called into question whether this 'Jean de Venette' was the same as the author of *Les Trois Maries*. The language and style of this work and the chronicle are radically different. Nonetheless, these scholars have concluded that this anonymous chronicler was also a Carmelite, also from the village of Venette, near Compiègne in the Beauvaisis, and may have even been named Jean.[75]

---

74 The castle of the duchess of Orléans.
75 See Erik Le Maresquier, 'La chronique dite de Jean de Venette, édition critique', *Positions de thèses de l'Ecole nationale des chartes* (1969), pp. 83–5; and *Dictionnaire des lettres françaises*, pp. 290–1. I will nonetheless refer to this chronicle 'dite de Jean de Venette' simply as by Jean de Venette.

THE JACQUERIE

While these cities and the city of Paris were being ill treated and little defended, there befell near Paris something hitherto unheard of. In the summer of the same year, 1358, the peasants living near Saint-Leu-d'Essérent and Clermont in the diocese of Beauvais, seeing the wrongs and oppression inflicted on them on every side and seeing that the nobles gave them no protection but rather oppressed them as heavily as the enemy, rose and took arms against the nobles of France. They combined in great numbers and appointed Guillaume Cale, an astute peasant of the town of Mello, their captain. Then, going forth with their arms and standards, they overran the countryside. They killed, slaughtered, and massacred without mercy all the nobles whom they could find, even their own lords. Not only this: they levelled the houses and fortresses of the nobles to the ground, and, what is still more lamentable, they delivered the noble ladies and their little children upon whom they came to an atrocious death. Thus, they destroyed the castle of Ermenonville, then the strongest in France, and slew many noble men and women who were in hiding there. This tribulation increased in strength until it reached even to Paris. A noble hardly dared appear outside his stronghold, for if he had been seen by the peasants or had fallen into their hands, he would either have been killed or would have escaped only after rough handling. The number of peasants eager to extirpate the nobles and their wives and children and to destroy their manor houses grew until it was estimated at five thousand. Therefore, the nobles kept themselves in seclusion and did not appear abroad as they had before. But this monstrous business did not long endure. For, since the peasants had begun it entirely of themselves, not of God nor of due authority such as that of an overlord, all their desire suddenly failed and came to an end. Those who had begun with a zeal for justice, as it had seemed to them, since their lords were not defending them but rather oppressing them, turned themselves to base and execrable deeds. It is said that they subjected noble ladies to their vile lust, slew their innocent little children, as I have said, and carried off such property as they found, wherewith they clothed themselves and their peasant wives luxuriously. What was so ill done could not long endure, nor was it fitting that it should. The nobles, perceiving this, began little by little to unite against the peasants with the caution of men skilled in arms. Thus the king of Navarre summoned some of the unsuspecting peasant captains to him with smooth words and slew them. After they had been killed, the king and his men with the count of Saint-Pol, near Montdidier, rushed upon many peasants who were in disarray and slew and destroyed them with the sword. Thus their whole fatuous faction and unjust stewardship vanished like smoke and ceased. Nor did this fatuous business remain unpunished. For the knights and nobles recovered their strength and, eager to avenge themselves, united in force. Overrunning many country villages, they set most of them on fire and slew miserably all the peasants, not merely those whom they believed to have done them harm, but all they found, whether in their houses or digging in the vineyards or in the fields. Verberie, La Croix-Saint-Ouen near Compiègne,[76] Ressons, and many other country towns lying in the open fields which I have not seen and do not note here, mourned their destruction by fire.

98 An outsider's view from the north of England

The Anonimalle Chronicle, ed. V. H. Galbraith (Manchester, 1927), pp. 41–2. Written in Anglo-Norman French by a monk at St. Mary's Abbey, York, this chronicle 'has been generally accepted as the single most important source' for the history of the English Peasants' Revolt of 1381. While this monk was 'exceptionally well-informed as to the origins and early course' of this revolt, the same cannot be said for the earlier rebellion across the Channel.[77]

In 1356, after the battle of Poitiers, the capture of King John, king of France, the great lords, and the aforementioned prisoners, a peasant [*une vilayns*] from [the Île de] France, named Jake Bonnehome, gathered round him a great throng of rustics [*vilayns*] and depraved ones of [the Île de] France and other counties, who began to wage war in [the Île de] France to take land. They went and ransacked cities, towns, and villages, doing great damage in various counties and places, ordering various citizens and bourgeois to hand over great sums of gold for their coffers and obliging them to send them their foot soldiers to aid them. In fear of the rustics' iniquitous ways and for their lives, these citizens and bourgeois were happy enough to give them great sums of gold to save their cities and property, and they also sent them their foot soldiers to aid them. When they [the rustics] had all assembled, they left in three battalions, the first with around 100,000, the second, 60,000, and the third, 30,000 men, and marched through many counties of the kingdom, destroying the property of the lords and of commoners, burning many villages and castles, taking great booty from

---

76 I cannot find this place on a modern map.
77 For the Anonimalle Chronicle as a source for the English Peasants' Revolt, see Dobson, *The Peasants' Revolt of 1381*, p. 123.

the land, and sparing no gentleman or lady. Once they had won over these castles and towns, they took the lords' wives, beautiful ladies and of great renown, and slept with them against their will. Then they shamefully killed the lords, the good folk, and the aforementioned ladies to the sound of great wailing and the terrible cries of their children. And in many places this Jak Bonehomme ripped babies from their mothers' wombs and with these babies' blood quenched their thirst and anointed their bodies in contempt of God and his saints. And because of this, in short order, great vengeance fell on him and his comrades.

At the same time, this Jak Bonehomme, a haughty and arrogant man with the heart of Lucifer in executing his deeds, had his people crown him with a circlet of gold in place of a crown as though he were the king or the conqueror. Hearing of this affair the lord of Fines,[78] as God had wished, assembled a troop of men-at-arms, knights, and squires, numbering at least a thousand, along with a great many commoners, to restrain the malice of the rustics. And eagerly this lord set out to face them in battle and fought against 30,000 of them. And these rustics knowing nothing of the ways of war and without battle skills were defeated like beasts and many were killed. Soon, the king of Navarre with his troops rallied in support of the lord of Fines and chased these rustics from the kingdom of France, killing a great many of them. They captured and punished this Jak for his evil, stripped him naked and put a hot and burning grille of iron on his body and another one on his head in place of his crown, finishing off his evil life as an example for the others.

99 An outsider's view from Florence

M. Villani, *Cronica*, II, Book Eight, chapter XXXVIII, p. 185.

How the people [*popolo*] of Paris began to stir up trouble.

The government of the realm of France, as we have said above, was divided into three estates, that is, the clergy, the barons, and the burghers. They held a council and decided what they wanted the crown to do, and the dauphin consented. This agreement lasted through March of this year [1358], when the provost of Paris and his supporters

---

78 This must be Robert de Fiennes; an old soldier by the time of the Jacquerie, he had been made constable of France in 1356. None of the other accounts attributes to him a principal role in the suppression of the Jacques.

took courage from the people, who were stunned after the massacre of the dauphin's counsellors, which [the provost] had plotted in secret with the king of Navarre.[79] With cunning he [the provost] sought to show the bourgeois of Paris that these affairs would be of particular profit to them, that the peace and the truce with the king of England would be prolonged, and that the king, their lord, would not be betrayed by it. And with this overture to the people, social order broke down, and the government of Paris was placed in the hands of the bourgeois, excluding first the barons, then the clergy. Other cities in Picardy and in other provinces of the kingdom followed their example. And with this began the nobility's hatred of the people, which caused great disruption across the kingdom, as we will soon discover. The dauphin was distressed but could do nothing to remedy matters and thus left Paris for Orléans.

Book Eight, chapter LXVII, pp. 214–15: Of the riots provoked by the people of Paris.

The bourgeois and lower classes [*popolo minuto*] of Paris were still armed, even if their weapons were of little use. The dauphin had not tried to contain their rage but instead had fled. As a result, their boldness mounted. And as the sun rises, one learns from experience: these wretched ones, their hearts burning with arrogance, became more daring against those who had fled. With the smell of victory and without resistance, they did not wait for anything to get them going. Seeing the foolish people armed and their hostile spirits uplifted against the royalty, those advising the king in these unfortunate matters thought that things would have to change dramatically before the people would lay down their weapons. And the people were very encouraged, animated by the hope of better fortune, and as an enraged and maddened people, they carried out one thing after another, seeing that they got what they asked for. And all of them were after palaces and the manors of the nobility, those that were near Paris and unguarded. And without any sense of their iniquity or measure of their crimes or of where they were being driven, they took many by surprise. The enraged people became so cruel that whomever they caught they put at the edge of their swords, not sparing even women or children. On top of murder they added arson, razing fortresses and manors with beastly savagery. And among various noble and wealthy

[79] See note 28.

buildings, they destroyed the beautiful castle of Montmorency and many other worthy castles. And with this mad victory that spilled citizens' blood, they returned to Paris, having made enemies of the nobles and barons of the realm.

Book Eight, chapter LXVII, pp. 215–6: How other towns copied the Parisians.

As the news spread through the country of the inhumane and beastly savagery that the Parisians showed towards the barons and nobility in the countryside surrounding Paris, other principal towns [*buone ville*][80] in Picardy and [the Île de] France took up the Parisians' example and quickly assembled in armed bands, left their towns, and went against their enemies, seeking out noblemen and their families on their manors, in their castles, and on their landed estates, where they had taken refuge. And they killed without mercy those who could not manage to escape and destroyed their castles and manors, when they could break in. And this storm arose so quickly and unexpectedly that many perished at their hands, giving justification that the nobility and barons were guilty of treason to their lord, the king. Certainly, the first cause of these wicked atrocities was the evil and treason of his lordship [the regent Charles] and of the kingdom, as the reader shall discover soon.

Book Eight, chapter CIX, pp. 274–5: On the justice brought to Paris.

The cruelty of tyrants is not so unusual, as wise and valiant citizens always suspect and fear. With the fearful severity of their boundless punishment, they even take delight in spilling innocent blood to maintain their envious control over their violent state, even if they become greatly distrusted and despised by their subjects, who are ensnared and ruined. But it is quite strange when this iniquitous spirit applies to royal blood, which by its title of natural lordship ought to be gentle and benign and treat its subjects with humanity, even if [the dauphin is] offended. This could be said to apply to the actions of the dauphin of Vienne [later, Charles V] in November of this year [1358], when he was in the city of Paris. Suspecting treachery, although he

---

80 The earliest known usage of the term – *bonnes villes* – dates to 1254. A royal ordinance of 14 May 1358 distinguished *bonnes villes* from ordinary towns as those with a cathedral, but in common usage, it simply meant a major city. *Bonnes villes* as places for which the king had a particular affections comes later in the eighteenth century; see Bernard Chevalier, *Les bonnes villes de France du XIVe au XVIe siècle* (Paris, 1982), pp. 8–9.

could find no clear proof, he imprisoned the count of Étampes [Stampo][81] – a kinsman of the king of Navarre – the count of Roucy,[82] and twenty-seven bourgeois of Paris, claiming that they had conspired with the king of Navarre against him. Because of the arrest of these burghers, the University of Paris was upset and became turbulent, and they sent a plea [*proposto*] from the merchants and other important bourgeois to the dauphin for these men's release, saying that they had not been guilty. The dauphin responded that where there was no guilt, there was no need to worry, and that matters would proceed fairly until the truth was uncovered. And this clever move cooled the initial temper of the crowd. A short time later, however, all of the bourgeois mentioned above were found guilty and beheaded and the counts kept in prison. This upset the community and they began to grumble, but out of fear and without a leader, they suffered this new infliction of his old sins without another insurrection, more out of servile patience than out of respect or love of their master.

100 A minor courtier's view

Eustache Deschamps, 'le Miroir de mariage', v. 11432–50, in *Œuvres completes d'Eustache Deschamps* (Paris, 1894), IX, pp. 367–8. Deschamps (1346?–1406) was born in Vertus, Champagne, studied law at Orléans, and was taught by the poet Guillaume de Machaut. He held several minor posts in the royal governments of Charles V and Charles VI.[83]

Then the three estates met
Which produced great division
In the people and a great stir
With the lesser ones against the nobility:
In the Beauvaisis they took
To killing women and children
Of the nobility, such were the times,

---

81 The county of Étampes is in the département of Siene-et-Oise, south of Paris. Louis of Evreux, count of Étampes, was also the cousin of Charles V. In 1359 he was instrumental in reconciling the differences between Charles of Navarre and the dauphin.
82 Robert, Count of Roucy, was a councillor of the king and one of the principal barons of Champagne.
83 See *Eustache Deschamps: French Courtier-Poet: His Works and His World*, ed. Deborah Sinnreich-Levi (New York, 1998).

And to demolishing their homes,
Burning, robbing, and tearing them down;
In Valois, Picardy, and Champagne
Such did the Jacquerie.
At Meaux, at Paris, and other parts
Many were hanged by the rope,
Many had their heads cut off,
Many lay dead in fields like beasts,
For the nobles set out upon them,
As they arose to the attack,
And in the end defeated
This people of poor stock.

101 Letter of Étienne Marcel to the Communes of Picardy and Flanders

Œuvres de Froissart, ed. Kervyn de Lettenhove (Brussels, 1868), VI, pp. 470–1. The original letter survives with traces of the seal of the city of Paris in the municipal archives of Ypres.

[...] My very dear lord and good friend, in so far as some along with their friends might wish to be excused for the evil things they [the Jacques] did in the Beauvaisis and also against us; in so far as some people from the lowlands [*gens du plat pays*] in the Beauvaisis began to riot against the gentlemen, killing them, their wives and children and tearing down their houses, saying that we came to their aid and support, in so far as this can and must be reported to the high and noble prince, monsignor, the count of Flanders, and to you for the sake of the truth, may it please you to know that these matters in the Beauvaisis were done without our knowledge or will. We would have rather died than have approved these deeds and the manner in which they were committed by some of those people of the plains of the Beauvaisis. Instead, we sent over three hundred troops from our people and confidential letters to them to stop the great evil they were committing. And in so far as they would not desist from the things they were doing, nor incline to our request, our people went after them and had our commands proclaimed in sixty towns: that under punishment of death by beheading, no one was to kill the wives or children of gentlemen, or any gentlewoman, unless they were enemies of the principal town [*la bonne ville*] of Paris; nor should they rob, pillage, burn, or knock down the houses where the nobility resided.

And at the time when Madame of Flanders, Madame the Queen Joanna, and Madame of Orléans were in Paris, we treated them all well and honourably, and even now there are thousands who have come and gone [to and from Paris] safely. We wish no evil to those good noblemen and women, who have not done any evil to the people, or wish to do so. And since these things have happened in the Beauvaisis, Monsignor of Navarre, who was there with his men-at-arms, has mowed them down and defeated them four times, captured their captains, cut off their heads, and restored the country entirely to peace. With the consent of the nobles of the Beauvaisis and the Vexin, who had been harmed and injured, and also of the townsmen in the plains of the Beauvaisis, he ordered that in each village four of the principal culprits who committed the excesses should be apprehended and punished. In addition, ten from the Beauvaisis should be captured who were involved in the harm inflicted on the gentlemen, the towns, and their residents. And this should be reported to the Monsignor of Navarre, and suitable reparations should be made to the gentlemen. With this, the good people of the plains of the Beauvaisis, the towns, and the countryside should be able to live in safety and peace. This notwithstanding, after Monsignor of Navarre and other nobles of these regions mentioned above, who were so hard hearted, had left, the gentlemen of the Beauvaisis and the Vexin assembled and destroyed and pillaged all the country of the Beauvaisis. Under the excuse of the deeds done in the Beauvaisis, the nobles in many and diverse places have held large assemblies and raided many places in the region on this side of the Somme and the river Oise. They overwhelmed those who had nothing to do with these deeds in the Beauvaisis, who were guiltless and innocent, invading, robbing, sacking, burning, killing, and destroying all the country, just as they are still doing day after day [...]

102 A soldier's view: the testimony of Bascot de Mauléon in 1388

Chroniques de J. Froissart, SHF, XII, ed. Léon Mirot (Paris, 1931), p. 97.

The testimony of Bascot de Mauléon in 1388:

The other year after I had been in Prussia with the count of Foix and his cousin the captal, whose command I was under, and on our return to Meaux in Brie we came to the duchess of Normandy,[84] at that time,

---

84 The wife of the regent Charles V.

and the duchess of Orléans,[85] along with a great number of ladies, maidens, and gentlewomen, whom the Jacques had enclosed in the Marché of Meaux, and would have violated and raped, had God not sent us there. It was well within their powers, since there were more than ten thousand of them [...] and the ladies were all alone. We delivered them from this peril and killed more than six thousand Jacques either here or fleeing through the fields; they never rose up again.

Documents 103–120 are letters of remission taken from the collections of the eighteenth-century advocate of the French Parlement and an archivist of Louis XIV, Denis-François Secousse (1691–1754) and from the nineteenth-century professor at the École des Chartes, Siméon Luce (1833–92). In far greater detail than the chroniclers the letters show the variety of leadership and participation in the urban and rural revolts as well as the means of cohesion, persuasion, and communication between leaders and followers. In addition, they provide us with another voice, that of the insurgents or at least those accused of rebellion. However, the form and purpose of these letters often led the supplicants as well as the king, his lieutenants, or councillors who adjudicated on whether to grant clemency to put as favourable a light on past crimes and revolts as was possible (see comments for [57]). On the other hand, others of these remissions are direct and detailed in their condemnations [103], perhaps as an argument to persuade the supplicants who escaped without paying penalties of corporeal punishment or banishment but were instead left with fines that they had been lucky in the bargain. Finally, not everyone could afford or had friends with influence or money to initiate such proceedings. Indeed, these letters of grace increase dramatically after 1350 and increase again in the early 1380s with the fiscal crisis of the crown, because kings realised that they were an effective means for raising royal revenues.[86] Nonetheless, we find letters from peasants, apprentices, and others who claimed to be impoverished as well as from villages, communes, and the principal cities of France that sought to lessen fines and corporal punishments for entire populations.

103 Letters of remission: annulment of penalties meted out to the city of Paris

Ordonnances des Roys de France de la troisième race, ed. Denis-François Secousse, IV (Paris, 1734), pp. 346–7, Arch. nat. JJ.reg. 86, no. 240, 10 August 1358.

Charles, the eldest son of the king of France, regent of the realm, duke of Normandy, and dauphin of Viennois, let it be known to all present and future that at the instigation, encouragement, and prompting of

85 The regent's sister.

the deceased Étienne Marcel recently provost of the merchants of the city of Paris, and of many other of his allies, adherents, collaborators, and accomplices, who proclaimed and supported all their deeds when they governed the good city of Paris and its surrounding district, that all they did was for a good purpose, for the ransom and deliverance of our lord [King John II] and for the public good. With these hopes, but without the authority, will, or consent of our lord or of us and unaware of the great treason and crimes, which the provost and his accomplices were doing in secret, a great number of the good people and loyal commoners of this city of Paris conceived and intended to do things against our lord, us [the regent Charles], and the Royal Majesty. They agreed amongst themselves to rebel and to hand over the government, its defence and leadership of the city, to the king of Navarre, in writing and on oath, and to make an alliance with him and his accomplices, aides, and supporters. They wore buckles of silver, half in vermilion and half in blue enamel with 'to a good end' written underneath, and hoods of these colours as a sign of alliance, to live and die with the provost against all others. They went to assemblies and congregations organised by the provost and took up arms against us; they usurped various royal rights from us and were rebels against our lord. They said words against us and reproached us. They put to death and killed in our presence and in our chamber, Lord Robert de Clermont, the Marshal of Champagne, and Lord Regnault Dacy, and others in this city. They took and occupied by force our castle of the Louvre, and also stopped and seized our artillery[87] which we were transporting to certain positions on the river Seine and deprived our troops, who were transporting it, of their power and used it for themselves. And they sent us nasty letters containing many rude, ugly, and ungracious words. They went along with and allowed the movement of troops, which the deceased Pierre Gilles led to Meaux to fight against us and our very dear army. They plotted a conspiracy and formed a great company, called the Confraternity of Nôtre-Dame, in which they had given and continued to give many sermons, organised secret meetings, and made alliances, without our authority or permission. Under the shadow and pretence of justice, they executed

---

86 See Michel François, 'Note sur les lettres de rémission transcrites dans les registres du Trésor des Chartes', *Bibliothèque de l'École des Chartes*, 103 (1942), p. 318; and 86; Charles Radding, 'The Estates of Normandy and the Revolts in the Towns at the beginning of the Reign of Charles VI', *Speculum*, 47 (1972): 83.

87 On the events of 22 February 1358, see Sumption, *The Hundred Years War*, II, pp. 312–13.

Jehan Perret and Thomas Forquant without reasonable cause. They seized, arrested, imprisoned, interrogated, and mistreated many of our soldiers and officers, their wives, families, and domestic servants. They seized many of the goods of our soldiers and officers, and used them to profit the city or for their personal gain. They rejected and refused the money for the purposes we had decreed at the assembly of Compiègne and instead minted their own money and forced our money to work to their advantage and the interest of our money to be added to their gains. They have torn down and burnt and have ordered [others] to tear down and destroy many castles, fortresses, and other homes of nobles. They have sacked and have ordered the pillaging of these nobles' goods, and have committed many other crimes, delinquencies, and misdeeds against the Royal Majesty and in other respects in that they led the said people to believe that we wished for our men-at-arms to destroy and rob them; that we had abandoned this city along with other cities and the countryside of the realm of France to these troops, and that we had no intention whatsoever of delivering and ransoming our lord ... And for this, many of the above could not be excused. If we wish to proceed strictly by the law, their property and bodies must be forfeited to our lord and to us, or at least we should pursue and charge them with great penalties and fines. Our good friends Gentian Tristan, presently provost,[88] the aldermen, bourgeois, and inhabitants of this city have humbly beseeched us to show pity and mercy and to find a gracious remedy. Thus considering the good love and loyalty, which the provost, bourgeois, and inhabitants of this city have always had towards our lord and to us and which has been demonstrated by the capture and destruction of these traitors, rebels, and enemies of the crown of France, we are inclined to grant them this supplication ...

Issued at Paris, 10 August 1358.

104 Authorisation given to the chapter of Meaux to close the gates of a street, July 1358

Siméon Luce, *Histoire de la Jacquerie d'après des documents inédits*, 2nd edn (Paris, 1894), p. 227; Arch. nat., JJ. 86, no. 150. The remission below illustrates that the extent of Meaux's destruction at the hands of the nobles and royal troops was not a wild exaggeration of the chroniclers.

88 Gentian (or Gencien) Tristan succeeded Étienne Marcel as provost until 11 December 1358, when he was succeeded by Jehan Culdoe.

The regent Charles authorises the dean and chapter of the church of Meaux and their servants – enjoying as they do royal protection – whose houses have been burnt and destroyed, as has the town and city of Meaux, by the men at arms who recently came to the said town and city by our command, to enclose with walls and to shut off day and night with the gates the street that goes from the cloister well of the said dean and chapter, on one side, and from the house which, before it was burnt down, served as the residence of Henri de Neuville, dean of the chapter, on the other side, up to the house of Simon de Villeneuil opposite the bishop of Meaux's palace, so that the said dean and chapter may proceed along this street, which runs alongside the cathedral, to celebrate their church services in peace and safety. At the same time high, middle, and low justice[89] is granted to the dean and chapter under the jurisdiction of the provost and viscount of Paris in the said street and in its surrounding premises. The command of the regent is addressed to the provost of Paris and to the chief officers of Troyes and of Meaux.

Although the king or his lieutenant granted blanket remissions to entire regions as with the region of Languedoc in return for a 800,000 franc fine imposed by John, the duke of Berry [64] or to entire cities as with the king's grants following the massacre of the Jacques to Meaux, Amiens, and Paris [103, 106, 107, and 118–20],[90] for the most part his grace pardoned individuals; on occasion the accused rebels were identified by occupation or by their social status [105–7, 112, 115–16].

105 Remission granted to Jean de Congi, bourgeois of the Marché of Meaux

Luce, *Histoire de la Jacquerie*, p. 228; Arch. nat. JJ. 86, no. 148.

Charles, etc. That Jehan de Congi,[91] bourgeois of the Marché of Meaux, has been accused and charged with being in the company of and aiding those of the city of Meaux and those of Paris who came to their aid to assail the said Marché, to capture, put to death, or hold to ransom those who were inside, if they could have been able to conquer and enter it. And for this, some charged the said Jehan de Congi, who

---

89 These are different grades of justice that an individual or corporate body could adjudicate. High justice was the right to sentence to execution.
90 Also, see Luce, *Histoire de la Jacquerie*, pp. 229–30: JJ 86, no. 240.
91 Probably from Congis, a village near Meaux.

had suffered corporally and lost all his property...[The usual phrases follow, granting the supplicant remission for previous criminal charges.] Issued at Meaux in the year of our Lord, 1358 in the month of July.

106 Remission granted to Guillaume de Chavenoil, priest and canon of Meaux

Ibid., pp. 228–9; JJ. 86, no. 274. The remission below is one of only two I have found granted to members of the clergy, regular or secular, from the cities or the countryside, accused or suspected of rebellion either in the Jacquerie or the siege of Meaux. Certainly, the view that clerics were prominent as leaders of 'pre-industrial revolts' does not fit the Jacquerie.

Charles, etc. To be made known to all present and future, that, recently we have forgiven and pardoned generally all the inhabitants of the town, city, and Marché of Meaux [...], except, however, a certain number of persons, including Guillaume de Chavenoil, priest and canon of Meaux. However, it has been reported and testified to us by many of the clergy [*degnes de foy*] that he was never guilty; nor did he give his consent to this said crime [...]

Issued at Paris, 11 August 1358.

107 Remission granted to Jean Chandelier, draper, resident of the Marché of Meaux

Ibid., pp. 230–1, JJ. 86, no. 211. Letters of remissions not only granted pardons; parenthetically and often disguised in the language of the king's proclaimed bountiful mercy, they inform us of penalties that the king and his counsellors imposed in the first place as well as those that were left intact.

Charles, etc. Let it be known to all present and future that we have heard the supplication made by our friend and faithful subject Jehan Maillart,[92] bourgeois of Paris, containing matters concerning misdeeds in the town of Meaux last Saturday, the eve of the feast day of Saint Barnabas, the apostle [11 June]. There were those inimical to us, who entered into this town of Meaux by the gate of Saint Remi to attack the Marché of Meaux to harm and humiliate nobles and non-

---

92 A rich draper who led the bourgeois of Paris against Étienne Marcel killing him on 31 July 1358; he then turned the city over to the dauphin, Charles; see Sumption, *The Hundred Years War*, II, p. 347.

nobles who were inside, thus breaking the fealty they owed to our lord and to us or at least so we presume, and were known to be opposed to the bourgeois and inhabitants of the aforesaid city and town of Meaux. In consideration of the harm that the bourgeois and inhabitants suffered from this misdeed and in consideration of our good friends the deans and chapter of the church of Meaux, and because several of the principal towns of this realm [*bonnes villes*] nearby have humbly beseeched us to grant our grace to these said bourgeois and inhabitants in order that this city and town can rebuild and restore itself to a good state as soon as possible, from these we have withdrawn all criminal and civil penalties that the said bourgeois and inhabitants of the said town and city might have incurred towards us for the abovementioned things by virtue of our special grace and authority, which we now invoke, and by virtue of certain information. We have reinstated them, pardoned them, and re-established their good name and reputation in their district and also to their property with the exception that the said town will not have the rights of a corporation and a communal government.[93] Nor is this pardon included in our letters of grace contained above extended to the named persons. Among those exempted and named is included Jehan Chandelier, draper, who then lived in the Marché of Meaux. This individual as someone suspected of the said misdeed mentioned above by the captain or chief officer of Meaux had been called to appear on punishment by exile from the benefits of this our lordship and our [kingdom]. Because the said Jehan did not appear, he has been exiled or put on the road of banishment from this kingdom as one says. In consideration of the losses and damages this man has suffered and sustained for the said deed and that he is a man of good behaviour [...] we have pardoned the above-mentioned Jehan of all punishments [...]

Issued at Paris, August 1358.

108 Remission granted to Hue of Sailleville, elected by the villagers of Angicourt as their captain

Ibid., pp. 253–4, JJ. 90, no. 288.

[...] on the part of Hue of Sailleville, it has been pointed out to us

---

93 Before the revolt, Meaux was a city corporation with rights to elect its own communal government.

that in the time when the people of the plains rose up and spread terror against the nobles of this realm, this Hue, forced by the people of the village of Angicourt, where he then lived, and by those of the region around it, and from fear of death, rode with them. And against his will, they made him their captain. And then, because of the great horror that he saw in the crimes and outrageous deeds committed by these people of the plains, which were against his desires and which he could not remedy, and to avoid the company of these people of the plains, he went before the provost of merchants, then in Paris, to give his views and request advice on how to end the matters stated above. Afterwards, when the people of the plains knew that the king of Navarre had come to Clermont, that the captain of the Beauvaisis [Guillaume Cale] and his accomplices had been placed in the hands and under the rule of the king of Navarre by those of Clermont, that their leaders had been put to death, and that this town of Clermont had been put under the protection of the king of Navarre, the people of Angicourt forced the said Hue to go before the men of the king of Navarre to obtain protection from him as had been granted to many other villages in the surrounding region, even if this protection was of little or no value in avoiding arson and destruction. As soon as the regions around had obtained [the protection], the nobles burnt, wrecked, and totally destroyed these villages. And still this Hue fears for his life because of these matters [...]

Issued at Paris, August 1358.

109 Remission granted to Colart du Four, a rebel of the Beauvaisis

Ibid., p. 260, JJ. 86, no. 308.

Charles, eldest son, etc. Let it be known to all present and future that we have examined Colart du Four called Melin, living at Feigneux in the Beauvaisis: when the people of the region of the Beauvaisis recently rose up and rebelled against the nobles of this region, these people and their captain forced this Colart to ride out in their troop [*compaignie*] to Mello, and if he did not do as they wished, they threatened to burn down his house and cut off his head. He left [with them] but returned to his home as soon as he could escape without riding out again or pillaging, setting fires, or engaging in other such crimes. But, because the nobles burnt, plundered, and ruined all his movable and landed property, he remains here only with his wife. Yet this Colart and his wife no longer dare to stay in this region on the property they have inherited, which they [otherwise could] farm out [*faire labourer*] and cultivate, but instead, from fear of these noblemen, they must stay in hiding in the woods and other such places and remain in great misery and poverty [...]

Issued at Paris, August 1358.

110 Remission granted to Jean Hersent, who announced Étienne Marcel's order to assemble all the men of the region to arm themselves

Ibid., pp. 263–4, JJ. 86, no. 231.

Charles, etc ... Let it be known to all present and future that we have heard the petition presented to us by Jehan Herssent of Châtres-sous-Montlhéry[94], ... that around John the Baptist day this year [24 June] he proclaimed and posted what was to be done in the village of Châtres. By virtue of the command given to him by the former Étienne Marcel, then provost of the merchants, this Jehan proclaimed in this village of Châtres that all manner of people allowed to bear arms [should] join together at Chaillilez-Loncjumel[95] to present themselves and their weapons and to parade in front of certain officers [*commissaries*], whom the provost of the merchants had appointed for this task, and to follow these officers' orders. Naively, this Jehan carried out the order, proclaiming it in this village of Châtres. He did not think that he had done anything wrong and greatly feared disobeying the order or being charged with negligence. Nor did he believe that he was acting wrongly towards our lord or to us; but later he realised his misdeed ... and from fear of imprisonment, punishment, and of what he imagined the captain[96] or provost of Montlhéry [Montleherry][97] would have done – that the bailiffs would seize all his property and put it into our hands – this Jehan left this region. Thus he has offered this humble supplication: he is as an old man[98] with a wife and three small children to bring up, who in the period mentioned above have

---

94 Today it is called Arpajon.
95 Today it is called Chilly-Mazarin.
96 'Castellan' has been crossed out.
97 Village where the dauphin had his massive keep.
98 'Poor man' has been erased.

suffered and still suffer great poverty, because he does not dare stay in the region. On this matter, we wish to grant our grace and mercy ...

Issued at Paris, August 1358

111 General remission granted to the villagers of Bettancourt and Vroil

Ibid., p.p. 266–8, JJ. 86, no. 346. The villagers of Bettancourt and Vroil in Perthois, condemned by the count of Vaudemont to pay a fine of 2,000 écus[99] for having participated in the terror against the nobles.

Charles, etc; let it be known to all present and in the future, that the inhabitants and residents in the villages of Bettancourt [Marne, arrondissement (hereafter arr.) Vitry-le-François, near Heiltz-le-Maurupt] and Vroil [Marne, same arr.] in Perthois, along with many other people of the surrounding plains have been involved in the terror that the people of the plains recently inflicted with great speed upon the nobles of the realm. They conspired and assembled with other people of these plains many times [but] without burning or knocking down houses, killing people, or mistreating anyone whatsoever. Although these inhabitants have been and are now being robbed and totally destroyed by these nobles, they did nothing beyond assembling, as reported. Nevertheless, our friend, loyal counsellor, and lieutenant in these parts, the count of Vaudemont[100] summoned them before him at a certain time and place. On that day and place these inhabitants did not dare appear in person out of fear of the great and cruel executions that our lieutenant had carried out and was continuing to do day after day against the people of this county. Instead they sent certain attorneys [*procureurs*] on their behalf to our lieutenant. Without knowing any more about these inhabitants, he condemned them to pay a fine of two thousand *écus*, even though they had done nothing wrong beyond assembling ... Out of fear and dread of bodily punishment, their attorneys did not dare to appeal against this condemnation. Thus Salehadin d'Angleure, lord in these parts and of these villages and inhabitants, humbly begged us, after we had come into our good city of Paris, to order all these nobles to forgive and pardon these people of the plains, and vice versa, for all they might have done wrong,

99 A gold coin initially worth 10 shillings Tournois (1266).
100 Henri, count of Vaudemont and lord of Joinville, lieutenant of the regent in Champagne.

one towards another, and to end all suits against these misdeeds and criminal pursuits in these parts. However, they might still be prosecuted for damages and injuries through the civil courts before my lord or our people or us [...] Following this, we have come to understand that because of this sentence and fear of the punishments from this count and our lieutenant, these inhabitants, who are on the borders of the county of Bar, are leaving the kingdom entirely, have crossed or are crossing from this county to others outside the realm, leaving their villages behind entirely empty, deserted, and without inhabitants. Thus, to these inhabitants, to each one of them, for the case stated above, we have remitted, forgiven, and pardoned [them] ...

Issued at Paris, September, 1358.

112 Remission granted to Jean Morel, curate of Blacy, who had been forced to follow his parishioners to an assembly of commoners

Ibid., pp. 270–2, JJ. 86, no. 355, fol. 121. Held at Saint-Vrain [Marne, arr. Vitry-le-François, near Thiéblement].

September 1358, in Paris.

Charles, etc ... Let it be known to all present and future that we have heard the supplication of master Jehan Morel, ordained priest and curate [*prestre, curé*] of the parish of the village of Blacy: that the commoners of the villages of the plains of Perthois recently organised many assemblies in various places to knock down and burn the houses of nobles in this region and to put them to death. It is said, and we believe, that the curates of the villages of these plains, and especially the said supplicant, were favourably disposed and obedient to these lords in this region. [Yet] they [the nobles] considered them all as traitors, and especially the said curate, who, they repeatedly said, had sold the bells of this village to the nobles of this region, and had acted falsely, treacherously, and lawlessly, as a result of which many of the said curates, and especially the named supplicant, were several times put in great danger and fear for their lives. And because of this, day after day, the said supplicant heard and saw so many rebellions [*mocions*] and such danger. And on various occasions, several of the parishioners and inhabitants of this village of Blacy said many threatening and menacing words so that he feared that these people would kill him. He went on horseback with these parishioners to an assembly organised by the commoners of the village of Saint-Verain. He carried no weapons except a short bat. And he danced with his parishioners, because they ordered him to dance, keeping him in line with his stick. Continuously, they exhorted him to show good cheer. When this supplicant was at this assembly in Saint-Verain, the people of the village of Blacy who had stayed behind stole a quantity of grain from him, which they used for their own purposes without his agreement or consent and to his great harm. He attended these assemblies only once and did not aid or comfort [the village insurgents] in anyway, except as described above. And in so far as the nobles of this said district keep the said supplicant in a state of dread, he does not dare to appear in the said village of Blacy for fear of his life. Day after day they have taken and go on taking his moveable goods and take over his rents and property, using the excuse [*soubz umbre*] that the said people of Blacy took his said grain, claiming that the said supplicant had abandoned all the grain he had in his house to the said commoners to help and comfort them. Yet in all this the said supplicant has done no misdeed, except for what has been stated above; that is, he attended the said assembly; no nobles or others were killed and no house burnt or destroyed any in anyway [...] even to get back and safeguard his own property [...] We therefore after our return to the good city of Paris, etc.

Issued at Paris, September 1358. This missive was sent to the provost of Paris and to the chief officer of Vitry.

113 Fragment of a letter of remission mentioning an attempt by Pierre de Montfort to spread revolutionary propaganda in the city of Caen

Ibid., pp. 291–2, JJ. 87, no. 321, fols. 204–5.

To all those who have received these letters, Henry, knight of Thieville, lieutenant general of the very noble and very powerful prince and our very distinguished Lord Charles, etc ... to those judges in the jurisdictions of Caen and Cotentin, greetings. We make it known from the testimony of the judges and other substantial bourgeois of the town of Caen and by various dear friends of Richard de Bray, Raoul Machue, and Jehan des Marez,[101] bourgeois of this town, that it has

---

101 The same name (Jehan des Marés) as the great lawyer of the Parlement who at the time of the Maillotins was outspoken against king, but not the same man.

been demonstrated to us that a man named Pierre de Montfort on many occasions while alive tried to provoke rioting [*comocions*], conspiracies, and discord among the people of this town by rousing and inducing the common people to subvert and obstruct what the judges and good people of this town ordered and commanded and to curse the subsidies and aids that had been collected for soldiers and others for the protection and defence of this town and country. For this purpose he gave many evil and disorderly speeches, as is apparent, to rouse and sow discord between the commoners [*menu commun*] and the big fish [*les gros*] of the town and to have them [the commoners] commit many crimes, for which they were not punished. Similarly, he drew in people from Picardy, who were put to death and perished in the market place of this town, where he had been one of the principal leaders [*facteurs*]. And at the time when the commoners of the Beauvaisis rioted against the nobles of that region, he wore on his hat a [model of] a plough made of wood in the place of a feather. In the end, with the intention so it seemed of implicating the commoners of this town and those in the surrounding countryside, he said that he was on the side of the Jacques [...]

Issued on 7 April, 1358.

114 Remission granted to Jean Flageolet of Favresse, elected as leader of several villages of Perthois

Ibid., pp. 293–4, JJ. 90, no. 292. Jean Flageolet elected as leader of several villages of Perthois to organise a defence against foreigners and, if necessary, against the nobles of the realm.

Charles, etc. Let it be known to all present and future, that we have heard the supplication of Jehan Flageolet of Favresse: during the revolts [*commocions*] which occurred in various parts of the kingdom last summer, the inhabitants of many villages of the region of Perthois organised meetings to plan how to resist the evil will of some from outside the kingdom,[102] whom they feared, and also the nobles of the realm, in case they might wish to harm them. To plan, carry out, and direct these matters, they appear to have elected the said supplicant as their captain in his absence. After the supplicant had accepted this office of captain, the lord of Saint-Dizier with a great number of soldiers rode towards Vitry in Perthois [Vitry-le-François or Vitry-

[102] The threat of English routiers and the forces of Charles of Navarre.

la-Ville]. This greatly enraged the people of the region. In many villages, they rang their [church] bells and assembled to go against this lord of Saint-Dizier, fearing that he wished to harm them. At the request of these people, the supplicant went with them, stayed with them, led them, and gave them orders when they went to the village of Perthes and other places. [But] as their captain, he had no intention of marching against and assaulting this lord or any others. He wished only to resist their evil will, if they should desire to do anything harmful. And then, without committing any crime, this supplicant and others approached this lord to find out if he wished to wrong them and to inform him that his men had threatened to burn them. And because he responded that he had no wish or intention of harming them, this captain and other good people said to this lord that they also wished him no ill will but desired to aid him, if he wished. Soon they returned to their homes without committing any crimes: as far as the supplicant knew, they did not burn any houses, knock down any castles, pillage or seize any property. They did not kill or mutilate anyone [...]

Issued at Melun-sur-Seine, July 1359.

115 Remission granted to Mahieu de Leurel, mason, condemned as an accomplice to the execution of Jean Bernier

Ibid., pp. 333–5, JJ. 98, no. 252. Mahieu de Leurel, mason, an accomplice to the execution of Jean Bernier, a non-nobleman, whom Guillaume Cale, captain general of the people of the plains, had handed over to be tried and judged.

Charles etc. Let it be known to all present and future that on behalf of Mahieu of Leurel, mason, a man subject to the justice of our friends the monks, abbot, and monastery of Beaulieu[103]: we have been shown in 1358 around the feast of Corpus Christi [31 May] that the people would seem to have forced him with many other people of this county and its environs to join the terror, which the people of the plains had brought against the nobles of our kingdom, to knock down many fortified places, wreck their property, mow them down, and kill them. For this, some of these nobles could have become hostile towards him and hated this supplicant, wishing to cause him bodily harm and damage his property. This was at the time when our dear lord and father

103 Beaulieu-les-Fontaines, a priory in the diocese of Noyon. The monks would have had feudal rights of justice over certain men in villages under their jurisdiction.

governed the realm – may God absolve him [of his sins][104] – and when we had returned and entered our good city of Paris. At that time, we desired and decreed that all the nobles give remission to and pardon the people of the plains as well as to those of the nobility who had and might have committed crimes against one another. All criminal suits and proceedings should cease between these parties; however, anyone could still bring civil suits for damages and injuries before us, our officers, and judges. And we proceeded against this Mahieu for the following reasons. Around the time of this feast day, Jehan Bernier, a non-noble, was allegedly accused of treason, because letters from the king of Navarre were found on him, and he was commonly known for such deeds in this region. For this, he [Bernier] was led to Guillaume Cale, then captain of these people of the plains, to be tried and punished. Guillaume handed him over to Étienne du Wès, then captain of the village of Montataire,[105] to be put to death, if he [Étienne], the villagers, and those of the surrounding countryside judged that he deserved it. Informed about [Bernier's] life and reputation and in the presence of two or three hundred people of this village and the surrounding countryside, this Étienne had him led barefoot in his shirt to the cross in front of the palace of these monks in Montataire, where he commanded Jehan le Charon to execute and put him to death; the command was obeyed. Bernier fell to the ground and died. The supplicant was present for this execution, holding a mason's rule, with which this Étienne commanded him to strike Bernier when he hit the ground. He did not dare disobey this order, since Étienne was their captain and would have put him to death or caused him grievous bodily harm [if he refused]. Thus he struck Bernier with his rule as he gasped his last breath. Because [Mathieu] had tremendous fear of the rigors of the law, etc, he fled [...]

Issued at Paris, March 1364 [5]

116 Remission granted to Guillaume le Févre, bourgeois of Paris and fishmonger, giving the false reasons the Parisians revolted against the king

D. F. Secousse, *Recueil de pièces servant de preuves aux mémoires sur les Troubles excités en France par Charles II dit le Mauvais, Roi de Navarre et comte d'Evreux* (Paris, 1755), 2 vols., I, pp. 83–5: JJ 86, no. 255.

104 '*que Dieux absoillé*: in other words, at the time of this letter's enactment, King John had died.

Charles etc. Let it be known to all present and future that at the instigation, prompting, and encouragement of the deceased Étienne Marcel, previously provost of the merchants of the city of Paris, many of his allies, followers, collaborators and accomplices said and maintained that during the whole time they governed the good city of Paris and its surrounding countryside, all that they did was for a good end – the ransom and deliverance of our above-mentioned lord [King John] – for the public good, and for the great number of good people[106] and faithful commoners of this city of Paris. Without the authority, will, or consent of our lord or of us and unaware of the great acts of treason, plotting, conspiracies, and other crimes which this provost and his accomplices did in secret, they resolved and strove to go against our lord, ourselves, and his royal majesty, agreeing to rebel [*eslever*] and take as their leader the king of Navarre, to make alliances with him and the English and other enemies of the crown of France. They wore a silver buckle [*fermeillez*] enamelled half in vermilion, half in blue, with 'to a good end' written underneath it. And they wore parti-coloured hoods as a sign to live or die with this provost, against all others, and took up arms against us to take away our royal prerogatives, that is, [they decided] to be rebels [*rebelles*] against our lord and us, and to say abusive words about us personally and commit many other crimes, misdemeanours, and felonies against the royal majesty. By these means, they wished the people to believe that we would order our soldiers to destroy and rob them, that we would abandon this city along with other cities and surrounding districts within the realm of France to these soldiers, and that we had absolutely no intention of delivering and paying the ransom for our lord, although these things are self-evidently false. For these crimes and felonies or some of them, Guillaume le Févre, fishmonger at les Halles of Paris and bourgeois of this city, who, as it is said, recently fled and is now absent [had been charged]. The provost of Paris, his lieutenant, or others appointed and deputed by us approached and summoned him to appear or face banishment within three days of the date of the present general pardon extended to all the inhabitants of this city for all their crimes, rebellions, misdemeanours that they might have committed against our lord and us for all the above-stated reasons, except for the crime of high treason. All his goods were

---

105 Near Creil.
106 Here, rather than the better-off, 'good' seems to suggest the vast majority of Parisians.

seized, even though he has not been convicted of any of these crimes. He has been banished because of failure to appear in court, for which we can certainly rule against him, for ignorance is no excuse. According to the letter of the law, we could proceed against him, forcing him to forfeit his property and life, if we should wish to pursue the case. But our good friends Gentien Tristan, the present provost of the merchants, the aldermen, bourgeois, and inhabitants of this city of Paris have humbly beseeched us to show pity and mercy on this matter. And considering the good love and loyalty, which this provost, the bourgeois, and inhabitants of this city have always had towards our lord and us, as they have well demonstrated in seizing and destroying these traitors, rebels, and enemies of the crown of France, we are inclined to accept their supplication ...

Issued at Paris, August 1358.

117 Letter of Charles, granting to the marshal Boucicaut the use rights of all properties that had belonged personally to Robert le Coq, bishop of Laon

Secousse, *Recueil*, pp. 85–6, JJ, reg. no. 525.

Charles, etc. To all those who will be sent these letters: salutations. Since Robert le Coq Bishop of Laon[107] has been and is a rebel, disobedient to my lord, to us, and the realm, and as best as he can has taken and receives advice, support, and assistance from our enemies and rebels and is still with them and a part of their military campaign, allied with the enemy of my lord, us, and our kingdom, and, because of Robert le Coq's treachery, we confiscate all the temporalities of his bishopric, which he holds within the kingdom of France; we place them in our hands and those of our lord [King John II], that is, all the furnishings and landed property of his patrimony, which he possesses and holds here, no matter where, whether [obtained] by purchase or by any other means or title.

We make it known that we depend on and esteem the fine, loyal, useful, and agreeable services which our friend, loyal knight, and coun-

---

107 For a sketch of Robert Le Coq as a radical of the estates general and the Council of Eighty in 1356–17 and his attacks against the king's men as 'slanderers, flatterers and boot-lickers', see Sumption, *The Hundred Years War*, II, pp. 256–8. On Le Coq's skills as an orator and politician and as the prime leader of constitutional reform from 1356 to 1358, see Funk, 'Robert Le Coq and Étienne Marcel'.

sellor of the king and of us, Lord Jean le Meingre, called Boucicaut, marshal of France,[108] has performed for us during the present wars, and which he continues to offer day after day, and which we hope he will render in the future. We have given, authorised, and delivered the house which the said bishop had in Paris on a main street, along with all and any furnishings and landed properties that he possessed in the city or county [*Vicomté*] of Paris that derived from his office as bishop, to our aforesaid counsellor. He is to have, hold, and possess [these properties] at our pleasure to the same extent and as long as Robert is bishop of Laon and now in rebellion against my lord and us. Moreover, we have given and granted all other furnishings and landed properties, inheritances, possessions, rents, and other revenues, which we have taken from the said Robert within the kingdom, no matter where they may lie, as is said, to the said Marshal. And we give and grant these properties by our special grace and sure knowledge, and by this particular order he shall possess them as his own, whether by fief, a pledge as a rear-vassal [*arréfié*], or otherwise, as long as he lives.

Issued at Paris, 11 August 1358.

118 Letter of pardon of King John II to the Parisians involved in the revolt

Secousse, *Recueil*, pp. 87–8; Register A of the Hôtel de Ville de Paris, fol. 223v.
Letter of King John II to the inhabitants of the city of Paris, declaring his intention to pardon those involved in the revolt

John, by grace of God, King of France. To our very dear and good friends, the bourgeois, inhabitants, and all the common people of our good city of Paris: Salutations and affection. It has come to our attention that in the past some, moved by evil intentions, have been won over by many false words, deceptions, proclamations, and by other malicious and deceptive means. Under the guise of good faith, [these evil ones have tried] to lure you fraudulently from our obedience and lordship and to push you into disobedience and rebellion against us and Charles, our son, urging you to submit to another government

---

108 This marshal of the French crown was a commander in the campaigns in Gascony in 1349–50, in Picardy in 1355, and at the battle of Poitiers in 1356. He died in 1368. According to Sumption (*The Hundred Years' War*, II, p. 50), 'his reckless courage and misjudgements' caused him to spend long periods in English prisons. His son (of the same name) was also a field marshal of the crown (Charles VI).

and lordship. Although in their great malice they pretended to be acting in the best interests of the public good, finally, inspired by the Holy Ghost, you have seen and have resisted their great treason and malice. You found the right path and challenged the power of these evil ones in their endeavour to fulfil their evil ends. Once [these evil ones] had disclosed and shown to all their treason and malice, you returned with loyalty and without hesitation the good city of Paris to our lordship and obedience and that of our son, paying your respect to us and to him and towards the crown of France as your good and loyal predecessors have always done. Once we had learned of this fact, we turned back with all our heart [to you], giving praise and thanks to Our Lord Jesus Christ who did not wish us to suffer the loss and destruction of so beautiful a joy that is our good city of Paris and its good people. Thus we believe that this deed has been achieved more by divine miracle than anything else, and that also you are indebted to God for all this. After thanking God, we thank you as heartily as we can, for your love, fealty, loyalty, and obedience, which you have shown us, our son Charles, and the crown of France, as good and loyal subjects. We want you to know that we recognise these things with all our heart. With the assistance of Our Lord, we trust that you will return to our kingdom and will also acknowledge our son Charles. And we and our successors will always remain loyal to you and to this good city. We pray as fervently as we can that you should always persevere to be better and better in loyalty and obedience towards us. In return our son will love, defend, protect, and support you with all our power, as we do ourselves, against all who might wish to trouble or harm you. And if anyone through simplicity has been deceived under cover of good faith, we choose not to enforce the letter of the law but to grant grace and remission, if they are worthy of it. Then stay firm and constant in your loyalty and good purpose, remaining united and of one will without division in your obedience to us and our son, as is pleasing to God and to the world. As testimony to this matter, we have placed our great seal on these present letters.

Issued at London, 14 August, 1358.

119 Remission granted to the inhabitants of Amiens, concerning various crimes and excesses they committed

Secousse, *Recueil*, pp. 97–9; JJ, reg. 86, no. 239.

Charles, etc. Let it be known to all present and future that in times past the aldermen [*esquevins*] and commune of the city of Amiens have been and, (we continue to hope) always will be good, loyal, and true in their obedience as subjects to my lord, to us, and to the crown of France. And they have realised that they have incurred our indignation for what has happened at several assemblies of the people of the three estates, which we found offensive, even if they were encouraged and advised by some who claimed at the time to be members of our council. These supplicants came to these assemblies by our command, and in these assemblies, the mayor [of Amiens], the town councillors, and the commune incurred the indignation of some of the nobility, who endeavoured to destroy and dismantle the decisions of those assemblies, which had been set up by the people of the three estates. In addition, during the present year, when we left Compiègne for Corbie, accompanied by many armed guards, we wrote to the mayor, many leaders of the guilds [*Majeurs de Banerez*],[109] and others of the city, ordering them to come to Corbie to talk with us. They did not obey or heed our command but sent us envoys, suggesting that we should go to the city of Amiens and that our men should go there unarmed. They said they feared the noblemen in our troops, because they had heard some of these persons make certain threats. Moreover, they feared that if these armed men in our troops entered their city, they would inflict great damage and bring shame on them. At the request of the common people of the Beauvaisis and without our permission, the mayor, aldermen, and the commune [of Amiens] sent their own people out [to join] the common people of the Beauvaisis, who had just begun to assemble.[110] In addition, many individuals of Amiens went by their own will, although it was said that those who were sent only went four, five, or six leagues outside the city and its environs and then immediately returned.[111] And because of this, others were ordered to leave that

---

109 *Bannières* were trades and crafts groups; each carried their own flag [*bannière*].
110 These townsmen were sent out to aid the Jacques in the countryside to fight against the nobles; see [94].
111 According to *La Chronique normande du XIVe siècle* [94], the reason they turned back was because of a division between the mayor and the city council of Amiens; the counsellors called for their citizens and commoners to return.

city against their will and permission and were plundered and robbed as soon as they left. Some fled, some were captured, and some were killed. Some sought justice to have the culprits beheaded and to restore the stolen property to those to whom it belonged. Moreover, in all the assemblies with the other principal cities [*bonnes villes*] of the realm, they requested the king of Navarre to be freed, hoping, it is said, that he would be good and loyal to my lord, to us, and to the crown of France. In addition, because of our letters, and for what they believed was good and loyal to my lord, us, and the crown of France, they came back to their city, and returned to their bourgeois, after Jean de Pinguigny and his accomplices had freed [the king of Navarre] from the prison of Arleux,[112] where the king [John II] or others on his behalf had imprisoned him.[113] Also they put on the hoods, part blue and red, as a sign of their unity and alliance with the city of Paris. And many of Amiens said and spread astonishing and injurious words against our state and our person. Moreover, after the treaty made between us and the said king of Navarre, when we were with our troops at the bridge of Charenton, they agreed that this king should be their leader, because the city of Paris had written to them that it had been among the things agreed to and negotiated between us and this king. And after this, over a period of time, those of Amiens wrote to many of the principal towns that they were united solidly together for the honour of the realm, for the king's deliverance, and for their own preservation and that of the city of Amiens. Also, when the said king of Navarre was freed from prison, he sent letters to the mayor, aldermen, and commune [of Amiens] that we did not authorise. And in this correspondence, those [of Amiens] might have said words against us, wishing to incur our indignation, without [considering] the consequences against my lord, us, and the crown of France. Their alliance with the said king of Navarre and others, beyond what has been said, is cause enough [to prosecute]. And by this event, if we should choose to proceed according to the rule of law and begin legal proceedings against them, they would not be able to escape from corporal punishment and the forfeiture of their property to my lord and us. We would have at least pursued these matters had the mayor, aldermen, and commune of the city of Amiens not humbly beseeched us to express pity and to be merciful towards them ...

Issued at Paris, September 1358.

112 10 km south of Douai.

113 The king of Navarre was indebted to the commune of Amiens because its men had freed him from imprisonment at Arleux.

120 Remission granted to those rebels who planned to seize the city of Paris

Secousse, *Recueil,* pp. 120–1; Reg. 90, no. 1.

Charles, etc. Let it be known to all present and future that we have been notified and it has been confirmed many times by sealed letters and in secret by word of mouth by many loyal subjects and good friends of the realm, that these enemies[114] desired to have and hold firmly the faith, support, advice, aid, and alliance of various friends of the deceased Étienne Marcel, former provost of the merchants of the city of Paris, during his lifetime, and of some of his aldermen and others of his adherents, supporters, and accomplices, who were sentenced as traitors to our lordship and to us and to be put to death along with several prisoners living in this city. These enemies have been thought to have been involved in secret meetings and in alliance with these traitors and their followers ... These enemies had the intention and were firmly resolved to come in as great a force as they could muster to the city of Paris, to enter with the force of arms, in treason, and to capture, imprison, or put to death ourselves, our men and officers, and the good people and commune of this city, to instil fear and to murder, kill, plunder, rob, and destroy this city, bringing it under their will and obedience. Many of the above-mentioned and others, who were faithful and loyal to our lordship, to us, this realm, and city, gave us the names of those persons living in Paris, whom these enemies held, called, and thought of as their friends and sympathisers [*bienveillans*] or allies, by word of mouth and authorized in writing, thus upholding and fulfilling their loyalty, good word, and faith, which they have for my lord, us, this city, and the crown of France, as they have said. Considering the arrogance [*les grans paroles*] and rioting [*murmures*] against us by the commoners of Paris, we could readily proceed against them, but we desire with all our power to resist the great peril and irreparable troubles that could fan their rage, and thus we avoid doing so. But we can no longer ignore, delay, or conceal what must now be employed to remedy these matters. Thus we have assembled the great council of our lord and us, with the provost of the merchants, the present aldermen, many persons and inhabitants of this city, our officers, and many other bourgeois, valiant men, and responsible people of Paris. After much deliberation, we have arrested

---

114 I suspect that 'these enemies' refers to the forces of the king of Navarre and the English routiers under his command.

and imprisoned many persons and inhabitants of this city in the Châtelet of Paris. We have seized and placed in the hands of our lord and ourselves all the property of those whom our officers and others held and named as the allies and supporters of our enemies ... From fear of these princes[115] and because of malice and jealousy and envy of the things of the world, certain members of the bourgeoisie and inhabitants of the city of Paris have departed. We have called these persons to justice before the king's court and continue to pursue and denounce other perfidious ones ...

Issued at the Louvre, December 1358.

115 I imagine that 'these princes' refers to the king of Navarre, the regent, and his uncles.

IV: THE REVOLT OF THE CIOMPI, 1378-82

The historiography on the revolt of the Ciompi is vast, international, and, more than other revolts documented above, divided. On the one hand, Gene Brucker,[1] Sergio Bertelli,[2] Mollat and Wolff,[3] and Raymond de Roover[4] have judged these insurgents as possessing little 'social cohesion' or class consciousness; their revolt arose from desperation and misery; their ideology, if they had one at all, was conservative or reactionary: instead of destroying the government, they strove only to ape their social betters by entering it, even going so far as to knight certain members of the previous oligarchy such as Salvestro de' Medici. On the other hand, Niccolò Rodolico,[5] Victor Rutenburg,[6] Charles de la Roncière,[7] Samuel Cohn, Jr,[8] John Najemy,[9] Alessandro Stella,[10] and

---

1 Gene Brucker, *Florentine Politics and Society 1343–1378* (Florence, 1962); idem, *The Civic World of Early Renaissance Florence* (Princeton, 1977); and idem, 'The Ciompi Revolution', in *Florentine Studies: Politics and Society in Renaissance Florence*, ed. N. Rubinstein (London, 1968), pp. 314–56.

2 'Oligarchies et gouvernement dans la Renaissance', *Social Science: Information sur les sciences sociales*, 15 (1976): 601–23.

3 Mollat and Wolff, *The Popular Revolutions*, pp. 142–61

4 Raymond de Rooner, 'Labour Conditions in Florence around 1400: Theory, Policy, and Reality', in *Florentine Studies*, ed. Rubenstein, pp. 277–313.

5 Niccolò Rodalico, *Il Popolo Minuto: Note di Storia Fiorentina (1343–1378)* (Florence, 1899; new edn, 1968); idem, *La Democrazia Fiorentina nel suo tramonto (1378–1382)* (Bologna, 1905); and idem, *I Ciompi: Una pagina di storia del proletariato operaio* (Florence, 1945).

6 Victor Rutenburg, *Popolo e movimenti popolari nell'Italia del '300 e '400*, tr. Gianpiero Borghini (Bologna, 1971; Moscow, 1958).

7 Charles-M. de la Roncière, 'Pauvres et pauvreté à Florence au XIVe siècle', in *Études sur l'histoire de la pauvreté (Moyen Âge–XIVe siècle)*, ed. M. Mollat (Paris, 1974), I, pp. 661–745.

8 Cohn, *The Laboring Classes in Renaissance Florence*; and 'Florentine insurrections, 1342–1385, in Comparative Perspective', in *The English Rising of 1381*, pp. 143–64.

9 John Najemy, '"Audiant omnes artes": Corporate Origins of the Ciompi Revolution', in *Il Tumulto dei Ciompi: Un momento di storia fiorentina ed europea* (Florence, 1981), pp. 59–93; and 'The Dialogue of Power in Florentine Politics', in *City-States in Classical Antiquity and Medieval Italy*, ed. A. Molho, K. Raaflaub and J. Emlen (Ann Arbor, 1991), 269–88.

10 Alessandro Stella, *La révolte des Ciompi: Les hommes, les lieux, le travail* (Paris, 1993).

Richard Trexler[11] have attributed more originality to the Ciompi – their social and economic demands, monetary and employment policies, and the creation of three new revolutionary guilds composed of workmen, which granted rights to previously disenfranchised men and women and gave them a voice in determining their economic affairs. These historians have not judged as reactionary the struggle of disenfranchised workers to obtain rights as citizens and the creation of a new government in which nearly all males possessed virtual representation by belonging to a guild [**122, 124**]. This revolution and the new government, it installed lasted considerably longer the Jacquerie's two weeks of terror or the six days during which the English Peasants' Revolt proved a serious threat to the English monarchy. In coalition with minor guildsmen (artisans and shopkeepers in trades outside the wool industry), wool workers with other workers in Florence formed a government that endured for three-and-a-half years.

There were four phases to the revolution and its governments. First, on 18 June 1378 Salvestro de' Medici and others from merchant-elite families sparked a constitutional struggle that challenged the Guelf Party's[12] control and manipulation of government elections through its denunciations [*ammoniti*] of those drawn from the purses [elected] for office. Secondly, on 20 July 1378 principally those in the wool industry with no guild representation stormed the town hall, the Palazzo Signoria, ousted governmental officials (previously elected on 18 June), and on the next day formed a new government, which for the first time included these disenfranchised workers. This revolution, however, left aspects of the Florentine constitution intact such as bimonthly elections for the priorate, and minor and major guildsmen still held offices in the various town councils. This government, nonetheless, brought in sweeping changes, most importantly, the creation of three new guilds, which meant that all workmen in the city, regardless of trade or status, had guild representation and thus became citizens; their names now could be placed in the electoral purses; they could be drawn and could hold the highest posts in government.

11 Richard Trexlar, 'Neighbours and Comrades: The Revolutionaries of Florence, 1378', *Social Analysis*, 14 (1983): 53–105; 'Follow the Flag: The Ciompi Revolt Seen From the Streets', *Bibliothèque d'Humanisme et Renaissance*, 46 (1984): 357–92; 'Herald of the Ciompi: The Authorship of an Anonymous Florentine Chronicle', *Quellen und Forschungen*, 65 (1985): 159–91.

12 On the Guelfs and Ghibellines, see ch. I, note 57. By the mid-fourteenth century, the Guelf Party had become an institution of upper-class reaction to initiatives towards more egalitarian measures and broader social participation in the Florentine government.

Unlike previous guilds, these much larger new ones were not occupationally specific; instead they cut across the occupational structures of the city, comprising guilds more of class than of trade: crafts as different as barbers and flag makers, or soap makers and weavers were combined as members of the same guild [128, 131].

At the end of August, a group of disgruntled aristocrats and wool workers primarily from south of the Arno [*sopr'Arno*], known as the Eight of Santa Maria Novella, plotted to push the revolution further and tried to force their proposals through the government [125–8]. They failed, and in reaction the government disbanded the third revolutionary guild – that of the *Popolo di Dio*, composed of the least skilled workers and apprentices of the city. Workers of the two other revolutionary guilds, however, maintained their newly won status and allied with minor and major guildsmen to form a new government (the Government of the Minor Guilds [*Arti Minori*]).

This regime continued to hold regular bi-monthly elections to the priorate, sent ambassadors throughout Italy, passed legislative reforms, and lasted until 24 January 1382, when aristocrats and *popolani grassi* (the fat cats of the old Florentine families), supported by foreign *condottieri* and foreign governments – Venice, Bologna, and Siena – overthrew it. The new regime of oligarchs abolished the two remaining revolutionary guilds of craftsmen – primarily those in the wool industry – reinstated the constitution that antedated the events of 22 July 1378, and restored the political status of those sent into exile by the governments of the Ciompi and the Minor Guilds over the past three-and-a-half years. Offices continued to be distributed between major and minor guilds, but as with most of Florentine history before and after the Ciompi, the old families were back in control [131]. In marked contrast to the Jacquerie, the Tuchins, or the German Peasants' War of 1524/5, however, no bloody repression with mass executions in fields or from town gallows followed. Nor is there any evidence of mass expulsion or emigration [121].[13] Indeed, soon after the change of regime, the government even reissued crossbows to the Ciompi who had been chased from town in September 1378! [187]

---

13 Rutenburg, *Popolo e movimenti popolari*, pp. 315–16 and 335–6, claims that the repression was brutal and that mass emigration ensued but he produces little evidence to back his claims. Only forty-four Ciompi were sentenced to exile in September 1378 following the fall of the Ciompi government. Furthermore, days later, any Ciompi who had left the city was invited back with safe passage [see 121]. With the fall of the Government of the Minor Guilds in January 1382, three were beheaded and only twenty-five sent into exile [121].

The documentation for the revolts of the Ciompi is radically different from the sources thus far studied in this volume. First, we begin with a diary of a prominent member of the Florentine patriciate, now considered to have been a member of the Machiavelli family and possibly Boninsegna Machiavelli, Niccolò's great-great-grandfather.[14] At any rate, the diarist clearly had been a member of the government and possessed a vast and detailed knowledge of the daily decrees, city crimes, and incidents of unrest even after the Ciompi had taken over in July 1378. His diary exhibits at every turn the patrician's vitriolic opposition to these workers and artisans entering office [121]. Yet his day-to-day, and on some days, hour-to-hour coverage of events supplies little overview beyond his personal hatred of the Ciompi, whom he regarded as common criminals: he condemned their desire to govern and determine their own destiny as outrageous arrogance. His *pointilliste* detail swamps the reader in the daily turmoil of new decrees passed by the revolutionary governments and new crimes that threatened the security of established merchants. We sense the emotional effects of this world turned upside down from the perspective of a stalwart of the old regime. Only in December 1378 did the chronicler allow himself a brief pause in this daily recounting to recall the apocalyptic prophecies of a Friar Minor for that *annus mirabilis* of 1378, supposedly made in 1368. The Ciompi's violation of the social order briefly takes on supernatural proportions.

Others such as Marchionne di Coppo Stefani (or Boniauti), who was a prior in 1379, had governmental positions during the government of the Minor Guilds but were not aristocrats or fat cats [*popolani grassi*].[15] They have left detailed reports, at times even showing some sympathy with some of the insurgents, especially their first leader, Michele di Lando [130, 131]. Others such as the second and third anonymous chroniclers, despite their antipathies towards the Ciompi, nonetheless had inside governmental information and reported almost verbatim the decrees and policies promulgated by the Ciompi government in July and August 1378 [122, 124].

---

14 Davidsohn, 'L'avo di Niccolò Machiavelli', 35–47; Brucker, *Florentine Politics and Society*, pp. 128 and 306, questions whether Buoninsegna was the diarist but concurs that he was a member of the Machiavelli family.
15 For Stefani's correct name, his political affiliations, and posts, see Green, *Chronicle into History*, pp. 91–6. Stefani was a prior in the government of the Minor Guilds in 1379.

Secondly, we find for the first time chroniclers who were workers [**129**] or even revolutionaries [**123, 125**], who did not disguise their political sympathies, even though with the defeat of the Eight of Santa Maria Novella in August 1378 such sympathies, had they been discovered, would have been curtailed by banishment or corporeal punishment.

Thirdly, the state archives of Florence conserve documents, such as criminal records, which do not survive in bulk in cities such as Paris or other places north of the Alps until the fifteenth century or later.[16] The criminal records describe events in a clinical fashion and from a lopsided perspective – that of the state bent on casting the criminals and especially rebels in the worst light possible even if they were acquitted. At the same time, however, they list those charged with rebellion, often identifying them by occupation and parish of residence so that the historian can now analyse the social character of these revolts and their governments, map out their networks of association, and speculate on interclass alliances with a rigour which is impossible for the north of Europe in the fourteenth century, Flanders included [**127**].[17] For this reason, I have presented in full some of the lists of condemned rebels.

Finally, the Ciompi did after all succeed, even if for a limited period, and as a consequence elected a new government, which passed laws that still survive in the vast *Provvisioni* registers of the Florentine state archives [**128**]. This source gives us a clearer view of insurgents' programmes and policies than is possible from failed revolts and the reportage of these programmes by prejudiced chroniclers from opposing classes.

---

16 Bronsilaw Geremek, *The Margins of Society in Late Medieval Paris*, tr. Jean Birrell (New York, 1987); Claude Gauvard, *'De Grace especial': crime, état et société en France à la fin du Moyen Age*, 2 vols. (Paris, 1991). For Florentine criminal records, see Rodolico, *La Democrazia Fiorentina*; Brucker, *Florentine Politics and Society* and *The Civic World*; and Cohn, *The Laboring Classes*.

17 For this analysis, see Cohn, *The Laboring Classes*; for a reconstruction of around a hundred insurgents in the English Uprising of 1381 from matching names in various sources with manorial records, see Dyer, 'The Social and Economic Background to the Rural Revolt'.

121 A diary of the Ciompi by an anonymous Florentine, 1378–82

Diario d'anonimo fiorentino dall'anno 1358 al 1389, ed. Alessandro Gherardi, in *Cronache dei secoli XIII e XIV*, Documenti di storia italiana, IV (Florence, 1876), pp. 207–588.

[p. 356] Today, in the name of God, 18 June, the sixteenth hour of this day and year [1378], our city counsellors [*Signiori*][18] wished to put forward to the Council of the People[19] a petition for the good, peace, and tranquillity of the city of Florence, so that merchants would not all be branded every day as Ghibellines[20] and made to repurchase [their status] from magnates and their followers. Every day the magnates threatened the merchants so that no one could speak out. And the office of the Signoria was worthless as far as we were concerned. It should muzzle these grandees, who are rapacious wolves. The good Salvestro, son of lord Alamanno de' Medici, a worthy and dear citizen, along with his supporters and the colleges of the Signoria [*Collegi*][21] submitted a petition to renew the powers of the Ordinances of Justice[22] against the magnates of the city, *contado*, and district[23] of Florence, and to curb the power of past captains of the Guelf Party, who wished to destroy Florence. Thus they wished to pass this petition through the Council of the People gathered in the Palace of the Signoria. Once the magnates knew that this petition was going before the council, many Guelf citizens along with a rather large number of magnates had gathered in the chapter house of the Guelf Party to hear the details of this petition that proposed to re-impose the Ordinances of Justice on the backs of the grandees. The people [*popolo*] and the guildsmen were in the Palace of the Signoria to support the

---

18 The Signoria was the supreme executive office of the commune, composed of nine elected officials – the eight priors and the standard-bearer of justice. They were advised by the two colleges – the Sixteen *gonfalonieri* and the Twelve good men. Collectively, these three bodies were called the *Tre Maggiori*.

19 One of two large legislative councils comprised of around 250 minor and major guildsmen and magnates. Petitions were first vetted in secret by the *Tre Maggiori* before they could proceed to be discussed openly and voted on by the two large councils of the People and the Commune; see Brucker, *Florentine Politics and Society*, pp. 59–60, and Cohn, *Creating the Florentine State*, pp. 172–3.

20 By the fourteenth century with Florence firmly established as a Guelf power, Ghibelline had become a curse word to brand any enemy of the state.

21 See note 18.

22 See [26].

23 On the distinction between *contado* and *distretto*, see chapter I, note 5.

stance of our governors [*Signiori*], the colleges, and the council, [but the magnates in the council managed to defeat the motion]. Salvestro di Messer Alamanno came down into the Chamber of the Council [of the People] and spoke: 'Councillors [*Signiori*], I have looked on, trying to bring concord and unity to this your city; up here there are some who have been against me for wanting to make peace and unity in this your city. They have not consented to bringing about this good. Therefore, I say to you that I am no longer the standard-bearer of justice [*Gonfaloniere di giustizia*][24], and I say to you, may God help you. And as for me, I'm going home, since you do not want my colleagues and I to bring about this good work for our commune'.

Once Salvestro started to leave the council chambers, the wise men of the council took it upon themselves not to let him leave. So they put forward the petition again to the council, and this time the Signoria and their colleges won the day. Our government and its councils, along with Salvestro, are and always will be worthy of praise. After having achieved these good and blessed manoeuvres, a small disturbance [*un poco di romore*] broke out. It began in the Palace of the Signoria and continued with those of the council, who saw that certain ones [standing] outside the [palace of the] Guelf Party were not happy, having realised that they could no longer rob the citizens, who every day had been threatened by the magnates and their followers. The disturbance spread to the Palace of the Guelf Party, where it picked up strength. Adoardo de' Pulci wanted to carry out the flag [*gonfalone*] of the [Guelf] Party to rouse the city to revolt. But it did not happen because of the good intentions of Foresse Salviati, who confronted him, and thus Florence was spared from having its citizens kill and be killed. And all those of the houses of the Buondelmonti, the Adimari, the Cavicciuli, and other magnates cried out for help [*almati*]. Had it pleased God that they should have then come out of their palaces, the people would have cut them to pieces. Further, [the people] threatened the Guelf merchants [*popolani guelfi*][25] in the Palace of the Guelf Party, drawing their swords against them; they threw many of them out of the Palace from the roof and out the back; in the house of Piero Fastigli, they were thrown out or forced to leave. Standing their ground on the steps of the Party's palace, with their unshielded weapons, the people challenged: 'We'll see who'll be chased out of Florence'? But once the petition had been passed, the

24 The highest officer in the Florentine Republic.
25 As opposed to the Guelf magnates.

discontent eased: not a drop of blood was spilled. [The chronicler then lists appointments to governmental offices from 1 May 1378.]

[p. 358] Today, 21 June 1378, at 3 in the afternoon,[26] a riot erupted in Florence. Because of suspicions stirring among the people [*giente*], many then came out into the Piazza della Signoria [the city's main square].[27] Among the many things happening in Florence that day, an olive branch arrived as news that the fortress of Fabriano had been taken.[28] Wishing to explain to the people why the rioting had arisen, our rulers [*Signiori*] quickly sent out a town crier, who explained that the commotion had arisen because of the arrival of the olive branch from Fabriano. On hearing the town crier's explanation, everyone withdrew from the Piazza della Signoria and returned to work in their shops and to do their own business.

Today, Tuesday, 22 June at 8 in the morning, all the guildsmen and their captains [*Capitudine*] went to the Piazza della Signoria, followed their artisans, who were all armed and with the banners [*gonfaloni*] of the guilds. They yelled: 'Down with these traitors'. Then suddenly they ran furiously to the houses of Carlo degli Strozzi, the Albizzi, Lord Lapo da Castiglionchio, Bartolo Siminetti, called Mastino, Migliore Guadagni, the Pazzi, Lord Filippo Corsini, Antonio di Nicolò di Cione Ridolfi, Lord Coppo di Lippo di Cione dal Cane, Niccolò and Tommaso Soderini, and Lord Ristoro di Piero Canigiani. They then went to the monasteries of the Hermits of the Angels [*Romiti degli Agnioli*][29] and to the Friars of Settimo in Cafaggiuolo,[30] where they killed a brother [*frate*] of the Angels. And at all the abovementioned places they burnt, robbed, killed, and cut down vines and orange trees and did great damage. At the house of Niccolò Soderini a wall collapsed on five men; all of them ended up badly. Boninsegna Machiavelli greatly feared that those of the Scali family were about to rob him and set him ablaze, and thus he stayed on his guard. In this mess, the Signoria sent for Giorgio degli Scali and Boninsegna and made them drink

26 The diarist, like other Florentines of the late Middle Ages, uses the twenty-four-hour clock, thus I have translated 'at 19 hours' as 3 in the afternoon; see Notes to the reader.
27 I have capitalised Piazza when it refers to the Piazza della Signoria to distinguish it from other piazze or squares of the city.
28 Guido de' Chiavelli with the help of the league of city-states against the papacy recovered the fortress on 24 June.
29 A hermitage of the Camaldoli order built between 1295 and 1305 in the parish of San Frediano.
30 A working-class neighbourhood on the western periphery of the city.

together;[31] peace was made and with the intervention of Michele di Vanni [de' Castellani] they put an end to it. Thank God.

On the same day, 22 June 1378, the disenfranchised workers [*popolo minuto*][32] broke into the Stinche[33] and freed all the prisoners, who collectively were sentenced at more than forty thousand gold florins as well as those who were condemned to death. They tore down and burnt the prison, causing great damage to our commune. God ought to make them pay.

And they went to the Treasury of Florence [*Camera del Comune*], where guildsmen stopped them from breaking the place apart; enough of them were wounded so that nothing was destroyed.

Today, 23 June 1378 they went in the morning at 8 o'clock to the church of the Friars of Santo Spirito and stole various things, large candles [*doppieri*] and relics of saints. Word of this was sent immediately to the Signoria, whence they quickly dispatched on horseback Piero di Santi, who was one of the Signoria, and Niccolò di Bono Rinucci[34], along with several of the government's bailiffs [*donzelli*]. They went to the house of these friars and quickly drove away these bad people from their thieving. Then these bad people wanted to go down the Via Maggio,[35] towards the house of Antonio di Niccolò [de' Ridolfi][36] to rob him and set his house on fire. But his neighbours had gathered at his house with soldiers, barricades, crossbows, lances, and shields and began to shoot. At this, these people turned and ran. Going down the Via Maggio, they shouted, 'Let's go to the house of the Biliotti'. But the people living in the Via Maggio pushed them back, and the robbers scattered. At this the Signoria sent out a crier

---

31 Although Giorgio degli Scali was descended from an ancient Guelf family, he became a leader of the popular forces against the old government when his cousin was declared ineligible for office by the Guelf Party. On the other hand, the Machiavelli were patricians of ancient lineage and in this period zealous supporters of the Guelf Party. Boninsegna may have even been the author of this diary; see note 14. At any rate, the diarist presents this feud as wholly devoid of any ideological difference.

32 See [13].

33 The principal prison of Florence.

34 He was a member of the Signoria and sat on the committee of Twelve, one of the colleges of the Signoria.

35 A main artery of Florence south of the Arno, running from the Ponte Santa Trinita to the piazza di San Felice.

36 He lived at the top of the street, near the church of San Felice in Piazza.

ordering all those from the countryside [*contadini*][37] to leave the city by five o'clock in the morning, or else they would lose a foot. However, they did not leave. Seeing the threat was of no use, the Signoria made a proclamation to stop the robbers. This order gave anyone without penalty or banishment the right to kill or hang anyone they caught robbing or carrying anything off. At this moment, several Flemings were off robbing: four were caught; one was hanged in the meadow of Ognissanti, another in the piazza of Santa Maria Novella from the iron grid of a window of the hospital of the Pinzocheri,[38] another in the Old Market from a column under one of the roofs of the loggia of the tavern-keepers, and the fourth was driven to the Piazza della Signoria, where he was quickly hoisted on the scaffolding and hanged. The other thieves and robbers, seeing these ones hanged, became more restrained. After five o'clock and with those from the country still in town, the Signoria passed another ban announcing that the peasants would have to leave by vespers or risk being condemned to death and having their property confiscated.

Today, Thursday, 24 June 1378, at eleven at night, the guildsmen went to the Signoria to request certain offices from our commune. Two of our Signoria stayed with them, while the guild artisans and the captains said they would arm themselves against a state of the people. On seeing this other people [*altro popolo*],[39] fearing the guild banners and that they might be burnt and robbed in the madness, [the *popolo minuto*] mounted many barricades throughout the entire city from vespers through the night as if to say: 'If this agreement falls apart with the captains, we will be prepared to fight them'.[40] Then all the citizens armed themselves and set up many barricades. They put them up here in the Oltrarno[41] to guard us,[42] at the foot of the Ponte Vecchio and on the bridge. At San Sepolcro, they put up

37 Literally, anyone who lives beyond the city walls in the *contado*, regardless of occupation.
38 Religious women who lived outside the cloistered life. The hospital of San Paolo was an institution for the care of the poor, located in one of the poorest neighbourhoods of the city.
39 I take this to mean the guildsmen.
40 That is, their alliance with the guildsmen, principally the craftsmen of the minor guilds.
41 The area south of the Arno, which comprised some of the largest concentrations of wool workers and other non-guild artisans in the city.
42 It is fairly certain that the author (even if not Boninsegna) was a member of the Machiavelli family, and their family palace was south of the Arno.

protective screens [*ventiere d'assi*] on the balconies and armed them with large crossbows. They took positions in the tower of the Mannelli family, the tower of the Guelf Party, and elsewhere on the Piazza, the bridge of Santa Trinita, at the palace of Michele di Vanni [Castellani], all along the Arno and under the arches of the church of Santo Stefano. With many well-armed soldiers and many crossbows and projectiles [*bombarde*], everyone was well protected. And the four Flemings, who had been hanged, were buried. On 24 June at night, another ban announced that all men should put down their arms, except those charged with guarding the neighbourhood banners [*gonfaloni*][43] and flags. And all those who had been banished or condemned were to clear out of the city or incur the penalties set out in this order. Then on this day the Signoria and colleges made an agreement with all the guilds and captains to condemn twenty-two men with penalties that would be more or less suitable.[44] They were inscribed in a book by name and family, their crime, and when they committed the crime.

Salvestro di Messer Alamanno de' Medici and the colleges had reformed the Florentine government and had removed from office those who wished to hand Florence over to the Church,[45] thus insulting Guelfs and the people of Florence.[46] And these are the ones who were so charged: Lord Lapo da Castiglionchio, rebel; Carlo degli Strozzi, Alberto da Castiglionchio, and all his family members [*consorti*] and the sons of Lord Lapo, all magnates; Attaviano di Boccaccio Brunelleschi, supermagnate;[47] Ser Taddeo and Francesco, magnates; Lord Ristoro di Piero Canigiani, magnate; Niccolò Soderini, were banned for life; Bonaiuto Serragli, magnate; Bartolo Siminetti, called Mastino, [were banned] for ten years; Piero Siminetti his brother, was banned

43 After 1342, the city was divided into sixteen districts or *gonfaloni*, each with its own militia and banners.
44 According to the editor, Gherardi, the meaning here is obscure.
45 This refers back to Florence's conflict with the papacy, sometimes called the War of Eight Saints.
46 With the radicalisation of the government of Salvestro de' Medici, even before the Ciompi of 20 July, the conservative Machiavelli had obviously changed his tune from his earlier admiration of Salvestro in late June, when Salvestro first challenged the excesses of the magnates and the Guelf Party.
47 In 1372 a law was passed that further penalised magnates found guilty of major crimes. As 'sopragrandi' they were forced to leave their homes and reside in another quarter of the city. They could also be made to change their names and their coats of arms. I wish to thank Mme. Christiane Klapisch-Zuber for this information.

for two years; Piero di Filippo degli Albizzi, magnate; Adoardo de' Pulci, supermagnate; Guerrieri di Tribaldo de'Rossi, supermagnate; Piero di Masino dall'Antella, were banned for life; Iacopo di Messer Francesco de' Pazzi, supermagnate; Lord Giovanni de'Ricci, were banned for three years; Alessandro di Messer Francesco Buondelmonti, supermagnate; Lord Filippo Corsini, Angnolo Serragli, Antonio di Niccolò di Cione Ridolfi, Annibaldo degli Strozzi, Pagnolo di Currado degli Strozzi, Lord Francesco Bruni, Giovanni di Piero Bandini, Filippo di Fornaino de'Rossi, supermagnate.[48]

Today, 25 June 1378, at eleven at night, the lord captain of the people, lord podestà, and lord executor of the Ordinances of Justice[49] issued a ban stating that no one should carry offensive or defensive weapons, and that all those who had been banished from the city, *contado*, or district must leave the Florentine territory, under the penalties described in the proclamation, and that anyone harbouring them would be sentenced to be burnt to death, and that everyone, skilled artisans and merchants, must open their warehouses and shops and perform or have others perform for them their trades under a penalty of 50 pounds [*lire*] for each shop that was not opened.

Today, 30 June 1378, fifty-two families, who had been banned from office[50] by previous captains [of the Guelf Party], were reinstated. [The chronicler then lists these heads of family, many by occupation, and then lists the newly elected officers of the government.]

[p. 362] Today, 5 July 1378, the captains of the Guelf Party requested that many citizens in the Guelf Party should try to restore the party's good image and that of Florence by being conciliatory, showing unity, resolving their differences, and refraining from fighting, rioting, and acts of arson.

In the first place, for the peace, unity, and concord of Florence, the Florentine government cancelled the privilege of previous captains [of the Guelf Party] to bear arms and to decide who could bear them.

And the government abolished the old Committee of the Twenty-Four;[51] now those on the Twenty-four had to be members of the college,

---

48 Although the chronicler says that twenty-two men were condemned, he lists twenty-six.
49 The three heads of Florence's three criminal courts and police forces.
50 Admonition [*ammonite*] meant that a person was barred from holding office.
51 A committee that could inspect the captains' decisions on sentences of admonition.

that is of the priors, the Twelve, the standard-bearer [of justice], a prior of the Party or secretary of the Party.

And that the officers called the little balls [*pallottole*] would be dismissed entirely.[52]

And that no one could be barred from office-holding while in office but only after a certain amount of time and only with serious matters could such an inquiry be made, and if no sound grounds were found, the person could not be condemned as a Ghibelline; rather it must be proven that the suspect was in fact a Ghibelline.[53]

In the name of God. Amen. These are the *pallottole* who have been made captains of the Guelf Party: [72 men are listed, mostly from the prominent families of Florence, but several are without family names and identified by occupations such as blacksmith, carpenter, cobbler, and butcher.]

[p. 363] Today, 8 July 1378, all the leaders of the guilds assembled in the Palace of the Guelf Party in front of their captains to make several demands. The captains answered the councillors and their leaders, saying they were willing to do anything they asked, and everyone was in agreement; our city remained in peace and harmony.

Today, 9 July 1378, the government issued a ban, decreeing that anyone who had been barred from office since 1312 had three days to bring a petition before the captains of the Guelf Party and immediately their rights would be restored; by these means our Florence should remain at peace.

Today, Friday, 9 July 1378, the petition of the councils and the captains of the guilds was put before the Council of the People, and they won what they asked for. And on the 10th of this month and year, they put the same petition before the Council of the Commune,[54] that is, on Saturday of this month, day, and year. It also passed this council for the honour of God, the well-being of the people, commune, Guelf Party, and the artisans of the city of Florence.

---

52 It is not clear what these officers did; nor does Gherardi or more recent political historians such as Brucker, John Najemy, or Guidubaldo Guidi discuss them, but I suspect that they were the ones who vetted the office pouches and barred candidates they did not like from office.

53 If condemned as a Ghibelline, a citizen could not hold office and might suffer other indignities.

54 After the Signoria and its colleges had approved a petition, the two larger chambers, first the Council of the People, then that of the Commune, would vote on it.

These are the ordinances which passed through the Signoria, the colleges, the captains and councils of the guilds, and the Councils of the People and the Commune on 9 and 10 July 1378.

First, no one who had been in the Signoria, the Twelve, one of the standard-bearers, the Ten of Liberty, the Eight of Power [*Balìa*],[55] or a guild captain, can be barred from office, neither he nor his descendants.

Second, the Guelf Party is stripped of its power to accuse, condemn, or banish anyone.

Fourth,[56] all the purses [*borse*] from today and in the past, selected by the Guelf Party, are to be burnt, and new names are to be drawn up for the purses [*fare inquittinio di nuovo*].[57]

Fifth, anyone who does not practise a craft or will not practise one shall not be placed in the purses [*imborsato*] for the minor guilds.

Sixth, [the number of] offices [reserved] for the minor guildsmen [*artefici*], that is, four, remains the same.

Seventh, the drawing of the names [*lo squittino*] for the priors is to be done at the usual time and manner; the selectors [*Arroti*] must have been members of the college, captains of the Party, a guild councilman, or a regulator.[58]

Eighth, all the guild counsellors at this time or their body guard [*compagnio*] may bear arms and may associate with present members of the committee of Eighty and the Signoria.

Ninth, the captains of the Guelf Party cannot bar any rector[59] from holding office for any reason.

Tenth, no one can be barred from office unless a request has been made three days in advance and on the same day taken to the committee of Twenty-four, and it must be proven to them that the individual has [been and] remains a Ghibelline. Then, the captains are to go to

---

55 The Florentine war committee.

56 The Third article is missing.

57 Elections were made by drawing those eligible for office whose names were placed in purses. In the past the Guelf Party had a role in the selection of officers, debarring those they found threatening to their conception of the Florentine state. Now they were stripped of this important privilege.

58 A 'regolatore' was a financial officer. I wish to thank Anthony Molho for this information.

59 These were the lower officers of parishes and communes in the *contado*.

the Signoria with the Twenty-four, and the Signoria will send for the accused with three companions within three days, and a two-thirds majority is required to decide if he is [to be condemned as] a Ghibelline.

Eleventh, no one who has been barred from office and then reinstated can be barred, condemned, or imprisoned again.[60]

Today, 11 July 1378, at night, certain scoundrels roamed through Florence wanting to rob. They went to the convent of the Hermit Friars of the Angels and climbed the walls until they were confronted with a crossbow and bolts. Immediately, they moved on to the neighbourhood of the Cafaggiuolo to the Friars of Settimo, and here entered through the gardens, tore down vines, and cut down several trees. And during the same night they went to the walled garden of Lord Niccolaio Alberti and entered with a ladder, shouting obscenities at the tenants and saying that they ran a brothel. And they entered the garden and caused great damage. And they did the same at the nunnery of the Cestello, calling them whores, and other obscenities. Finally, they left; there were more than a hundred of them, all armed and carrying ladders.

Today, 12 July 1378, they began to make the selections for the Guelf Party at the monastery of the Servites ... [61]

Today, 18 July 1378, between 2 and 4 o'clock in the afternoon a messenger on horseback arrived at Florence. Entering the gate of San Piero Gattolino with an olive branch in his hand, he announced that peace had been made between us and the papacy. Once the messenger had delivered the olive branch to the Palace of the Signoria and the governors had read the letters sent by the pope and our ambassadors reporting that a peace had been signed between us and the pope, the olive branch was hung from a window of the Palace and the great bell was rung to call an assembly of the citizens [Parlamento]. The entire city staged a great party and was filled with joy; everyone rejoiced. They began by putting up the drapery [capoletto] on the rostrum

---

60 The chronicler's record of these laws deviates from those preserved in Register LXVIII of the *Provvisioni*, c.57, which contains eighteen laws; for these, see *Diario*, pp. 364–5. These were the principal constitutional reforms of the first phase of revolt before the Ciompi stormed the Palazzo Signoria.

61 According to the *Cronaca* d'Alamanno Acciaioli (once attributed to Gino Capponi), *Il Tumulto dei Ciompi: Cronache e Memorie*, ed. Gino Scaramella, RIS, XVIII/3 (Bologna, 1917–34), p. 18, they moved from the Palace of the Guelf Party to the friary of the Servites because of the great heat.

[*ringhiera*]⁶² to prepare for the assembly. Then with great ceremony the Signoria sounded the trumpets and made many bonfires, which many people and citizens came to. Here, the notary of the Signoria presided over the assembly and read aloud the letters of the pope, the agreement made between him and us, and the letters from our ambassadors. And that evening, in the Piazza in front of the Palace and in the Piazza and throughout the city of Florence, numerous bonfires were lit and festivities were held in honour of God, the pope, the people and the Guelf Party. And curses and death threats were made against all those citizens, magnates, and merchants [*popolani*], who might wish to destroy or betray the people and commune of Florence. And as should be, these matters [the curses against the enemies of Florence] would have been pleasing to God. Amen.

Today, 20 July 1378 at 7 o'clock, a riot broke out in Florence. Our government officials heard that in Camaldoli and other places, such as San Piero Gattolino and Belletri,⁶³ many had come together and sworn an oath to do great evil, that is, to burn all the houses of the merchant class [*popolani*] and of those who from their positions in the Guelf Party had ruined Florence by barring others from office. Along with them [the rebels of the *popolo minuto*], guildsmen, and their leaders [*capitudine*] wished to punish those who had wanted to ruin Florence. The captains of the guilds listened to what their members wanted to do about these matters but said nothing to our government counsellors [*Signiori*]. Meanwhile, on Monday, 19 July this year, the Signoria had four of the ringleaders [*caporali*], who must have been of these troublemakers [*brigata*], pulled out of their beds in the night.⁶⁴ The next morning the guild artisans and their captains heard that the Signoria wanted to condemn these men to death and sent for a Ser Nuto to execute them. All the captains of the guilds woke up and rushed into the Piazza fully armed and shouted: 'You must hand those

---

62 See Rubinstein, *The Palazzo Vecchio, 1298–1532*: 'In order to make it possible for the *Signoria* to appear before the people in conditions which guaranteed a modicum of safety, a platform was built in 1323' in front of the Palace between its two doors (p. 15).

63 These were some of the poorest neighbourhoods of the city with high concentrations of wool workers. Camaldoli and San Pier Gattolino are located across the Arno, near the walls of the city; Belletri was north of the river in Florence's largest parish, San Lorenzo.

64 The most important of these named by other chroniclers was Sinoncino called Bugigatto from the gate of San Piero Gattolini. The others were from the same working-class parish near the Porta Romana in the southern tip of the city.

men over to us, or we will burn down the Palace'. Then, the crowds of the *popolo minuto* all chanted: 'Long live the People and the Guilds'. The Signoria was then preparing to hand them over, but it did not appear so to the *popolo minuto*. Suddenly they shouted: 'Let's go to the house of the standard-bearer of justice (who was Luigi di Messer Piero Guicciardini)'. And they went and burnt down his house and those of his relatives. And with all this, those four, who had been captured, were released. For the rest of the day, these people went through Florence, burning and torching. The next day, this gang of the people, the captains of the guilds, and the guild artisans took Salvestro di Messer Alamanno, led him to the rostrum, and made him a knight. He went to the houses of Giovanni Dini and Tommaso di Marco and made them knights along with Guccio Dino Gucci and many other citizens. And they [the *popolo minuto*] went to attack the Palace of the Podestà; many were killed and wounded inside and outside the palace. They burnt the door of the palace and created great havoc. They seized the podestà and his men, and then left, having killed and robbed them. Then they went to the Palace of the Executor [of the Ordinances of Justice] and did similar things; then to the Captain of the People and did the same.[65] They then proceeded towards the Palace of the Signoria and proclaimed: 'We want to hang Ser Piero of the *Riformagioni*,[66] and Ser Nuto,[67] who lives in [the parish of] San Giorgio'. And they constructed gallows in the Piazza della Signoria, which they said was to hang the fat cats [*popolani grassi*], and six hangman's ropes were attached to the gallows.

And the Ciompi[68] sent out an order that anybody caught wearing a cloak would be killed without a trial or warning.[69] The people [*giente*] who were in the Piazza and throughout Florence all took off their cloaks from fear of death; and one could not put them back on with them around.[70] On Wednesday, throughout Florence, the *popolo minuto*

65 These were the three tribunals and police forces of Florence.
66 The Government's principal notary, who drafted laws and decrees.
67 The commune's executioner.
68 The rebels of the *popolo minuto*. The chronicler Stefani maintained that the word derived from the time of Walter of Brienne's dictatorship of Florence (1343; see [42, 43]), when workers overheard the French soldiers calling one another 'Compar, allois a boier' and garbled it, by calling themselves '"Ciompo, Ciompo'," and suddenly they were all Ciompi, that is, comrades'. However, most linguists now dispute this interpretation.
69 I do not understand the reason or significance of this law; nor does the editor Gherardi explain it.

were told that Migliore Guadagni⁷¹ was coming from the Valdinievole and would invade Florence with five thousand soldiers. The news touched raw nerves, and for the entire day the *popolo minuto* did every sort of evil: they tore up all the official documents in the palace; they broke into government buildings, burnt them, and did all sorts of evil. On Wednesday night, when the soldiers of the Signoria went to lock the gates of the city, they [the rebels] grabbed them and took away their keys, because they were nervous about those soldiers they had heard were coming from the Valdinievole. As a result, this gang and the people stayed up all Wednesday night guarding all the gates and bridges. They took over any place that might be vulnerable in case this army might arrive. And they stayed up all night in fear. On Thursday morning, in the middle of the first third of the day, they discussed among themselves [and decided that] all the purses, from which the names of the ruling class of Florence [*reggimento*] were drawn, should be burnt and new selections [*squittino*] made. And they demanded that two [new guilds] of the *popolo minuto* should be called into being, and that Tommaso Brancacci and Brancazio [di Berto Borsi, the two priors from the Quarter of Santo Spirito], should be forced to leave the Palace [of the Signoria].⁷² If they refused, they'd be cut to pieces. Seeing that this was their order, the Signoria sent Lord Guerriante Margniollo out of the Palace to bow to the gang's desires. And thus these knights [*cavalieri*] were saddened; painfully, they returned to their houses, one after another, saddened and in pain.⁷³ Immediately, they sent for Lord Salvestro and this people [*popolo minuto*] entered our Palace of the Signoria. They sent for Giovanni Dini and other citizens to make new laws for the country and to call up whomever they pleased to comprise this *popolo minuto* and their Guild. God give them whatever it takes to keep this city at peace. On Thursday they sent for their comrades who had been guarding the gates and made them return the keys of the gates to the Palace of the Signoria. And immediately they arrested the notary Ser Nuto Pieri from Città di Castello or Assisi,⁷⁴ who had come to execute those four

70 I do not understand the significance of these cloaks, except that they were worn by the rich and could be used for concealing weapons.
71 A wealthy cloth manufacturer of Florence, who came onto the political scene in 1358 when elected as one of the four *popolani* of the eight captains of the Guelf Party; see Brucker, *Florentine Politics and Society*, pp. 165–6.
72 In other words, resign their posts.
73 I believe he is referring to the rulers in the Palazzo Signoria.
74 All the other chroniclers identified him as from Città di Castello in Umbria.

THE REVOLT OF THE CIOMPI, 1378-82

who had been captured.[75] He left the Palace along with the priors with his face and head shaven and dressed in the armour of the commune so as not to be recognised. He checked into an inn in the via Vinegia.[76] Meantime, a soldier emerged and went into the Piazza of the Signoria and asked a standard-bearer of the *popolo minuto*,[77] and then the others: 'What will you give me, if I tell you where Ser Nuto is?[78] And they asked, 'What do you want?' He answered, 'I ask for no more than the money in his pockets'. They responded: 'it's a deal'. This soldier then came forward and people followed him. When Ser Nuto heard this rioting of the people, he took off his armour and threw himself under his bed in the inn. They went up the stairs and gave him many blows, but he would not come out from under the bed. Wounded, they dragged him out of his inn and led him by the arms to the entrance of our Office of the Gabelles.[79] He cried, 'Oh, me, will I be hanged? Go ahead, kill me'. Then, someone unexpectedly jumped up and gave him a big blow with an axe across the head, chopping him in two; then they tore him apart at the armpit with his brains spurting out and blood spewing all across the street where the lions were kept.[80] They then dragged him along the ground to the foot of the gallows in the Piazza of the Priors, where they hanged him by the feet. Here all the people cut off little pieces of him and stuck them to their lances and axes and carried them around the city, through the streets, and into the suburbs. And in his breeches were found four gold florins and perhaps forty shillings, which were given to the soldier who had informed the *popolo minuto* of Ser Nuto's whereabouts.

Then, these men who were in the Palace of the Signoria sent messengers out to all the citizens and to all the churches, ordering them to bring their banners and pennants to the people who were up there in the Palace [of the Signoria].

---

75 The four leaders of the *popolo minuto* apprehended in the early hours of 19 July but released later that day.

76 A street still so named running north from the Piazza della Signoria.

77 In concentrating on the political violence, the chronicler fails to report that those from the new guilds of the *popolo minuto* now had rights of citizenship, to elect and be elected to the highest echelons of the Florentine state.

78 None of the chroniclers identified this Ser Nuto with any clarity; see Gherardi, 'Prefazione', and note n. 5, p. 368.

79 The office for drawing up and collecting indirect taxes.

80 The via de' Leoni, still so named, behind the Palazzo della Signoria, where the Commune kept its lions – vital symbols of the republic.

That evening at 6 o'clock, the standard-bearer of justice sent an order from the councillors of the guild of the *popolo minuto* that no one of whatever status or condition was to commit any villainous deeds against our podestà, the captain of the people, or the executor [of the Ordinances of Justice] on pain of loss of life and property, that is, the *popolo minuto* should not in their fury commit any villainous deeds against these three rectors.

Today, 23 July, this year, the priors were called to step forward, that is, the Twelve and the standard-bearers of the companies [the sixteen *gonfalonieri* or districts of the city]. These priors were Michele di Lando, the standard-bearer [of Justice],[81] Giovanni d'Agnolo Capponi, Lioncino di Francino, Salvestro, a dyer, Bonaccorso del Lamiera, Benedetto di Tendi, a slipper maker, Giovanni Bartoli, a drug wholesaler, Spinello Borsi, and Salvestro, a kiln builder.

The standard-bearers [of the neighbourhoods were]: Bruno di Pagolo, stable master, Lorenzo di Donato, dyer, Lionardo di Iacopo, money changer, Gottolo di Ciardo di Banco, Giovanni di Cambio de' Medici, Baldo di Lapo, wool-cloth finisher, Michele Ciapi, armourer, Filippo di Forbosco, bed-cover maker, Mezza di Iacopo di Mezza, Lorenzo Pucci Cambini, Lorenzo del Toso, linen-maker, Niccolò di Vanni, tanner, Giovanni di Giovanni, Guido di Filippo Fagni, Bonaiuto di Giovanni, napper [*cardaiuolo*].[82]

The Twelve: Francesco Fantoni, vintner, Priore di Feduccio Falconi, Lorenzo di Riccomanno, wool carder [*iscardassiere*][83], Niccolò di Lorenzo, blacksmith, Duccio di Caroccio degli Alberti, Domenico Chiavaccini, washer of wool, Giovanni di Cione, stable master, Francesco di Chele, furrier, Piero d'Andrea, weaver, Agniolo di Bindo, carder, Simone di Biagio, armour maker, Giovanni Panoli di Ser Bartolo.

And today, 24 July of this year, this *popolo minuto* put their own men in the respective palaces of the Signoria, the Podestà, the Captain of the People, and the Executor. And that night the standard-bearer of the guilds and the priors of the people decreed that anyone could buy

---

81 The highest elected officer of the Florentine republic.

82 *Cardaiuolo*: a dealer in teasels used to make the loose fibres of woollen yarn rise up into a nap by scratching; see Florence Edler, *Glossary of Medieval Terms of Business, Italian Series 1200–1600* (Cambridge, MA, 1934), pp. 63–4.

83 One of the most menial or proletarised tasks in the wool industry, the *scardassatori* or *scardazzieri* worked for day wages and in central workshops under the control of an industrial entrepreneur; see Edler, *Glossary of Medieval Terms of Business*, pp. 259–60.

and sell grain and flour without paying the gabelle from that day for the next six months.

And today, the same day, they were given their banners [*gonfaloni*] in the usual way with the same insignia as before. And they crossed the Piazza [of the Signoria] with their patrol and swore allegiance on the rostrum in the usual manner. Then the banners and pennants were passed out in the usual way. The Piazza was filled with all the guildsmen, and the *popolo minuto* was armed with every sort of weapon; the Palace was filled to the brim, all the way up to the great bell above and stuffed with all the banners of all the guilds, pouring out of the windows, hanging over the rostrum. Banners and flags of all the guilds and of their captains were everywhere, and yet there was no conflict.

And on this day, the government issued a decree: when the banners were returned and hung from the houses of the citizens, the guild artisans, and the *popolo minuto*, everyone must open their shops and warehouses and practise their trades. And everyone, regardless of standing or condition, must now disarm, since now none of the rich and powerful [*le famiglie*] would try to do anything rash.

And today, 25 July in the morning, as was the custom, the banners were handed out to the companies.[84]

That night at midnight, a decree was issued that all those banned from city and *contado* of Florence could stay in Florence until the middle of August, when they would be sent again into exile, and that no one should harm them, on pain of losing their lives and property.

And late that night, other decrees were issued: no one should transfer or carry any of their goods from one house to another, and no one should create any disturbance or go to a friend's house armed on pain of death and loss of property.

And today, 27 July 1378, our Signoria decreed that those who owed *prestanze*,[85] gabelles, or other taxes, would have until the middle of August to pay them at the given rate without incurring any penalties. But those who did not pay within that time would be arrested and their property confiscated.

Also, they issued an order for all the crossbowmen and their captains to go immediately with their arms and crossbows to the Piazza, where they would be paid.

84 These would be the sixteen neighbourhood militia of the city.
85 Forced loans levied on those living within the city walls of Florence.

And today, 28 July 1378, the crossbowmen were fully armed in the Piazza della Signoria with their arms and crossbows, all waiting in the courtyard of the lord captain [of the people]. Immediately, their names were recorded; they were inspected and paid. In all there were a thousand crossbowmen under the command of forty constables with forty pennants. Two-hundred-and-fifty were assigned to each brigade with various pennants for the quarters of the city – ten pennants for the quarter of Santo Spirito, and the same for Santa Croce, San Giovanni, and Santa Maria Novella. They all formed a squadron [*drappello*] in the Piazza della Signoria. As soon as this had been done, they marched through Florence, making a fine show and displaying how well they were equipped. And it is said that they did the same in the *contado*.

When they were parading in the Piazza della Signoria, soldiers from Rome arrived, who were asked for news and they said it was positive, but I don't know what they said. In the morning the Signoria issued a decree, ordering all weapon makers to open their shops; similarly, moneylenders must allow people to buy and exchange money.

Also they decreed that all the podestà in our *contado* are denied further offices but they may remain in office until the completion of their terms but for no longer.

And that no one should dare to take up the office of podestà or castellan without first swearing an oath of office to our Signoria, under a certain penalty.

And today, 31 July 1378, the *popolo minuto* burnt all the names that had been put in the electoral purses. That is, those eligible for the offices of the priors, the Twelve, the standard-bearers of the companies, and all the castellans and podestà in the countryside [*podesterie*]. They wished to draw new names for all these offices.

The first of August 1378.

On this day at 5 in the evening our Signoria issued a decree announced by their crier that all merchants and guild artisans in the name of God were to practise their trades, open their warehouses and shops, and ply their trade diligently, and no one of whatever rank or condition should abuse anyone and should know that such an act would be punished severely.

And that no one was allowed to say anything against our Signoria or else suffer whatever penalties the Signoria might wish to impose.

And today, 3 August, our Signoria decreed that a bushel [*staio*] of salt would cost 60 shillings and a bushel of unrefined salt [*saline*], 40 shillings, and those in the *contado* would pay 40 shillings per bushel of salt and 30 for unrefined salt.

And today, 5 August of this year, news arrived at 9 in the morning that we were no longer excommunicated.[86] And at that hour mass was sung at Santa Maria Novella, which was on the feast day of Saint Dominic and Saint Mary of the Snow.[87] It was hailed as though we were in heaven.

On the night of the same day, our Signoria set a bonfire in front of their palace, and similarly throughout the city in praise of the Almighty God and all the saints of heaven.

Today, 6th of this month, at 10 in the morning our Signoria sent a notice through Florence that anyone who possesses [any fortress in the *contado* or district of Florence, which is not under Florentine custody] must appear before the Signoria within eight days and swear allegiance with a handshake.[88]

And no one of whatever rank or condition should presume to say anything against the state on pain of loss of life and property.

Anyone knowing someone who possesses illegally any property belonging to the commune must inform the commune and he will be compensated well for the information.

And on the 8th a decree ordered everyone to go to [Baptistry of] San Giovanni[89] to accompany the members of our Signoria and to hear a mass for peace, the honour of God, good fortune, and the state, and to support the people, the guilds, and the commune of Florence.

Today, on 9 August 1378, a new selection for the Signoria began.

Today, the 9th, it is said in Florence that a treaty or indeed a true peace was signed in Lombardy between Lord Bernabò,[90] the lords of

---

86 During Florence's war with the papacy, Gregory XI had excommunicated the city-state.
87 These two feast days happen to fall on 5 August.
88 The meaning is vague in the chronicle, but Gherardi has provided the original Latin version found in *Il Libro di Deliberazioni*, p. 372, and I have translated the essential parts in brackets.
89 Florence's baptistery, across from the Cathedral in the Piazza del Duomo.
90 Lord Bernabò Visconti, the lord of Milan.

Verona,[91] and the marquis of Ferrara. We know no more about this. God help us.[92]

Today, the 9th, our Signoria announced through Florence that all citizens of Florence who happened to be in the *contado* or within ten miles of it must return to Florence within four days; those wealthy citizens [*popolani*] who did not return within this period would be made magnates and those who were magnates would be turned into supermagnates, except those who were in exile or had been sent outside the city for their bad behaviour.[93]

Today, the 9th, the Signoria announced through Florence that all those taxed in the *contado* must pay their tax [*lira*],[94] less one-third of what they were assessed in their survey [*del loro estimo*].

Today, the 9th, the Signoria announced through Florence that anyone who possessed grain or wheat in the *contado* must deposit it in the city of Florence by 18 August, or the grain would be confiscated; no excuses would be accepted ...

Tuesday morning, 10 August, the grain officials [*Ufficiali dell' abondanza*] issued a notice that all the rectors in the *contado* and district of Florence must appear before our Signoria within four days to swear an oath of allegiance or else be penalised.

And today, 10 August 1378, Friar Agostino from Scarperia, our preacher,[95] announced in [the church of] Santo Spirito, that we were reunited with the church and absolved from every excommunication and are blessed again. (He showed us the papal letter [*brivilegio*], which he received from the pope and his vicar general.) We can now go everywhere in spiritual health and be saved, and we can buy and sell merchandise throughout the world. Praise be and thanks to the Omnipotent Lord, his Blessed Mother, Our Lady Mary, all the saints

---

91 An ancient city and major medieval town about 100 km west of Venice.
92 It turned out to be only a temporary ceasefire, not a peace; see Gherardi, note 5, p. 372. Such a peace would strengthen the hand of Florence's rival Milan, even though the war against the papacy had brought the two sides together.
93 On the special conditions and penalties for being declared a magnate, see earlier documents on the Ordinances of Justice [26, 28–9] and the introductory remarks to the Italian section of chapter I.
94 A combination of a head and property tax based on a land survey or *estimo*.
95 Davidsohn, 'L'avo di Niccolò Machiavelli', p. 45, uses this reference as further proof that the anonymous diarist was Buoninsegno Machiavelli, because the Machiavelli palace was nearby Santo Spirito.

of heaven, and to the people of Christendom that God always allows us to adopt His will. Amen.

Today, 10 August 1378, at 6 at night in Galluzzo[96] a Lord Michele de' Pigi of Volterra with eight horsemen and three foot soldiers attacked four men from Volterra, who were coming to Florence, trespassing their boundaries of exile. And on that very day they were attacked and fatally wounded. A young man accompanying Lord Michele stood at the door of an inn in Galluzzo, waiting for these four victims of Volterra and alerted Lord Michele: 'Here come your enemies'. Lord Michele and his gang then came out [of the inn] and fatally wounded these men from Volterra. One of the foot soldiers later returned to retrieve a lance he had left with the innkeeper at Galluzzo. He was recognised and taken to Florence. I do not know if he will die or be spared.[97]

Today, 11 August 1378, our Signoria decreed that all who had been taxed by the tax to raise forty-thousand gold florins must have paid it in full by 12 August.

Today, 13 August 1378, a law was passed forbidding anyone transporting grain out of our *contado* under the penalty of losing the grain, his fodder, and animals.

Today, a law was passed forbidding anyone of whatever rank or condition from speaking out against the state of our Signoria, or against the *popolo minuto*; anyone who accuses another will be believed.

Today, 14 August, a decree was issued that anyone possessing or knowing the whereabouts of rebel property must make it known within eight days and the same for those possessing or knowing about goods belonging to the commune. The informers will be paid two shillings per pound [of the property's value].

Today, 16 August, a decree was issued that anyone who owes money or has contracted to pay someone must keep to the agreement.

Today, on the morning of 17 August, the Emergency committee of Twelve (*XII della balìa*) issued an ordinance that if anyone knows of anyone in possession of any quantity of money belonging to the commune of Florence and makes an accusation, he will be believed.

Today, 17 August, it was decreed that anyone possessing land in the

---

96 A suburban village south of Florence.
97 This case appears in the criminal records of the Capitano del Popolo.

contado must come before our Signoria and declare it [for tax purposes] within eight days on pain of loss of life and property.

Today 18 August, a decree announced that each and every citizen who possesses grain or wheat in the *contado* must deliver it to the city of Florence during the month of August, and if he fails to do so within this time, he will be forced to forfeit the grain or fodder. Every [village] rector and syndic[98] must bring charges [against such offenders] or be fined 25 florins, and the same goes for any man who fails to give evidence.[99]

Today 18 August, letters arrived from Rome addressed to merchants in Florence; thirteen cardinals acused the pope of being a heretic and lacking spirituality [*paterino*].[100]

Today 19 August, the officials of the crossbowmen [decreed that the crossbowmen] of the quarter of San Giovanni should go immediately to the square of their officials with their arms and crossbows, receive their pay, and go with good will wherever they are ordered.

Today, 21 August, the electoral process was completed in the name of God.

Today, 25 August, our Signoria decreed that any citizen or person from the *contado* who possesses a fortress, must swear allegiance [to the commune] by 28 August, and this should be done before the judge of the gabelles with good and sufficient numbers of guarantors. And he who does not pledge his fortress within this time will suffer whatever penalty they wish to apply.

And today, the same day, a ban was issued that anyone owing money or taxes [*prestanze*] to the Commune must pay at the established rate by the end of the month.

---

98 A locally elected secular official. On these officers and their duties, see Cohn, *The Laboring Classes*, pp. 198–200.

99 The commune was always anxious about the supply of grain to the city and the hoarding of stores. Most of Italy and places north of the Alps had experienced severe crop failures and scarcity in 1375. However, 1378 was not a year of dearth in Tuscany and 1377 had in fact produced a bumper crop.

100 *Grande Dizionario della lingua italiana* (Turin, 1961–2002), XII, p. 816; The encyclical of the thirteen rebel cardinals, the French cardinals who declared themselves to have excommunicated Pope Urban VI. On 20 September 1378 they elected in his place Robert of Geneva, who took the name of Clement VII and the schism began; see *The Popes: A Concise Biography*, pp. 276–7.

Today, 27 August, the office of the priests [*avillari*][101] and the emergency committee of Sixteen[102] decreed that anyone who had deposited money derived from the property of the priests must identify it as property of the priests.

Today, 27 August, the Officials of the Property of Rebels decreed that anyone wishing to purchase the property that had belonged to Lord Lapo da Castiglionchio[103] should come before them; they will sell it to the highest bidder. [He then lists thirty-one Florentines from prominent families with the towns presumably where they were then in exile.]

Today, 28 August, at noon, a riot [*rumore*] broke out in Florence after all the guilds found out that the syndics and the Signoria had agreed to pass certain decrees [*provigione*] – concerning [governmental] salaries, who was allowed to bear arms, who could band together, form an army, and carry their own insignia. Once those outside heard this, the *popolo minuto* and all the guilds armed under their banners, flags, and insignia, assembled in the Piazza [*della Signoria*], and said to the syndics and the Signoria: 'We are not happy with what you have done'. Then the Signoria replied to the guilds and the *popolo minuto*: 'Tell us what you want from us and we will more or less do it'. And Lord Luca da Panzano, who was a knight of the people [*popolo*] of Florence, resigned from the government and wanted to be made and was made a knight of the *popolo minuto*; a great uprising ensued.[104]

And with matters as they were, the wool merchants with the banner of the wool guild [*l'arte della lana*] entered the Piazza. The *popolo minuto* all chanted: 'We do not want you'.[105] Then Gentile di Salvestro Bonfiglioli, who had the banner of the wool guild in his hand, carried it up front to place it on the rostrum alongside the banners of the other guilds. But the others did not want to let him hang it there. At

---

101 Office that oversaw the confiscation and sale of church property during Florence's war against the papacy (1375–78).

102 Should be the Twelve.

103 From one of the ancient clans of Florence; from the 1360s he had been the leader of the aristocrats in the Florentine *contado* and a stalwart of the Guelf Party; see Brucker, *The Civic World*, pp. 31–3.

104 The turncoat magnate became the leader of the last and most radical phase of the Ciompi revolt, that of the Eight of Santa Maria Novella, whose coup to change the constitution failed at the beginning of September.

105 Those of the wool guild were the bosses, who had lorded over the *popolo minuto*, most of whom had been underlings [*sottoposti*] in the wool industry.

that moment, a crossbowman pulled his bow and shot his large bolt at the young man; it passed through his breastplate and two [padded] doublets, seriously wounding him on his side and remained stuck in his side as he was carried off wounded on a plank to his home. They then tore off a piece of the banner of the wool guild. And then, with this piece in the hands of people and the guilds, they felt guilty and put it back on the wool-guild banner. And when it [the banner] came into the Piazza, they were friends. From the middle of this, Lord Luca with his brigade pushed their way towards the Palace of the Guelf Party, some reluctantly, to grab the Party's banner and take it into the Piazza. But many did not like this and refused to follow. And had Lord Luca returned there on Sunday [the next day], I fear he would have caught some heat other than that from the sun. Already, the people were beginning to ask: 'Do you wish to betray us'?

Today, 29 August, our lord priors waited all day for the results of those eligible for office [*tratta*]. The Piazza was completely filled with armed men with the banners of all the guilds. And all day rioting broke out and many questions were asked of our rulers. Finally, towards night our lord priors drew the names. Many times, those who were armed wanted to fight; many times, they hurled villainous words against citizens in the Piazza and in the [street of the] Vacchereccia.[106] They were prepared to shoot arrows into the unarmed crowds. Once night fell, all returned to their houses. But things stayed tense that entire day.

Today, 31 August, at 7 in the morning, the *popolo minuto* assembled in Santa Maria Novella, San Frediano, and Sant'Ambrogio[107] to organise an uprising and disgrace Florence. With uprisings of the *popolo minuto* happening every day, guildsmen began to ask themselves: 'Who is it who every day creates unrest in our country?' They agreed that these people did not want peace, and that those in the Palace were not unified. Suddenly, as intelligent men, the guildsmen rallied: 'Let us all take the bit between our teeth; otherwise we and Florence will be defeated'. Thus with the grace of God, all the guild craftsmen [*artefici*][108] assembled together in the Piazza with their guilds, their arms, banners,

---

106 A small street that leads from the Piazza della Signoria to Por Santa Maria, named after the tower of the Della Vacca family; see Piero Bargellini and Ennio Guarnieri, *Le strade di Firenze* (Florence, 1986), VI, p. 186.

107 Parishes comprised largely of artisans and workers in the wool industry.

108 These would have been minor guildsmen and not the *popolani* or wealthier shopkeepers and merchants of both the minor and major guilds.

THE REVOLT OF THE CIOMPI, 1378-82

and insignia, ready to defend the people and the guilds of Florence. And in the midst of this, our standard-bearer, Michele di Lando, came forward as the sage of the Palace, carrying the banner of Justice in his hand. With one of his comrades in the Signoria, he mounted his horse, and they rode through most of Florence, screaming: 'Long live the *Popolo Minuto* and the Guilds' and afterwards returned to the Palace. And all day the guildsmen stood armed in the Piazza and nearby were the forces of the *popolo minuto* with their insignia of the angel. As intelligent men, sensing the tension and trying to avoid anything bad from happening, our Signoria ordered all the banners and insignia of the guilds to be put in the Palace to end this disgrace. Meanwhile, one of our Signoria, named Lioncino, saw that the *popolo minuto* did not wish to give up their standard, the one of the angel, and went over to them and asked: 'What do you want to do? Can't you see that all the other guilds have given us their banners, but you refuse to give up yours?' They responded: 'We will then be left without an insignia'. And they demanded: 'Then give us another banner'. And Lioncino said to them: 'But there is no other one, except the one of justice'. They replied: 'Then, give us the old one'. But he said it was no longer there. Then Leoncino returned upstairs to his comrades, who said: 'Let's do what they want'. Our Signoria became indignant seeing that the guilds were obedient but that there were malcontents among the *popolo minuto*, who wished not to obey. And in this mess, the *popolo minuto* made threatening moves against the guild craftsmen, taunting them: 'We'll see who'll chase us from the Piazza'. Then a brigade of the *popolo minuto* began drawing back their crossbows. Seeing this, the guild artisans said among themselves: 'We will no longer tolerate their treachery'. Then, all the guildsmen, who were well armed, threw themselves on them, pushing them back as far as the church of San Pulinari.[109] They gave it to them, cutting them down, killing many; that is, around twenty were killed and more than thirty wounded. Having been well punished, they returned home at night; some here, some there. And at midnight, our standard-bearers woke us, calling us from one house to another, to make us all aware of what was going on.[110] And they [*popolo minuto*] said they would set the place ablaze. On hearing that they wished to burn down the city, our Signoria

---

109 Sant'Apollinare: a small parish church in the Quarter of Santa Croce within the Roman walls of the city centre, about a hundred metres from front entrance to the Palazzo Signoria.

110 As Gherardi indicates, the text is obscure at this point.

sounded their bells and those of all the churches of Florence for a good two hours. Now, with day breaking, a decree was issued commanding everyone to arm himself under his banner and come into the Piazza of the Signoria, and whoever refused could be killed without a trial or authorisation.

Today, Wednesday, 1 September, in the name of God, our Signoria entered office. They were Bartolomeo di Iacopo Costa, wool comber, standard-bearer of justice,[111] Michele Carelli, barrel maker, Agnolo Tigliamochi, wool manufacturer, Taddeo, embroiderer at the Terme,[112] Giovanni d'Ugolino, blacksmith, Giovanni del Tria, wool carder,[113] Domenico di Bindo Gili, Becco, blacksmith, Benincasa di Francesco, shearer. Ser Luca Bambocci, their notary.

Today, Wednesday, 1 September in the morning, the Signoria commanded all the crossbowmen of the city of Florence to assemble with their crossbows immediately in the [church] of San Piero Scheraggio; they must hand over their hooks [for bending the crossbow] and their bolts, or be penalised with the loss of a foot.[114]

On that day at nine [in the morning], a master carpenter was murdered on the rostrum.

Later in the day, everyone was ordered to be armed behind their neighbourhood banner and march into the Piazza della Signoria on pain of loss of life and property. Then, with these forces fully armed behind their banners, all were present in the Piazza. When the *popolo minuto* saw this handsome assembly with their banners, immediately they decided to have nothing to do with the Piazza, and all of them left with dignity; no one was hurt. With all the banners thus in place, news came that people had gathered outside the gate of San Frediano[115] and had put ladders against the city walls. Carrying their banners, all the forces [in the Piazza] went on horseback in search of these men; they looked everywhere but found none of them.

On the morning of 2 September, the standard-bearer of justice[116] and Lord Giorgio degli Scali as prior of the Quarter of Santa Maria Novella

---

111 Corrected to Francesco di Chele, dealer in second-hand clothes.
112 A street in central Florence that passes parallel to the Arno on the northern side.
113 Corrected to Lord Giorgio degli Scali.
114 This and the following decrees are not found in any other chronicler.
115 A working-class district at the far western part of the city, south of the Arno.
116 Francesco di Chele, a used-clothes dealer.

were drawn [elected]. God grant them the courage to do their jobs, to restore the good and peaceful state of the people and the guilds of the commune of Florence, and to bring all the traitors of the city and *contado* of Florence to a bad end and death.

Today, 2 September, our lord priors decreed that all the crossbowmen of the city of Florence must bring their bows, hooks, and bolts immediately to the armoury [*Camera del Arme*] and should know that whoever refuses will have his house torched by those carrying the banner of liberty and will be worse off than sold slaves.

Today, the same day, a decree was issued at vespers: between now and Sunday all wool carders, wool beaters, and wool finishers must bring all their weapons, both offensive and defensives ones, to the Treasury of the Commune of Florence, or be fined 25 pounds and, if they should try to hide them, 50 pounds.

And on that day, those from the district [*gonfalone*] of the Golden Lion[117] marched through Florence, went towards Cuculia,[118] and destroyed a house belonging to a wool carder.

And on that day a Fleming named Giannino was killed in the house of a certain dell'Asino; a son of Pieruzzo della Petraia, named Antonio, killed him. At once, the murderer's head was cut off in the piazza of Sant'Apollinare [*San Pulinare*]. Today, one must always be on guard not to inflict wounds or commit murder.

Today at 6 in the evening, a letter was put in the hands of Lord Vieri di Gherardo [de' Bardi][119] and the messenger fled immediately. Lord Vieri then brought it straight to the Palace of the Signoria.

That night, a decree proclaimed that a new council would be formed, comprised of certain syndics who would advise on what should be done.

On that day, the captains of the Guelf Party presented Michele di Lando with a beautiful horse, a flag bearing the arms of the Guelf Party, and a beautiful helmet of beaver fur [*barbuta*]. They did well in doing this excellent deed, which he certainly deserved.

---

117 One of four of the gonfaloni of the quarter of San Giovanni.
118 An area to the west of Santo Spirito towards the city walls with vineyards and olive groves; see Davidsohn, *Storia di Firenze*, I, p. 1122.
119 One of those who had been knighted by the Ciompi in July.

Today, 3 September, our Signoria issued a decree ordering all the captains of the crossbowmen and their men to turn in their insignia, crossbows, hooks, and bolts at their offices in Santa Cecilia[120] by the end of the day or be punished by losing a foot ...

Today, it was decreed that no one should injure anyone who had been banished.

And on this day, it was ordered that all crossbowmen must carry their bows all day long or be fined 50 pounds.

And no one should attack another regardless of status or condition on pain of loss of life and property; anyone who turned in someone who had offended another of the city, *contado*, or district could collect 500 pounds from the commune of Florence, if brought back alive, and 200 pounds, if dead. And any person ordered by his district standard-bearer to stand guard must do so or be fined 20 shillings for every time he failed to show up; 10 shillings going to the one who reported him and 10 to the commune of Florence.

Today, 3 September at 6 in the evening, our Signoria issued a decree, that all the wool workers, that is the beaters [*iscamatini*] and cleaners [*divettini*][121], must take all their weapons, both offensive and defensive ones, to the armoury by Sunday, the 10th of this month, or be fined 100 pounds. In order to find out who had not turned in their weapons, the officials would launch a secret inquiry and would not accept any excuses.

Today, 4 September 1378 our Signoria issued a decree prohibiting anyone from the city, *contado*, or district harbouring any wool carder, comber, or beater on pain of loss of life and property.

Today, the same day, the committee of Eight responsible for the safety of the city, *contado*, and district [called the *Otto di Guardia*][122] issued an ordinance that no one in the city should dare to assemble ten or more persons, unless authorised by the standard-bearers of the companies or the standard-bearers of the guilds, on pain of loss of life and property.

120 A small church located in the centre of Florence.
121 One who removes the knots and bits of skin from raw wool.
122 The *Otto di Guardia*: a new criminal magistracy created in September, 1378, that practised summary justice, avoiding the due process upheld by the three medieval criminal magistracies of Florence – the podestà, captain of the people, and the executor of the Ordinances of Justice. It lasted through the early-modern period. Although it focuses on this court's early-modern history, see John Brackett, *Criminal Justice and Crime in late Renaissance Florence, 1537–1607* (Cambridge, 1992).

Today, the same day, the Signoria decreed that all those residing in the *contado* of Florence must pay their taxes [*estimo*], less a third of what they usually paid and must pay half the salt tax in the usual manner. Similarly, citizens of Florence must pay the salt tax at the rate of three pounds and at 40 shillings for raw salt [*salina*]. And any of the Ciompi who wishes to return to his home in Florence may do so.

Today, 5 September, the heads of two men, who had been members of the committee of Eight of Emergency, were cut off in the Piazza Signoria – Matteo di Ser Salvi Gai and Tambo, who stayed at the end of the piazza of Santo Spirito. They had tried to bring Florence to ruin. Good riddance!

Today, 6 September, the Eight of the Guard [*Otto della Guardia*] for the city, *contado*, and district of Florence decreed that no one of whatever rank or condition could go about at night with or without weapons after the third ringing of the bells, unless authorized by the deputies of the Eight; and if so deputised, he cannot bring others along with him or be fined 10 pounds per violation. And the name of anyone who has not been authorized or who passes by force will be handed over to the Signoria.

[After 6 September, the chronicler returns mostly to business as usual and to news from elsewhere in Italy. I have selected only those reports that reflect the social and political tensions that remained in the city.]

[p. 384] 10 September, all the captains of the guilds came into Florence to the Palace [of the Signoria]. They came for their banners, which were in the Palace, and left with great celebrations and honour to the irritation of the Ciompi, thieves, traitors, robbers, murderers, assassins, gluttons, and felons.

Today 9 September 1378[123] our Signoria declared that all the crossbowmen of the city of Florence who had been paid from the first of July 1378 until now must deposit their bows in the armoury by 11 September or lose a foot ...

Today, 16 September, our Signoria declared that no one could bear arms, offensive or defensive ones, or play games of chance [*zara*], or go about at night, unless they have been deputised by the Eight. Anyone

---

[123] This entry of the 9th is out of sequence, following the previous one of the 10th of September.

of the *popolo minuto* may return and work in the city of Florence, except rebels, those under investigation, and those condemned or in exile from the city, *contado*, and district of Florence. And every man must bring his weapons to the armoury, that is, all the crossbows that were commissioned by the commune of Florence, and swear before the lord executor [of the Ordinances of Justice] to maintain the state and honour of the people, the commune, and the guilds of the commune of Florence. Amen.

Today, 17 September, forty-four men, who had been among the Ciompi – wool carders, thieves, robbers, murderers of every sort – were exiled from the entire [territory of] Florence.

Those mentioned below had been against the state of the commune of Florence. [36 of the 44 are listed, starting with Lord Luca di Totto da Panzano, leader of the final and radical phase of the revolt of the Ciompi – the Otto di Santa Maria Novella; Stefani makes a similar list. There are discrepancies between the two; the original sentences no longer survive.]

Today, 25 September, our Signoria declared that anyone who had been attacked in person or in property by another since the first of June could submit a petition to the Signoria, and it would be acted on sympathetically ...

[p. 386] Today, 1 October, our Signoria decreed that no one of whatever rank or condition should leave the city through the walls or by the Arno at night or he would be shot and killed by the crossbowmen on guard without trial or warning ...

Today, 15 October, Matteo son of Lord Luca da Panzano was captured ... and fled. They say he confessed that certain plots had been hatched to take place in Florence. For this reason, the city's horse race [*il palio*] will not run ...

[p. 387] On 25 October at midnight, it was decided to send Lord Lapo da Castiglionchio into exile at Barcelona. If anyone should kill him outside Barcelona, he would receive a thousand gold florins from the commune of Florence ...

[p. 389] Today, 20 December, a riot broke out in Florence at vespers, but nothing came of it.

Today, 22 December, at nine in the morning, another uprising was staged, but it amounted to nothing.

Today, 27 December 1378, Lord Luca da Panzano arrived in Santa

Maria Impruneta[124] with many of his troops. Once he arrived, news travelled to Florence, and soldiers rode there immediately. Having heard that he had been discovered, he marched out. Many scattered but who knows where. The Florentine troops chased them and led five back to Florence. The next day, the 28th, they were beheaded. Good riddance! ...

In 1368, a Friar Minor prophesised what would happen in the future, claiming it came from the prophecies of the prophet Daniel; the pope threw him in prison. [He predicted the following:] ...

That year [1378] will be filled continually with strange novelties, fears, and horrors, such that the worms of the earth will cruelly devour lions, leopards, and wolves. And blackbirds and other small birds will despise the greed of birds of prey.

Also, at this time, the wealthy citizens [*popolani*] and commoners [*giente minuta*] will kill all the tyrants and false traitors, which will include many princes and powerful lords, deposing them from their status and grandeur.

And he foretold that at this time there will appear one from the East, who will be called the Antichrist. Followers from Judaea will say and believe that he is their Messiah, and they will bring great afflictions to the Christians, such that all the churches in many places of the world will be destroyed; few, hardly one in ten, will remain faithful to Christ.

Also, at this time the Turks, Saracens, Tartars, and other infidels will rise up against the Christian people, devastating part of Italy, conquering Bologna and many other regions of Italy; they will also stay in Hungary and parts of Germany. And this will last for three-and-a-half years.

Also at this time, great and wondrous torments and storms will descend from the heavens, causing floods greater than any since the Great Flood. And there will be great famine and death, killing off some of the evil ones. And the churches will be despoiled of all their earthly wealth. And false prophets will lead the common people to do these things. Only then will the clergy and wealthy citizens be happy to have only the necessities of life.

[Between 1379 and 1382, the Diarist describes numerous attempts by Florentine exiles to bring down the government of the Minor Guildsmen:]

---

124 Hill town 16 km south of Florence.

[p. 406] Today, 19 December 1379, Sunday night, certain men carrying the insignia of the Guelf Party and other insignia were captured inside and outside the gate of San Niccolò.[125] As a result, on Monday morning, shops and warehouses did not open. It was said that many people were plotting to bring this state down. Thus, in the same morning, Lord Benedetto degli Alberti and Lord Tommaso di Marco degli Strozzi rode through Florence, all morning long with our soldiers, both on foot and on horseback, to guard the city of Florence. And the Genoese crossbowmen were placed in the Palace to protect our Signoria and the Palace.

Today, from 19 to 20 December, unrest spread through Florence when certain plots were disclosed ...

[p. 407] Nencio del Cieco and his troops [compagnia] carried the Guelf Party's coats of arms and other standards, but he was defeated along with his men by Lord Cante di Messer Iacopo de' Gabriele of Gubbio on 24 December. All six were beheaded. ...

[22 December 1379] A woman screamed in the Piazza and the entire Piazza rose up in a riot. Some had their heads cut off. The Piazza was flooded with men and children, so great was the crowd, so many people were in the Piazza della Signoria.

[p. 435, The End of the Government of the Minor Guilds] Today 16 January 1381[2], messer Obizzo degli Alidosi [Captain of the People] from Imola cut off the head of Lord Giorgio degli Scali [and stuck it] on the wall of his courtyard. Further, he outlawed twenty-five men ...

Today, the 18th of this month at night, Lord Donato de Ricco and Feo Cane, a maker of plate armour, were captured and led to the Palace of the Captain of the People.

Today, on the morning of the 20th of this month Lord Obizzo our captain cut off their heads [and placed them] on the wall in the captain's courtyard and a great revolt ensued. During the morning, all of Florence rose up in a great revolt, screaming: 'Long Live the Guelf Party'. And this continued for several days. And many new knights were created. And on this day the twenty-one guilds assembled in the New Market,[126]

---

125 South of the Arno on the eastern side of the city.
126 In the centre of town about 60 metres from the old grain market previously housed in the famous church of Orsanmichele. Thus the two guilds of workers and artisans, which continued to exist and played a role in government since September 1378, were no longer included.

and all were in agreement. And they made Vanni di Michele di Vanni
[Castellani] and Lord Vieri di Gherardo de' Bardi knights.

Today, the 20th of this month, our Signoria issued a decree that all
those exiled, condemned, and outlawed would have their sentences
cancelled, and for the month of February to the first of March they
are to stay in the *contado* but not in the city. And the practices of
making denunciations against the magnates by placing them in the
tamburo[127] and by petitions were taken away. The Signoria, the colleges,
and all other offices confirmed these decisions. And the wool bosses
were armed and for three days stood guard in the New Market. On
the evening of the 20th of this month they broke into the offices of the
twenty-second and twenty-third guilds,[128] took them over and broke
their tables, chests, and coats of arms, and to show their contempt,
threw these guilds' papers out into the streets. On the 22nd and 23rd
of the month, the wool bosses armed themselves heavily and were able
to push through an agreement ruling that only the twenty-one guilds
and the *popolo* would remain.[129] And they threw to the ground that
stone that had been in the Palace of the Merchants' court [*Mercanzia*][130]
and each of those [who had been members of the twenty-second and
twenty-third guilds] were content once again to be subject underlings to the guilds [*sottoposti*] as they had been before.[131]

Today, in the morning of the 24th of this month, all those owning wool
shops [*Conventi*][132] suddenly shut their shops and went armed into
the New Market and asked who was in power. They wanted to have
all the purses in all the quarters torn up and new selections made,
comprised of good men who would govern the city of Florence in
peace, love, and harmony. Thus, on that day, the coffers were opened
and all agreed to tear up the names in all the purses for all the
quarters [of the city]. And together they all returned to their homes

127 The *tamburo* was the box where anyone could secretly denounce another.
128 The two remaining of the three new revolutionary guilds created in July 1378.
 The 24th guild, that of the most abject workers, the *Popolo di Dio*, had been
 abolished in early September 1378.
129 In other words, the two revolutionary guilds were now suppressed, and the *Popolo
 Minuto* were barred from entering office.
130 I do not understand what this stone was or what it symbolised; nor does Gherardi
 explain it.
131 Principally, they were *sottoposti*, under the thumbs once again of the wool bosses,
 the *Arte della Lana*.
132 The wool shops of Florence were divided into three neighbourhoods or *Conventi* –
 San Martino, Garbo, and via Maggio; *Grande Dizionario*, III, p. 720.

that evening in harmony. Florence was at peace. The deal was done; for now on, all those artisans who previously had been underlings [*sottoposti*] would again be underlings, subject to the councils of their guilds and to the guildsmen's will.

122 Petitions granted to artisans and other workers, 21 July 1378

Cronaca seconda d'anonimo, in *Il Tumulto dei Ciompi*, pp. 110–11.

The petitions approved by the priors who were chased from the Palace and granted to the craftsmen and other workers [*minuti*]:

That the wool guild shall no longer have the official of the *forastiere*.[133]

That the petitions made against the magnates shall be implemented entirely.

That those who have shares in the Commune's *Monte*,[134] shall not be paid any interest, but beginning now their capital shall be returned to them over the next twelve years, one twelfth per annum.

That the office of the priors shall be comprised of four craftsmen [*minuti*], two of the skilled craftsmen [*artefici*], as has been the custom,[135] and two *minuti*, who previously did not possess a guild. And there shall be three *minuti* among the Twelve,[136] and four among standard-bearers; and these must be selected by drawing names from the purses. Craftsmen in minor guilds [*artefici*] are not included in this count of *minuti*. And these *minuti* have the right to be elected as the standard-bearer of justice[137] as do other guildsmen, and no one can possess this office if he has another office, except that of consul.

That the *minuti* shall have a guildhall worth 500 florins,[138] where their

---

133 The official who presided over the workers (previously the *sottoposti*) of the guild, adjudicated over conflicts and misconduct, and delivered summary justice. He was a hated figure. Unlike in other guilds, the wool artisans had no recourse over decisions made against them.

134 The Monte del Commune was the Florentine funded debt. Principally the rich and those from the prestigious families of Florence owned government bonds issued by the Monte, which paid interest at high rates. Thus this petition was a serious economic blow to the rich *rentiers* of Florence.

135 That is, those from the formerly recognised fourteen minor guilds.

136 The committee of Twelve, or twelve good men, one of the colleges that advised the Signoria and vetted petitions and laws.

137 The highest office in Florence.

138 In 1378 such a sum would have purchased a modest palace.

eight consuls shall meet.

That all those who have been banished shall be readmitted without fines, except rebels, counterfeiters, and those condemned [to death]. With a payment of one florin to the priors' notary, their banishments will be cancelled.

That the forced loans on citizens [*prestanza*] shall not be imposed after six months; then a tax survey [*estimo*] will be carried out.[139] Those charged a *prestanza* of four florins or less are to pay 20 shillings on the florin and are not obliged to pay the rest.[140]

That Lord Salvestro de' Medici should have the rents from the Ponte Vecchio for life, and Lord Giovanni di Mone, 400 florins a year for life from the licences [*deschi*] of the stalls in the market.

That Lord Guido, a wool beater, who has been made a knight, is to have 2,000 florins from the property of rebels or from the treasury.

That the officers of grain distribution [*abbundanza*] are to be removed and the office terminated.

That no one should be arrested for indebtedness for the next two years.

That anyone who commits a crime, no matter what his status, must pay the accustomed penalty.

That forty of these lower *minuti* should have the same pre-eminence as those of The Eighty of the Emergency Council [*balià*] had before the revolution.[141]

That Lord Rosso and Ughiccione de' Ricci are to have their status restored.

That the florin should be valued at no more than 68 shillings in common coin [*piccioli*].[142]

That ten artisans of the lowest ranks of craftsmen [*artefici minutissimi*] per quarter shall draw [the names to be elected (*s'arroga*)] to the Council of the Commune.

139 The forced loans were advantageous to the rich; the *estimo* was a more equitable tax, charged on the value of one's possessions, mainly real property.
140 In other words, the poorest households were granted a tax break; twenty shillings on the florin would have meant that they were charged less than a third of the face value of the tax. In 1368 the value of the florin was 68 shillings or more. In effect, both by lowering the rates of the *prestanze* on the poorest and changing the tax system to the *estimo*, these reforms introduced a more progressive tax system.
141 These privileges are not spelled out.
142 The money of every-day market transactions.

That no one who is a member of the [Guelf] Party can be a rector of the commune of Florence.

That Spinello of the Treasury and Ser Stefano di Ser Matteo Becchi should have the same pre-eminence as members of the Eighty.

That no rector of the commune of Florence or any other person can try [*conoscierne*] anyone for acts of arson or robbery committed from 18 June 1378 to today.

That no one who had his house burnt can ever hold office, except for Lord Luigi Guicciardini.

That the captains of the [Guelf] Party cannot appoint any elector [*arroto*] for any position on the Councils of the People or the Commune but can for the colleges.

That the banner of the [Guelf] Party is to remain in the Palace of the Priors and must never be returned to them for any reason.

[The list of decrees then concerns individuals or families from the previous elite, those penalised by being branded as supermagnates and deprived of honours and offices. The last petition returns to a major constitutional change.]

[p. 112] That no magnate can be in the Council [of the People or the Commune], and in their place, ten from the *minuti* are to be elected.

123 On Michele di Lando

Cronaca prima d'anonimo (called the *Squittinaio*)', in *Il Tumulto dei Ciompi*, p. 75. The document below describes the single most important event in the rise of the Ciompi to power. In contrast to revolts in the north, where firebrands such as Peter the king, an old man in the crowd of Tournai in 1364, or later Jean des Marès, Philippe van Artevelde, and the surgeon Jean de Troyes moved crowds to action by 'sweet words', Michele di Lando by all accounts said nothing; rather it was his possession of a flag that brought him to lead the Florentine wool workers. With the fall of the radical wing of the Ciompi forty days later, again Michele was leader and again it was his possession of a flag, not rhetoric, that mattered. The only words he uttered were in unison with the rest, the Ciompi chant: 'Long live the *Popolo Minuto* and the Guilds' [121, 126].

[22 July 1378] Then one Michele di Lando, a wool comber, son of the woman Simona, who sold vegetables in front of the Stinche prison, came out into the piazza [of the Signoria] without any weapon at his side or on his back; and the banner of justice [*confalone della giostizia*] was taken and thrust into his hands. And he took it into his hands to preserve it for the *popolo minuto*. Then he ordered that the governors [*signori*] be told to clear out of the Palace [of the Signoria]. The Palace had been well supplied for any eventuality, but, as with those who are afraid, they thought it best to leave. Then all the people went up and entered, carrying with them the banner of justice. They went through all the rooms, finding many nooses, which had been bought to lynch the poor who went looting once the first fires of the revolt had been lit. And they found many other things. And many of the youngsters climbed up the tower. To honour God, they rang all the bells announcing their victory and seizure of the Palace. Then, they got down to the business of doing what was necessary for their defence and the liberation of the *popolo minuto* ...

p. 77: the 28th [July] 1378. The [new] lord priors passed a decree that lifted the bans of exile, so that each could return safe and sound to the city, *contado*, or district of Florence ...

Also, to strengthen the *popolo minuto*, they appointed 1500 crossbowmen in the city of Florence with a leader for every twenty-five crossbowmen. And they ordered twelve banners bearing the arms of the quarter to be made for each quarter: for Santa Croce, the cross; San Giovanni, the church; Santa Maria Novella, the sun; Santo Spirito, the dove. It took three days to assemble all these crossbowmen, and they were paid six pounds a piece. And when they were on guard duty, they were paid 13 shillings a day. And each quarter had to guard the Palace of the Signoria for two days, during the day but not at night. They guarded the city with the utmost security day and night ...

In contrast to the anonymous chronicler from the patrician Machiavelli family [121], who gives us few hints of what the *popolo minuto* was after (other than violence and evil), two other anonymous chronicles, known as the third anonymous chronicler or the 'Cronichetta Strozziana' and '*lo Squittinaio*' [124, 125] list in detail the practical but revolutionary objectives and innovations of the *popolo minuto*. These two chroniclers, however, were on opposite sides of the political spectrum in their views towards the Ciompi.

124 Economic and social policies of the Ciompi

Cronaca terza d'anonimo (1378–1382), in *Il Tumulto dei Ciompi*, also known as 'Cronichetta Strozziana', pp. 130–1.

On 3 August [1378] they [the government of the Ciompi] reconfirmed the petitions that penalized any magnate who caused anyone civil or criminal injuries. The same day, they set the value of the Monte shares, which had previously been frozen. They authorised a thousand crossbowmen from their ranks, with a payment of five florins per month apiece, and every day they stood guard, shouting villainous words against other citizens. Again, they made the citizens repurchase [their status],[143] under the threat of burning down their houses. They ordered that all the grain and wheat harvested in the *contado* be brought to Florence to be sold, under great penalties, and beyond Florence's borders no one could sell as much as a single strand of hair, since they wished to rob the city as they showed on many occasions.[144] Then they held elections for the officers of the Signoria and the colleges, and not a single person from any of the [prestigious] families was chosen. Then they re-assessed all over again the value of Monte shares and authorised a tax to collect forty thousand florins from certain citizens. And they collected a large part of it, because they threatened to burn [alive] any who refused to pay. They passed ordinances that all the wool bosses must produce [at least] 2,000 wool cloths [*panni*] a month, whether they wanted to or not, or suffer great penalties. They ordered that none of those who had been made knights could hold office. They banished thirty-one [citizens] to various places. They elected syndics, ruling that nothing could be decided without them and that they would receive six florins a month in perpetuity; however, the officers of the Signoria and the colleges did not approved. They [the Ciompi] distributed all the grain of the *contado* among themselves. They removed [all those elected] from the Councils of the People and the Commune and sacked all those appointed to offices in the commune and the Palace [of the Signoria]. New elections for the priors were ordered on that day [3 August], and they stayed armed in the Piazza and yelled from the windows: 'So

---

143 The chronicler is asserting that citizens as in the former regime controlled by the Guelf Party were blackmailed into giving money not to be condemned as Ghibellines, magnates, or super-magnates.

144 The accusation being that the government was 'robbing' the patrician landowners of their grain and property.

be it'. If the votes went their way, they would stick; if not, they would tear them to pieces. On many occasions they went to the standard-bearer of justice to take away the banner, and they wished to have two full days to rob the city. But they never gained this consent. They swaggered about arrogantly as was the way of this rabble [*di loro ginea*]. And it was thus truly said, had it not been for the wise ones who restrained them, they would have brought this city to a bad end. And this standard-bearer [of justice] who was able to bring things under control was named Michele di Lando.

125 On the Eight of Santa Maria Novella, 27 August 1378

Cronaca prima d'anonimo, in *ibid.*, p. 80. [27 August, 1378, after the assembly in Santa Maria Novella and the election of the eight]. The third wave of the revolt of the Ciompi.

All the people, well armed, and also with many skilled artisans, assembled in the piazza of San Marco,[145] and here they deliberated on what was the best course of action for each individual. They negotiated to draw up a petition, taking on a suitable notary, whom they told to write down the following: 'Because of the syndics' failures, none of them should hold office for the next ten years; the Eight of War should be paid a salary of no more than 5 gold florins a month. They have been paid 15 a month and have done nothing for it. And he who is not worthy or has failed in his duty is to be banished. And the clique [*consorterie*] that has formed [among them] should no longer be tolerated. And Lord Salvestro should no longer have the rents from the Ponte Vecchio, nor Lord Giovanni di Mone, those from the market.[146] No magnate should be allowed to hold any office.[147] And no poor person of the minor guilds should be arrested for any debts of 50 florins or less from now until two years hence. And Lord Luca di Totta da Panzano, who was a magnate, is now to acquire popular status, and Betto di Ciardo is to be paid ten florins a month and he and his bodyguard should be given weapons.

---

145 In the north-central part of the city; it became the famous church of the reformed Dominicans in 1435, sponsored by Cosimo de' Medici.
146 See [122].
147 Although the first revolt of the Ciompi had restricted the number of seats magnates could occupy in the government's councils, they had not been excluded entirely from government.

126 The revolution betrayed, 27–29 August 1378

Cronaca prima d'anonimo, pp. 81–2. This radical chronicler of the Ciompi, who clearly supported the demands of late August, then goes on to describe Michele di Lando's betrayal and how the traditional guildsmen defeated the third wave of the Revolt of the Ciompi, that of the Eight of Santa Maria Novella, and outlawed the guild of the 'People of God' or 'the Ciompi'. For another perspective of these events, that of the old families, turn back to the account by the Machiavelli [121].

[27 August, 1378] All the guilds and especially the fat cats [*popolo grasso*] among the citizens schemed to undermine and strip the privileges and power from the *popolo minuto*, that is, that from that guild they called the Ciompi.[148] The Eight of War met with the standard-bearer of justice [Michele di Lando] and plotted their attack. First, they bribed the standard-bearer; then he convinced the other members of the Signoria who were members of the *popolo-minuto* guild that they would not lose their offices. Each one was happy with the plan. You will now hear how and why it succeeded. First they ordered all the banners of the guilds to be brought into the Piazza [of the Signoria] and hung them on the rostrum on 29 August. Then all the banners of the companies [the neighbourhood militia] were to appear in the Piazza, and all the entrances to the Piazza were to be sealed off. Next the officers of the Signoria were to send for all the leaders of the crossbowmen and have them ready. With these plans in place, they would explain [to the officials] what they wanted them to do, that is the plot. Thus they convinced them to swear to keep this plot secret by persuading them that they would be able to retain all the honours of their office; thus they agreed. After hatching these plots that night, they counselled Michele di Lando to call in all the fat cats to let them in on it, so that each would know what was happening. The next morning Michele di Lando left with Benedetto da Carlone on horseback with the banner of justice in his hand and rode around the entire city, shouting: 'Long live the People and the Guilds; death to those who want a dictatorship [*Signore*]'. And they shouted that these Eight were the ones who wanted a dictatorship …

---

148 This was the short-lived twenty-fourth revolutionary guild comprised of the lowest members of Florentine society. Unfortunately, I do not know of any document that specifies who exactly belonged to this guild. Other than carders [*scardassieri*] it is not clear which occupations were included. Still, guild recognition survived for other previously disenfranchised crafts in the wool industry; see [128].

[29 August, 1378] Many people of every rank, rich and poor, but especially the fat cats and the minor and greater guildsmen, poured into every part of the Piazza, because they were the ones who knew how the plot would unfold. They ordered all the banners of the guilds and all the companies to be brought to the Piazza of the Signoria. And all the flags of the guilds were put on the rostrum, and all the banners of the companies were placed in the corners of the Piazza, at every post. And at 5:30, the standard of the angel[149] came into the Piazza with a great swarm [*istuolo*] of the *popolo minuto*. They entered the Piazza and nothing was said to them, because it was apparent to everyone that they were too strong to challenge ...

[p. 82] At 3 in the afternoon, the officers of the Signoria asked for all the banners of the guilds, which they wanted placed in the Palace, thus leaving the *popolo minuto* isolated without their own insignia to follow. All the other guilds brought their insignia, because they knew the plot. And if they [the *popolo minuto*] had given up their flag [*la segnia*], as had been the plan, they would have been cut to pieces and hounded out of town, and all the bowstrings of their crossbows cut. Thus, on hearing this request for their flag of the angel to be handed over, they did not want to do it, saying: 'If we did this, what would we have to run behind?' So they gave them nothing.

127 Criminal proceedings against the Ciompi and the radicals of the Eight of Santa Maria Novella, August 1378

Niccolò Rodolico, *La Democrazia Fiorentina nel suo tramonto (1378–1382)* (Bologna, 1905), Doc. I, pp. 441–5: ASF, Atti del Capitano del Popolo, Sentence of 17 December 1379.

Piero di Ciro, carder of the parish of San Frediano of Florence, has been accused.

With Lord Luca di Totti da Panzano, Luca di Melano, Bartolomeo di Lorenzo called Meo the Fatso, Bartolo di Niccolò di Betto, a dyer, his son Zanobio, and many others,[150] he met and assembled in the city of Florence in the quarter of Santo Spirito, in the neighbourhood [*contrata*] called Camaldoli, in a certain field in this neighbourhood

---

149 The flag of the *popolo minuto*.
150 Rodolico does not list them but adds: 'almost all were from the parish of San Frediano'.

beyond the nunnery of the converted whores [*convertite*][151] [...] with Angiolo di Cenne, Nofrio di Cinello, Niccolò di Bartolo, Matteo di Ser Salvi, Simone d'Andrea, Domenico di Bonacorso and a great multitude of their followers numbering two hundred or more from the guild of the carders. They made plans to disturb and upset the free and popular [*popularem*] state of this city and also to destroy this city, depriving the lord priors of their authority and governance ... And to accomplish this, the abovementioned Eight who had been elected and this Piero together with the others and their followers elected themselves as the representatives and most important governors, as if they were the lords of the entire city of Florence, and they called themselves openly in public 'the Eight Saints with the Authority of the People of God'.[152] This occurred at the time and place contained in the inquest of this case [now lost].

Item ... the said Piero, together with those mentioned above, planned that these Eight so elected were to see to it and to ensure that the priors of the guilds, who served at this time and were currently in power, should pass each and every petition that had been brought before them by these Eight at the instigation of this Piero and the others mentioned above and their followers, and that these Eight, so elected, should become the sovereign power as if they were the lords over the entire city of Florence, above the lord priors and the colleges and every one of their officials ... such that altogether these abovementioned in the inquest, the Eight, their followers, and this Piero swore with their hands touching the Holy Gospel, passing it from one to another, that they would be in life and death one body united; each one would stand steadfast and act in unison to conspire and revolt against the syndics of the guilds, presently in power, and against the rule of the city of Florence.

Item ... this Piero together with the others named above and the Eight and their followers ... held a meeting and conspired together with many others numbering five thousand or more in the church of San Marco and in the city of Florence. And here ... this Piero with the Eight and their followers negotiated, commanded, and planned that they should go with their iniquitous and unjust petitions to the Palace

---

151 The Augustinian Beato Simone Fidati and the confraternity of Santo Spirito founded Sant' Elisabetta delle Convertite in the first half of the fourteenth century. It was located in the via degli Serragli, south of the Carmine.

152 'The People of God' was the name given to the poorest of the Ciompi, who comprised the third and at this point outlawed guild of the Ciompi or carders.

of the lord priors to ensure that these petitions would be approved and passed by the lord priors of the guilds and the colleges ... While these proceedings were taking place, a riot and revolt [*rumor et tumultus*] broke out suddenly in the city of Florence, especially around the Palace of the lord Priors of the Guilds with this Piero, the others named above, and their followers, shooting bolts from crossbows against the lord priors ... and shouting and yelling loudly: 'Death to the syndics of the Guilds' ...

Item ... while the newly elected lord priors of the guilds, the standard-bearer of justice, and the standard-bearers of the neighbourhoods were coming out [of the Palace], these Eight and many others with a great crowd of armed men pushed towards the great Palace of the Priors and next to the door of the palace ... shouted and rioted, creating a disturbance, and they blocked these priors and standard-bearers from coming and going from their offices as they pleased, according to the customs and laws of the city of Florence. And in the midst of this shouting and rioting, one of the priors or a standard-bearer shouted: 'We do not want this'. And similar things were committed and perpetrated against the free and popular state of the city of Florence ...

Item ... this Piero with the others and the Eight and their followers with the intentions and spirit described above gathered and congregated in the church of Santa Maria Novella ... and once assembled and after discussions among themselves ordered and planned that two from the Eight along with several of their followers should go to the Palace of the Priors and make them swear by shaking hands with each of the Eight and their followers that each and every petition, the just and unjust ones, would be sent to and voted through the colleges. After giving these orders and having these talks and plans, those of the Eight, that is, Simone d'Andrea called Morello, Domenico di Totto, Francesco di Bartolo, and Matteo di Ser Salvi with several others and some of their followers, all of whom are named in the inquest, deliberated and that evening went to the Palace of the lord Priors, where they met with the present lord priors, who had been newly elected and had assembled to carry out affairs for the well-being, peace, and tranquillity of this city. This Simone and his associates ... addressed these newly elected priors: 'We come representing ourselves and our lords, that is, the Holy Authority of the People of God and their followers. And for us and our party, we desire that you swear full-heartedly by shaking our hands and touching the Holy

Gospel of God, that you will approve, vote through, and make sure that everyone of our petitions becomes law and that you will not act against the will of these Eight and their followers'. Then these lord priors and others who had been recently elected, not being powerful enough to avoid these oaths because of the assembly of people [outside] brought by the said Eight of the People of God and their followers, obeyed them [the insurgents] and took an oath in the presence of this Simone and the others just named: touching the Holy Gospels, they swore to implement and observe in every detail everything these two and their associates wanted ...

Item ... this Piero with the aforementioned others together with these Eight and their followers, after discussions and plans, assembled many armed men and crossbowmen in the said church of Santa Maria Novella, where they persuaded, ordered, and planned that those of the said Eight of the People of God, together with their followers, should go to the palace of these lord priors, where they told the lord priors of the guilds and the standard-bearer of justice: 'We come before you on behalf of ourselves and our lords and their followers, and we want to see that our petitions are passed through and become law'. Because of this, a massive riot broke in this Palace and in the city of Florence; the people revolted [*et tumultus in populo*]. And on this day, those indicted above along with those Eight and their followers, comprising a massive crowd, went immediately with crossbows and other defensive and offensive weapons to the square of these lords [the priors] with their flag raised bearing the figure of the angel. They entered the square, weapons in hand, all shouting loudly: 'Long Live the *Popolo Minuto* and Death to the syndics of the Guilds'. And with this the entire city of Florence was aroused to take up arms and riot; many deaths and an infinite number of injuries inflicted on the people of the city of Florence followed.

Item ... the said Piero with the aforementioned and the Eight and their followers, however, were not strong enough to accomplish their malicious plans or implement their most evil deeds. Another crowd of armed men assembled and rang the bells of many churches, and those of the people and commune of Florence united to prevent them [the Eight, etc.] subverting and destroying the free and popular state of the city of Florence. [The indicted were condemned to death in their absence; the sentence was decided on 17 December 1379.]

128 The laws transforming the government of the Ciompi to that of the Minor Guilds

Ibid., doc. II., pp. 445–52: Provvisioni Reg., n. 68, cc. 24 ff, 22 September 1378. The petition below, which became law on 22 September, for the most part simply ratifies the privileges of two of the three revolutionary guilds won two months previously on 21 July. However, for that date, we have no surviving documents that specify with any detail the rights of election, office holding, or the occupations that comprised the members of these two new guilds (and nothing for the third new guild). Only at the end of this petition does it specify the consequences of the failed revolt of the Eight of Santa Maria Novella at the end of August – the outlawing of the third revolutionary guild, that was variously called of the carders, the Ciompi, or *Popolo di Dio*, and their prohibition to join any other guild or have guild or citizenship recognition.

On behalf of the councillors of the two newly created guilds described below, that is, the guild of the doublet makers, shearers, tailors, barbers, those who sell small pieces of cloth [*retaiuoli, ritaglio*[153]], hatters, flag makers, and others connected to this guild, and the guild of the dyers, those who cut the nap on woollen cloth, those who make the cards, make soap, other types of carders and those who raise the nap, the combers, the drawers of wool and the finishers, the weavers of cloth, those who wash the newly-shorn wool, and others connected to this guild, the following petition is humbly and reverently submitted before you, the magnificent and powerful lord priors of the guilds and the standard-bearer of justice: that all these consuls, described below, who have been and are elected to the office of consul [of the guilds] and their successors in this office should have the power, jurisdiction, control, and recognition to rule and govern over these two guilds sufficiently and according to custom. Therefore, on the part of these consuls and the men of these guilds, we devoutly and humbly beseech you to provide, decree, decide, and solemnly put into law through the Councils of the People and the Commune of Florence the following: that the two guilds mentioned should exist and flourish in the city of Florence and shall be understood as joined with the other twenty-one guilds of this city, and that in turn the city should denominate and list twenty-three guilds in the way it formerly denominated and listed twenty-one guilds in this city. And that each and every one of these below-listed consuls described above should be understood to be consuls of the guilds for the time and term of four

---

153 See Edler, *Glossary of Medieval Terms of Business*, pp. 241 and 248.

months, beginning in the present month of September; and that these consuls and their successors in office during their whole term and [by a vote of] two-thirds of them ... ought to have and be understood to have total and full control, authority and power, jurisdiction, and recognition in this office concerning the operation of these guilds and over their crafts, that is: each of the said consuls in his guild should have the same powers as those of the other consuls of the fourteen minor guilds of the city of Florence; and that each and every statute, ordinance, and law of the People and Commune of Florence that confers authority, rights to hold office, and control on those consuls of the said fourteen guilds in this city should be the same for the said consuls of these [two new guilds] for their terms in office. [There follows great detail and regulation over the procedures for electing these consuls.]

[p. 448] Item, to be a member of one of these two guilds, each and every craftsman must practise or make things with a member of one of these two aforementioned guilds who has matriculated[154] and has been written down in the book of the matriculated members of one of these two aforementioned guilds, and once understood to be in one of these guilds, he is then freed, totally absolved, and fully exempted from the obligations and subjugation to any other guild in any manner whatsoever and to any penalties or offences [they might wish to inflict].[155]

And in turn these other guilds or their consuls or officers cannot order, tax, question, indict, or in anyway molest them, or [they shall] be fined [...] pounds in Florentine currency ... .

[p. 449] Item, both these guilds are to have their own coats of arms and insignia, which are to remain theirs ...

Item, the number of consuls of these two guilds ought to be as follows in perpetuity and for the future; that is, six for the guild of the doublet makers – two for the members who are doublet makers and one for the members who are tailors for the first term of office, and two for the members of the tailors and one for the doublet makers for the second term; and for the next term of office, there should be two for the shearers and the hat makers, and one for the barbers. And for the guild of the dyers, those who cut the nap, those who make the cards, the soap makers, other types of nappers, combers, tenterers, finishers,

154 That is, formally enrolled as a guild member.
155 Previously these workers in the wool industry were subject to the decisions and tribunal of the wool owners' guild, the *Arte della lana*. These workers had no say over their work routines or affairs.

weavers, and washers of raw wool, there should be twelve [consuls]; that is four for the dyers, three for the nappers and soap makers, two for the other sort of nap cutters and combers, one for the tenterers and finishers, one for the weavers, and one for the washers of the raw wool.

Item that these guilds, both of them, and their consuls and craftsmen ought to have, enjoy, and possess each and every benefit, favour, and privilege enjoyed and possessed or that can be and should be enjoyed or possessed by each of those fully privileged as members of the fourteen guilds of this city.[156] [The consuls of the two guilds are then listed again by name and occupation.]

[p. 450] It is added and decreed that none of the members of the [guild of the] *Popolo Minuto*, that is, any member prohibited and excluded from the benefits examined and made in August this year, ought or may at any time be admitted, enrolled, or in any way be received into the matriculated members of these two guilds under penalty of one hundred pounds in Florentine coin [that will be charged against] each consul in office at the time of such an admission, reception, or registration.[157] However, if someone is acted against and is in the right, no one should or may act against his admission or matriculation so long as the craftsman is listed and drawn up in one of these guilds. Similarly, anyone who does not practise one of the crafts of these guilds or of their members should not be or may not be admitted, received, or inscribed in anyway as a said matriculated member under the penalty stated above.[158] ... [The petition was decided and made into law on 21 September 1378; it passed the Council of the Commune with a vote of 223 black beans for and 60 white beans against it.]

129 The chronicle of a worker

Pagnolo di Ser Guido, wool shearer (ASF, Strozziane, 2nd series, LIX, fols. 98r–101r), transcribed by Alessandro Stello, *La révolte des Ciompi: Les hommes, les lieux, le travail* (Paris, 1993), pp. 271–5. The following account is monotonous, written in a rough style, adds nothing new to our knowledge of the

---

156 That is, the fourteen minor guilds (and not the seven major ones).
157 In other words, those workers who were members of the short-lived twenty-fourth guild, the *Popolo di Dio*.
158 This was to block those from higher social status matriculating into lower guilds to win elections to governmental posts – a practice that became widespread in the fifteenth century.

Revolt of the Ciompi, and according to its editor, Alessandro Stella, contains errors (although he does not specify them). Nonetheless, it is remarkable since its author came from the ranks of the Ciompi. He was a shearer in the wool industry, an occupation that before the revolt had no guild recognition and afterwards was a part of the new twenty-third guild of the doublet makers [131]. Indeed, given that he was made an election supervisor in 1379 by the new Ciompi regime, he had to have been from the lowest ranks of the disenfranchised workers, one of the *artefici minutissimi* [125]. He is the first worker I know of to have left a description or commentary on a revolt. The next such worker (although from an agrarian setting) who comes to mind is Gerrard Winstanley (?1609–after 1660),[159] nearly three hundred years later. The account below gives us some insight into the perceptions and anxieties of a worker in the heat of the revolt. Despite its style and small errors, I find it a remarkably accurate narrative sweep of the events from 15 June 1378 to February 1379, highlighting the major events in such a short report. Even more remarkable and in sharp contrast to the other chroniclers is this author's nonjudgemental reportage. Finally, the report shows the importance of the newly-won rights of citizenship and powers to serve in government – how proud this shearer was to have become a functionary in the Florentine government.

On 15 June 1378 a cry was heard many times in the Palace of the Priors, 'Long live the People'; the shops were locked and this was on Friday at vespers. Then on Tuesday an armed riot broke out with the People and all the guilds running with their banners into the Piazza of the priors,[160] chanting; 'Long live the People'. At nine in the morning the guild of the furriers[161] left with their banner, went to the house of Lord Lapo da Castiglionchio, and robbed and burnt [his house] and that of his kinsmen.[162] And they went to the house of il Mastino and robbed and burnt it. Then they went to Carlo's and robbed and burnt it; then to the house of the Albizzi and burnt [the house] of Piero di Filippo and the sons of Pepo d'Antonio, and the sons of Uberto d'Antonio di Jacopo d'Alesso, and several of their kinsmen; and they burnt [the house] of Migliore Guadagni and burnt

---

159 On Winstanley, see among other places, Christopher Hill, *The World Turned Upside Down: Radical Ideas During the English Revolution* (London, 1972). By the early-modern period, artisan diarists became fairly numerous; see James S. Amelang, *The Flight of Icarus: Artisan Autobiography in Early Modern Europe* (Stanford, 1998). For a Florentine writer from the working class, who was critical of the Medici duchy, see the diary of the tailor, Bastiano Arditi, *Diario di Firenze e di alter parti della Cristianità (1574–1579)*, ed. Roberto Cantagalli (Florence, 1970).

160 Another name for the main square of Florence, the Piazza della Signoria.

161 It was one of the seven major guilds.

162 According to the Anonymous Diary [121], these events took place on the 22nd and not the 19th of June.

[the one of] Jacopo, Simone, and Sandro de' Pazzi[163] and then burnt [that] of the Bondelmonte.[164] Then they went to break open the Stinche[165] and then burnt [the house] of Niccolò and Tommaso Soderini, then robbed Lord Filippo Corsini, then Bonaiuto Serragli and his brother, and Lord Coppo of [the parish] of San Frediano; then they burnt the [house] of Lord Ristoro Canigiani; then robbed [those of] the Agnoli [family]; then they tried to break into the Florentine Treasury, defended by the grocers' guild;[166] then they rested that night. The next morning a brigade of Flemish foreigners gathered by a chapel, went to [the quarter of Santo Spirito],[167] and began to rob. At this point, the podestà was the leader and led the executor [of the Ordinances of Justice] and the captain of the people;[168] he unfurled the banner of liberty and marched with all his soldiers on horseback. They were followed by the flags of the sixteen [neighbourhood militia] with fifty men under each flag. They searched the city with the block, henchman's axe, and the hangman's noose, captured the five Flemings[169] and hanged one in the Piazza of the priors, another in the market[170], another at Santa Maria Novella, another in Borgo Ognissanti, and the other at Santo Spirito.[171] Then they rested, blocking all the [gates] of the city, and they guarded every city-district [*Gonfalone*] night and day until Wednesday. They then reopened the shops and laid down their arms. It is worth mentioning that two were robbed on Tuesday: Vieri di Messer Pepo Cavicciuli in the Via Larga and Francesco Martini in Borgo di Santa Croce. Then on Friday, 2 July, the guilds presented their petition against the [Guelf] Party and the magnates and on many other matters, but it failed to pass through the colleges.[172] As a

---

163 One of the old magnate families of Florence.
164 Another ancient noble family of Florence.
165 The Commune's prison.
166 Unlike the Guild of Grocers in northern European cities such as London, this guild was comprised of middling sorts, who operated small shops selling prepared foods; they were not wealthy dealers in foodstuffs.
167 The district south of the Arno.
168 Until 1378 and the creation of the Eight of the Guard, these were the three juridical groups of the city responsible for law enforcement.
169 According to the Anonymous Diarist, only four were caught [121].
170 Most likely, the New Market [*Mercato Nuovo*].
171 Thus they distributed the hangings over most of the city.
172 Before coming to a vote in the two legislative councils of the People and the Commune, the elite inner council of the three colleges [*Tre Maggiori*] of the priors, the sixteen standard-bearers, and the Twelve good men vetted petitions in secret.

consequence, all the guilds armed themselves to get what they wanted. The next Sunday, 18 July 1378, at eight in the evening, an olive branch of peace came from the Church [ending] a war that had lasted three years.[173] Then on the next Tuesday, 20 July, the priors captured three poor men and wanted to cut off their heads in the Piazza,[174] but a riot broke out with [people] running into the Piazza, shouting: 'Long live the *Popolo Minuto* and the Guilds'. They struggled against the Palace [of the Signoria] for a while. A brigade of them then left and went to burn down the houses of the Lords Luigi and Piero Guicciardini. The latter was the standard-bearer of justice.[175] As a result, they freed the three poor men, and as a result of this, the insurgents left the Palace of the Priors but went and attacked the [Palace of] the Executor [of the Ordinances of Justice], where they ripped off the banner of justice. Then they burnt [the house] of Alessandro di Niccolaio degli Alessandri;[176] then [those of] the Ridolfi and Corsini families, Lord Coppo, Andrea di Segnino, Moscone and Simone di Rinieri Peruzzi, Ser Piero, the government's notary, Domenico di Berto and Ser Nuto.[177] They then went to the house of Salvestro di Messer Alamanno de' Medici and led him to the Piazza of the priors and made him a knight of the *popolo minuto* and the guilds along with another sixty or so other citizen [whom they made] knights. Then that night Lord Stefano brought the banner of justice back to the Palace. On Wednesday morning, they called forth all the guilds except that of the wool bosses,[178] thus they amounted to twenty [guilds] in all, and with the banner, they stormed the Palace of the Podestà; the fighting lasted for more than an hour. The podestà gave himself up with oral agreements made to the priors. Except for these ones and the government functionaries who had slipped out [*uscinne*], all the guildsmen entered the palace with the banner and burnt all the furniture, books, and charters. Then they rested for the rest of the day. Then on Thursday after the first third of the morning, they marched with their banner into the Piazza of the priors and demanded to speak

173 Florence's war against the papacy began in 1375; see Richard Trexler, *Economic, Political, and Religious Effects of the Papal Interdict on Florence, 1376–1378* (Frankfurt-am-Main, 1964).

174 According to the Anonymous Diarist, four were hauled in and tortured [121].

175 In fact, it was Luigi who was the standard-bearer of justice [121, 122].

176 An old magnate family.

177 The commune's executioner; see [121] on his fate.

178 The Ciompi were comprised mostly (though not exclusively) of workers in the wool industry, the underlings [*sottoposti*] of the wool guild.

to those priors who had refused to leave the building. These priors asked for a guarantee that they would not be harmed; it was granted; they left, and the banner entered into the palace with the *popolo minuto*. Then between five in the morning and vespers they came out onto the town rostrum [*Aringhiera*] and created an emergency government of the people to change the laws of the land. Ser Coluccio[179] drafted these proposals. Then at vespers Ser Nuto was sighted; those under the pennant of the wool shearers ran him down, seized and killed him, dragged him into the Piazza of the priors, and hanged him by his feet. Blessed were the ones who could have a little piece of him; no more than a foot and half a leg remained of him. They burnt the [house] of Michele di Vanni [Castellani] and the furnishings of Bonaccorso di Lapo and destroyed his house. They burnt all the books and furnishings at the office of the wool guild. They burnt the furnishings and books of the tax office [*Grascia*]. On the same Tuesday they burnt other buildings and on Thursday entered the Palace of the Priors and burnt all the furnishings and books in the offices of the executor [of the Ordinances of Justice] and the captain [of the people]. Then on Friday they drew the names for the priors, the Twelve, and the standard-bearers [of the neighbourhoods],[180] who then entered their offices on the following Saturday, 27 July. On that day, they began their official duties in honour and for the preservation of the guilds and the *popolo minuto*, that God would always maintain them in peace and in a good state. Except for rebels, they liberated those who had been exiled either without any payment or for a florin each to cancel their condemnations.

Then on 25 August 1378 a riot broke out through the city; they came armed into the Piazza of the priors, chanting: 'Long Live the *Popolo Minuto* and the Guilds' and immediately sent eight Ciompi to the Palace of the Priors with a petition, which would cancel decrees made to citizens and the rights to bear arms and hold office made to knights, along with many other petitions.[181] All were passed. Then on Friday night these eight went into the Palace of Signoria with various sealed petitions and made the old priors swear to the newly elected ones and to the colleges that all their petitions had been passed, and all of them swore this oath. Then on Wednesday morning two of

179 The famous humanist and later chancellor of Florence, Ser Coluccio Salutati, was the principal notary of the commune in 1378.
180 That is, those who comprised the three colleges, the *Tre Maggiori*.
181 The author does not seem to have a clear idea about these petitions of the Eight.

these eight went into the Palace of the Priors, and the standard-bearer of justice[182] drew out his sword and wounded one of them in the head and arrested him. He then armed himself and unfurled the banner of justice and mounted his steed, and with blood dripping from his sword he searched [for the others] throughout the city, shouting: 'Long live the People and the Guilds'. Then at vespers all the guilds placed their banners inside the Palace of the Priors, except for the wool combers and the carders, who did not wish to give theirs up. For this, the other guilds attacked and beat them up, killing four of them and wounding others. They chased them from the Square and immediately took out the banner of liberty. They searched for them through the [parish of] San Pier Gattolino, Camaldoli, Belletri and Sant'Ambrogio.[183] Then they took the banner back inside [the Palace], and they returned all the neighbourhood banners back to their proper homes. Then, at eleven, the bells of Sant'Ambrogio began ringing and rang for at least an hour. Then the bells of the priors and the podestà began to ring and then all the other bells of Florence, calling the people and the guilds to arms. And they stayed armed all night. And the next day, remaining armed, they searched the city, blazing through [the shops of] the wool beaters. And at vespers the bells sounded for a public meeting of the citizens [*parlamento*]. The priors and members of the colleges came out onto the public rostrum and confirmed [the legality] of the two new guilds, that is, that of the dyers and of the doublet makers with their members, and joined these with the fourteen [as members of the minor Guilds]. But, they outlawed the guild of the carders, preventing their members as well as those who had ever matriculated in this guild from holding office. The sixteen [minor] guilds were to have five priors, and the seven [major guilds] and the idle rich [*scioperati*], four priors. For one term, the banner would be kept by the sixteen; for the next, by the seven; to the sixteen would go nine [offices of] the standard-bearers of the militia [*Compagnia*]; to the seven, seven standard-bearers; to the sixteen, seven [offices] of the Twelve [Good Men]; to the seven, five [of the] Twelve; and thus by agreement all the other offices were distributed as above. On Sunday, 30 August, at vespers, the priors and

182 Michele di Lando.

183 Four of the major working-class and artisan districts of the city: San Pier Gattolino is located sopr'Arno down the via Romana; Camaldoli, roughly is in the same zone around the Carmine; Belletri, in the parish of San Lorenzo in the western part of the city and Sant'Ambrogio is in the northeastern corner of fourteenth-century Florence.

the standard-bearers came out before all the guildsmen, who were armed in the Piazza with their banners raised. The guild of the wool beaters remained at the gate of the [Palace] of the Priors, and they wanted to know who had been placed [in the purses for electoral offices, the *tratto*]. And if they did not like it, they would tear up [the names in the electoral purses], and three wool beaters tore them to ribbons. On 10 September 1378, the banners were returned peacefully; where once there were twenty-one, now there were twenty-three guilds; the fourteen had grown by two – that is, the guild of the dyers and the guild of the shearers. Then on 27 December 1378 a plot involving the fat cats [*grassi*], magnates, and wool carders was discovered; they were captured, and twelve of them lost their heads. Among them was Lord Ghirigoro di Pagnozzo de' Tornaquinci, Pippo di Forbaino de' Rossi. The others were poor men. Many others were sentenced to corporeal punishment, fined, or banished. Among them were Mariano and Alesso degli Albizi, Luca di Piero and his son, and one of the Strozzi [family]. Then in March 1378[9], another plot was discovered, in which Guerriante Marignolli and his son were outlawed and a number of poor men killed [*guasti*]. Then in December 1379 Filippo di Biagio degli Strozzi, Nanni di Piero Anselmi, Carlo Mangioni, Lord Jacopo Sacchetti, Piero di Filippo degli Albizzi, Mastino Siminetti, Cipriano di Lippozzo Mangioni, Lord Donato Barbadoro were killed; above all the rest Giannozzo Sacchetti was killed for treason and Piero Canigiani, Guido della Foresta, Bonifazio de' Peruzzi, Antonio da Uzzano were fined 2,000 florins each; Bonifazio de' Peruzzi and Antonio da Uzzano paid it.

1378.

In February 1378[9] the selection [*squittino*] of the priors was made. I, Pagolo di Ser Guido, was appointed to supervise the elections [*Arrotto*] by Bartolomeo di Giovanni, saddle maker and standard-bearer of the [neighbourhood district] of the ladder [Scala][184] ... I, Pagolo di Ser Guido, shearer, drew these names from the purses. 1379.

---

184 Sopra'Arno in the Quarter of the Santo Spirito; its biggest parish is the largely working-class neighbourhood of San Frediano.

130 Dissension between the guild of dyers and the wool bosses, 1380

Stefani, *Cronica fiorentina*, r. 887, p. 386. On Stefani, see [39]. Perhaps it is surprising that someone who served as a prior in the government of the Minor Guilds (in 1379) could have been so opposed to the principles on which that government rested – inclusion of the two revolutionary guilds, which meant that most working men of Florence had at least virtual representation in governmental affairs. Was this chapter written at the time or after the fall of the government of the Minor Guilds in 1382?

How conflict arose between the guild of the dyers together with [its] other members and the guild of the wool bosses

In December this year [1380], the guild craftsmen's tempers reached their boiling point [*lo soperchio homre*], sparking big disputes in Florence, so much so that their complaints reached the Palace of the Priors. As I have already said many times before, the cause of these conflicts derived from the two guilds that had been added onto the fourteen minor ones; that is, the doublet makers, tailors, barbers, etc., on the one hand; and the dyers, shearers, other wool carders, washers, and others, on the other. This guild of the dyers became so audacious that they lost sight of who they were in relation to others in the city and in terms of their own worth. They had been ruled and had been under the thumbs [*retti e sottoposti*] of the wool bosses [*lanaiuoli*], obliged to accept their laws and be ruled by their statutes; now they acted with such arrogance: while all the other guilds were required to take on only a certain amount of work and no more, or face a penalty of a certain number of pounds, these people made laws that gave workers the right to accept any amount of work [they wanted] and those who gave them less were penalised. This struck the wool bosses as very bizarre and the citizens as abominable; it was beyond all reason. Because the rich dyers acted so immoderately, they failed to profit from their trade. With this, apprentices had become the guild counsellors, not the masters, and wherever the masters went, their colleagues laughed at them. Things were so mixed up that out of fear shopkeepers had to submit to apprentices. This state of affairs was detestable, and the city was weakened from within by these revolutionary notions [*novità*]. It even reached the point where the priors had to acquiesce and accept these ideas, but it did come into being. As a consequence, almost the entire city was armed. But it ended to the detriment of the wool bosses and the rich; the poor acquired rights and prestige.

131 The end of the two revolutionary guilds of workmen, February 1382

Stefani, *Cronica fiorentina*, r. 904, p. 397.

How those on the emergency council [*balìa*] destroyed the two Guilds, recalled those who had been banished, lifted the restrictions [*divietati*] on government offices and seats within the city chambers, and extended privileges to the magnates.

In this year [1382] during February, those of the Emergency Committee [*balìa*] assembled and immediately overturned all the decisions taken from 18 June 1378 to today regarding sentences of exile and restrictions on assuming governmental posts; these individuals would regain their previous rights. Moreover, they renounced all other innovations introduced from that time by law, emergency decrees, or reforms; such matters were to return to their previous state. Immediately, the two guilds, that is the guild of the dyers and many other trades, and the guild of the doublet makers, barbers and other members, created by the Ciompi in that year 1378 and ordained by the city councils, were annulled and cast aside. They now returned [as dependents] to those guilds to which they had formally been attached before creating their own guilds in 1378. The wool bosses brought about this change by a petition [to the Signoria]; they had been in conflict with those from the guild of the dyers and their members every day, even though these workers had two council members on the board of the wool guild. With this done, they passed a law liberating and recalling from banishment all those sentenced to exile for reasons of state or rebellion from 18 June 1378 to 22 January 1381[2], except for those who had performed indecent acts; they were to remain outside the city walls of Florence until the end of February. This Emergency Committee also freed from exile those who had committed civil offences; they were compelled only to come to peace and reach an agreement with the offended parties. Moreover, all those who were incarcerated, held under examination, sentenced, or imprisoned in the palaces of Florence, or in any other place, from the above-stated day when the rebellion began, were understood now to be free and to assume their previous status. This did not, however, apply to those sentenced or held under suspicion from 16 January [1382] to today or to those held for private debts or those of the house of the Ubaldini.¹⁸⁵

185 A magnate family that ruled the mountainous regions of the Mugello, the Alpi Fiorentine, and the Podere, bordering the territories of Bologna and the Romagna. In 1373, Florence declared 'a war of extermination' against this family, and except for a few branches, they became outlaws of the Florentine state; see Cohn, *Creating the Florentine State*, pp. 19–21, 159–60, and 174–7.

V: THE CLUSTER NORTH OF THE ALPS, 1378-82

One of the most enduring of the conclusions drawn in Mollat and Wolff's work on late medieval popular rebellion has been their notion of a pan-European clustering of revolts a generation following the Black Death, that is, between 1378 and 1382. I have already called into question this conclusion for Italy, and even for France as a whole, but for northern France it applies best, where a period of relative social peace may have followed the Jacquerie until the crisis of the French state at the end of Charles V's reign.[1]

More clearly than in 1358 these revolts, 1378-82, arose from the demands of war, forcing the king to exact new taxes.[2] The first wave of revolt erupted in the last years of Charles V's reign, when with rapid succession he jacked up the hearth tax [*fouagio*] from two to five to twelve francs per annum per household in Languedoc.[3] The increase sparked tax revolts in Le Puy, Montpellier, Lodève, Alès, Béziers, and the surrounding countryside [**169-74**].[4] Unlike the rustics and small townsmen of the Jacquerie, these insurgents made their demands clear and attacked directly the objects of their oppression — tax collectors and the king's officers in these regions.

---

1 Even in the Beauvaisis, however, the brutal repression of the Jacquerie did not kill off all rebellion or peasant resistance. In the year following the Jacquerie, peasants around Longueil, near Compiègne, lead by the peasants Guillaume l'Aloue and Grandferre, defended their village against the violence of English troops and defeated them in two battles. Also, Charles' tax increases to fund war in the 1360s were not accepted without protest as witnessed in Tournai in 1364 [60] and in 1369 (*Chronique des Pay-Bas*, pp. 248-9) and in other places in France; see *Chronique Latine de Guillaume de Nangis*, II, p. 230; *Chronique des quatre premiers Valois*, p. 202; and *Richardi Scoti chronici continuatio*, p. 157.

2 As we have seen in chapter III, the surviving documents, both the chronicles and letters of remission, give little sense of the Jacques's demands. Only one of these documents shows any protest against taxation, but this one comes from a town — Caen — and not the countryside [113].

3 Delachenal, *Histoire de Charles V*, V: (1377-80) (Paris, 1931), p. 288.

4 In addition to these cities, a remission to rebels of Clermont de Lodève [173] suggests that the uprisings had spread to smaller towns and villages for which no remissions survive: 'Finally, the lord of Clermont realised the seriousness of these crimes, that such crimes were now common in his territory and were beginning to increase and to inflame others, and would lead to evil consequences'.

Another element that distinguished this round of revolt from the Jacquerie and most other revolts thus far examined was the explicit complaint and description of poverty as a cause in both the narrative sources and the appeals in letters of remission [**169, 172**]. The most significant of these revolts was in Montpellier on 25 October 1379. The town's chronicle, *Le chronique romane*, saw the revolt arise not only because of the intolerable burden of the hearth tax at 12 francs, but also because 'the people [*pobol*] were already entirely devastated and broken by the great dearth that had for a long time run through this region' [**172**].

These tax revolts in southern France came to an end by 1381 and do not seem to have affected the north of France. Few of the northern French chroniclers noticed them and those who did, kept their comments short [**170, 171**]. Charles V made matters better for his subjects on his deathbed in 1380, at least in the north [*Langue d'oïl*] with his extraordinary last guilt-ridden legacy.[5] On 16 September 1380, he abolished the hearth tax, from which about a third of the royal revenues derived.[6] With the dead king's brothers raiding the royal coffers and renewed difficulties and pressures from the English incursions in the Hundred Years' War this gift placed severe strain on the dauphin and king-to-be, Charles VI, then twelve years old. In 1380 he sought new means for raising taxes [*aides*] to support the war but was repulsed violently by commoners of the 'bonnes villes' (or principal cities) of the north, especially in Paris. These popular insurrections forced him to approve an extraordinary ordinance as compromising to royal finances as his father's last legacy: on January 1381 all the taxes set since the reign of Philippe le Bel were abolished [**152**].

The *Chronique du Religieux de Saint-Denys*, now known to be the work of the Abbey's cantor, Michel Pintoin, was a new type of chronicle, more a humanistic history than a medieval chronicle, replete with

---

5 Harry Miskimin, 'The Last Act of Charles V: The Background of the Revolts of 1382', *Speculum* 38 (1963): 433–42, challenged this view held by Delachenal and others. Miskimin maintained that it followed 'wise' governmental management, that royal coffers were full, that Charles saw his subjects suffering, and that before 1380 various royal ordinances had reduced the hearth tax for various towns. Inconsistent with this argument and not explained by Miskimin is Charles V's rapid increase in the rate of the hearth tax by 400 percent in less than a decade leading up to his death and the revolts in the cities of Languedoc before his renunciation.

6 See Radding, 'The Estates of Normandy', pp. 79–80.

classical references, invented speeches, and socio-psychological analysis and commentary.⁷ It sets the emotional landscape for understanding the 'pestilence of revolts'⁸ of the next several years. The dreaded subsidies or new excise taxes that Charles VI imposed on basic commodities against his earlier ordinance was only the spark. According to the *Religieux*, 'throughout the kingdom of France, the appetite for liberty was burning ... a burning rage was brewing'. Moreover, in its origins, this burning rage or new self-assertiveness came not only from the 'most abject *plebes*' but like the Ciompi or later the French Revolution, from those at the top of society; rich burghers and even noblemen spearheaded the protest [132]. But according to Pintoin, the bourgeois had not led the *plebes* by their noses; rather, it was often the other way around. Thus in Paris 1380 two hundred of 'the most base sort' led the provost of the merchants 'despite his reluctance', to the royal palace to argue their case against the regent.⁹ Further, aided by the street violence outside the palace, their intervention proved successful: the king was forced to back down from his fiscal demands and to reform the tyrannical practices of his tax collectors [132, 133, 135].

The chronicles show the interconnectedness and networks of communication among insurgents across vast areas of northern France and Flanders – how a revolt in one place inspired tax resistance and disobedience to the crown in another. In 1382 the *Religieux* pointed to Paris as the example and epicentre [136, 146]: 'In Paris these risky things began; the rest then followed the capital' [136]. But later it was 'the daring' of the Rouennais, their *Harelle* in 1382, that set off a new round of revolt, which emboldened the Parisians to break into the Châtelet, steal the lead hammers, and revolt [136, 144, 145]. For others, it was the example of Bruges's and Ghent's defiance against the French crown [140, 151].¹⁰ But their major onslaught against the French king came in 1383, after those in northern France had already revolted and had been repressed¹¹ [140, 151]. The geography of

---

7 For a detailed study of Pintoin's classical references, his definition of the historian, and his use and moderation of the chronicle form, see Guenée, *Un roi et son histoire*, esp. chapters 1 and 5.

8 Of all the writers on the wave of revolts 1378 to 1382, Pintoin is the only one to think metaphorically about these revolts as contagious or as a plague. The notion was much more commonplace in chroniclers of revolts prior to the Black Death.

9 This was the king's uncle, Louis, duke of Anjou.

10 Also Froissart thought that those of Rouen and Paris took their cue from the 'men of Ghent', who 'so valiantly maintain their liberties'.

11 In 1381 the people of Ghent had risen against the count of Flanders.

revolt in northern France of the 1380s is much broader than that of the Jacquerie (even if Rouen's defiance of the dauphin's representatives, seizure of its royal castle, and raids against the noblemen of its surrounding country is considered part of the same revolt [57]).[12] Further, these revolts of the 1380s are in a different world from the uprisings in central Italy, where no significant evidence of inter-city support or communication can be found, except from the perspective of the ruling elites, who sought and received soldiers and aid to repress the uprisings of their commoners.

The two principal revolts of the opening years of the 1380s were the tax revolts and theatres of disrespect directed against the king and his officers, the *Harelle* in Rouen, followed by the hammer men in Paris. Despite the rich narrative and archival documentation, including even the chance survival of a charter the insurgents imposed on the barons of Rouen (Saint-Ouën) and whose dicta remained in force for less than a twenty-four hours [153], these revolts have received scant attention from recent historians. Since the work of Alphonse Chéruel published in 1843–4 and Léon Mirot at the beginning of the twentieth century,[13] they have received hardly any specialised treatment outside general surveys of the later Middle Ages. Thus, unlike the Jacquerie, the Ciompi, or the English Uprising of 1381, no current debate rages over the *Harelle* or the hammer men.[14] Nonetheless, given the influence of Mollat and Wolff's work certain views are now widely accepted: first, the years 1378–82 constituted a remarkable clustering of revolts not only across France but for all of Europe. Yet, as we have seen, in terms of its timing, the Revolt of the Ciompi was the exception in Italy. Even in France, there were two clusters; one for the south in the last years of Charles V's reign (1378–80), another for the north with the crowning of Charles VI and his urgent need to replenish his war chest (1380–2).

Secondly, Mollat and Wolff have distinguished this cluster of revolts from the earlier 'révolutions des métiers' circa 1250 to 1330, as revolts

---

12 On these events, see Sumption, *The Hundred Years War*, II, p. 325.

13 A. Chéruel, *Histoire de Rouen pendant l'époque communale 1150–1382*, 2 vols. (Rouen, 1843–4); and Léon Mirot, *Les insurrections urbaines au début du Règne de Charles VI (1380–1383): Leurs causes, leurs conséquences* (Paris, 1905).

14 Radding, 'The Estates of Normandy', has challenged earlier views of historians at the turn of the twentieth century – the royalist Léon Mirot and the liberal Alfred Coville – by insisting that the Estates General played no role in inspiring or leading the urban revolts, that instead they fully supported the attempts of the king to re-impose taxes.

of economic misery. But except for the revolts in the south there is little sign of it. Indeed, Froissart blamed the revolts of 1382 on the wealth of the lower classes and thought that the hammer men were 'the rich and powerful' of Paris, more elaborately armed than any 'knight could afford' [149]. Although Froissart grossly exaggerated the wealth of the hammer men, letters of remissions for these accused insurgents show a wide spectrum of professions – a furrier's apprentice or journeyman, a goldsmith, an image maker, and a salt merchant [161, 162]. While those involved in the street theatre of the *Harelle* with their trumped-up king for a day, their drunken orgies in the wine cellars of ex-mayors of the city, and their solemn oaths and charters imposed on the barons of Saint-Ouën may have been mostly journeymen, the local chronicler of Rouen, Pierre Cochon, reports that they were comprised of 'the scum as well as notables, drapers, and people of cheap cloth' and 'secretly supported by several big merchants and vintners' [145]. Moreover, such city-wide support, even involvement is suggested by the insurgents' objectives, which centred not on the poor or the disenfranchised but instead on upholding the interests of the bourgeois commune – its independence from the barony of the Saint-Ouën and from the privileges of other ecclesiastical institutions, such as the chapter of Nôtre-Dame and the monastery of Fécamp [136, 137, 145, 154]. Further, the ultimate penalty imposed on Rouen was the symbolic disgrace of cutting the tongue from its communal bell (which had called the rebels to action) and the abolition of Rouen's communal privileges [137, 146, 155] – symbols and rights more to do with the bourgeois and respectable artisans than the wretched of the earth.

Thirdly, it is questionable whether Philippe van Artevelde's 'revolt' of Ghent,[15] this city-state's conflict with Bruges, and the ensuing protonationalist struggle against French overlordship should be labelled as popular protest; rather, it is better seen as civil war and the efforts of one ruling elite to establish hegemony in Flanders. First, Philip reestablished his family's dynastic control over the city, using his first month in power to settle ruthlessly old family scores; then he used his thugs, the 'White Hoods' of Ghent, to ambush the Bruges workers, then digging a new canal authorised by the anti-Ghent count (Louis

---

15 Philip van Artevelde was the youngest son of Jacob van Artevelde, who had ruled Ghent from 1336 to the storming of the city by the young count Louis de Male in 1349. In alliance with England, Jacob was able to gain domination over Flanders and challenged the powers of Count Louis of Nevers and the French crown. Philip strove to do the same but his hegemony as a self-styled Prince of Flanders lasted for less than a year. On these rulers, see Nicholas, *The van Arteveldes of Ghent.*

de Male) that would have damaged Ghent's shipping advantage; then, in alliance with England Philip mobilised his forces to achieve regional hegemony in Flanders [151]; then he sought to free Flanders from the burden of Charles VI's new subsidies and the impositions of the French crown [140, 141, 151].[16] After Charles VI's victory, the confiscations of property show that it was the Ghent elite and not the poor who were the principal forces behind Ghent's 'rebellion' and resistance to the French.[17]

Fourthly, one of the most prominent historians of late medieval France has recently classified these late-fourteenth-century insurrections as 'revolts of the excluded', that 'they rose up against corrupt representatives of the law, the ruler's evil counsellors, but their confidence in the monarch – source of all justice – was unshaken'.[18] But direct acts of disobedience, insults to and attacks against the king, as well as indirect ones such as the attacks on Jews as a means of insulting the king, because they were perceived as his personal property [134, 136, 142], abound in these documents and horrified contemporary chroniclers such as the king's own historian, the *Religieux de Saint-Denys*.

Finally, historians need to rethink the links between the Black Death and the remarkable increase of popular protest across large areas of Europe. More than a narrow clustering of revolts from 1378 to 1382, the Black Death and its subsequent strikes spurred on an increasing number of revolts over a thirty-year period. These did not begin immediately after the plague's first strike, but rather around 1353 in Flanders, 1355 in Italy, and after the plague's second strike of 1357–8 in France and then with increasing regularity from the 1360s through the 1370s. Unlike before the plague, when no synchronisation in the timing of revolts north and south of the Alps occurred, for the thirty years following the Black Death, the trends ran roughly along the same tracks, even though their causes and forms varied radically from place to place. Certainly, the Black Death changed the balance between labourers and employers and resources and consumption, but as historians of the 1970s and 1980s have argued, these shifts were by no means uniform.[19] As with the English Uprising of 1381, these

---

16 See Nicholas, *Medieval Flanders*, pp. 228–31; and *idem*, *The van Arteveldes of Ghent*, chs. 6–8.
17 Nicholas, *Medieval Flanders*, pp. 230–1.
18 Guenée, *States and Rulers*, p. 195.
19 See *The Brenner Debate: Agrarian Class Structure and Economic Development in Pre-industrial Europe*, ed. T. H. Aston and C. H. E. Philpin (Cambridge, 1985).

documents for continental Europe show peasants and artisans in a privileged bargaining position because of the demographic catastrophes of the previous thirty years. On the other hand, the most famous of the revolts south of the Alps – the Tumulto dei Ciompi – turned on just the opposite demographics: the decline of the Florence's wool industry outstripped the fall in Florence's population. Thus a key demand of the Ciompi was the imposition of production quotas on their bosses in order to secure employment [128].[20] Labour surplus, not scarcity, was here the problem. Nonetheless, the Ciompi along with the vast majority of post-plague revolts show 'revolutions of rising expectations', 'a new self-assertiveness',[21] and not revolts of misery and desperation. It is to that psychological vein that historians must now turn their explorations.

Northern France and Flanders

132 The first popular uprising [*commocione*] before the crowning of King Charles VI

Chronique du Religieux de Saint-Denys, VI/1, Book I, Chapter II, pp. 16–23 [1380].

When the tempest of discord had settled, the people heard with happy exuberance that the dukes had decided to hasten the crowning of the king. The princes, however, delayed their departure for Reims[22] for some time because their troops, having abandoned their pursuit of the English, devastated the diocese of Paris and its surroundings, inflicting intolerable harm. Touched by the pleas of those of the city and the countryside, the new regent [the future Charles VI] summoned a meeting of his most important captains: 'Serious news', he told them, 'and rather strange words, my lords, have come my way about the men who serve under your military banners; it is reported that they are inflicting deployable violence on the subjects of our lord the king.

---

20 Giovanni Villani, *Nuova Cronica*, III, Book XII, chapter XCIV, p. 199, reported that around 1338, 200 wool shops in Florence were producing between 70,000 and 80,000 woollen cloths a year, worth more than 1,200,000 florins. Also, see Hidetoshi Hoshino, *L'Arte della Lana in Firenze nel basso medioevo: il commercio della lana e il mercato dei panni fiorentini nei secoli XIII–XV* (Florence, 1980), pp. 194–5.

21 For the English Uprising of 1381, see R. H. Hilton, *The Decline of Serfdom in Medieval England* (London, 1969), p. 35.

22 The city where the kings of France were crowned.

As a consequence, we beseech you by virtue of the oath that you have sworn and which binds you to demand that they end these practices. Thus to stop these disgraceful crimes and to arm us with a just and healthy law, we order that if a robbery is committed [by one of your men] it will be permissible to kill the thief and the murder will not be considered a capital offence, and if the thief is guilty and can be tried, he will be executed'.

This decree was made public everywhere in the king's name by the cry of heralds. But the troops remained insubordinate and undisciplined. They failed to take any notice of the law and continued to commit even greater atrocities. Soon they had infested all the surrounding territory, and, as a consequence, almost all those who worked the fields fled their villages in terror with their flocks and herds. They went hiding in isolated spots covered in brambles or in walled towns, fleeing as though from the English; truly, the deeds of these bands [the French soldiers] resembled those of the English in every respect, except for the murders and acts of arson. What's more, rather than respecting laws of hospitality, some robbed the peasants, stripped their houses bare; moved by their thirst for gain, they broke into all their rooms, searching every nook and cranny. With unbounded lust they looted everything they could carry with them. Others, thinking up other evil deeds, attacked the merchants who brought farm produce to Paris. If they encountered rustics or citizens, they would rob them immediately as well as extort large sums, saying it was owed to them in compensation for their trouble and to reimburse their expenses. Some went into the territory of others under the pretext of taking back what on previous occasions had been pillaged from their native soil; others so entranced by this pestilence that had struck these people gave their libidos free range and violently raped young girls, who had preserved the seal of their virginity. Also, these officers possessed a latent hatred of commoners [*ignobiles*], who obstinately refused to pay their royal taxes called the subsidies.[23] The royal tax collectors of Compiègne and of the county of Picardy pursued more ruthlessly than was the custom the collection of the salt tax, the sales tax on merchandise, the fourth on wine, and the rights of entering and leaving towns. After a lapse of a certain time, those [who had not paid] were cruelly expelled from their towns and villages, warned not to attempt similar things in the future, and to

---

23 These were excise taxes on wine, foodstuff, and other merchandise.

thank God that this time, out of respect for the king, they had been lucky to escape death.

Throughout the kingdom of France, the appetite for liberty and the desire to throw off the yoke of the subsidies were burning; a burning rage was brewing. Thus at Paris, more than two hundred men or more of the most base sort [*ex abjectiori plebe*] went to the royal palace. Despite his reluctance, they took along with them the provost of the merchants, John called Culdoe,[24] a modest man of proven loyalty. Surprised to see him in such a crowd, the duke [the regent Charles] asked why he had come in such a disorderly fashion and against custom. On his knees, the provost responded that necessity had no law; forced by the fury of the people, he had come to beseech him to abolish completely the burden of those taxes that the deceased king had imposed and had increased beyond measure.[25] He showed in many ways that the commoners [*plebs*] had been taxed intolerably. As soon as he had finished speaking, the crowd arose with a terrible cry, shouting that they would not pay the taxes any longer, that they would die a thousand times rather than suffer such dishonour and harm. The duke waited in fear, knowing that nothing was easier than for the disorder of the crowd to spill from anger to acts of violence. Thus, hoping to avoid exposing his majesty to the consequences of the crowd's disorder, he [the provost] flattered them with sweet words, and when they insisted with greater rage, he calmed them down with a prudent speech and obtained what he had asked of the new king, now absent.

Thus this colloquium had ended, and now with the spirit of liberty kindled within the commoners [*ignobiles*], they sought to hold nocturnal meetings and organized secretly in bands to plot revolt [*commocione*]. With their heads held up and scowling in wild rage, they attended these insane and dangerous assemblies. Their pride swelling, they attacked the rights of nobles and churchmen and in their extravagance thought that they could direct civil administration better than their natural lords. And even worse was their envy of

---

24 Jean Culdoe became provost in October 1380 and remained in office until 27 January 1383, when Charles VI returned to Paris and abolished the office of provost of merchants in Paris. Culdoe died in 1415; see *Dictionnarie de biographie française*, IX, pp. 1368–9.

25 Pintoin seems unaware that Charles V on his deathbed had abolished the hearth tax reducing royal revenues by a third and tax demands presumably by a comparable amount. Was the cause of these rumblings not instead Charles VI's need to compensate for this loss by raising revenue from indirect taxes, the subsidies?

their lords' wealth; so only with the greatest reluctance and occasionally with murmurs mixed with threatening words did they hand over the dues from their landed property. In short, this lust for new things was so incessant that only the absence of a leader prevented them from rebelling [*ad rebellandum*].

133 The king eases the tax burden imposed by his father on the people

Ibid., VI/1, Book I, Chapter VI, pp. 44–53 [1380]. The humanist chronicler uses invented speeches to capture the mood and reasoning of the artisan rebels.

In the same way that we look with pleasure at the sky as it clears after a storm, we rejoiced in the peace following the dispute among the dukes.[26] But while they were reaching agreement in the government, unexpectedly a civil uprising [*civili motu*] erupted. The spirit of the crowd was impelled by the desire for change; with an extreme burning the people sought to be free of the heavy burden of the subsidies. Parisians hoped not to be cheated of this favour by the king's accession to the throne. Until now the duke of Anjou[27] had not scheduled when it [the question of taxes] would be discussed. To speed up his reply, the youth, blaming the slowness on the old men, said the matter could not be put off without violence. And as a matter of fact, internal strife spread throughout the city between the powerful and the weak with their hatred blazing. Already skirmishes had broken out between them, and a revolt [*sedicione*] was about to explode. So the provost of the merchants called the aldermen [*scabinos*] and the notable bourgeois to assemble and attend to the matter. They met in the Parlour of the Bourgeois, in front of the Châtelet. All were of the same mind, to throw off this yoke and reclaim their liberty. However, so as not to upset the recent joy[28] of the royal majesty with these troubles, the provost asked them to wait a little while for the reply because of the

---

26 The dispute among the dukes of Anjou, Berry, and Burgundy, the brothers of Charles V, after Charles's death; it concerned who would be regent and tutor of the Dauphin (Charles VI); see A. Coville, *Les premiers Valois et la Guerre de Cent Ans (1328–1422)* Vol. 4 of *Historie de France depuis les origines jusqu'à la revolution*, ed. Ernest Lavisse (Paris, 1902), p. 269.

27 The uncle of the regent and a chief advisor of the future Charles VI. After Charles became king, the duke was made regent.

28 The peace among the dukes.

current circumstances. The wisest went along with this judgement, and the words of one man even began to appease the confused *plebes* and won the good graces of the king. But then a tanner, a coarse man, full of himself, incited the *plebes* with these seditious words:

> Will we ever get to enjoy prosperity and peace? Will we cease to see the greed of the lords ever increasing, which with numerous and unjust taxes crushes us without respite, reducing us to such misery? Riddled with debts, we are forced every year to pay more than we earn. Do you understand, citizens, in what contempt you are held? If they could, they would without doubt deprive you of light. If you breathe, if you utter a word, if you appear, or if you go out into a public place and stand near them, they are indignant and say: why do they confuse the sky with the earth? Without doubt, these men to whom we are forced to grant homage, of whose health we are ever mindful, and whom we feed from our own sustenance, have no other thought than to polish their gold and jewels, be surrounded by a great entourage of servants, build lofty palaces, and invent taxes to weigh down this mother of cities. For a long time, the patience of the *plebes* has borne these evil taxes. Unless we are soon freed from this intolerable yoke, I predict that the entire city will soon be roused to armed revolt; everyone would rather die many times than suffer such indignities.

After he had finished these insolent words, more than three hundred men like him soon assembled. Men incapable of being ruled by reason, with their daggers drawn, led the provost to the Palace, despite his refusal, resistance, and many excuses. And with great shouts, they demanded that the duke of Anjou lend a sympathetic ear to the petitions of the *plebes*. Constrained by the king's order, the duke came forward with my Lord Miles de Dormans, bishop of Beauvais, whom King Charles had made chancellor, a man remarkable not only for his eloquence but also for his wisdom and loyalty. When both had taken their places around the marble table, they agreed to let the provost say what he wanted. Speaking on behalf of the crowd, he pointed to the enormous burden of the subsidies, exposed the wretched state and poverty of the *plebes*, and concluded that even under pain of death, the people could not tolerate much longer the weight of the taxes that the dead king had placed on their heads, and that they all would rather die than lose their ancient liberties. All this was developed in a long speech. When he had finished, an immense cry arose from the confused crowd, a sign that those assembled had been pleased. The duke, a very prudent man, who knew how easily such people were aroused and moved to sudden violence, reflected on this enthusiasm and was known to have been terrorised by it. He feared they would rise up in violence, and more terrible riots would ensue. He also judged that any refusal would be dangerous and sought first to appease them with sweet words. Finally, with so many rebels staring at him, he ordered the chancellor to speak:

> Long experience has taught you that it is reasonable to boast of the generosity of the kings and the lords of France. You know that the city of Paris has been privileged from ancient royal decrees, embellished with monuments from a wise administration of public funds, and that it has always been – dare I say it – without equal among all the cities of France, treated with the highest honour and love. Nothing has ever been refused to you, whenever you have shown submission – certainly a quality that you lack at the moment. What do you wish to say to the king, that he should dare come here before this disorderly assembly, which is entirely consumed in anger, to address your demands when you order threats rather than pleas with respectful words? Then, without doubt, you deserve to be refused, for you have offended your natural lords. But the habitual clemency of kings, which always knows how to mix sweetness with severity, pardons you this time for this offence. To relax these subsidies, the royal majesty by custom does nothing without first taking counsel. You should now withdraw; the rage of the people [*populi*] must be curbed. Tomorrow, you will be given a hearing. You are to come here and perhaps your desires will be satisfied.

When the rioting of the people had quietened, [royal] counsellors appeared who wanted the people's demands to be refused. This concession, they said, would make the people more intractable rather than submissive; their first success would lead to more and more unjust demands. But the next day, they heard the same words as before – the *plebes* would rather die a thousand times than submit to these humiliating taxes. Then, the chancellor, in the name of the king and the duke, agreed to meet their demands and ended his speech thus:

> The peaceable exercise of the king's commands has always made the realm flourish, and we believe that everyone knows that God looks upon power without pride with benevolence and favour and would go against the plebes, who are haughty and insolent. The strength of an empire depends on the lawful obedience of its subjects [*regnicolarum*]. For kings are right to deny a hundred times that their rule derives from the will of the people [*suffragio popularum*] or that the strength of the people makes kings formidable. But at the same time, the sweat of his subjects gives the king his esteem, and his vigilance must ensure the health of his subjects so that they can enjoy the joys of peace and the luxury of leisure. Therefore, as you know, the king never wishes to abuse the greatness of his power; rather, he wishes to govern his subjects with clemency and gentleness. He

has thus decided to lift the yoke of slavery from your lives without demur so that you can enjoy the fruits of peace, which all mortals yearn for. Therefore, because of his paternal munificence, he withdraws the subsidies and all those taxes on importing and exporting merchandise that used to be levied on subjects of the realm and foreigners. Henceforth, no one under any pretext can be forced to pay any of these taxes; each will have the right to buy and sell freely. The king has also decreed by his special grace that tomorrow he will have this edict posted on every street corner of the city.

It seemed that the chancellor had satisfied the people; but noblemen, who were intermingled in the crowd and regretted that their property was being squeezed by excessive usury, instigated the people to terrible rioting again, demanding that the Jews be expelled from the city. But, by the king's goodness, they were made subject to an annual tax [*tributo*] and, because of this, were allowed to remain in his cities. Attentive to these riots, the chancellor felt obliged to calm the *plebes* with sweet words, promising to intervene with the king to obtain what they desired as soon as possible.

134 Crimes committed by the Parisian insurgents, particularly against the Jews

Ibid., VI/1, Book I, chapter VII, pp. 53–6 [1380].

After these words, the violence of the crowd quietened. Great thanks were given to the chancellor. Everyone extolled his prudence, praising to the stars his diplomacy and the wisdom of his judgement. All were happy beyond measure to have grasped the chance to regain their liberty. But the commoners took their pleasure to extravagant and immoderate lengths, tumbling into intemperate crimes, whose details are rather gruesome; however, since it is the historian's duty not to pass over the slightest detail worthy of being known, I have judged it proper to include them.

These aforementioned men animated by a beastly rage refused to wait for the next day when the concessions made in the name of the king were to be promulgated. Moved by their fury they soon rampaged through the city in a drunken rage, forced open the coffers containing the tax monies, seized the records of the royal tax receipts, tore them to pieces, and destroyed them. Then, still driven by the same impetuous spirit for change, they entered with fury into the quarter that the king had granted to the Jews, comprised of forty houses. Pressing on, they abandoned all individual traits of human character, age, and other distinctive qualities. Some forced open the doors of the Jews' houses, searching them thoroughly to plunder and steal anything that appeared useful. Others took necklaces, rings, belts, and other feminine ornaments, which were easy to carry off. They searched greedily for silk cloaks and other expensive clothing. They threw from the windows silver vases, which they took to their homes. Others preferred to cancel their debts to nobles and bourgeois, believing this to be more lucrative. Several nobles, who had joined them, incited them to go further. Given the free range of their cruelty, many killed all the Jews they encountered. There would have been a horrible carnage had these terrified people not fled to the king's Châtelet, where they immediately claimed their immunity in the house of the king and demanded to be protected with the other prisoners. While these massacres were taking place, pleas and cries of women and children in panic could be heard throughout the city. In this violence, some with their husbands succeeded in finding asylum. Others confided in the good faith of Christians, to whom they gave money. But these iniquitous people of the crowd, worthy of divine vengeance, stole everything they had, and more deplorably, kidnapped their children and forcibly baptised them.

On hearing the news of these crimes, the king was angered but was advised to conceal his vengeance for the time being. The next day he ensured the Jews could return to their homes safely, and by the cries of his herald and the sound of trumpets, he publicized throughout the city that he had issued an edict commanding all the stolen goods of the Jews to be returned under pain of death. Few, however, obeyed this royal ordinance.

135 The lords try in vain to re-impose the subsidies on the *plebes*

Ibid., VI/1, Book I, chapter X, pp. 66–9 [1380].

While these events were taking place [the English siege of Nantes], the funds of the royal treasury, as we have said, had become exhausted; the uncles of the king, his troops, and their captains could no longer be treated with the same largess. The sumptuous palaces begun by his father remained unfinished. In effect, the people were no longer subject to paying the subsidies. Recently, the duke regent had been denied these revenues.[29] But he reckoned that because the whims of commoners are so fickle it takes little time for the people to change their mind. Therefore, he called the most important bourgeois, nobles, and bishops to gather at his palace in Paris to accept a law that would reintroduce the general subsidies, but he did not succeed. Only his assistants [*assistencium*] agreed to a law that required a payment of twelve pennies on the pound on the sale of all merchandise. By the order of the king, this decree was posted in Paris, Rouen, Amiens, and the principal cities of the realm. But the bourgeois of the kingdom held it in contempt, adding that its implementation would require spilling much blood. Everyone desired fervently to cast off this burden; that is, they wished to live in liberty. Fearing dangerous and sudden revolt, the lord duke accepted this refusal, but only on the surface.

136 The uprisings at Paris and Rouen because of the subsidies, 1382

Ibid. VI/1, Book III: Chapter I, [1382], pp. 128–43.

Seven times in the past year, the duke of Anjou, regent of France, had called the most noteworthy men of the two estates [the nobility and the bourgeoisie] for advice to know how and when to decree a new levy of public subsidies to meet the needs of the king and the realm. Without doubt, those to whom it brought no disadvantage and those who made a profession out of flattering royal power and hoped to enrich themselves by sticking their hands into the king's gold sought arduously [the passage of] this measure. But the most notable of the bourgeois looked on it with deep suspicion, knowing that the people [*populus*] with their noses in the air and their inflated words had shown their disdain for it and wished to hear no more of it. In these gatherings, the knight Pierre de Villiers[30] and Lord Jean des Marès,[31] men of advanced age, great prudence, and highly respected by the

---

29 The Religieux fails to spell out here that Charles VI was forced to end royal exaction of these subsidies in January 1381; see [152].

30 From fear of attacks by the dauphin Charles, Étienne Marcel employed Pierre de Villiers as captain of the Parisian city guard – in effect, chief of police – in January 1358. Already in 1358 Villiers, a Norman knight, was an experienced soldier, who had served in campaigns in Brittany and Scotland; see Sumption, *The Hundred Years War*, II, pp. 305–6; and Delachenal, *Charles V*, V, p. 76.

31 Jean des Marès or Jehan des Marets or Mariez was advocate general of the parlement and one of Charles V's most able advisors; see Delachenal, *Histoire de Charles V*, II, p. 127.

plebes, often tried to change the *plebes'* opinions, arguing that it would provoke the king's anger. But the headstrong were bored by all this talk. Their unhappiness was like a spark that lights an inextinguishable fire. They remained steadfast in their opposition, declaring that they now considered the promoters of the subsidies as enemies of the state. Then, in each city, to show they would defend their liberty with force, the people took up arms, closed the city gates, stretched iron chains [across the streets], called up their neighbourhood militias of the tens, fifties, and sixties [*dizeniers, cinquanteniers,* and the *soixanteniers*],[32] and ordered close surveillance of those who entered and left their cities.

These thoughtless acts began in Paris; the rest then followed the capital. Everywhere, the presumption of citizens grew beyond bounds; these most untrustworthy men hoped they could gain their liberty in spite of the king. Those from Rouen fell into daring crimes better cast in the lugubrious tones of a tragedy than by a straight retelling. But to avoid such errors in the future, the historian cannot remain silent. Thus I judge it appropriate to speak now of these matters.

More than two hundred of the most insolent sort, workshop assistants in various crafts,[33] were emboldened no doubt by having drunk too much wine. By force, they seized a simple bourgeois, a rich vendor of cloth, nicknamed the fat one because of his obesity. Impertinently, they placed his name at the top of their acts and threw themselves headlong into this insane enterprise without any calculation of where it might end; immediately, they made him their king. They raised him up onto a throne as though a monarch, placed it on a chariot, and paraded him through the city, parodying the acclamations that would be made to a king. When they arrived at the market square, they asked him if the *plebes* should be freed from the yoke of all the subsidies, and he granted it. This franchise of short duration was made public through the city by the cry of a herald – a scene so ridiculous that it even justifiably made prudent men laugh. A huge crowd of the

---

32 For Nîmes, the citizenry was divided into fourteen units of fifty householders, each under a *cinquantier* with five *dizaniers* under him. Each 'fifty' was charged with the defence of a particular section of the walls. See Sumption, *The Hundred Years War*, II, p. 396. In Paris, the city districts were divided into units by forty, fifty, and sixty households; presumably, as in Nîmes, the tens were under the heads of these various divisions.

33 The editor, Bellaguet, calls these workers '*compagnons des metiers* (journeymen)'; the Latin is 'et qui publicis officinis mechanicis inserviebant artibus'.

most wretched sort quickly ran towards him and forced him to listen to their pleas as he sat in judgement. If anyone conceived of a riotous act and asked him his advice, he would be compelled to approve it and say: 'Do it; do it'. Then, driven not solely by audacity but by a beastly rage, they rose up against the royal tax collectors, killed them mercilessly, and unreasonably divided their belongings among themselves.

With this crime committed and approved, they went with the same authority to inflict great damage and losses on the Church. At Saint-Ouën, where the monks had obtained a writ entitling them to keep all their privileges against the wishes of the citizens, these nefarious men, fully deserving God's wrath, violently broke into the tower where their charters were kept, disrupted and tore to pieces the monastic privileges, which would have caused irreparable harm had they not been restored shortly by the king's authority. Pushed on by the same fever and without any fear of offending the king, these stupid and unarmed men charged against the king's castle to destroy it. But those inside repulsed them, killing or mortally wounding several.

This evil daring not only won over those from Rouen, it spread through almost all the people of France, who were roused to no less a feverish pitch. According to public opinion, it came from the Flemings, who had laboured under a similar plague of rebellion [*peste similis rebellionis*], spread by their messengers and letters, and by the example of the English, who, at the same time, were rebelling [*rebellantes*] against their king and the knights of the realm. The English forced them to flee and led an armed charge into the royal palace. In the king's presence, they violently dragged out five famous knights and the chancellor, the Archbishop of Canterbury, and in a public spectacle they were beheaded for disrupting the peace. At the time, I was in this kingdom, defending the cause of our church and heard with indignation that the *plebes* had kicked the sacred head of the archbishop through the streets of the city on that day. A bystander said: 'You know that in the kingdom of France even more horrible things are about to happen'. I only added: 'God forbid that such monstrous behaviour should befoul the [*plebes'*] continual loyalty to France!'

I return to my subject. My lord of Anjou saw clearly that the crime committed by the people's fury in October would eventually affront the king. Nonetheless, he held back his vengeance until March and in the interim made several attempts to collect the subsidies from the Parisians. Seeing that his efforts had not succeeded by embassy or gentle words, with the advice from his council, he tried to get his way by action. In January, he passed an ordinance behind the closed doors of the Châtelet in order not to spark a revolt [*tumultus*] from the *plebes*, who were not yet pacified. Immediately those hungry to profit from the tax farms stepped forward. But fear of death prevented anyone coming forward to make the proclamation in public. The matter dragged on for a long time and threatened to stall. But seduced by money someone took the offer to end the delay and began selling these tax farms in the market on the last day of February. Taking all necessary precautions for his safety, he assembled the people and began a sophistic discourse, shouting vigorously that someone had stolen some of the golden plates from the king's palace and that the king promised forgiveness, praise, and compensation to whoever returned them. This excited the people to begin laughing as though it were slightly unbelievable. While the town crier saw the people embroiled in these confused words and occupied in quibbling, he suddenly kicked his horse and confirmed that the collection of the tax would begin the following day. Not surprisingly, these things upset those who heard them and immediately wild rumours spread throughout the city. Most believed it was a lie; others were stunned and decided to wait until the matter was made public. Then, lit by the spirit of rebellion, they were drawn out by frightening oaths and conspired to kill those who had decreed the tax. The conspirators set to work without wasting time. And their oaths, O for shame! were soon followed by their crimes.

In the first hour of the first day of March, they gathered in les Halles [the principal market of Paris] and saw a woman selling greens, called *cresson* in French [watercress], being asked for the tax; they quickly charged against the royal tax collector and wounded him in many places, which led to his death. With this crime committed the revolt was no longer confined to les Halles but spread here and there throughout the city. From all over, the insurgents ran to les Halles and made a tremendous noise. The crowd swelled on all sides, an immense clamour arose everywhere, filling the ears of everyone. Thus the awful stench [*dirum virus*] of sedition [*sedicionis*] gushed out everywhere. Through the squares and streets of the city, the uprising soon filled the heads of men, and worthy of God's wrath, the dreadful rumblings of voices called their men to arms with swords and other weapons that fanned the people's rage for the liberty of their country [*ob libertatem patrie*]. A small number had incited the multitude into this insanity. Drawing in one after another, they recruited everywhere those who volunteered to join the sedition. In no time, five hundred of a similar spirit had joined them.

News of these crimes became known to all, spreading to all parts and filling everyone with fear. As a consequence, several counsellors of the king, the principal bourgeois of the city, the bishop, and provost of Paris, fearing for their safety, left the city and afterwards sent their belongings to other places. Indignant over these uprisings, they thought they would insult the king less by being absent than in contact with the seditious crowd. One saw these miserable men, viler in their manners than in their poverty, on foot and leaderless, marching in troops ready to overthrow the city. If the stupidest of them proposed some criminal act, all the rest of these miserable ones followed, resulting in the wickedness seen below.

Since they were unarmed, they went first to the Town Hall [*domum ville*], where they snatched swords, sabres, hammers of lead, and other arms from the city's armoury. As a prelude to the massacre, they put to death all the tax collectors they met. With greater cruelty, they violently seized someone from the church of Saint-Jacques, who, fearing for his life, was found at the altar, clutching a painting of the blessed Mary. They hemmed him in and cut his throat, violating the sanctity of the church. Then, pleased with their criminal acts, they went pillaging the property of their victims, destroyed the front of one house, violently broke into other houses, knocked down doors, carried off all the gold, silver, documents, and precious objects they found, and tore to pieces other belongings and threw them out windows. They also poured out the wine in cellars, drinking beyond measure. Inflamed with drunkenness, they then committed their crimes with greater audacity and went to Saint-Germain-des-Prés.[34] Knowing that those tax collectors who had escaped their blows were in hiding, they hunted them down. If any refused to obey, they violently broke into their houses. Those inside vigorously repulsed them. But the crowd's fury drove them on. No doubt, provoked by shouts from the most abject of them, as before, the wickedest went after the Jews, whom the king protected; they killed some and stole their most valuable possessions. Adding to their infamy, they felt no shame in violating the house of the king, incurring for a second time the crime of treason.

---

34 One of the oldest and wealthiest monasteries in France, located on the left bank.

Many of the men in this mob [*concione*] were criminals who had accomplices imprisoned in the royal Châtelet. The dumb crowd were led to this place and broke into the prison, freeing two hundred men or so, some charged with indebtedness, others held for capital offences. The insurgents perpetrated similar crimes at the episcopal prisons of Paris, where they found Lord Hugues Aubriot, recently charged for his misdemeanours.[35] With insolent rejoicing, they led him back to his house and made him their leader. He thanked them graciously and promised them great things. But being a modest man and distrustful of these seditious *plebes*, he seized the first opportunity to escape, sneaking out in the dead of night. These miserable people increased steadily in number, a crowd of almost incalculable size followed in their footsteps, not so much to imitate them as to wonder at this strange uprising. The following night they made several attacks against the citizens. Thus the squadron leaders of the militia companies of the fifties and the sixties assembled ten thousand bourgeois armed to the teeth. At first, these tried in every way to bring the agitated *plebes* to their senses. But seeing that sweet words would not move them, they thought it wise not to confront the crowd's blind rage head on. Instead, they divided their men into small groups and spread them through the city on street corners and squares where they could repulse the insurgents' violent actions when they were committed. After spending the evening in debauched eating and drinking, this haughty and boisterous crowd fell into an insane frenzy. They went to the house of Hugues Aubriot, and not finding him, burst into a beastly rage; a horrible clamour rang through the city. They rushed rapidly to destroy the bridge of Charenton. Gripped by fear of death or repentance, they failed, or more likely, the conciliatory words of Lord Jean des Marès, whose eloquence had often swayed them and whose advice they followed, stopped them.

---

35 Prior to becoming provost of Paris, Aubriot had been the chief royal officer [*le bailli*] of Dijon until 1367 when he came to Paris. With the funeral procession of Charles V, he came to blows with the University of Paris, and on 24 September 1380 his police badly injured thirty students. Because of his quarrels with the church and the university on questions of the jurisdiction over clerics, he was accused of heresy and jailed on 1 February 1381; Delachenal, *Histoire de Charles V*, V, pp. 423–4; and *Dictionnaire de biographie française*, IV, pp. 241–4.

137 The people of Rouen are punished for their crimes

Ibid., VI/1, Book III, Chapter III, pp. 144–5 [1382].

Infuriated by the insolence of those from Rouen and not wishing to close his eyes to their crimes or to encourage them to become more audacious and commit new ones, the king soon entered the city with his uncles and an entourage of many noble lords. The principal perpetrators wanted to refuse him entry unless he first promised them immunity. This only made the king angrier, and from anger he raced to vengeance, razing the gate through which he entered. Passing by the town's belfry, he dismantled the bell that had called the commune to action. He ordered all the citizens to hand in their weapons in person to the royal castle, which they did regretfully and unhappily. The following day, the king's council condemned to death the principal culprits, sentencing them to capital punishment as a spectacle for the commune. Then the royal commissioners were given the authority to collect the tax on drink and the sale of cloth.

138 The king pardons the Parisians for their offence

Ibid., VI/1, Book III, Chapter IV, pp. 144–9 [1382].

The king had hardly taken three days to reform Rouen, when he heard the news of the Parisians' crimes. This doubled his anger, and he immediately left Rouen to punish the offence. However, he was persuaded to soften his vengeance for the moment, yielding to pleas and the intervention of the University of Paris, his venerable daughter. Knowing that his resentment was not without justification, the wisest of the citizens sent representatives to meet him in the Bois de Vincennes.[36] As envoys to negotiate the peace, the city elders with the most prestigious doctors and masters [of the university] went and asserted their innocence. Allowed to have an audience with the king, they persuaded him little by little of their position in the following way:

> Your royal grandeur and eminence knows much better than us that in every assembly – not only in the cities and the grand meetings of men – all do not sparkle with the same prudence; nor are they endowed with

36 A large royal park on the southeastern fringe of Paris, where the kings of France had a castle that stands today.

equal learning. Rather different passions and *mores* produce different tastes, as the wise saying goes: 'there are as many opinions as there are men'. Not that the heated imprudence of the inconsiderate *plebes* necessarily damages the better off. Indeed, it generally happens that the confused *plebes* have no regard for rules and by habit indulge in fights and sedition. Surely, the inconsiderate *plebes* must explain themselves to the wellborn and those who conduct important affairs.

After developing these points at length, humbly kneeling at the king's feet, they described the impassioned actions and damages inflicted by these most nefarious men. By their pleas, they finally obtained exemptions from the subsidies for the *plebes*, and the commoners were pardoned for their public errors, provided that those who had broken into the Châtelet were seized and punished severely.

They were delighted with these conditions and accepted his gracious actions. Then Lord Jean des Marès went through the streets of the city in a litter, because he could not walk, and made it known to everyone that the king had been appeased. However, as might be expected, they took little notice of his intentions or the ordinances. Already the provost of Paris held those who had offended the royal majesty, but when he was leading one of them to be punished, the people suddenly ran from all parts of the city, shouting in rage that they should not suffer such an insult. With such a crowd, justice could not be rendered so quickly. New and dangerous uprisings would have flared everywhere, had the king not magnanimously capitulated and not ordered the provost to defer the execution. The provost obeyed only in appearance. By another order from the king and over many days, he secretly had many of the condemned forcibly drowned in the Seine.

139 The Parisians refuse the subsidies with a new stubbornness

Ibid., VI/1, Book III, chapter VI, pp. 150–7 [1382].

While these affairs were being treated in this cloudy whirlwind [the debates in the regional assemblies over the subsidies], several courtiers did not cease bending the king's ears with vehement and earnest pleas: that by his benevolence he should condescend to forgive the offences of the Parisians and to bring about peace by coming to Paris. The king sent an envoy[37] to say that he would enter the city only on

---

37 According to Froissart, the lord of Coucy went unarmed to Paris to begin negotiations.

the following conditions: that on the arrival of the king and his entourage the people would put down their arms and open all the gates of the city. As long as he was in residence, the iron chains would not be stretched [across the streets] at night; the Parisians who served the lords of France would be the only ones permitted to bear arms; and finally, he would enter decked out in armour without any hindrance. He also ordered that within three days the Parisians should send six or seven hundred of the wealthiest citizens to him at Meaux to let him know what had been decided.

The conditions of the treaty were read out to the general assembly of citizens, and most of the populace, who were there in great numbers, were ready to reject them out right. Stirred by the spirit of rebellion, they enjoined the notables under threat of losing their lives and property to see things their way. In addition, only with great difficulty could six, justly filled with terror, be found to bring this news to the king and plead humbly that he would not treat them too harshly but with clemency would weigh the dangers they constantly faced when conciliatory words failed to dampen the people's rage.

This response was not taken kindly. However, the king let the envoys go without doing them any harm. Holding himself back, he buried the injury of this refusal until he knew for certain whether the people were really agitated enough to revolt. He placed Lord Pierre de Villiers in charge, whom the *plebes* held in esteem. The king suggested that he mention to them only the salt tax and the tax on the sale of merchandise. But seeing how such things sparked sedition within the city, he did not fulfil his mission. He returned with news that was more outrageous than what the king had already heard. Thus the king was pushed to use naked force and received counsel on whether to attack the city or the countryside around it. For this, the duke of Anjou assembled a large force of men-at-arms from anywhere he could. They pillaged the entire diocese of Paris with all the atrocities that one enemy levies against another, except for murder and acts of arson. Urged on by an irreconcilable hatred, the soldiers ran here and there, driven by greed to carry off everything they could and would not end their raids or plundering unless paid to go away. They destroyed the property and by force robbed every bourgeois or peasant they encountered and crushed them into paying ransom. If refused, they cut down the fruit trees in their orchards and the wheat in their fields. In a word, they ravaged the surrounding countryside to such an extent that the inhabitants not only had to transport all their goods from the countryside to walled towns but also their animals; no one dared step outside his door. These intolerable damages fell principally on the most powerful citizens, who possessed considerable properties and mansions in the suburbs outside the city walls. One night, various signs were secretly marked on their doors so [the perpetrators] could see more easily which houses would give them the greatest spoils. Rightly, this increased the terror, especially since they did not know if it came from the rebels within or from the combatants outside.

Finally, the citizens saw they did not have the means to resolve these pressing troubles, of which they informed the citizens of Rouen and many other cities. With pleas, sweet words, and attempts to buy them off with money, they persuaded the *plebes* to put an end to all this agitation and thereby to enjoy at last the comforts of peace. Further, to ensure that this matter was arbitrated by prudent men and brought to a good conclusion, the king sent Lord Arnaud de Corbie, the first president of the Parliament with Lord Jean des Marès, deputy of the citizens of Paris, to Saint-Denis towards the end of May ...

To cut a long story short and get to the point as I strive to do, I will not indulge in an eloquent discourse or use sweet words to express how this Arnaud conveyed the needs of the king and kingdom and asked the *plebes* for a subsidy. Lord Jean des Marès responded at greater length, giving a thousand examples of the loyalty and affection that the Parisians have always shown the king and ended by saying that as proof they would generously give the king by unanimous consent one hundred thousand gold francs. Thus the conference ended to the great satisfaction of both parties. It was ruled that all those who had assisted would go and give thanks to God before the bodies of the blessed martyrs,[38] and the venerable monks of the abbey were beseeched to sing loudly a *Te Deum laudamus*[39] for bringing peace. The following day a herald publicised the peace through the squares of Paris.

All settled, the king made his entry into the city two days later to the great joy of the citizens. They sang his praises with sweet melodies played on musical instruments to acclaim his entry. However, they delayed for a long time to pay the promised sum, blocked by the insolence and stubbornness of a wicked company [*comitiva*] of the

38 At the abbey of Saint-Denis, where the kings of France are buried.
39 First line of the hymn of thanksgiving: 'We praise Thee O Lord'.

people, who did not cease demanding that members of the clergy pay taxes as they did. They were unaware that they would soon receive their just deserts for this and their other rebellious acts.

140 Philippe van Artevelde vigorously urges the Flemings to fight valiantly, 1383

Ibid., VI/1, Book III, Chapter XV, pp. 204–11 [1382].

Those from Ghent and their allies, exhausted by a great number of battles, could no longer endure the cruelties, pillaging, and massacres, which the French inflicted on them everywhere; nor could they repulse them by force. They called for Philippe van Artevelde, who pushed aside any excuses and led his armed men into the interior of Flanders to come and decide on what was to be done. He abandoned the siege of Oudenaarde,[40] which had gone on for three months. He left some of his troops there and went as secretly as he could with four thousand Flemings to join his other troops and to keep them tightly bunched to give the French the impression, if they saw them, that they were few in number so [the French] would not retreat in terror. The people [*populo*] of Ghent received him with great honour and gratitude. He quickly held a general assembly; the pressing circumstances did not allow for any delay. They debated whether to resign themselves to a humble capitulation or to continue with the fortunes of war. Philippe took the floor and with the most arrogant words disparaged the French and exhorted everyone to resist valiantly to the end:

> Friends and compatriots, when will you realise your own strengths, which nature does not even wish wild beasts to ignore? At least count how many you are compared with the enemy. When you must fight one against one, I am persuaded that you would show more energy in defending your own just cause than the foreigner can in sustaining a tyrannical domination. Only by threatening war, will you gain lasting peace. Some might say that you are about to enter the abyss, but God should prevent it. To be sure, He will never descend from the heavens to mingle in your affairs. But He must give you the courage necessary to make such an audacious strike. I could talk to you for a long time on how to fight the French and on the vanities they deploy. Vain appearances contribute nothing to success. You will see an army glittering in gold and silver, their helmets with their plumes, knights dressed in golden tunics and in many colours. But for a

---

40 About 27 km south of Ghent.

long time you have known this apparel of shining insignia, and your enemy is no more terrifying for it. You have nothing to fear unless the French, overwhelmed by cowardice, terrorised by your numbers, should flee or refuse to fight. Thus, I have no doubt that you can easily hem them in. Therefore, if you can lift up your heads, under my command I can ensure you happiness. In war you must deploy all the courage you can now muster to achieve victory. If hope should deceive me, I would not have you follow me at all, and I would make myself endure every imaginable torture.

With few words he recommended that after victory they take no hostages, that all be killed, except the king, who should be led captive to England, if he were to take part in combat and should fall into their hands, and that the French domains be divided among the Flemings. Raising their right hands, they swore to fulfil all these daring deeds. Then, certain of victory, he marched against the French with the raised standard of Saint George followed by many others, on which the tools of all the craft guilds were painted.

141 The French pursue the Flemings as they flee

Ibid., VI/1, Book III, Chapter XVII, pp. 228–31 [1382]. The chronicler describes the slaughter of the Flemish forces, calling their actions seditious and 'crimes of rebellion'; nearly all their leaders were killed, including Philippe van Artevelde, who, the chronicler says, was offered a pardon if he would become French to which he answered: '"Your efforts are in vain; now with my blood and life about to abandon me, I was and always will be Flemish" ... And as seen throughout his life, he would rather die than be given liberty as a Frenchman'. The chronicler continues:

Afterwards, the king left the field of battle with great ceremony and headed for Courtrai, as had been decided, to punish these people for their revolt. He entered by removing the city gates from their hinges and knocking them down. The four leaders of the sedition were led in front of him and the following day endured their last anguish. He rested for several days in this city to provision his troops with wheat, which they found in abundance, and by the cries of his herald and the sounds of trumpets made it known publicly through the squares of the town that the inhabitants were not to suffer any damages or injuries. But the frenzy of the French was great and uncontrollable. The memory of the golden spurs and military banners suspended in the cathedral [of Courtrai] as trophies of their victory over the French in

[...]⁴¹ provoked such resentment that the king's order was disobeyed once he had left. They sacked the town, rampaging through it indiscriminately, penetrating into the most secluded houses, flushing out hiding places, and seizing the most desirable booty for the French. They attacked those who fled and hid and led them to a dishonourable death. They massacred all they found, sparing none because of rank, age, or sex, so it could be said: 'They slew the widow and the foreigner, murdered orphans, young men, and virgins alike, babies at their mothers' breasts, and old men'.⁴² Once the carnage ended, they consumed the town in a torrent of hungry flames.

Now the fame of the king's exploits had spread throughout Flanders. On hearing of the defeat, the princes of the counties regretted having been thrown into the rebellion [*rebellionis*], cursed the author of their defection, and prayed to God that he be condemned to eternal fire with Dathan and Abiron.⁴³ They did not take up arms to avenge him but unanimously chose to ask forgiveness for their errors. They sent ambassadors [to the king] with words and gifts carefully chosen to please him and promptly offered to submit in any way. With his inexhaustible clemency, the king did not refuse the grace they prayed for. Rumour then spread that someone had discovered a letter at Courtrai sent by the citizens of Paris, which proposed an alliance of mutual friendship between the two cities. This provoked the king's anger. Thus the citizens of Paris and all others responsible for defending their cities were seized with terror and renounced any such designs.

142 Tax revolts and attacks on Jews in Paris, 1380

Chronique des quatre premiers Valois, pp. 291–2.

After the king [Charles VI] had arrived in Paris,⁴⁴ some of the nobles and the people of Paris did not wish for the subsidies to continue to be imposed, taxes such as those of twelve pennies on the pound, the salt

---

41 The year was 1302 during the popular revolts across the Low Countries from 1299 to 1302; see [12, 13].

42 The core of this citation, 'viduam et advenam interfecerunt, et pupillos occiderunt' comes from the Vulgate, *Psalms*, 93:6.

43 Sons of Eliab who joined the conspiracy against Moses and Aaron and were swallowed up by an earthquake.

44 The young king had just returned from his coronation at Reims.

tax, and the fourth and the thirteenth.⁴⁵ The Parisians went to petition the king and the duke of Anjou to repeal the subsidies, [pleading] that they would ruin and reduce to poverty all the people. The new chancellor said they would have an answer the next day. And, as the chancellor was leaving the palace, a great throng of people seized him and shouted at him, saying that they [the royalty] would hear from them [the people] if the evil subsidies were not ended. The Chancellor was frightened and answered that the king and my lord of Anjou wished to end them all. Then they led the chancellor to the cash boxes, where these subsidies were collected. Afterwards, the Parisians led the provost of the merchants to the Palace to gain confirmation that these subsidies would be abolished. More than twenty thousand men had gathered there, dressed in white and green. Monsignors the dukes of Anjou, of Berry, of Burgundy, Monsignor of Clichon, the new constable, the chancellor, and a great number of the great lords went to the marble table in the Palace. And the Parisians were told that the king wished to end and abolish all the subsidies. Then the Parisians shouted very loudly: 'Noel! Noel! Great Plenty! Long live the King of France! Glory to Saint-Denis!'⁴⁶ Then someone cried out in this assembly: 'After the Jews, After the Jews, After the Jews!' And they went after them and robbed the Jews, killing one of their rabbis.⁴⁷ But the king quickly sent my lord the duke of Bourbon, who declared that the king had taken all the Jews of his realm under his protection. And the Jews in other cities of the kingdom were put under his safeguard. After these evil subsidies and taxes had been quashed, it was agreed and decreed that a certain tax [*aide*] would be granted to the king for the defence of his realm, and that the provinces and regions would follow suit [in paying the taxes], that my lord the dukes of Anjou, of Berry, of Burgundy, and the council would be taking care of this matter for the king.

143 Tax revolts in Picardy, 1380

Chronographia regnum Francorum, ed. H. Moranvillé, 3 vols. (Paris, 1893–97), II, p. 397. This was a compilation of earlier texts assembled at the Abbey of Saint-Denis at the beginning of the fifteenth century. It goes from the history of the Franks to 1405.

45 The fourth was a tax on wine. I do not know what the thirteenth was.
46 A French war cry.
47 The chronicler says 'evesques' or bishops.

And then in certain of the principal towns of Picardy grumbling began because they were now forced to pay all the taxes [*tailles*] and aids, except the hearth tax [*fouagio*], which they had paid at the time of Charles [V], the last king to die, who had declared that they would not have to pay these in any form. Those of [the town of] Saint-Quentin were especially opposed to paying them. Thus on the feast day of Saint Denis [9 October], a market day, royal commissioners came to collect the sales taxes [*auxilia*] and pressed forward to collect them. The townsmen and those around the market square came out, beat these men up, and threw them out. Then, they knocked down the house where these taxes were received. Thus those in the market place remained free without paying these taxes.[48]

144 The *Harelle* of Rouen and its ramifications for the commoners of Paris

Chronique des quatre premiers Valois, pp. 297–301. As a resident of Rouen, this chronicler would have been particularly well-informed about the *Harelle*; most likely, he was an eyewitness to the events; see [93].

In this year, 1381, the dukes of Berry and of Burgundy with the advice of the king of France wished to impose the tax of twelve pennies on the pound along with other subsidies. It happened on Saint Mathias day [24 February], Monday, the first day of Lent. Some of the commoners [*menu commun*] of the city of Rouen rose up against the bourgeois and the people of this estate, because the latter wished to go along with the king's new tax. For this reason, wrongheaded and badly-advised commoners headed for the houses of several notable bourgeois of the city and broke into their houses, smashing the doors, windows, trunks, coffers, walls, and glass lanterns. They took, seized, sacked, plundered, broke, and smashed the property of several of these bourgeois. From fear of these badly-advised people, several of the worthiest bourgeois left town. Constrained as much by fear for their wives and children as for the houses and property they possessed in the city, having been threatened with the loss of all these things, the bourgeois conceded to obey [the commoners]. Over the next few days, these badly-advised ones organised three large assemblies in the

---

48 The incident is also mentioned in a letter of remission; see Douet d'Arcq, *Choix de pièces inédites*, I, p. 20, granted to Gervaise de Grenges, a carpenter, accused of having taken part in this riot.

chapter house [*l'ettre*] of Saint-Ouën in this city. In these assemblies they forced the monks to bring out their property charter, which gave the dean and chapter of the church of Nôtre-Dame in Rouen revenues from the markets and mills of this town, granted to them by Charles [V], who had just passed away. In addition, these ones who had been badly advised wished to force the monks, abbot, and monastery of Saint-Ouën in Rouen to surrender and renounce all claims and end all their law suits against the city and in general to acquit the city of anything these monks might demand. After doing these things, along with forcing the monks to draft many invalid ordinances, they were advised to send an envoy to the king of France to appease and excuse the good citizens before him and his council. For this purpose, they appointed to represent the city clerics as well as lawyers, bourgeois, and nobles to go in the company of my lord of Blainville. Because of the great troubles the royal court was going through, they returned empty handed.

In this year Saturday 1 March in the city of Paris, the commoners also revolted because they wanted to put down the new tax and other subsidies. And the common people [*menu gens*] attacked the tax collectors, killing some. They also rose up against several of the king's officers concerned with taxes and committed many crimes, breaking, taking, and pillaging all the property and houses they could find belonging to these officers. Then they went and broke into the royal prison of the Châtelet, freed the prisoners and ripped up the registers, acts, and charters they found there concerning the king, his jurisdiction, and his officers. They then went to the bishop's palace and similarly freed the prisoners kept there, among them Hugues Aubriot, who had been provost of Paris ... They led him through Paris and left him; he then escaped outside the city.

After these things had happened, the king of France, who was a child, with the duke of Burgundy, his uncle and chief advisor, left the Bois de Vincennes and travelled to Pont-de-l'Arche, four leagues outside Rouen, where they stayed for part of Lent. Here several bourgeois of Rouen came to plead on behalf of the good bourgeois and citizens of the city of Rouen. And after the king, my lord of Burgundy, and the king's council had been well informed about what had happened in this city, they became favourably disposed towards the bourgeois and people of this city. And so that each should have his just deserts, they seized those who were and could be shown to have been the most culpable of the wrongdoers and threw them in prison. Of these, the king, my lord of Burgundy, and the king's council ordered six to be beheaded. Of the others in prison, twelve were taken to the castle of Fontaine-le-Bourg, which belongs to the abbey and monastery of Fécamp.

After this, the king with his uncle, the duke of Burgundy, and many notable men who were his advisors, left Pont-de-l'Arche for Rouen. And with his joyous arrival,[49] the citizens – at least six hundred on horseback – went a good two leagues outside the city to receive the king joyously and to accompany him into his city. These bourgeois with many others of the city dressed in robes of the same colours, the heraldic blue and green with the blue on the right. The king was very honourably received and gave his full grace to the entire city. He stayed here for all of Easter week, leaving after Easter. Before entering Rouen, the king ordered the townsmen to take all their weapons to the castle of Rouen, which they did obediently. And they took down the defensive devices [*manteaulx*] of the gate of Martainville, where the king was to enter. And the king removed the office of the mayor and Rouen's jurisdiction and control over its commune and placed them into his own hands; then he entered the city on the eve of Palm Sunday. While in Rouen, he had the barons, prelates, and bourgeois of Normandy agree to the tax so that the other provinces of the realm of France would then accept it.

At Easter 1382, the king of France held his full court in his castle at Rouen with the nobles of Normandy. He made My Lord Guillaume de Bellegues captain of Rouen, and the day after Easter, the king left Rouen. On the following Friday the weapons were returned to the men of Rouen because of their good behaviour. And on the Monday after Quasimodo,[50] of the twelve who had been taken to the castle of Fontaine-le-Bourg, before the king had entered Rouen, as was said, six were hanged on the gallows of Rouen and the other six remained in prison at the castle of Rouen and were later freed by the king's grace. All these were people of the lowest estate [*petit estat*] and of bad behaviour.

The king and the duke of Burgundy, with the king's council, went from Rouen to Compiègne in order to impose these taxes and [even] on most of the nobility of Picardy. And some of the principal towns of the county agreed to the new tax.

49 The 'joyous arrival' of a king was a grand ceremonial entry.
50 The first Sunday after Easter.

145 The *Harelle*, according to Pierre Cochon

Chronique Normande de Pierre Cochon notaire apostolique à Rouen, ed. Charles de Robillard de Beaurepaire (Rouen, 1870), ch. XI, pp. 162–6.

In 1381 on Saint-Mathias day, the first Monday of Lent [24 February], when Sir Robert Deschamps was mayor, a revolt comprised of the scum [*merdaille*] as well as notables, drapers, and people of cheap cloth [*gens de poure estoflé*] began in the town of Rouen. Secretly supported by several big merchants and vintners, they charged through the streets of Rouen. And the city's grandees felt it necessary to go into hiding, and they were robbed and pillaged. And thus a great number, who were rich, now are poor, and those who had nothing are rich. Because of the [king's] fine the rich were ruined and those responsible for these wicked deeds were asked for nothing. And it all began because the king and his councillors wanted to have once more all the taxes as in the past. During this riot, all the gates of Rouen were locked for three days and none of its bells was rung, not at Notre-Dame or Saint-Ouën, except for those of the commune. And no sergeant of the mayor dared to carry the staff [of the commune] about the city. And every day they [the insurgents] gathered in the cemetery of Saint-Ouën. And in all this mayhem, only one man died, named Guerart Poullain, and a Jew was drowned in the Seine. And they freed the prisoners from the town hall and those of the vicar general [*official*], and they tore up the privileges of the barony of Saint-Ouën[51] and they took over the rights of appointing the priests for Notre-Dame of Rouen. And everything they demanded they drew up in a charter of the rights and liberties of Normandy. And they went to the home of Gueront de Marromme, who last year had been mayor of Rouen when he had done much harm to the poor of the city in his time as mayor: they still remembered him and threw his belongings out on the street on the Big-bridge, where he lived, and hurt him as best they could. They broke up his house and drank his wine, and when they could drink no more, they smashed the casks filled with wine and let them roll down the cellar. The damage they inflicted amounted to between two thousand and three thousand pounds. They then proceeded to the homes of Sires Guillaume Alorgem Eude, Clement, and Sir Jehan Le Triffillier – all past mayors of this town[52]

---

51 See [153].
52 They had been mayors respectively in 1375–76, 1359–72, and 1376–78.

– and did great damage. Thus because of the rage of this scum, no one dared to come out; rather they stayed in hiding at the Cordeliers [Franciscans] and other religious houses of the city as best they could. And on that first night, a large number of people were robbed, especially priests, Jews, and moneylenders [*presteurs à usure*], who were in the city at that time. And with these evil things still going on, the bourgeois reflected that if they did not put an end to these matters, they would all be ruined. So in the evening they armed themselves and set as good a watch as they could. And stationing themselves at the cemetery of Saint-Ouën, Notre-Dame, Saint-Lô, and Saint-Godart, they seized a large number of these thieves that night. And all this was done in agreement with the masters of the rioting, like one named Jehans Le Cras of the cloth industry and another named La Caune. They fled and have never been seen since in this country. Another among them named Mahiet Beaudouz, who had worked as a guard [*sergenterie*] for Pierre Poolin, did not flee, which was foolish for his head was cut off. And these ten leaders led their allies to the field of Rouen at the cross of Saint-Ouën, where they assembled. And they refused to pay the 300 pound rent they owed [for their stalls] in the market of Rouen. And similarly they forced [the monks of] Saint-Ouën to renounce its rights of barony and jurisdiction over the city and made them admit that these rights were held by the city of Rouen and that the city would no longer be obliged to pay the fine of 200 pounds, which it had been condemned to pay by an act of parlement. And these things said, after all that had happened, matters returned to their rightful order. In addition, on the following Wednesday, these masters called another assembly in the cemetery of Saint-Ouën [carrying with them] a charter of the Normans sealed with silk strings and green wax, which they took into the treasury of Notre-Dame in Rouen and had it read out to all assembled [*fu leue en general*]. A lawyer named Thomas Pougnant, the chief officer of Harecourt, read it out under threat of having his house knocked down if he disobeyed. And neither the great nor the small refused to swear on the Holy Gospels that they would uphold the agreements [in the charter] as best they could. Everyone present swore to it: the abbot of Saint Catherine, the dean and chapter of Rouen, the vicar general, his prosecutor [*promoteur*],[53] the priors of

---

53 A ecclesiastical law enforcer trained in canon law who reprimanded crimes and misconduct made by individual denunciations or by public outcry; see Robert Fawtier and Ferdinand Lot, *Histoire des institutions françaises au moyen âge* (Paris, 1957), III, p. 359.

the priory of the Madeleine, those of Mont-à-Maladez, along with all the lawyers and bourgeois of Rouen, and the procurator of the king, who was in Rouen at this time. And in addition, they pardoned and ceased proceedings against all those who had caused damage or done worse things at the time of these revolts. And the officials present at the time in the ecclesiastical and lay courts passed these matters and drafted them correctly. With this everyone was appeased. Afterwards, they sent letters to the king seeking pardons and did so many times without a reply. They were told that the king would come to Rouen and here he would find out who had broken into the larder [*aroit mengié le lart*]. Enough said about this riot. I will return to the king's entry.

146 The hammer men of Paris and the spread of tax revolts through *Langue d'oïl*

Chronographia regnum Francorum, III, pp. 24–33 [1382].

And then all the gates of the city [Paris] were closed and the chains were stretched across the streets. The king, Charles [VI], was then at Saint-Denis, about to set out for Rouen to reconcile and pacify those of this city who like the Parisians had risen up. They killed their mayor[54] and demolished his home along with many other crimes. Therefore, the king with the dukes of Burgundy and Bourbon, Lord Coucy[55] and Arbeti, and many other knights, soon returned to his castle in the Bois de Vincennes. He dispatched the duke of Burgundy and Lord Coucy to the castle of Saint Antoine to pacify the Parisians.[56]

When they approached this castle, many Parisian bourgeois came; among other matters, they made three demands: first, the four bourgeois imprisoned in the Châtelet for fifteen days for speaking out against the newly imposed taxes were to be freed; second, the king should keep his promise made by him and his council immediately after his consecration; that is, he should withdraw the subsidies from the aids and taxes, [restoring taxes to what] they had been at the

54 The revolt in Rouen lasted three days, from 24 February 1382; the populace did not kill their mayor, Robert Deschamps, nor the former one, Guérout de Maromme.
55 Enguerrand VII, lord of Coucy. For his earlier career in the brutal slaughter of Jacques, see [91].
56 According to the Religieux de Saint-Denys, these events took place after the king had returned from Rouen.

time of Saint Louis[57] and Philippe le Bel;[58] in this way the kingdom of France would be freed and exempt from all taxes; third, the king should in general refrain from all wrong-doings, murder, and crimes from this day on; finally, the Parisians declared that they would fight to their death to prevent the king of France from levying these customary taxes again.

But of these demands, only the first was granted, that is, the liberation of the bourgeois from prison. On hearing this, the Parisians gathered in great numbers with their hammers, went to the Châtelet, broke into the prison, and liberated all the prisoners, those for theft and murder as well as those for any other crime. Further, they tore to pieces criminal records, charters, and registers deposited here. Then they went to the court of the officials of Paris and also liberated those locked up in the jails of the bishop. Among those freed, was Hugues Aubriot, who immediately left the city.

Further, at vespers, early that evening, these Parisians went with their hammers to [the abbey of] Sainte-Geneviève, where they broke into the prison and liberated all the inmates. Among those confined were the chancellor and a canon of this abbey along with another cleric named Brule, imprisoned for violating the king's safeguard by beating almost to death Master Peter Soulas, the king's procurator at the Parlement.

Not content with this, the next day these Parisians ran and attacked the Abbey of Saint-Germain-des-Prés, until they were allowed to enter. They searched through the abbey to see if they could find any who had taken refuge here because of the taxes; none were discovered, however, since they had all left during night. From here they returned to the city, going street by street, destroying many homes and killing many Jews as well as Christians.

Weighing up these vile acts, the bourgeois of the city met in a secret council and ordered each to arm secretly at home and to attack those men with the hammers; some soon left to ward the hammer men off. Moreover, they ordered certain armed men to go through the quarters of the city to take the hammers from these men as they passed down the streets, one after another. By these means, the bourgeois kept the city at night under maximum alert; the gates were locked

---

57 King of France from 1236 to 1270; canonized in 1297.
58 King of France from 1285 to 1314.

and the chains stretched out; all who entered and left were watched to know what was going on at every gate.

Then rumours spread through the city that similar riots were cropping up in all the principal towns of the kingdom of France, as had already occurred in Rouen, Amiens, Reims, Orléans, and Meaux.

The king then ordered all foodstuffs to be barred from crossing the bridge of Charenton.[59] As at result, the Parisians were most upset and said that if the king were to do this, they would march out and destroy everything. The Parisians then stood on alert from Saturday to Tuesday to see what would happen. At noon on this Tuesday, the king's council and the Parisians negotiated and made public the following agreement: the king would restore all the customs and liberties to Paris and everywhere else in the kingdom, to what they had been at the time of Saint Louis and Philippe le Bel, ending in perpetuity all the taxes, aids, *tailles*, and any other fiscal imposition. Further, he would refrain from all the murders and other crimes mentioned above. He honoured their request and sent letters to the Parisians, those of Rouen, and to other cities confirming the agreement.

It was then left to Lord Jean de Fleury,[60] who remained in the Bois de Vincennes to prepare the documents for the Parisians. They were delivered not in the usual fashion in vellum sealed with green wax and waxed strings. Rather, they were sealed in yellow wax with a tail hanging down the parchment. These contained the agreement that the king with his council and members of his family had for the time being withdrawn the imposition of the customary taxes.

When these documents were brought to Paris and read out in the presence of citizens, they were unhappy, declaring that with their hammers and the support of the commoners of Paris they would defend their liberties, those of the city, and of all the kingdom of France. And considering their numbers, they were not about to suffer any punishment. Moreover, they demanded that if the king did not uphold these charters dismissing the taxes, he would have to abdicate, since he could do nothing else. And they wished to have letters renouncing his crimes, which he refused to give them. For these reasons, they again sent for the king and the duke of Burgundy, who then was in charge. The duke and the royal council dragged their feet

---

59 In other words, to blockade the city.

60 In 1378 he had been one of four échevins of Paris; Delachenal, *Histoire de Charles V*, V, p. 76.

day after day without giving a final decision. Then, the Parisians sacked the property and treasures [that the king and his family had] in Paris.

It is said that the king then fortified his castle in the Bois de Vincennes and sent for the dukes of Anjou and of Brittany to come with innumerable armed men to bring the Parisians under the yoke. Because of this escalation, the Parisians were on guard every night with many on the watch. In the midst of this tight security, Lord Coucy, then with the king and one of his major councillors, fled, prompting rumours that he was planning to lay siege to the city.

Therefore, certain Parisians then went to the king and the duke of Burgundy, hoping to negotiate. Finally on Sunday and Monday [9 and 10 March 1382], all those of the forties, fifties, and tens of Paris [the citizen militias] were called before the king; many consented to the king's wish that those guilty of wrongdoing would be punished appropriately. For this reason, the king allowed the offence committed against him to be made public the next Tuesday, as is explained below. Then, on this Monday, under the cover of night, the leaders of the forties, fifties and tens caught these criminals, imprisoned them in the Châtelet, and led them to judicial executions, as is made clear below.

Finally, on the following Tuesday, 11 March, peace was made and cried out from the scaffolds [*in fallis*] and in the squares of Paris. At the request of Lord Valesio,[61] the king's brother, the duke of Burgundy, the University of Paris, and many others, the king pardoned all the delinquents above, absolving them from all criminal and civil punishment, which they had incurred against him, except for those imprisoned in the Châtelet. On the same day, two were beheaded in the presence of Lord Coucy and many armed knights and bourgeois of the city; on the following Wednesday after lunch, five of these criminals were beheaded at the same place.

The Parisians began to grumble about this, since it caused them a great deal of shame. Because of this rioting, the next day, Thursday, at the gate of Saint-Denis, five others in turn were led to the gallows next to Montefalcone and beheaded, which left many Parisians indignant. On the following day [14 March 1381(2)] it was rumoured in Paris that the king had decreed that each of the guilds of the city should assemble to hear what taxes they owed the king, either for the

---

61 I have not discovered who this lord was. In 1325, a count of Valesio was the captain of the king's army in Languedoc; *Histoire générale de Languedoc*, X, col. 656.

tailles or in some other form. They responded that they would by no means consent.

On the following Saturday, the provost of Paris sent two executioners to aid the executioner at Paris in beheading or hanging the criminals for their crimes. With this the provost made a big show of it on the scaffolds and elsewhere. Then, shortly after the king's proposition, because of rioting by commoners in the district of Saint-Denis, he pardoned all those who had committed crimes against him so that none would now be killed for his sake. With this act, the grumbling of the Parisians ceased.

Before Easter, the king left the Bois de Vincennes with the dukes of Burgundy and Bourbon to go to Rouen and stayed for about eight days at Pont-de-l'Arche, outside Rouen. Then, on the 28th [March], he entered Rouen with the citizens' consent; they greeted him with honour.[62] Later, he entered the gate [of Martainville] and ordered the people to throw themselves on the ground before him, remove the chains fastened across the streets, and bring their weapons to his castle. In addition to this order, he took the tongue from the town's bell.[63] Afterwards, he ordered the decapitation and quartering of six men of the city. Having done this, he decreed that those taxes imposed on Paris should be extended to Rouen and throughout the duchy of Normandy.

Then, with the feast of Easter over,[64] the king went to Compiègne,[65] where he sent for the nobles, clergy, and men from the principal towns, especially from the province of Reims. But many from the towns sent only their representatives [*procuratores*]. The nobles, clerics, and men of the principal towns, who came, consented to the king's taxes and subsidies. But the procurators from the cities of Reims, Châlons-en-Champagne, Laon, Soissons, and Tournai, since they had not been consulted, refused to consent to anything coming from the king.

With this achieved, the king sent sealed letters to Paris, reporting the need to resist the English, who were about to invade. He wished to find out what help he could get from them, what would be most useful

---

62 The *Religieux de Saint-Denys* gives a very incomplete version of these events.

63 According to the *Partie inedite des Chroniques de Saint-Denis*, ed. Baron J. Pichon (Paris, 1864), p. 4, he took it back to his castle.

64 The *Religieux de Saint-Denys* says the repression of the revolt of Rouen lasted three days; according to Pierre Cochon, the king did not leave until 7 April 1382.

65 He arrived there on 12 April and stayed to the 17th.

for his domestic affairs [*pro statu suo*] and for the waging of war but less burdensome for the people, and what would be the fastest way to collect these taxes. They responded by sending on Sunday 20 April 1382 four bourgeois to Meaux, who came to an agreement with him like the one he made with those of the province of Soissons. But, in Paris many of those of the forties, fifties, and tens had met and consulted among themselves before and after things had been decided on this Sunday, agreeing to send nothing to the king.

Then the king sent Lord Coucy to the Parisians, who was told that they would not grant any aid to the king other than twelve thousand francs for his domestic affairs, but swore to give nothing for his wars. On receiving this news, the king went immediately to Meaux, where he assembled a great crowd of men, whom he sent to the bridges of Saint-Claude and Charenton to block any foodstuff being brought to Paris by water. In addition, he sent many nobles and armed men, lusting to pillage Parisian property, to fight them.

Afterwards, the king sent sealed letters to Paris, stating that on a certain day they were to send him their heads of the militias (forties, fifties, and tens) with certain other bourgeois to discuss these matters that concerned the honour and condition of the king and decide which aids they could readily provide him. On that day, several Parisians went to him and informed him that the commune of Paris would pay some of the aids [*auxilium*]. Then the king urged them to come to a swift conclusion on which taxes they would pay and to reply to him by a certain day.

147 The hammer men according to Pierre Cochon

Chronique Normande de Pierre Cochon, pp. 169–70.

When the Parisians heard the news that those of Rouen had revolted, they heard it with great joy, because they had begun their own revolt. They had marched out with so many mallets of iron, steel, and lead, that they equipped most of the city with them. They had stripped bare the town hall and the big garrison entirely of these hammers. And they charged through the city, proclaiming that they should no longer suffer under such high taxes as the *tailles* that were robbing and ruining everyone. And the extent of their rioting was truly astonishing. The king and his counsellors stayed out of Paris for the time being, daring not to be around until the fury of the town had been appeased.

And with them [the Parisians] there was one of their opinion, one of the greatest lawyers of the Parliament, named master Jehan des Marés, who proclaimed that neither the king nor his counsellors could make of them a people, but that the people could very well make a king. And when all the rioting had calmed down, they put themselves at the mercy of the king and repented. On Sunday 11 January 1382 the king's troops entered the city with their weapons unleashed, and Paris was greatly subjugated ... But the following February they refused to pay the taxes imposed on them of twelve pennies on the pound ...

148 The hammer men according to Cousinot le Chancelier

Guillaume Cousinot I, *Geste de Nobles*, ed. Vallet de Viriville (Paris, 1859), pp. 106–7. The chronicler, who lived from c. 1370 to c. 1440, was chancellor of Charles duke of Orléans at the height of the civil war between the Armagnac princes and the Burgundians and in 1422 became chancellor of the exchequer for the Dauphin Charles VII. No doubt, his experiences during the civil war, when the Cabochienne butchers murdered, imprisoned, and destroyed the property belonging to nobles like himself who supported the Armagnac cause (see [180]), would have redoubled his natural aversion as a nobleman to any uprisings from the lower orders.

On 1 March 1380[2][66] while the king was at Vincennes, on the instructions and advice of duke Philip of Burgundy, the taxes, *quatrièmes*,[67] and sale taxes [*gabelles*], which had previously been cancelled by the king, were proclaimed at the sound of the trumpet and made public in les Halles of Paris. Because of this, the commune [*la commune*] of les Halles rose up in revolt and inside Saint-Jacques-de-l'Hôpital pursued one of the commissioners, pulled him out of the church, and killed him in the street. Craftsmen came forth from all parts, raising a standard of white cloth, which they carried before them, their numbers growing constantly. And angrily they marched on the town hall, taking many hammers and other weapons stored there, and went after the Jews, broke into all the prisons, and freed the prisoners. They sacked the townhouses of some of the officers previously involved with the subsidies and smashed the wine casks in their cellars. They pulled the chains across the squares and placed guards on the city walls and at the gates to prevent anything being taken in or out of Paris without

66 It should be 1381, which would be 1382 by our calendar.
67 Sales taxes of a quarter on certain commodities, principally wine.

being inspected. Among the prisoners who were freed was Lord Hugues Aubriot. They put him on a mule and made him ride through Paris until evening, when they led him to his house at the rear of Saint-Pol and left him master of his possessions. But that night, he found a way to cross the Seine and escaped to Dijon, where he was from, leaving the people without a leader. To placate them, Philip duke of Burgundy wrote to them that the king wished to restore the liberties of his good subjects, which they had enjoyed at the time of King Philippe le Bel, and thereby end the fracas in Paris and in all the other cities of the realm that followed Paris's lead. The only ones who had not risen up were nobles, ecclesiastics, and notable bourgeois of the cities of Chartres, Senlis, and Troyes, who on this occasion were with the king and at odds with the commoners. Of these aides, no levy was put on anything; except only the tax paid in small silver coin [*blans*] levied at that time.

149 The hammer men according to Jean Froissart

Jean Froissart Chroniques, Livres I et II, ed. Peter F. Ainsworth and George T. Diller (Paris, 2001), pp. 853–4: This single paragraph on 'the hammer men [Maillotins] of Paris', does not even constitute its own chapter; rather it comes at the end of his chapter 'On the famine in Ghent and the Gantois ... '

At that time [1382][68] those of Paris rebelled [*rebellèrent*] again,[69] to such an extent that the King of France did not come to Paris at all but remained on the outskirts of Paris to take his pleasures. The Parisians feared the king would send his men-at-arms to Paris and at night would charge through the city, killing whomever he wanted. So they guarded their streets and squares at night with great care; then they revolted and stretched the great chains across the streets so that no one could pass on horseback or on foot. And anyone found at the sound of the eleventh hour who was not of their company or men was a dead man. The rich and powerful men of the city of Paris armed themselves from head to toe at a cost of 30 thousand [francs ?][70]

68 If Froissart is using the Parisian calendar, he gets the year wrong. Previously, he has been discussing events in Ghent in 1382 and then continues 'en ce temps ... '
69 Earlier (but still for 1382), Froissart has a short chapter entitled 'How the Parisians and Those of Rouen Refused to Pay the Taxes and the Gabelles to the King of France', pp. 834–5, but mentions neither the theatrical events of the *Harelle* nor the hammer men. As the modern editors note, his treatment is 'rather thin' (p. 835).
70 Froissart does not specify the currency.

They were so well armed with all the pieces of armour as no knight could afford, and had their valets armed to the nines: they wore suits of iron mail and carried hammers, dangerous batons for breaking apart cauldrons. Throughout the parishes, they were in such great numbers that, without other assistance, it would have taken the greatest lord in the world even to fight them. These people were called the soldiers [*routiers*] and hammer men of Paris.

150 The eyewitness account of the Florentine Buonaccorso Pitti

Bonaccorso Pitti, *Ricordi*, in *Mercanti Scrittori: Ricordi nella Firenze tra Medioevo e Rinascimento*, ed. Vittore Branca (Milan, 1985), pp. 383–5. Pitti is the only eyewitness at least to leave a written record of both a northern European and Mediterranean revolt in the post-plague period. In 1378 he was forced to flee Florence after murdering a Ciompi insurgent, who was a stone-cutter.

Before I write about the king and what he did on entering Paris, I will record why this battle took place. In 1381 the inhabitants of Ghent rebelled against their lord, the count of Flanders, who was the father of the duchess of Burgundy. They attacked Bruges, captured it, hunted for the count, and robbed and killed all his officers. They did similar things in other principal cities which they seized in Flanders. Their leader was Philippe van Artevelde. The Flemings who rebelled against their lord increased in number and power. They sent secret ambassadors to Rouen and Paris, urging them to do the same to their lords, offering them aid and assistance. For this reason, these two cities rebelled against the king of France. It began with the *popolo minuto* in Paris: the spark of the revolt came when a tax collector tried to impose the gabelle on fruits and vegetables on a woman hawker of greens in the square; she began screaming: 'Death to these taxes', that is, the gabelle.[71] As a result, all the people rose up and ran to the houses of the tax collectors and robbed and killed them. Seeing that the *popolo minuto* was unarmed, one of them led them to the Châtelet, where Lord Bertrand de Guesclin,[72] a former constable of France, had ordered three-thousand leaden mallets to be kept to fight a battle he

---

71 Excise taxes or 'subsidies' on the sale of commodities (not only salt as is often assumed).
72 Spelled as Beltran di Crichin by Pitti: Bertrand de Guesclin was the great constable of France, famous for rendering military services to King Charles V in the struggle against the English.

thought would be waged against the English. They broke through the locked gate of the tower, where the mallets called hammers [*maglietti*] were kept.[73] Once these hammers were in their hands, they went throughout the city, robbing the king's officials and killing many of them. The fat cats [*popolo grasso*], that is, the good citizens, whom they called the bourgeois [*Borgiesi*], feared this *popolo minuto* called the hammer men, who were people like the Ciompi rioters of Florence. The bourgeois, however, thought they would not be robbed if they armed themselves and made themselves look strong so that the hammer men would then obey them. They [the bourgeois] passed decrees in support of the people and pursued the rebellion against the royal lords. For this reason, the king and his court retreated to the Bois de Vincennes to hold a council. To remedy the situation and make sure that the entire realm would not rebel, his council advised him to order all the barons, knights, and esquires of the realm to appear with all their forces and follow him wherever he wished. But although he made the request many times with commands as strict as he could muster, they did not arrive, except those, as I have said, who were already enlisted. Thus in the following year, that is, 1383, among the many sad mottos one heard, it was said: 'Long live whoever wins'.

151 The 'troubles' in Flanders in 1379 to 1382

Chronique rimé des Troubles de Flandre en 1379–1380, ed. Henri Pirenne (Ghent, 1902). I have used the extract, notes, and commentary of Véronique Lambert, *Chronicles of Flanders 1200*–1500 (Ghent, 1993), pp. 70–2. The 'troubles' in Flanders in 1379 to 1382 in rhyme. The commentator closest to being an eyewitness of the 'troubles' in Flanders in 1379 to 1382 and to leave a surviving narrative was the anonymous chronicler in rhyme. According to Henri Pirenne, he most likely lived in Bruges and probably knew some who led the uprisings. Although he called himself a 'Flemish Fleming', he wrote in French and dedicated the chronicle to Duke Philip of Burgundy.[74] Unfortunately, much of the text has been lost, but the chronicler's introduction translated below lists the events he covered and gives his notions on how they unfolded.

How first they rose up
Those of Ghent, and outside the city they did go.

---

73 Hammers with wooden handles and two leaden heads.
74 Nicholas, *Medieval Flanders*, p. 252.

How they conquered the entire country,[75]
Smashing mansions and breaking prisons;
How the peace was made
And soon after broken.
How the cities came into conflict
Arming one against the other.
And of the battles that came to pass,
And how those of Ghent held their own,
And controlled the supply of food.
How they won the battle
Outside Bruges[76] against their lord.[77]
How they robbed and offended
Their rightful lord and his men.
How they strove with all their wits
To put all the goods and people
Of Flanders in their mitts.
How they sent for England
And with the English they allied.
How afterwards the noble flower[78]
At Rozebeke won the day
God be praised for the victory![79]
How the English entered
Our country, wearing the cross,[80]
In aid of the city of Ghent.
How they won a battle,[81]
And before the walls of Ypres laid their siege.

75 By 29 September 1379, Ghent occupied Courtrai, Ypres, and Bruges, and other smaller towns soon followed.
76 Ghent won the battle of Beverhoutsveld on 3 May 1382.
77 In other words, the count of Flanders.
78 The 'fleur de lys'
79 Charles VI won at the battle of Rozebeke on 27 November 1382.
80 The English under the Bishop of Norwich thought of themselves as a crusade against one of the claimants of the papacy, Robert of Geneva, who took the title of Pope Clement VII. Since 1378, following the disputed election of a successor to Gregory XI, the papacy had been divided by papal rivals supported by various national parties of cardinals. Robert of Geneva was the choice of the French determined to remove the Italian Pope Urban VI. The division in the papacy was not resolved until the Council of Constance elected Martin V in 1417. But as we shall see [204], this resolution did not end disunity among rival national factions jockeying to contest and elect their own popes.
81 The battle of Dunkirk between the English and the Flemings.

How they were driven out
So that they have no longer had a foot in this country.
How those of Ghent conquered
Oudenaarde[82] and left it empty.
How the treaties were signed.

152 Ordinance of the three estates of *Langue d'oïl*, abolishing all the taxes set since the reign of Philippe le Bel

Ordonnances des Rois de France, VI, pp. 552–4, Arch. nat. JJ reg. 118, no. 12.

Charles by grace of God, king of France. Let it be known to all present and in the future that we have made and held a convocation and general assembly at Paris of the men of the church, nobles, bourgeois, and inhabitants of the principal towns of our realm in the Langue d'oïl. When giving advice on the defence and provision of the realm, they made complaints about the aides, subsidies, and subventions that our very dear lord and father, now deceased, may God absolve [his sins], had imposed and levied on them as well as about many other things, which they said had been done to their detriment in the time of our said lord and father and his predecessors [and] by the kings' soldiers and officers acting against their immunities, nobility, freedoms, liberties, privileges, constitutions, practices, and customs of the country, and against ancient royal ordinances. Thus they have requested an agreeable remedy should be provided, wishing us to re-establish, re-instate, restore, maintain, and protect these immunities, nobility, freedoms, liberties, privileges, constitutions, practices, and customs for these people and subjects. And with all our power, we should protect them from all injustices, taxes, and sundry acts of oppression. From the counsel, advice, and discussions with our very dear and amicable uncles, other blood relatives, and our great council, we wish, decree, and grant by our manifest power and royal authority and understanding, that the aids, subsidies, taxes, and various subventions of various names and sorts, which were and in various ways have been imposed on these our people and have endured in our realm from the time of our lord and father and other of our predecessors since the time of King Philippe le Bel, our predecessor, shall he repealed, removed, and abolished. Thus we remove, repeal, and abolish them and impose no new burdens at all by these present letters. And

---

82 Won on 17 September 1383.

we wish and understand that neither we, our predecessors, successors, nor any of us, should have by any right collected these taxes, subsidies, and subventions, which have been in force in our realm, or have injured our people or infringed on their immunities, rights of nobility, freedoms, liberties, privileges, constitutions, practices, and customary rights, or have restricted them in any manner. Moreover, we wish and judge by our power, full knowledge, and royal authority, that all the immunities, rights, freedoms, liberties, privileges, constitutions, practices, ancient customs, and all the royal ordinances, which these men of the church, nobles, principal towns, and the people of our realm in *Langue d'oïl* in any of these estates have enjoyed and practised in the time of King Philippe le Bel until the present, should be restored and re-established to them. ... But we do not include in this any of our rents, revenues, tolls, and profits from the exportation of food and merchandise. These remain ours, and will be levied by various ways and means as decreed by our officers with the least possible inconvenience for our subjects. Also, these do not include the taxes placed on the Genoese, Lombards, and others across the Alps or born outside our kingdom and on their goods ...

Issued in Paris, January, 1380 [1381]

153 Renunciation imposed on the abbey of Saint-Ouën during the uprising of the *Harelle*, 25 February 1381[2]

Chéruel, *Histoire de Rouen*, pp. 544–6; Archive départementale, 1er cart. de la Harelle.

To all those who will see or hear these letters, brother Arnault, humble abbot of the monastery of Saint-Ouën by divine permission, and the entire convent of this place [wish you] salvation in Our Lord: as discord has been stirred up for some time between our good friends the mayor, the peers, the commune, and the inhabitants of the city of Rouen, on the one hand, and our abbey and this convent, on the other, arising from the fact that we have claimed to possess the baronage over the city of Rouen and its district, while the mayor, peers, commune, and inhabitants have maintained the opposite. As a result, we have brought lawsuits, one against the other. But let it be known from today by our common accord and consent that we renounce these claims, and by this present charter and of our good will, we withdraw entirely without any reservation, thus ending any claims to the particulars and dependencies of baronage over the mayor, peers, commune, and inhabitants. Further, we promise never to bring new lawsuits or claims of baronage over these matters or dependencies. Nor will we ask anything from them, nor make claims of jurisdiction by petitions, laws, force, or appeals to parlement or the exchequer, nor by any other avenues or means, either now in force or which may be instituted afterwards. With this agreed, we are obliged to renounce our claims to all of the property of our church, moveable goods as well as landed possessions for the present and future, to all indulgences granted or to be granted by the pope, the king, prince, prelates, and all others who are or could be present, and generally to everything and all assistance, by which by deed or by rights we could be aided, and which may avail us against the claims of this charter, and especially any law proclaiming that this general renunciation is invalid. And we swear by our conscience that we will not act against openly or by covert means what [has been] said. And we are obliged by what is said to pay any costs, damages, and expenses, if we should do so. We wish the bearer of these letters to be believed by a simple oath and not have to prove it by any other means. Moreover, by this obligation we promise to recognise and confess [that we have agreed to the matters above] before any judge or royal notary [*tabellion*] that the mayor, peers, commune, the inhabitants or the bearer of this charter would wish that we promise to free them [of the obligations of baronage] by the next Ascension day[83] and to guarantee them as much to our lord the king as towards any others. And if we possess any low justice[84] in this matter, we admit that we hold it under the said mayor and by the authority of his jurisdiction, except for the right of the king in all matters. As testimony to what we have put in these letters we close them with the usual seal of our Church. This has been done in the year of Our Lord 1381[2], Tuesday, 25 February.

154 Charter of Charles VI granting pardon to those of Rouen for the uprising of the *Harelle*, 5 April 1381[2]

Chéruel, *Histoire de Rouen*, pp. 547–9; Archives municipales, drawer 3, no. 2 and 3.

Charles, by grace of God, king of France, let it be known to all present

---

83 In 1382, Ascension day fell on 15 May.
84 On different levels of justice, see chapter III, note 89.

and in the future, that some of the inhabitants in our city of Rouen have recently committed and perpetuated certain acts of rebellion, disturbance, and disobedience. During this rebellion and disturbance, they broke into many prisons and destroyed houses and committed and perpetrated murders, robberies, plots, conspiracies, assemblies, soundings of bells, locking of gates, carrying arms, crimes of treason, infractions of safeguards, acts of sacrilege, violations against the church and holy places, and other acts of evil and impropriety. And for this reason, the bourgeois and inhabitants of our city have humbly petitioned us concerning these matters that we should wish to give and benignly impart our grace. Considering the humility and repentance of these bourgeois and inhabitants and for the honour and reverence of God and the Holy Week, in which we are at this time, and the gracious and beautiful gathering they have made for our joyous entry into this our city, we have dismissed, pardoned, and forgiven the bourgeois and inhabitants, each of them with regard to all aspects of their involvement. By our special grace, authority, and royal power, we dismiss, forgive, and pardon the crimes and misdemeanours stated above, along with all corporeal, criminal, and civil punishments that we have imposed or which they might have merited on this account. And we restore to them their good name and reputation to their lands and properties, except for those who because of the rebellion and these disturbances are absent and have become fugitives, and those who have been detained in prison in Rouen or elsewhere for this [revolt] ...

Issued at Rouen 5 April, Easter eve, 1381[2]

155 Charter of Charles VI suppressing the Commune of Rouen

Chéruel, *Histoire de Rouen*, pp. 550–5; Archives municipales, drawer 3, no. 2 and 3, drawer 2, 1. This pardon pertains to what Chéruel has called the second *Harelle* or tax revolt in Rouen during 1382. Without much pruning, I have left the long-winded, repetitive, and tangled clauses stand as they are presented in the original.

Charles by the grace of God, king of France: on Friday the first of August last year, certain taxes [*aides*] which we have imposed to conduct our wars were to be collected by our order and statute in our city of Rouen on Friday, which is always the market day in this town. On this first day of August, they knocked down the table on which these taxes were to be collected, and all our men, officers, sergeants, and tax farmers here were terrorised and frightened and saw fit to flee and hide; thus, as a result, the collection of these aides ceased and were prevented from taking place in our city and could not be carried out here for some time afterwards. Following these things, they committed further acts of rebellion and crimes of treason against us, and in so doing set a bad example for those of other principal towns and places in this country. Because of these matters, our high commissioners and officers, previously appointed by us in the county of Normandy, apprehended and imprisoned many of these inhabitants of our city of Rouen and its environs. Further, by the request of our procurator, the entire commune of this town was put on trial, in which certain criminal and civil judgements against them were reached. Moreover, our procurator reached verdicts against those who committed and perpetrated the above-stated crimes in Rouen, as has been said, that is, certain rebellions, disturbances, and other crimes committed and perpetrated by these people and others against us and our royal majesty, for which we had [previously] given our pardon on 5 April before Easter 1381[2] by our letters with our seal in green wax. Our procurator has judged that these pardons must now be declared null and, with this, they are accused of many crimes of treason [*lèze-magesté*],[85] disturbing the peace, rebellion, disobedience as much for seizing and assaulting our castle of Rouen as for other crimes committed and perpetrated in the time of our previous kings of France by those of Rouen or some of them or by their predecessors. Thus our said procurator concluded that these high commissioners and officers might sentence these people of Rouen in these cases with justice and reason. Some of the bourgeois and inhabitants of this our city, who were present, have responded that they were innocent and are without guilt for these misdeeds and crimes, and that supposing anything had been done in the past by them, then they claim that they had received pardon and remission from us and our predecessors, the kings of France, which ought to avail them and should be sufficient and of service to them as much as they might have need of it. As for the accusations of these later disturbances and rebellions, as has been described, when the tax-collector's table was overturned, they claimed that it was not done by them or the good people of this town;[86] rather, against their will, foreigners and those living outside the town who

---

85 On the legal meaning of treason in late medieval France in regard to popular rebellion, see S. H. Cuttler, *The Law of Treason and Treason Trials in Later Medieval France* (Cambridge, 1981), esp. ch. 2.

86 In other words, the bourgeois.

had come to the market did it. Further, they could not and dared not remedy the matter, since they did not possess or have the power over the commune or any jurisdiction, since these matters had been placed in our hands and these powers are still kept from them.[87] Thus they did not dare arm themselves or assemble and still do not dare do so without our authorisation and licence. They gave many other reasons for claiming not to act, which they said were lawful and reasonable. And after many debates and discussions among themselves, before the high commissioners, and with other officers, these bourgeois and inhabitants, acting on their own behalf and in the name of their commune, chose not to proceed any further against our officers and us. Always hoping to receive our grace and mercy, they confessed to have sinned and committed the crime of treason against us. They admitted their guilt to all the deeds, crimes, and misdemeanours listed above clearly against our will and laws. And afterwards, certain notable persons of this city have come before us, humbly beseeching us, saying that they and the other bourgeois and inhabitants of the city have always been and wish henceforth to be good, loyal, firm, and obedient towards us and the crown of France. In regard to each of the deeds and cases stated above ... we would wish to offer them our grace and mercy. Thus let it be known to all present and in the future, based on the report of these high commissioners and officers, and having considered the obedience and humility of these supplicants, and given that corporeal punishment has been inflicted on some of these bourgeois and inhabitants for this reason in addition to the penalty of sixty thousand francs, of which the inhabitants and commune of this city of Rouen have already paid twenty-five thousand francs to our friend and loyal knight Bertrand Aladent, the principal collector of the aides for conducting war, as indicated in his letters concerning these matters, that they must pay him immediately five thousand francs, along with another thirty thousand francs, according to the schedule we have decreed. To these bourgeois, inhabitants, and the commune of this our city of Rouen and its suburbs, to each of them, except all those bourgeois and inhabitants who against the orders of the high commissioners and officers did not come forward and have left this city of Rouen, considering themselves to be at liberty or staying in a holy place out of fear of justice, and wish not to be included in our present pardon but to remain entirely outside it, we

---

87 That is, as a consequence of the *Harelle*, the king had punished the inhabitants of Rouen by taking from them the rights and privileges of being a commune; see [137, 144].

have dismissed, pardoned, and forgiven [them] ... by our special grace, royal authority, and full powers from the crimes and cases above that they committed, perpetrated, and experienced, those before 1 August last year, as with those on that day, and since, and all that ensued, and any other rebellions and disturbances committed and perpetrated by them against us and our predecessors and during all times in the past ...

Issued in Paris 18 June 1383.

156 Remission to a vendor of vinegar for acts of rebellion during the hammer men's revolt

Léon Mirot, *Les insurrections urbains*, pp. 35–6; Arch. Nat., JJ, 131, no. 47, fol. 27v, June, 1387.

During the first revolt in Paris against the Jews,[88] the petitioner [*exposant*, who in this case was Jean le Conte] went down the street of the Jews in Paris to the townhouse of Chère de Châlons, a Jewess, to whom he had given many goods such as cloaks, hoods, overcoats, bedcovers, pillows, and pewter dishes as collateral for a three-franc loan she had lent him. In this townhouse, he found certain goods wrapped in his bedcover. Thinking they were his, he took them away to his house. Immediately, certain law officers arrested him and took him outside the house of the petitioner. Then this cover or parcel was taken to the town hall by order of Master Dreuz d'Ars, the commissioner for this matter. And when the sergeants unwrapped it, the petitioner found none of his goods. Assuming there were things to be found, he returned to the Jews quarter [*juifverie*][89] that day without any intention of taking anything or of causing any harm. He only bought from a man he knew three pieces of a wooden bedstead for 2 *sous*,[90] which he brought back to his house. After this and the great riot [*grant commocion*] had occurred in Paris, the petitioner was seized and locked up in the Châtelet on suspicion of having been at the riot but was released as pure and innocent. Also, after we had returned from Flanders, the petitioner, seeing the great swarms of soldiers

---

88 In 1380, see [133, 134, 142].

89 There were two 'juiveries' or streets of Jews, one on the Île de la Cité, the other on the right bank of the Seine between the Grève and the Châtelet. According to R. Delachenal, the riots of 1380 concerned the latter; see *Chronique des règnes de Jean II et de Charles V*, ed. R. Delachenal (Paris, 1910–20), III, pp. 2–3.

90 A copper coin worth a half-penny.

making arrests and serving summary justice, feared he could be
blamed and imprisoned for this case of the Jews. So he left Paris and
did not appear in court within the announced time and thus was made
an outlaw. Sometime later, during the second Lent after the riot, the
petitioner was in the church of Saint Martin at Harfleur and saw Jehan
Labice, Jehan d'Estampes, Antoine Pasté, and another, all sergeants of
the cavalry of the Châtelet of Paris. He addressed them and wished
them well, since he knew them. As soon as he told them he was Parisian, they tried to grab and drag him out the church. But he demanded
his freedom and was allowed refuge in this church, according to the
customs of the region. After staying there for thirty-four days and
realising that on the fortieth he would be forced to leave and would be
taken to the place of justice as was the custom and as these men
threatened him every day, he considered his options when these
guards were in one of the chapels; he shut them in and left the church.
Since this time, he has been a fugitive and has not dared to return to
his place of birth or travel about our realm [...]

157 Remission to a furrier's journeyman for acts of rebellion during the hammer men's revolt

Mirot, *Les insurrections urbains*, pp. 112–3; Arch. nat. JJ. 142, no. 64, f. 38.

Charles, etc. Let it be known to all present and in the future. It has
been made known to us by the close friends of Philippe Melite, a poor
journeyman [*valet*] furrier, presently in prison in our Châtelet in
Paris, that [...] about two years ago, just after we had decreed that
these taxes should be levied and imposed again ... many bourgeois of
this city and this Philippe, along with others who assembled in the
church of the Holy Cross and elsewhere, held meetings concerning
these taxes. And when each was asked his opinion, many of these
bourgeois and this Philippe said that they would not tolerate in the
least any of these taxes being charged, since we [the king] had cancelled them, and that if we needed money, we should levy taxes
[*tailles*] that each could pay according to his means [*taux*] and ability
[*faculté*], and had they been of a reasonable amount, then they would
have paid them willingly. But, despite what they said and did, these
taxes – no more or less – were laid down and levied. After they had
begun to be collected, causing many commoners of Paris, foreigners,
and others, to assemble and commit many wicked and unseemly acts,

this Philippe did all he could to fan the troubles and disturbances, doing the evil deeds, which they suggested and wanted to have done. And he was with our friend, loyal knight, and chamberlain, Maurice de Trèsiguidi,[91] then captain of this our city, to keep him company and to search for and seek out these commoners in Paris who had brought on the trouble, to bring them to justice and punish them. And by chance as they passed towards the hospital of Saint-Antoine-le-Petit, this Philippe and many others of this captain's company came upon a Jew and told him that he should become a Christian and renounce his false faith. The Jew refused, telling them that his faith was worth more than the Christian's. And as a sign of his great contempt, he spat in their faces, which very greatly incensed them. They were so roused that they beat the Jew savagely [*à coup de chaude colè*] and killed him. This Philippe then went to another assembly, where it was decided that he and the others would lock the boxes for collecting these taxes, and in fact the deceased Jacques de Hangest (at that time alive) by an order from the bishop of Beauvais, at that time our chancellor, had them closed. Moreover, following an order given by the captain of his militia of the fifties [*cinquantenier*], this Philippe stood guard at the gate of Saint-Denis. And while there, he and the others on guard, searching for weapons, inspected many bundles, pack animals, and other things, and if they found any, they would send these people back home and not let them pass. And among others, they seized a soldier [*bacinet*] of [the force of] our friend, loyal knight, and chamberlain Boucicaut[92] and guarded him closely [*au sofflet*] at the gate of Saint-Denis and then sent him back to Boucicaut's valet. Also during this rioting [*commocion*], this Philippe with Garnot Rabiole and others, went to get timber to make barriers at the gates of Saint-Antoine and Saint-Denis. Also, a little after these taxes were to be levied, he and others went to the knight Jehan des Marès and begged him to tell Master Jehan de Chatou that these taxes should certainly not be exacted on the date they had been decreed. Concerning the case of this dead Jew ... he has already obtained remission ... but has not received grace or remission for the other cases and was put in prison for three months in the Châtelet, where he has suffered and continues

---

91 An esquire, partisan of the house of Blois and previously a commander of soldiers of fortune in the Auvergne and the Limousin in the 1360s.

92 Jean II Le Meingre, dit Boucicaut (1366–1421), the son of marshal Boucicaut to whom Charles V in 1358 had granted the use rights of all properties that had belonged to Robert le Coq (see [117]). Jean became the governor of Genoa between 1401 and 1409.

to suffer great misery and poverty to the point of death, thus we take pity and compassion on him ...

Issued at Paris, February 1391.

158 Remission to a poor man for acts of rebellion during the hammer men's revolt

Mirot, *Les insurrections urbains*, pp. 116–17, Arch. nat. JJ. 124, no. 332, fol. 188v.

Charles ... having received the humble supplication of Jehannin le Feure, a poor man born at Montfort l'Amarry: on the first of March 1381[2] a riot of the people [*commocion du peuple*] occurred in our good city of Paris, when a great number of the commoners of this our city staged a very great uprising. As they passed in front of the house of this supplicant, who was then living in the great street of Saint-Denis, they made a great noise and disturbance [*tumulte*]. Whereupon the supplicant went to his door to see what was happening. And as they passed, he saw that they led along with them everyone they met. Thus he was forced to go with them as far as les Halles, where he saw one knock down a wooden post at the inn of the Sign. And afterwards, he left and went with the crowd in front of the inn of the Golden Coin [*Chayère*], where many of them broke apart a latticed bench [*bant treilliz*]. Yet he was in no way involved in these incidents beyond observing them and looking on, as did many others. And afterwards, he left this crowd at the inn of the Golden Coin and went straight to the church of Saint-Jacques-de-l'Hôpital, located in the great street, where the supplicant followed them and a great many of them climbed up the bell tower. A journeyman in his company, whose name he does not know, found a chaplet of pearls ... which the supplicant took half of [...] Then we announced publicly in this our city that anyone who had taken or found anything during this rioting, whether it belonged to Jews or Christians, were to bring it to the city hall on pain of death. Obeying the law, this supplicant brought what the journeyman had given him ... to our friend Master Guillaume de Nevers, a commissioner who had been appointed for this matter. [The supplicant fled but was given remission.]

Issued at Paris, October 1383.

159 An innocent bystander swept up in the crowds of the hammer men

Mirot, *Les insurrections urbains*, p. 117: Arch. nat. JJ 123, no. 710, fol. 38v.

Charles ... having received the humble supplication from Guillaume Chevalier: on the day that the revolt [*commocion*] of the hammer men took place in Paris, he was a man plying his trade and residing with his wife in this our city. On that day, he heard a vast crowd approaching, making a great and horrible noise. He went to the door to see what was happening, and while in the doorway, a great many of these people made straight for him, demanding, 'What are you doing here? Come on, come with us'; he replied, 'And where am I going?' They bullied him and did not let him out of their sight. Because of their deceitful instigation and fear for his life, he grabbed a hatchet and went along with them without any intention of doing anything, except return to his house as soon as he could. And he went with them to the fortifications [*bastilles*] of Saint-Denis, Saint-Antoine, and Saint-Martin, and also to the square between the two bastilles, where they executed one or two men, also to the bishop's bakery, in front of our Châtelet of Paris, to the prisons of the bishop of Paris, and around many places, but without entering them or doing anything wrong in the world; he was only following along, contributing nothing, without imposing on anyone or engaging in any villainy. [He left Paris, then was banished, and then given pardon.]

Issued at Saint-Denis, August 1383.

160 A wool shearer and the massacre of Jews in the hammer men's revolt

Mirot, *Les insurrections urbains*, pp. 119–20: Arch. nat. JJ. 126, no. 281, fol. 174.

Charles ... We have been informed about the case on behalf of Thomas le Barillier, called Dangiers, a wool shearer, who recently had been our sergeant on guard duty in our city of Paris. At the time of the riots [*commocions*] in the city of Paris, he attended the assemblies of the people of the commune as did other inhabitants of this city and was armed as a guard by the city as were the others. And among the other cases of unrest [*émovemens*] in this city on the day when many men of this city carried hammers of lead and killed many Jewish men and women of Paris, all under our protection, and went rampaging and robbing in this city, causing much damage and rebellion [*rebellions*], this one being investigated, who was our sergeant on guard duty, was passing down the street of the Jews or near it, where he found many of them dead. He then entered the house of Giles du Boulay, our sergeant of the cavalry of the Châtelet of Paris, where many Jewish men and women had come to hide in fear of their lives. Then these Jews begged the petitioner and several others with him to protect them, for which they would willingly pay. The petitioner and those with him protected these Jews all day and led them to our Châtelet to guarantee their safety and to prevent them from harm. But our jailor did not dare take them under his protection, because the men with the hammers had broken in and liberated the prisoners. At great peril and fear, they brought these Jewish men and women back to the house [of Giles]. And for this, the petitioner received six or seven francs or so from these Jews. Afterwards, the petitioner and his comrades drank in this house, and this Giles allowed them to take certain clothes and other things belonging to these Jews, which they wrapped up in a sack and sealed with his sign. Of these, the petitioner took only one woollen shirt. After our public announcement, they brought these things to us in the townhouse of Baudet at the Black Head. And as his comrades had led him to believe, this booty was put in the hands of justice. This petitioner never broke into prisons or committed other crimes, except to the Jews and being armed with his ten comrades to guard the city, as has been said. But when we returned from our first trip to Flanders, because of this case, he feared he would incur our anger and that of our soldiers and officers; thus he left town. [He was pardoned.]

Issued at Cambrai, April 1385.

161 Remission to a salt merchant for acts of rebellion during the hammer men's revolt

Mirot, *Les insurrections urbains*, p. 125: Arch. nat. JJ. 123, no. 120, fol. 64v.

Charles ... the case on behalf of Jehan le Grant, called Saunier [the salt merchant], responsible for a wife and four small children, has been humbly put before us: on the first of March 1381[2], when rioting broke out in Paris, this petitioner was delivering white salt to us, as we had ordered. Out of hatred for what he was and what he had been doing over the last sixteen years as the clerk responsible for the excess tax on the sale of animals in Paris, those who rampaged through Paris, when the revolt called the hammers raged, attacked and drew swords and other weapons on him. As a result, it was expedient for him to flee and hide in the church of Saint Germain-l'Auxerrois.[93] Afterwards, he went home, all frightened and terrified. Hearing the great crowds, which passed in front of his house, shouting 'let's go and shut the gate of Saint Honoré' and seeing that all of his neighbours were going there, the petitioner was in great fear for his life because of their hatred for his services to us. Hoping to escape the city, he left his house, and, because he was unarmed, he took a hammer (of which he possessed three before this revolt, when Robert Knolles [*Canole*][94] last came to France) and stuck it under his cloak. And he went along with those rebels, assuming that he could pass through the gate and slip out of Paris. From fear of bodily harm and not being able to pass through the crowds, he found a fellow salt merchant, who was carrying a large axe and warned: 'Friend, don't do anything wrong'. For his misdemeanours the petitioner has since been brought to justice. Afterwards [...] some of the rebels took his hammer, and at the first chance, frightened out of his wits, he fled to [a place called] the Fifteen Score[95] and hid himself. When he could, he returned home without going out again in the city on that day. [He was condemned, fled, and later pardoned.]

Issued at Ravensberg, September 1383.

162 Hammer men pardoned for crimes of rebellion on 1 March 1382, identified by occupation

As in Rouen and other towns in Normandy, those first to revolt in Paris appear to have been predominantly commoners – small shopkeepers, apprentices, and workers. In the absence of surviving judicial registers, our best source for the social composition of crowds, despite drawbacks, are letters of remission kept in the king's *Trésor des chartes*. Mirot, *Les insurrections urbains*, p. 114

93 Across from the Louvre, it was the king's parish and the largest in Paris.
94 An English knight and routier from Cheshire of humble origins, who was a commander of English troops with the Earl of Buckingham at the siege of Nantes in 1379–80.
95 It was a hostel for the blind in the rue St-Honoré, founded between 1254 and 1261 by Louis IX. It appears in François Villon's *Le Testament Villon*, ed. Jean Rychner and Albert Henry (Geneva, 1974) I, p. 132, line 1728. I wish to thank Dr Jim Simpson for this reference.

(from National Archives, series JJ).⁹⁶

Adam Pellerin, worker of picture making [*imagerie*]
Colas Pavillon, seamster
Colin Adam, cutler
Dimanche Cruchet, last-maker
Étienne Bièvre, called le Hongre [the castrated one], wool shearer
Gassot Mauparlier, wool shearer
Guillaume Cabot, cobbler
Guiillaume le Maire, money-lender's assistant
Guiot Manglout, furrier
Jacot Maucorps, minstrel
Jaquot de Banville, almoner
Jean le Conte, called du Preel, vinegar vendor
Jean Fromage, money lender
Jean de Louvre, goldsmith
Jean de Mons, store-room guard [*cellier*]
Jean Polet, doublet maker [*doubletier*]
Jean de Sepmons, smith [*maréchal*]
Michel Rassigot, servant
Nicaise Preudhomme, brewer
Perrin Hure, engraver of seals
Philippe Mélite, furrier's apprentice
Philippot du Val, tallow-chandler
Pierre Guiot, leather dresser
Pierre de la Mote, pastry maker
Remondin le Fessu, embroiderer's apprentice
Richard langlois, coppersmith
Maciot Testart, almoner
Thomas le Barillier, wool shearer

163 Tax revolts in Laon, 1380

Léon Mirot, *Les insurrections urbains*, pp. 19–20. Already, before the death of Charles V, unrest had erupted in several cities of northern France, such as Laon. We have much less information on these revolts than those of a year or

---

96 Mirot has not included all the remissions, even of those presented elsewhere in his text, for instance: Jehannin le Feure, 'a poor man born at Montfort l'Amarry, Guillaume Talent, mayor of Arcueil, and Jehan le Grant, le Saunier, salt merchant (pp. 119 and 125). Nonetheless, this is the best list I know of those who were hammer men.

two later in Paris and Rouen, but as [164] shows several of these earlier ones succeeded and could not be put down by royal forces. The remission below illustrates various ways in which towns disobeyed the king and resisted royal orders – refusal to allow royal troops to enter their city walls, to send soldiers requested by the king, to show their merchandise to tax collectors, to pay other taxes, and to make loans to the king. Moreover, such towns were not afraid to make their own threats against the military might of the crown or to the king's lieutenants; Arch. Nat. JJ 123, no. 85, fol. 47.

Charles ... let it be known, that he has seen letters with the following information. The officials [*les généraulx reformateurs*] ordered by the king our lord in the province of Reims [...] have reproached the captain, governors, bourgeois, and inhabitants of this city, town, and the county of Laon for committing many acts of disobedience, rebellion, and other crimes against our king, this lord, and against his sovereignty and lordship, especially last August and for the past three years or so, when the English under the command of the earl of Buckingham,[97] enemies of this lord and his realm, were raiding this kingdom. They [Charles' troops] were then at Crécy-sur-Sère and in the county of the Laonnais in the viscounty of Meaux, whom the lord of Coucy of happy memory,[98] recently deceased, then lieutenant of King Charles [V], may God have mercy on him, sent with a certain number of armed men to this city [Laon] to support and protect it. He arrived with his armed troops at one of the city gates at night about an hour before dawn and requested the gate to be opened. The captain, then in charge, and the others on guard that night refused them entry into the city, and therefore [the lord of Coucy] was obliged to retreat with his armed men to Bruyère, within the jurisdiction of Laon.[99]

Also, they had failed to send messengers in advance to the clergy, nobles, and the inhabitants of the principal towns of his realm as was customary when calling such assemblies and convocations ordered by the king before requesting taxes [*aides*] for the defence of his realm. This authority and power was to be agreed on through deliberation. Such convocations usually took place only some time after they had heard the reports from the Parisians and the inhabitants of other principal towns of the realm, who first dealt with such matters; such proceedings would not start with those of this province. Also, they

---

97 The Earl of Buckingham (Thomas of Woodstock) led the last great cavalry charge against the French in 1380 before that of the duke of Clarence in 1420.
98 In other words, recently deceased.
99 Today, Bruyère-et-Montbérault, 6.5 km southeast of Laon.

[those of Laon] refused to loan a thousand francs to the king to contribute to his [military] expenses on the frontier of the Ardre,[100] which would be deducted from their taxes when ordered. Moreover, they wanted Lord Arnaud de Corbie, first president of the Parlement, sent by the king to collect the tax, to be seized; it was said that some spoke strongly against the payment and tried to persuade others not to pay. Finally, although they promised to make a loan of 200 francs, they authorised nothing, and although the king had ordered them to send thirty crossbowmen to serve in his cavalry and army, recently sent to Flanders, they had sent none. Instead, they had only paid the king's war treasury the sums [*des gaiges*] to keep these crossbowmen in the field for a certain period. In addition, they said or had others say to the lord of Saint-Dizier or to some of his men, who were serving in this lord's army or cavalry and who were being billeted [in Laon] and the soldiers who were in his company at Vaux-Montreuil in the territory of Laon, that if these men troubled this town and its countryside, they [the townsmen] would send out their crossbowmen and other soldiers of this town. In addition, these and others of the province had recently granted the king certain aids charged on the wholesale and retail sale of wine to support the costs of war and for their defence. Some of these inhabitants refused to show their wine to the collectors and to these tax farmers. They were charged with these matters and found guilty of disobedience and rebellion against their lord, the king, and for this, it was concluded that they should be sentenced to great punishments and fines. On these matters, the bourgeois and inhabitants made many excuses to secure their innocence and said among other things that they had always paid the usual taxes [*aide commune*]. Finally, they requested that we should not proceed against them with the full force of the law but should grant them grace and mercy ...

164 The troubles in Saint-Quentin, 1380

Léon Mirot, *Les insurrections urbains*, p. 21; Archives municipals de Saint-Quentin, laisse 2, no. 20.

Charles, etc. Let it be known that we have heard the supplication of our good friends the mayors, aldermen, and magistrates [*jurez*] of our

---

100 This was a castle somewhere in the region of Calais, Hesdin, or St.-Omer; see Sumption, *The Hundred Years War*, II, pp. 171–2. He does not locate it on his maps.

town of Saint-Quentin in the Vermandois, reporting that because the town is a walled city of importance, situated on the frontier of the Empire, where it protects, fortifies, and provides for [our kingdom], the supplicants have paid greatly, employing their resources in times past so that many creditors still hold them accountable for great sums of money. And again they have been presently summoned to pay out great sums for the expenses of repairing the fortress of this our town for its defence and government. In addition, they are harassed and hounded for great sums of money, which they are obliged to pay to many creditors, which at present they cannot pay, because they cannot easily levy a tax [*taille*] on anyone in this town out of fear of insurrection [*commocion*], and for this reason the tax [*aide*] recently ordered to fight our wars must be delayed.

Issued at Paris, 1 May 1381.

165 Tax evasion in Dieppe, 1382

Remission granted to Ricart de Saint-Morice, from Dieppe, charged with concealing wine from the tax collectors. Léon Mirot, *Les insurrections urbains*, p. 96; Arch. nat. JJ. 123, no. 262, 130v.

About two years ago, soon after the taxes [*aydes*] had been struck down generally throughout our kingdom, the elected officials and treasurer then appointed in this region and ordered by us to collect the new aides in the county of Normandy, approached the said supplicant in his town house. They told him that he must show them the wine he possessed. He responded most graciously that he did not sell wine, but he had some, which was good, left over from his wife's giving birth [*la gezine*], and from it he would willingly give them a drink, if it pleased them. They responded that this was not what they had come for and ordered him two or three times to show them his wine stocks. As before, he answered that he did not sell wine, but if they wished to drink what he had, they were welcome to do so. Otherwise, if he sold wine retail [*à détail*], he would pay just like everybody else. Then, while the supplicant was standing at his door, his cousin and friend, who had taken on the tax farm[101] of wine for Dieppe, came down the street and said to the supplicant that he would come see him

---

101 With a tax farm, an investor would buy the rights to tax a certain commodity in an area at a fixed price. His profit came from the taxes he could collect above this outlay.

after dinner, and the supplicant asked him if he were his master to which he responded, 'why yes'. And thus the supplicant joked and spoke pleasantly with his cousin, without intending any harm: his cousin said it had been a bad week for his tallies and asked whoever had sold him his tax farm [...]

Issued at Melun, December 1383.

[The case was summoned before the king's commissioners, but it was refused a hearing, because the defendant was on bad terms with the seneschal of Eu. He was summoned again to return to prison at Arques[102] and to the high commissioner of Caux to answer accusations: 'touching on the prevention and obstruction of our taxes [*aydes*] and certain acts of rebellion against our soldiers and officers'. He fled.]

Although the *Harelle* and the *Maillotins* were the most famous of the revolts sparked by Charles VI's renewal of the subsidies, other towns staged major revolts and some were severely punished in the early 1380s. Most prominent of these was the important port of Caen in Normandy. Like Rouen, it lost its rights and privilege to govern itself as a commune.

166 A rope-maker stirs up rebellion in Caen, early 1380s

Remission granted to Jehan Garin; Léon Mirot, *Les insurrections urbaines*, pp. 97–8; Arch. nat. JJ 123, no. 225, fol. 136.

Charles [... .] on behalf of Jehan Garin, a poor man and rope maker, responsible for a wife and children, recently living in our town of Caen [...] After hearing that the taxes [*aydes*] had been thrown down and rejected through our kingdom, we ordered them to be reinstated in order to pursue our wars. And when these aids were announced, made public, and proclaimed in this town of Caen, many of its inhabitants began to riot, committing many acts of rebellion [*rebellions*] and disobedience towards us, our soldiers, and officers over the issue of these aids. To punish and correct them, we sent certain of our commissioners into our county and duchy of Normandy. Before these commissioners entered this town of Caen, we announced throughout the town and its suburbs at the customary places where such matters are proclaimed that none of these inhabitants should leave this town or its suburbs or they would be banished, and that if any left they should return within eight days or face the same penalties.

102 A suburb of St. Omer, about 18 km south of Dunkerque.

Garin fled; his property was confiscated. [He was granted remission.]
Issued at Melun, December 1383.

167 Collective fine against the bourgeois and commoners of Caen because of their rebellion, early 1380s

Mirot, *Les insurrections urbains*, pp. 208-9: Arch. nat. JJ. 123, no. 51, fol. 29.

Charles[...] Because these rebellions, riots, armed insurrections, and assemblies, which occurred since the death of our very dear lord and father – my God have mercy on his soul – have been committed against us and our royal majesty in our good town of Caen by the bourgeois, inhabitants, and commoners of this town or some of them, our friends and faithful councillors, the general commissioners and officers appointed by us for the province of Rouen have ordered the seizure and imprisonment of many of these bourgeois and inhabitants. And they have taken or have been ordered to be taken and placed in our hands the privileges, rights to nobility, exemptions, liberties, rights, and customs, which these bourgeois, inhabitants, and commoners enjoyed and were accustomed to enjoying and using ... before these commissioners and officers came to Caen. Because of the town's treason [*ce trais*], these bourgeois, inhabitants, and commoners have wished to make a plea before us and have drafted an agreement with these learned commissioners and officers, agreeing to pay us 22,000 florins in gold francs. In return, these learned commissioners and officers have promised them in writing ... [the remission details when certain portions of the fine must be paid] that they will be given a pardon and remission from us for all these cases, and with the restitution of all their privileges, rights of nobility, exemptions, rights, and customs ... we restore to them their good name, reputation, and property. And with this, we restore entirely their said privileges, rights of nobility, exemptions, liberties, and customs ...

Issued at Paris, July 1383.

[The inhabitants of Caen delayed in paying the fine; by March, 1384 it had not yet been paid.]

168 Eustache Deschamps's ballad of the hammer men

'Ballades inédite d'Eustache Deschamps sur la sédition des Maillotins 1382', *Bibliothèque d'École des Chartes*, 2ᵉ ser, I (1844): 367–70. This ballad is perplexing and difficult to translate. I do not understand all the allusions and word plays.

The year thirteen-hundred-and-eighty-one [*quarto vini*][103]
On the first day of that fearful month of March,
A great wind of thieves and scoundrels rose up
And in Paris ran through all its parts.
At Les Halles its first sad havoc struck.
Then they stripped the Châtelet of its prisoners.
And one of the dandies said to me:[104]
'Flee! flee! for here come the hammers of lead!'

I was frightened; to the wood[105] I went;
Nor would I have stayed in Paris for a hundred Marches;[106]
But, thank God, I took horses and armour,
And I fled like a cowardly hare.
There you'd see the king's men dispersed all over
Fleeing far and wide.
And as they left, the servants cried:
'Flee! flee! for here come the hammers of lead!'

Prelates and the noble council, by morning,
Leave Paris, like foxes darting,
One by the Seine, others by other roads
Even the gouty jumped like leopards
Once burnt, twice shy;
One had to yield before the rabble,
And when the time comes, let us all cry against such pillagers:
'Flee! flee! for here come the hammers of lead!'

In the end they'll come to grief.
On this point, the prince held firm,

103 Deschamps puns on the year; *quarto vini* was an excise tax on wine; see doc. [169]
It was 1381 by the French calendar which began each year with Easter, 1382 by our calendar.

104 *Une coquars*: the name given to dandies at that time, because they dressed in hoods in the manner of a cock's comb.

105 Bois de Vincennes; see note 36.

106 The month of the revolt [1 March]; perhaps also a pun on marks.

And let neither favour, friendship, nor fine gold
Be a shield against his honour, nor darts
To these unfortunates, give them nothing other than the gallows
To be hanged or drawn on the block
As an example to such imbeciles.
'Flee! flee! for here come the hammers of lead!'

For they did worse than Saracens:
The fools assailed Saint Germain[107]
Destroying goods, guzzling wines,
Breaking into houses, killing innocent flesh,
Their doors locked and the carriages of
The king's uncle of Burgundy held back. And according to
What I see, I say to myself:
'Flee! flee! for here come the hammers of lead!'

Prince, I am inclined to write to you
That justice for long has had no friend,
That all went awry and away
In the city where you were named prince
You ought to strike down those (who have wronged) and keep saying:
'Flee! flee! for here come the hammers of lead!'

Southern France

169 Tax revolt sparked in the cathedral at Le Puy when the Virgin was unveiled, 1378

Histoire générale de Languedoc, cols. 1609–12, no. 648: JJ. 113, no. 101.

Louis etc; it has been reported, etc. Members of the council and the notable people of the city of Le Puy [*Anicii*] have humbly brought to our attention the following: recently, on the first of April [1378] by our own command, Bernard of Area, knight, chief officer of Le Velay, and our commissioner, and Master Pierre Jules, judge and chief officer of Beaucaire and Nîmes, summoned an assembly of royal officers and the aldermen of the commune of this city. By our command, these aldermen, along with many bourgeois, notaries, and other notable people of this city, were to attend diligently to the implementation of

107 See [136, 146].

the hearth tax [*fornatgio*], the tax on wine [*quarto vini*], and other taxes, which had been agreed in the last council by the communities of Languedoc for the defence of the realm. Because of their poverty and the desperate state of their inhabitants, these communities had not been accustomed to paying royal subsidies or the hearth tax for some time. On behalf of these commoners, they sent us many frequent dispatches to explain matters. Along with the chief officer and principal judge, these townsmen authorised one of their officers, a notary, and a council member with two or three from the bourgeoisie and the notables of this city, representing its various pockets [*insulas*] or districts, to draw up a tax survey according to the instructions of this edict. Diligently and obediently, they attended to our command and began their work. On the morning of the next day, those assigned to this task along with many other bourgeois and good citizens with the chief officer and judge met in the church of Le Puy to finish their assignment.

During the celebration of mass in this church, when the image of the Virgin Mary was uncovered as is the custom at the end of Lent, a loud uproar came from the people of this city. Filled with laments and tears and gathered here in great numbers, they rose up [*insurrexit*]. In front of the image of the Virgin Mary, they implored loudly: 'Blessed Virgin Mary, help us! How can we live and feed our children, since we cannot bear these heavy taxes imposed on us to our harm, which strip and siphon off our property?' Hearing this tearful clamour, the deputies were saddened and disturbed but nonetheless diligently sought to fulfil their orders. Nevertheless, before the chief officer, judge, and deputies had left the church, certain good men[108] went to them to argue that our officials should not collect the tax, because the town councillors favoured the wealthy of this city to the detriment of the people and collecting the tax would drive them into poverty.

Some of the commoners said: 'Let us approach our lord the duke;[109] he will look after us and not let us be stripped of our possessions and die of hunger'. And among other places, they went to the house of Pierre of Monterevello, a bourgeois and alderman, who was said to have procured favours from us. They broke in, overturning this and that, causing much damage and injury. For this, this Pierre quite rightly was frightened and fled with his family. And the crowd went to the home of Pierre Gaselas, another alderman, and as at the homes of

108 Good not in the moral sense but as substantial, the bourgeois of the town.
109 The king's uncle and lieutenant in Languedoc, Louis of Anjou.

other aldermen where they went, they revolted and created a major disturbance [*magnum tumultum & commocionem*]. And the son of one of these wicked people rang the city bells, which greatly upset the aldermen and other good men of this city and ended by insulting the officers and those appointed to set the taxes. Yet many of them went to the chief officer and on their knees, hands clasped together in prayer, and weeping bitterly, they beseeched him for God's sake to look after them and not tax and afflict the people so. Otherwise, they would die of starvation or be forced to go begging from place to place. They would willing pay us this tax if it had been assessed according to the value of their property or by another means, or if by our grace we had given them a remission beforehand. This was an impoverished people; many were workers or vagabonds from foreign places [*diversarum nacionum*], who because of this pilgrimage site had ended up here. Many committed crimes, assembled illegally, carried weapons and other things. On many occasions they insulted the aldermen and bourgeoisie and have violated the defence of our realm. Further, they have gone against the announced edict regarding the payment of the above-mentioned taxes and other matters. Their aldermen have beseeched us for God's sake and mercy that we should consider it worthy to pardon them from all corporeal, criminal, and civil punishment ... [The remission was granted, except for certain ones who were prosecuted for treason.]

Issued at Montpellier, 13 May 1378.

170 A notice of the revolt in Béziers, 1381

From the *Chronique des quatre premiers Valois*, p. 297.

In Languedoc, the citizens of Béziers rebelled against the dukes of Anjou and of Berry. As a result, many of Béziers, who had revolted against the duke of Anjou, uncle of the king of France, were put to death.

171 Rebellion in Montpellier according to the official chronicler of King Charles V, 1379

Chronique de Jean II et de Charles V, II, pp. 368–9.

Of the rebellion of Montpellier: item, a general uprising [*commocion universal*] of the inhabitants of the city of Montpellier erupted on Tuesday, 25 October that year [1379]. They put to death Lord Guillaume Pointel, a knight and chancellor of the duke of Anjou, brother of the king and his lieutenant for all of Languedoc, Lord Guy of Lesterie, seneschal of Rouergue, Master Ernault of Lair, governor of Montpellier, Master Jehan Perdiguier, magistrate and governor of the king's finances, and many other officers of the king as well as of the duke of Anjou, numbering eighty or more. Afterwards, they threw many of their victims' bodies down the wells of the city. And they did this because the above-mentioned councillors had requested taxes [*aide*][110] from them on behalf of the duke of Anjou so he could wage war in Languedoc, for which he was very much threatened and not without reason.[111]

172 Rebellion in Montpellier according to a local chronicler

La chronique romane, in *Le Petit Thalamus de Montpellier* (Montpellier, 1840), p. 398.

On Tuesday 25 October [1379] at evening and all through the night some of the commoners [*popolares*] staged a revolt [*gran insult*] in Montpellier, in which several high officers of our lord the king and of the lord duke of Anjou, his brother and lieutenant in Languedoc, were killed, because they had made large and intolerable demands, especially the imposition of the tax of 12 francs per household a year. The people [*pobol*] were already entirely devastated, broken by the great dearth that had run through this region for a long time. For this reason, these matters came to the attention of our lord the pope on the following Tuesday. And immediately afterwards on Wednesday, after dinner, Monsignor, the Cardinal d'Albana, the brother of Pope Urban of Holy Renown went to hear the people and console them, to bring an end to all this rioting and restore the people to peace.[112]

---

110 This was the recently ordered *fouage* of 12 francs per household per annum.
111 All of the above were royal officers sent to the towns of Languedoc to quell resistance because of the increase in the hearth tax to 12 francs per household per annum. It had not been imposed by the duke of Anjou, who was retained in the service of the king in Brittany, but by the men of the king's council.
112 For a similar account, see Jacme Mascaro, *Le 'Libre de Memorias'*, ed. Charles Barbier, in *Revue des langues romanes*, 4th ser., 34 (1890): 36–100, p. 72; and for a brief account, *Chronique des quatre premiers Valois*, pp. 281–2.

173 Revolt of Clermont de Lodève[113], 1379

Histoire générale de Languedoc, cols. 1632–9, no. 648; Arch. nat. JJ. 117, no. 37.

Louis, etc. Let it be known, etc that the noble Déodat, son of William, lord of Clermont and its barony, of the district [*vicarie*] of Gigniaci, and viscount of Narbonne, has reported to us that last October [1379] the common people [*popolares*] of Montpellier perpetrated murders and other nefarious crimes against our venerable and renowned men of our councils of the district of Rouergue and other officials and councillors of our kingdom. Some of the residents of this castle of Clermont, that is, Pierre del Royre, master Jehan Colletti, and many of their followers, filled with a malignant spirit, wished to follow in the footsteps of those of Montpellier, and held Jehan de Clonchis, Bertran of Ausaco, Berengar Vallete, and many others of Clermont in mortal hatred. On Sunday before All Saints' Day, the last day of October, around vespers, while the inhabitants were leaving church, they conspired to create a horrible riot [*tumultum*], shouting: 'Ring the bells, ring the bells, let's kill, kill, kill the traitors, who have sold this place to the English [stationed at] Carlat'. They had previously plotted with Paul Cayreli and many others from this place as well as elsewhere, comprising a hundred men or more, that at this hour they would appear armed, would attack, and try to murder Jehan of Clonchis, Bertran of Ansaco, Berengar Vallete of Clermont, and others as planned. And on this Sunday after this hour, this Paul Cayrelli and others in this crowd armed with various weapons performed what in French is called a *touquesain* [tocsin or sounding of the bells]. And in this assault on Jehan de Clonchis, they killed him in his own house by setting it on fire, burning him alive.

And afterwards that night, since Bertran de Ausaco and the others, whom they had conspired against could not be found, they formed an armed squadron and ran throughout this place through the night, searching many houses and especially those belonging to the men they were conspiring against, intent on murdering them. And among other things they searched the house of Berengar Raynaudi, whom they wished to kill, and also because they believed that a royal judge of the [duchy] of Berry was a guest there, and they wished to kill him

---

113 Popular protest was not new to Lodève. Seventeen years earlier the people and councillors of the town had revolted against paying a fine of 1,300 florins imposed by the sénéchal de Carcassonne for an earlier revolt. They succeeded in lowering the fine to 800 florins; Arch. nat. JJ 91.

as well. The next day, at the instigation of Pierre del Royre, Master Jehan Colletti, and their followers, these murderers went to the house of Beregar Vallete. On finding out about it, he fled over his roof but was pursued and killed on the terrace belonging to Pierre del Royre. And even though the chief officer [*bajulum*] of this place tried to restrain these men from committing other wicked crimes or daring to carry weapons, the aforementioned Pierre del Royre, Jehan Colletti, and their followers – murderers – continued to go about armed, searching many houses to ferret out those they planned to kill, bringing to fruition their murderous plans. In the interim, Master Jehan Colletti held the keys to the principal gate of the town, which he kept locked. Seeing that on this day, they could not find any of those they wished to kill, they marched with a great number of men, armed with various weapons and with a war horn or trumpet that led their assembled crowd. With great insults, they shouted and declared: 'Open, open, open up the gate of the castle, so we can enter, and hand over those traitors you are hiding among the thieves, or we will make war on your castle'. With pickaxes or battleaxes they began knocking down the gates of the castle, yelling: 'To the assault, to the assault'. In the midst of this revolt, the chief officer of this place, who was the captain inside this castle, tried with pleas and exhortations to persuade those in pursuit to end their siege. Negotiating with many good men of this place, who under fear of death and by force had been forced to arm, the chief officer opened the first and second doors at the front of the castle, allowing seven or eight of these murderers to enter. And he negotiated with them and had them promise to spare Berengar, son of Raymund, Berengar of Balma, and several others inside, whom they had planned to kill. After these men had been so favoured, the murderers had retreated, encouraged by the threat of death. Then the murderers with many of their comrades, armed and marching with the sound of trumpets at their head, went to the house of Bertran of Ausaco with the idea of killing him. But they did not find him there; nor did they find him later that day or at night. So they rioted and made attacks, which continued to the next day, All Saints' Day, and, around sunrise that day, they found and killed him. Having accomplished this, Pierre del Royre and Master Jehan Colletti ordered an end to the rioting and the actions of these armed men.

Fearing the law, Pierre del Royre and Jehan Colletti immediately held discussions with the other murderers to ensure that the gates of this castle would be guarded. Satisfied with what they had accomplished, they now ordered that if any officer of the king or commissioner or lord of this place should come collecting information against them or others to capture them, they would immediately lock the gates, begin to riot, and have them killed. These murderers guarded the gates of the castle for twelve days or more and plotted many other enormities, nefarious crimes, and conspiracies. Finally, the lord of Clermont realised the seriousness of these crimes – that such crimes were now common in his territory and were beginning to increase and to inflame others, and would lead to evil consequences. As a consequence, the officers of the king, temporal lords, and other good men were now in grave danger of being killed in the countryside and the towns. Commoners [*populares*] in other places were shouting: 'Let's kill, let's kill all the rich, let's do just what those of Montpellier and Clermont have done!'

Dreading that the strict rigour of the law would not restrain any of these commoners of Clermont, [the officials] presumed that the commoners would subsequently commit even worse crimes ... [The case then turns to the lord of Clermont's suppression of the ringleaders, all of whom were sentenced to be hanged by the neck. Rather than being professional or common 'murderers' as the rhetoric of this document portrays these insurgents, we learn that in the year of the revolt Pierre del Royre was a town councillor of Clermont and a bourgeois of the royal town of Aigues-Mortes, that Master Jehan Colletti was the notary of the bishop of Lodève and a town councillor of Clermont, and that two others condemned to death by hanging, Jehan Podi and Raymund Galani, had served as royal inquisitors in the year of the revolt.] Issued at Montpellier in February 1379[80] and confirmed by the king in April 1380, after Easter.

174 Revolt in Alès, 1380

Histoire générale de Languedoc, cols. 1630–2, no. 648: Arch. nat. JJ. 118, no. 326.

Louis, etc. We have been faithfully informed by our worthy officers orally that the people in several parts of Alès in the district of Beaucaire assembled unarmed, numbering about three hundred persons or more, around All Saints' Day of this year [1 November 1380]. Seditiously, they forced the councillors now in office here to summon the vicars of the lords of this place. Thus summoned and from fear of those assembled, they compelled Salvator Peleti, Michael Boveri, Jean

Mimelta, Étienne Radulfi, Étienne of Sinolis, Bernard of Alairac, and several other men of this place, who previously held government offices here and whom those assembled alleged to be in possession of large sums of money both from the commune's tax accounts as from other governmental income, to spend these sums on behalf of the commune. Aggressively, the people compelled these aforesaid councillors to take provisions of grain, wine, and other possessions of the commune from their homes and put them on sale before those assembled, where they were sold at any price the crowd pleased. By so doing they [the people] were committing the crime of treason and sedition and were violating the king's safeguard protecting these councillors as well as committing many other crimes. Because of these crimes, these people and some of their accomplices were brought to us at our district court of Beaucaire and before the lords of this place, where we tried and indicted those who appeared before us. Recognition and punishment of these crimes pertained to our lordship because these insults and their seditious and unjust congregation were crimes of treason. But the town councillors and friends of these people from other surrounding places came before us and asserted that these people at other times had been faithful and obedient to me and our lordship; they had caused this great damage because of the wars in my territory and the burdens that these events had placed on them. Further, the barren harvest that has persisted over the past year has left them extremely destitute. Perhaps it was easy for them to believe that the rich and powerful of this place possessed great sums of money belonging to the commune and for this reason their anger was roused. At any rate, they did not come carrying arms or kill or wound anyone. Thus, they have beseeched our grace and mercy on behalf of these people ...

Issued at Montpellier, January 1379[80].

175 Rebellions and raids in the region of Toulouse in 1381 and 1382

Histoire générale de Languedoc, X, col. 1744–7: Arch. nat. JJ, 133, n. 53. This document might be called 'Tuchins without the name' and shows that cattle raiding and private wars extended over vast terrains of southern France in the early 1380s.

Charles, etc. Let it be known to all present and in the future that we have been informed on behalf of the dear friends of Pierre Vaquier from the village of Gargas in the district of Toulouse, how in 1381, when the rebellion [*commocion*] of the communes in our region of Languedoc had begun, certain soldiers of the garrison of the castle of Cabrières, who were opposed to these communes, went off raiding and pillaging this place Gargas, where they killed, captured, and led off many people and animals, with Vaquier losing twenty-seven head of cattle or thereabouts. And because of the sorrow and anger aroused by this loss, he and others of the region assembled and started off on the road for this castle, sending some ahead on foot to set an ambush. But these stopped the next day at a village where they slept late into the next day when those with Vaquier found them. Seeing that the ambush had failed, Vaquier wanted to return to his village. But some of the others said that he should go with them to the castle and town of le Causé under the lordship of Terride. They then set off to go there. But, since it was reported that this scoundrel of Terride had only recently run raids against the communes in the region of Toulouse, Vaquier said that the men of le Causé had not done him any wrong; thus he left with his men to return home. But soon after he had gone about a league from the others, Vaquier heard them sound the trumpet, which led him to think that his company was in trouble and needed help. He returned to join the others with his men, who took two men and ten or twelve head of cattle along the way and led them to Villemur[-sur-Tarn], and these were returned and freed soon afterwards with no profit to Vaquier and without any harm to those of le Causé.

After five months or so, the men of Toulouse and of the surrounding countryside attacked the castle of Cabrières, which did injury to Vaquier and others. The siege lasted three or four weeks. Recalling the damages he suffered, Vaquier stayed armed and as a cavalry for twelve days but did nothing else there. Then in the following year, 1382, Vaquier took the side of the lord and knight of Aigues-Vives against Nicole de Lettres, a knight, who was then in charge of our forests and rivers in Languedoc. He held the village of Capendu, which the knight of Aigues-Vives contested. In the dispute, Aigues-Vives, along with many armed and mounted men, among them, Vaquier, went one night to attack and capture the village of Villar-en-Val in the district of Carcassonne, which lay in the lands of this lord of Lettres, as is well known. Once they took this place, they gutted it, pillaging and ravaging all the property there. Some of the company of this lord of Aigues-Vives used the booty for their own gain but not Vaquier. They held this place for ten days or so, and from it they went forth many times, mounted on horseback and armed as though for war. They raided the area of Capendu with the intention of capturing it if they could. And in doing so, on several occasions, they took many prisoners and led them back to the castles of lord Aigues-Vives, where they were ransomed and their cattle sold for these men's own gain or at least in part. A day or so after this cattle raid, Vaquier and several others from his company rode from Aigues-Vives and Marsaillete to Capendu, where de Lettres was staying. Vaquier asked to speak with him, but de Lettres refused to come out and sent instead his men. Vaquier told them that he should give this place to the lady of Aigues-Vives and her children, who were his kin on his or his wife's side or he truly would not cease making war on him, inflicting bodily harm, destroying his property, seizing his castles and fortresses, and harming him as much as he could.

Of the cattle mentioned above, the lord of Aigues-Vives handed over to Vaquier several plough animals and between a hundred and 120 sheep, which he was supposed to sell to raise money. The plough animals were led to Vaquier's house and then transported into the districts of Carcassonne and Toulouse but soon afterwards law officers seized and returned them to their owners. But the sheep did not get as far as Vaquier's house. Rather, he stayed on the road in a village, where a servant of Aigues-Vives heard that the law had taken the plough animals, of which the servant quickly returned and told his master. Because he was ordered and from fear that the sheep could not be kept safely, the servant sold them at whatever price he could fetch without letting Vaquier know about it or receive anything. Instead, the servant handed the money for the cattle over to Aigues-Vives, his master, except what he and his servant with their two horses had lived on from the goods taken from Villar, which was taken by them by escalade as is said above. And if anything was kept for his own use, of which there is no proof, it would have amounted to very little, and if there were anything, he offered to make full restitution for any of it.

In this matter, he had not committed murder, sacrilege, rape, or arson. The two knights mentioned above [Vaquier and the lord of Aigues-Vives] had come to a working agreement and negotiated a marriage between their parties. However, because of these matters and because some claimed to be under our safeguard, although it was never specified, he [Vaquier] feared that he might suffer in the future if we did not provide for him. Thus he humbly beseeched us to consider what has been said and that he had previously received a remission from our very dear and loving uncle, the duke of Berry, our lieutenant in Languedoc, and that we should desire to impart our grace to him and include him in the general remission we granted awhile back to the inhabitants of the districts of Carcassonne, Toulouse, and Beaucaire. He thus claimed to have paid his part and portion of the expenses for this remission, the eight hundred thousand francs imposed on these communes ... [the usual clauses in letters of remission ensue].

Issued at Paris, June 1388.

176 The ravages of the companies in the Velay

Histoire générale de Languedoc, col. 1792–4: Arch. nat. JJ. 137, n. 108. This document points out several things inherent in a number of other documents – that individuals and villages resisted threats and the arrogance of marauding soldiers of fortune, that harassment of the poor by royal officers was endemic, that even the poorest of peasants kept legal and royal documents and were expected to present them to royal officers, and that the poor had a weapon that touched sensitive ears and concerned the king after the Black Death's toll on population, peasant threats of flight that would lead to the further erosion of the tax base and labour supply of the kingdom.

Charles etc. Let it be known, etc. We have been humbly informed on behalf of Girart and Peronon del Rieu, poor manual labourers under the command of Bonas in the diocese of le Puy Notre Dame. They woefully lament that around 1380 Loys de Bugny, then captain of certain armed men, held a fortress in the Auvergne and constantly made raids through the countryside, stealing cattle and capturing country people, forcing them to come to terms with them or to flee. Nonetheless, one day this Loys moved from this castle because he heard that Ponchot de Langac, chief officer of the mountains of Auvergne, wanted to attack it. So he and his men went to lodge in a church in a village called Chambon-le-Château in this diocese. This Ponchot assembled his men-of-arms and foot soldiers from the countryside, and they pursued and attacked Loys at Chambon. In the struggle that ensued Loys was killed in the village along with most of his men. Those, who could, fled. The two petitioners named above were present and returned to their homes a half league outside Chambon. When they returned home, they found a squire [*valet*] of Loys, who was a part of his company and had also fled, and who said to them: 'Up peasants [*villains*]; make me a good welcome and go fetch some wine and fix me something good to eat, or I'll set your house ablaze tomorrow morning'. The petitioners asked if he were one of Loys de Bugny's men, to which he said yes. Then, with another called de Montillet they got together to discuss the matter and went to a wood near the village, where they planned to kill the squire. Another called Blaye would be a lookout, while the petitioners accompanied the squire to the wood. Meanwhile, the squire slept and supped at the petitioner's home, and the next morning, when they brought him to the edge of the wood, this Blaye appeared with a mace and hit the squire on the head with such force that he died instantly. Then, they returned to their homes. Because of this, Ponchon obtained a remission for himself and for all those who needed one for this incident. But these poor petitioners, in part because of their stupidity and in part because of their great poverty, had not been able to get a copy of this remission. As a consequence, they have been constantly harassed and bothered by commissioners and sergeants. If we do not bestow our grace on them, they will flee our kingdom ...

Issued at Avignon, January, 1389[90].

177 Tax revolt in Lyon, 1382

Remission to Ymbert de Rousillon, stable master; Léon Mirot, *Les insurrections urbains*, pp. 110–1; Arch. nat. JJ. 121, no. 257, fol. 153v. The revolts against taxes clustered first in Languedoc, 1379–81, then in *Langue d'oïl* – Rouen, Amiens, Reims, Paris, etc – from 1380 to 1382, but scattered evidence suggests that they flared in other regions of France as well. When the castellan of Lyon assembled the inhabitants of Lyon 'to impose and place on them certain subsides', the townsmen replied with the same refrain heard elsewhere: 'we'll pay nothing'.

Charles [...] Ymbert de Rousillon, stable master, inhabitant of Lyon, has pleaded to us that on a day around Lent, last year [1382], along with a great number of other inhabitants he went to the chapel of Saint-Jacques, where it was customary to hold the council of the commune of this city. He went with others to see and learn what was happening. He was in this chapel with the town councillors and many others of the good sort of this city, who were assembled to respond to our trusted friend Pierre de Thury, guardian of Lyon and our commissioner in this region. He brought certain royal letters from us to be read out to the councillors and inhabitants of this city, which imposed and placed on them, as it is said, certain subsidies on this city. And all those assembled let loose great insults and shouts, declaring that they would pay nothing. But this supplicant did not say then or at any other time villainous words against us and our majesty [...] even if it is very true that he left the chapel with many of these inhabitants and followed Leonart Carronier[114] in his cart to his house, where they harassed him, saying many injurious words, because he [Carronier] had said certain words in the chapel, which appeared to them to harm the cause of the commune [...]

Issued at Paris, November 1382.

---

114 It is not clear who this Leonart was, whether he was simply another commoner who disagreed with the others or had some authority from the crown, but because he left in his own cart perhaps he was a man of substance and authority.

EPILOGUE:
AFTER THE CLUSTER, 1382-1423

After the 1380s the rhythms of revolt north and south of the Alps again went their separate ways. The duke of Berry may have brutally smashed the Tuchins of the Massif Centrale in 1384; yet the Hundred Years War, poorly enforced truces, and the mountainous terrain, allowed townsmen, rustics, dissatisfied noblemen, and ex-soldiers to continue to form armed bands in pursuit of economic and political ends. Such acts of banditry remain rife in the letters of remission. The only thing that appears to have changed after 1384 in a letter of remission presented here [185] was the absence of the term *Tuchin*. Yet the word and its legends survived in descriptions of other raids well into the fifteenth century.[1]

Similarly, in the north of France, serious threats to the crown and the *échevins* or city aldermen did not die with the hammer men. In 1403 the epicentre of a new wave of tax revolts erupted in Reims and as in 1380, the king had to abolish his fiscal plans 'because of the people's protest [*propter murmur populi*]'.[2] One of the most remarkable uprisings in the history of Paris came in 1413 in the midst of the civil war between the Armagnacs and the Burgundians. First, 'the people' threw out one provost of the merchants and replaced him with another; then the butchers and animal skinners took advantage of the factional strife between the dukes and their struggle for royal favour. Supported, perhaps even 'used',[3] by John the Fearless and the Burgundians, commoners – 'a jumble of men of the lowest origins' to use the words of the *Religieux de Saint-Denys* – forced the city aldermen and the crown into negotiations [180–2]. In May 1413 Charles VI was forced to capitulate and signed an extraordinary set of compromising reforms (even if they were never implemented). Containing 258 articles, these acts – *L'Ordonnance Cabochienne,* named after the animal

---

1 *Histoire de Languedoc,* X, col. 1735, nos. 698: 'Lettre de remission pour un partisan des Tuchins', JJ 131, n. 226, November 1387; and Boudet, *La Jacquerie des Tuchins,* p. 110.

2 *Le Religieux de Saint-Denys,* III, pp. 38–9; and Guenée, *L'opinion publique,* p. 60.

3 See R. C. Famiglietti, *Royal Intrigue: Crisis at the Court of Charles VI, 1392–1420* (New York, 1986), pp. 117–19.

skinner and insurgent Simon Caboche – seriously challenged royal prerogatives and gutted administrative extravagance [183].

Nor was Paris the only town in northern France to experience new forms of popular insurrection. In 1418 Regnault le Moqueur, a manual worker and labourer in the vineyards, conspired to oust the town council of Châlons-en-Champagne. As we have seen, such conspiracies by workers to overthrow city councils and other regimes were not new, but what appears new in this document are this worker's methods and objectives and the length of time he spent as a revolutionary, in effect a practising politician. 'For five or six years' he had held assemblies with others 'of the lower estate at Châlons', making political speeches to convince the *petit peuple* that the current town councillors were no good and should be thrown out. His speeches not only 'scorned' these rulers but also their laws and argued for reform. Presumably, he and 'his accomplices', like Caboche and his followers, had new laws in mind that they would have implemented had their rhetoric and plots borne fruit [184].

In Italy, popular insurrection post-1382 was different. The greatest number of popular riots, at least for Tuscany, is known for Florence. They were comprised of Ciompi remnants following the fall of the government of the Minor Guilds in January 1382 but hardly matched the force or sophistication of what had come before. Stefani paints a picture of their rag-tag formations: 'like animals, they did not wait for their ranks to form, but instead dribbled into the square ... hopping this way and that' [186]. Three weeks later a similar band fared no better: they came into the Piazza della Signoria, but it was enough for the famous *condottiere* John Hawkwood and his crossbowmen only to appear to set the fifty Ciompi with their stolen flag of the Guelf Party running; 'one had never seen such a sorry group of soldiers' as these ex-Ciompi [187]. Into the 1390s, ex-Ciompi on occasion brought out their illegal flags from concealed closets and marched to restore their lost rights and guilds but without serious threat to the ruling oligarchy [188–90, 195]. Only one of these incidents – a failed uprising of minor guildsmen led by a goldsmith in 1393 – caught the eye of a non-Tuscan chronicler.[4]

---

4 *Corpus Chronicorum Bononiensium*, III, p. 442, dates it a year later (1394). According to Brucker, *The Civic World*, p. 17, this was 'the last moment in Florentine history when guild loyalties and aspirations played an important if ultimately unsuccessful role in a political crisis'.

Popular urban revolts in other places in Tuscany are even harder to find. Siena's last major popular insurrection reported by its town chronicles was that of the wool workers' Club of the Caterpillar in 1371. By contrast, only two incidents that might be defined as popular protest emerge in the published Sienese chronicles between 1371 and 1425 (and probably beyond). In the first, villagers southwest of Siena in 1423 formed a vigilante group to apprehend 'the monster' they suspected of killing a neighbour's baby boy. But even they abided by the law, handing over their suspect to the executor of justice in Siena [**203**]. The most serious of the post-1382 riots documented here was that of the wool workers from the neighbourhood of Sant'Angelo in Perugia. After a failed revolt in March 1383 [**191, 192**], they succeeded in toppling the oligarchic government of the Raspanti in 1393, but instead of replacing it with members from their own ranks they turned to the Papacy, which led to the rule of another oligarchic regime – that of the Guelf Michelotti [**193**] and their henchman Biordo, who successfully and egotistically co-opted the revolution for his own vainglory [**194**]. No doubt, the rich archives of Italy conserve many more insurrections, and new research might change the contours of what now must be largely drawn from published chronicles.[5]

The most widespread and numerous revolts in Italy post-1382 come from the least likely section of the population given the current historiography, which holds that the city-states of Italy may have had their share of urban riots but the countryside remained compliant and complacent.[6] Instead, archival sources reveal that Florence's war with Milan unleashed widespread peasant insurrections across the northern mountainous frontiers of Florence. Against the mounting burdens of Florentine taxation with drastically fewer to pay them than before the plagues, these mountain peasants found the 'tyranny' of their former feudal lords preferable to Florence's 'liberty' and unequal taxation.[7] With rare exceptions [**200**], the chroniclers either pretended that these revolts against their Florentine 'liberators' had not happened or,

---

5 Cities such as Rome, Genoa, and Ferrara can count numerous and important rebellions against taxes and oligarchic governments in the late fourteenth and early fifteenth centuries, and more work is needed on rural insurrections.

6 See most recently *Protesta e rivolta contadina nell'Italia medievale*, ed. Giovanni Cherubini in *Annali dell'Istituto 'Alcide Cervi'*, no. 16 (1994).

7 For a revolt which interchanges these words and makes the choice explicit, see my translation of the court case against the rebels of Rocca di San Casciano in the Romagna, 1399; *Women in the Streets: Essays on Sex and Power in Renaissance Italy* (Baltimore, 1996), pp. 122–3.

as in the case of Gregorio Dati, rewrote Florentine history, portraying its mountaineer rebels as instead protectors of Florentine liberty [201]. Archival records – the criminal cases and the *provvisioni* (or almost daily register of Florentine decrees) – however, tell another story – one of revolt and peasant victories, in which the Florentine oligarchy had to make major concessions to rebel ringleaders and mountain communities, including perpetual tax exemptions, rights to carry arms, sinecures as officers of the Florentine state and rights to elect whomever they wanted to settle in their communities enticed with tax exemptions and privileges [198, 199].[8]

Florence was not the only region to experience such a sudden upsurge in peasant resistance and insurgence towards the end of the fourteenth century. The tax rebellion of peasants northeast of Ferrara may have involved even greater numbers [197], and between two thousand and four thousand peasants from the *contado* of Parma conspired with artisans within the city, rebelled against taxes and their provision of salt, and invaded the city, killing tax officials and noblemen [196]. Similar invasions by peasants and others who resided outside city walls appear to have heated up also in Genoa: between 1393 and 1419 the city experienced at least six threats to its hegemony from the peasants of its neighbouring three valleys and many more came from towns and villages further along the mountainous Ligurian coastline.[9] As the case of Florence and its peasant unrest suggests, the archives once tapped hold surprises, but a survey even of the published chronicles promises new interpretations for Italian social history.

France

178 How the University of Paris had a big quarrel with Lord Charles of Savoy, 1404

La Chronique d'Enguerrand de Monstrelet, ed. Douët-d'Arcq, I (Paris, 1857), pp. 73–5. Born around 1390 Enguerrand de Monstrelet would have been a teenager or younger when this serious town-gown battle unfolded. As a chief officer and provost of Cambrai and servant to Philip, duke of Burgundy and Flanders, Enguerrand set himself the task of continuing the chivalric chronicle of Froissart where Froissart left off on Easter day 1400. Longer and fuller

---

8 For many other examples see Cohn, *Creating the Florentine State*.
9 Georgius and Iohannes Stella, *Annales Genuenses*, in 1393, 1394, twice in 1400, 1405, and 1419, pp. 207–8, 243–4, and 344.

versions of this incident can be found in the *Chronique du religieux de Saint-Denys* and the *Journal de Nicolas de Baye*[10] but this one sketches the course of events in a spirited way.

Chapter XIII. At that time [1404][11] while the University of Paris was making a general procession to Saint Catherine in the Vale of the Students,[12] a quarrel arose between some of the University and the soldiers of Lord Charles of Savoy, the king's chamberlain.[13] The soldiers were taking their horses to drink along the river Seine. And this riot erupted because they galloped violently into the procession, wounding several of the students. Not content with this, the students hurled stones at them and pushed some violently off their horses. After this assault, they returned to the palace of this lord of Savoy, where they armed, grabbing bows and arrows. They then led other soldiers, assembled at the palace, and attacked the students again, shooting arrows at them and beating others with clubs, even in the church [of Saint Catherine]. Thus began a great riot [*hutin*], and finally the students, because of their great numbers, were able to push away the soldiers but only after many of them had been beaten and badly wounded. And what's more, after the procession had disbanded, a large number from the University went to the king to file a complaint against the offence that they had suffered. The rector made an urgent plea that the soldiers be punished according to their crimes. And what's more, they said that if their plea were not granted, they would leave the city of Paris and go somewhere else where they could live peacefully. The king responded, saying he would grant them a decision that would be sure to please them. Finally, after several days of pursuing this request before the king and his relatives as well as before the great council, they received an ordinance from the king that appeased them. As punishment for the offence committed by his

---

10 *Le Chronique du religieux de Saint-Denys*, III, pp. 185–94; and *Journal de Nicolas de Baye, Greffier du Parlement de Paris 1400–1417*, ed. Alexandre Tuetey, SHF, 222, 2 vols. (Paris, 1885), I, pp. 110–14.

11 Monstrelet mistakenly dates the event 1403; the attack occurred on 14 July 1404.

12 The procession began at Saint-Mathurin to celebrate mass at Saint Catherine's.

13 In the account of the *Journal de Nicolas de Baye*, p. 107, the students were not as innocent as they are portrayed in Monstrelet's version: several of Charles's soldiers passed a group of young students (*enfants ... escoliers*), 'who were screaming [*pipoient*] as they sometimes do', which startled the horses and caused some to fall off. Afterwards, the children taunted two of Charles's valets, causing them to be bucked off their horses. The students then threw stones and mud at them, and enticed others to follow suit, yelling 'get the rocks [*ad lapides*]', ending up with the valets badly wounded.

soldiers, as reported, the lord of Savoy would be banished and ejected from the king's palace, along with all his kinsmen. Further, he would be deprived of all royal offices. In addition, his mansion was to be demolished, knocked down from roof to floor, and he was charged to found two chapels with an income of a hundred *livres* [per annum] to be placed under the University's dominion.[14] After this sentence was implemented, Lord Charles left the realm of France to live in a desolate foreign place with great displeasure. But, thereafter he behaved so well and honourably that the king of France and others of the great lords decided to make peace with him, and he returned to the king's household by the grace of those of the University.

179 A student brawl in Orléans, 13 November 1408

Choix de pièces inédites relatives au règne de Charles VI, ed. L. Douët D'arcq, SHF (Paris, 1864), II, pp. 29–31, Arch. nat. JJ. 162, no. 112. The document below presses the margins of what might be considered social protest. It is probably better labelled simply as social violence, but it shows the civil disruption that students could inflict on a community, the centrality of taverns for their organisation, and the surprising ease by which they could obtain serious military weapons to carry out their private vendettas.

Charles, etc. Let it be known to all present and future that we have received the humble supplication of our dear friend, Jean Pitoyte, twenty-three years old or about, bachelor of law, a student studying at the University of Orléans, containing the following:

On Friday 25 October [1408] Pitoyte and several other students of this university, about nine or so, were dining together in the city of Orléans, at an inn and tavern called the *Brissete*. While eating, one of them, whose name Pitoyte does not remember, said that Pierre Langloiz, a student at this University, had in the past hit, hurt, and insulted Henry de Marte, another student who was then dining with them. Langloiz had recently arrived in Orléans and was lodging with Pierre Pépin, an innkeeper living in Orléans, at the sign of the Arms of Burgundy, in front of the church of Saint-Lieffart. After these words, one of them, whose name Pitoyte does not remember, said:

14 In addition, the duke of Savoy was fined one thousand pounds, which was given to the University and an equal sum paid to the wounded. Further, to avoid the destruction of his art collection, he 'built magnificent galleries on the walls of the city, which were decorated with paintings of every sort (*Le chronique du religieux de Saint-Denys*, III, p. 193).

'Let's go and beat him up'. The others responded: 'We'll go, once we've eaten, and we'll discuss what we'll do'. After supper, all six of them left the inn, including Pitoyte. Together, they went to an inn called the Little Ring [*Petit-Anneau*] There, the six – including Pitoyte and Henry de Marte, who as we said had previously been beaten up and wounded by Pierre Langloiz – were all involved in the plot and agreed to go and beat up Pierre Langloiz. With this plot hatched, they left and each went to his house to get armed and to borrow any equipment they could muster such as mail coats, padded jackets [*jaques*], swords, daggers, battle-axes, guisarms [*guisernes*],[15] and other weapons. And especially this Pitoyte wore a padded tunic [*gippon*] made with many layers of cloth and carried a sword, dagger, and a weapon called a falcon's beak. And they gathered at the corner called 'the corner of the former Jehan Giresme', near the church of Nôtre-Dame-de-Bonnevoiz, and from there went to the inn of Pierre Pépin, the innkeeper, which they found open. And four of them, including Pitoyte, climbed to the top of the stairs to reach the room where Pierre Langloiz lodged. He was still eating supper with four or five other students ... And when they had reached the top, Pitoyte stopped in a hallway in front of the room while the three others, including Henry de Marte, entered the room, and as he sat eating they immediately began beating Pierre Langloiz with their guisarmes, swords, and batons. They wounded him in many places, as much on the head as on the body and arms. And he was beaten so hard that he died four or five days later. Because of this, Pitoyte feared the rigours of justice and left the country.

Issued on the river Loire in front of Orléans, 13 November 1408, by the king, the Grand Master of the town hall [*Hotel*], and others present.

180 The revolt of the butchers and the people of the wretched estate [*vil estat*] of Paris, March 1413

Guillaume Cousinot I, *Geste des Nobles*, in *Chronique de la Pucelle ou chronique de Cousinot*, ed. by M. Vallet de Viriville (Paris, 1859), p. 145. This source presents the origins of the Cabochien revolt as though it were completely lodged within the high politics of the internecine conflict between Armagnacs and Burgundians. As chancellor to Charles of Orléans and administrator of

---

15 'Long-handled weapon with curved blade and spike, combination of spear and battleaxe' *Old French–English Dictionary*, ed. Alan Hindley, Frederick Langley, and Brian Levy (Cambridge, 2000), p. 345.

EPILOGUE: AFTER THE CLUSTER, 1382-1423

his property while Charles was imprisoned in England, Cousinot naturally gave the events of 1413 an Armagnac view. Not only does he have no sympathy for the butchers, he gives them no voice of their own or any reason why they may have been aggrieved in 1413.

At this time [March 1413] the butchers and others of the wretched estate of Paris and in other cities in the realm rose up with pride and extreme arrogance, spurred on by the duke of Burgundy, who desired to take over the government and endeavoured to break the peace. And they were supported by the duke and tried by all means to assemble all the princes inside Paris in order to kill them all. In the name of the king, they [the butchers] immediately wrote to the princes and the three estates to come to Paris on a certain day. The princes excused themselves and sent their councillors in their place, which hardly pleased the butchers. They began to grumble and set off against the princes and Lord Pierre des Essars, provost of Paris, who did not wish to break the treaty of Auxerre[16] for their sake. For this, the duke took to hating [the provost of Paris], even though the provost had advanced his interests so that the duke could lead a life grander than that of any knight alive.

181 Rebellion of Paris and the imprisonment of the dukes of Bar and of Bavaria, April 1413

Ibid., pp. 146–7.

At the end of April 1413, by the will and approval of the duke of Burgundy, the commune of Paris rose up in arms and revolted. The leaders were Thomas le Gouais and his children, butchers; Caboche, a skinner; Philippe du Mont, a furrier; Master Jean de Troyes, a surgeon, and others. They went to *la petite Guyenne*, the palace of the duke of Guyenne, attacked Monsignor Guyenne, and in his presence seized and imprisoned in various jails the dukes of Bar and Bavaria, Master Jean de Vesley, chancellor of Guyenne, Lord Jacques de la Rivière, Lord Regnault d'Angennes, the lady of Quesnoy, the lady of Montauban,[17] Guillot du Mesnil, and many other knights, esquires,

---

16 Peace treaty drawn up at the end of August 1412 in Auxerre among the princes of Armagnac, Burgundy, Charles VI, and Henry IV of England. It was short-lived. As the treaty was being negotiated, English troops had been dispatched in the Cotentin and had advanced as far as the Loire; see Coville, *Les premiers Valois*, pp. 338–9; and Famiglietti, *Royal Intrigue*, pp. 107–12.

ladies, and damsels, who waited on the king, queen, and the Monsignor of Guyenne. From this offence the latter took particular displeasure as well as those imprisoned in the Royal Palace. One day, the knight Lord Elion of Jacleville [Léon de Jacqueville] and the skinner Caboche went to the prison and killed this Lord de la Rivière. And the next day, they brought Guillot du Mesnil, along with the dead de la Rivière, to the central market, where they were beheaded.

182 The first revolt of the Parisians, sparked by the most squalid, April 1413

Chronique du religieux de Saint-Denys, VI/5, Book 34, chapter II, pp. 6–13 [1413].

Most Parisians, who in the previous year had shown great attachment to the provost, regarding him as the father of the people and the principal defender of public interests, then changed their minds, which I do not understand. One cannot explain this love of change, which always torments the capricious rabble [*vulgus*]. They became deeply resentful of him, harboured a mortal hatred of him, and demanded that another provost replace him immediately. Their demand was easily granted ... and from then on Pierre des Essarts was considered an outlaw. Everywhere it was made public that monsignor the duke of Guyenne had not pardoned him for squandering the revenues of the duke's august father [Charles VI]. Such was the mood, when five days after Easter, 27 April, a troop of knights and esquires on orders from the duke of Guyenne took away this provost from the castle of Saint-Antoine.

... Suddenly, the duke became master of this royal fort, which was almost impregnable and abundantly supplied with every sort of weapon and siege machine. With it, one could bring a great number of troops into Paris, to the disgust of the citizens and detriment of the city. With the disasters that ensued it is better to write them in the form of a tragedy than with the pen of the historian ... A jumble of men of the lowest origins, whose names I must make known to stain them forever – the two brothers Legoix, common butchers, Denys de Chaumont and Simon Caboche, animal skinners in the butchery of Paris – ran through the streets of the city all day long spreading rumours to whomever they met. They were with others, whose names

17 These were the queen's ladies of honour. The lady of Quesnoy was especially close to the queen and was entrusted with the care of her books.

escape me for the moment. One was the famous doctor, Jean de Troyes, an eloquent and crafty man, already advanced in years, from whom they regularly took advice. These poor ones, who had instigated and led revolts in the past, posted throughout the city that the duke's objective in taking over of the castle was to ruin the city and instigate its armed seizure by the king and his eldest son, the duke of Guyenne. By their vain clamour they had already deposed the provost, Pierre Gentien, director of the royal mint, under the pretext that he had altered the [values] between new gold and the greatly depreciated old silver currency. And they had named in his place a worthy bourgeois, André d'Eperneuil. Following this, they went immediately to see the new magistrate and, against his wishes, made him put back the flag of the city, called the *étendard*, and obtained authorisation to request the city militia, the fifties and the tens, with the men under their orders to give up their weapons in the *place de Grève*. They would have executed and finalised their sinister designs, had it not been for the courage of the clergy, who refused repeatedly to sign the decrees of the provost. This man [Jean de Troyes] did not yield to threats or violence; he was always content to respond with a smile and without any rush. He knew well that the provost, the aldermen, and the principal defenders of the city had sworn to the duke of Guyenne that they would not rouse the citizens to take up arms without giving him word of it two days in advance. Thus the authorisation of the provost was annulled, and on the same day a great number of the *plebes* refused to obey them.

On the next day, 28 April, the leaders of the fifties, wise and moderate people, and some of the most notable bourgeois of the city, unarmed, as was their custom, held a meeting at the town hall with the provost of the merchants and the aldermen to discuss the current state of affairs. Considering how much trouble the last incidents had caused the public, they proposed that those who had taken up arms without permission of the king or the duke of Guyenne should lay them down. Then, a man entrusted with pleading to the masses, enjoined the inhabitants to stay peaceful and to devote themselves to the usual matters of their crafts and shops, and not to be swayed by vain disturbances and outside provocation ...

But desiring to talk reason to these leaders was like telling a story to a deaf ass: they responded with a seditious uproar [*tumultuosis clamoribus*]. 'It is in vain', they said, 'we have warned the king, the princes, and their councillors in secret and in public of the dangers, which these dishonest traitors have brought us. Since they have not taken any account of our advice, we have the right to take vengeance ourselves'. Soon agitated by this fury, nearly three thousand of the most miserable sort [*abjectissimorum*] were armed and drawn along with them to the gate of Saint-Antoine; inside and out they encircled the city with a blockade to prevent Lord Pierre des Essarts from escaping. Some from the knightly orders were involved, who gave advice on these manoeuvres. Soon, as time went on, the Lord of Helly, Léon de Jacqueville, and Robert de Mailly, soldiers of the duke of Burgundy, freely offered their assistance to the astonishment of many. I don't care about their motives, but I learnt that this Léon de Jacqueville yearned for the post of captain of Paris, which he later obtained, and that the two others nourished a vindictive hatred of Pierre des Essarts.

183 The laws inspired by the butcher Caboche, May 1413

From the Preamble, *L'Ordonnance Cabochienne (26–27 Mai 1413)*, ed. A. Coville (Paris, 1891), pp. 2–3.

... that the abovementioned clergy, knights, squires, bourgeois, and our very dear and much loved daughter, the University of Paris, and others assembled before us should give us their advice, help, and support ... Our true and loyal subjects, the provost of the merchants, the aldermen, the bourgeois, other governors, and inhabitants of our principal city of Paris have presented us with this particular roll of parchment, which they have had read publicly in our presence and before many of our kinsmen and lineage, our great council, the clergy, knights, esquires, bourgeois, and other subjects of all the estates assembled here in great numbers. With this roll, they have made us mindful of the many great abuses, evils, and improprieties that exist and have arisen in our realm. These have arisen in many areas and various ways because of the great and excessive number and poor conduct [*petit gouvernement*] of our many officers and others responsible for government and administration, which concern the finances of our royal domain, taxes charged for warfare, the judicial system, and other things touching the government and administration of the commonweal [*la chose publique*]. These abuses have caused harm and irreparable damage to us, have greatly sapped and dissipated all our finances, have led to the excessive diminution of our domain, contempt for and harm to our justice, and the sad oppression and vexation of our people. They have also made us aware of the many ways in which these evils and improprieties can be corrected... [The 258 articles that follow reduced or annulled royal administrative offices, specified maximum salaries for guards, castellans, and other royal officers in various parts of France, placed heavy penalties on those who received bribes or made corrupt profits from their offices, limited the king's hunting grounds, charged with treason any soldiers who took property without payment or collected booty from the countryside, annulled all the king's tolls that had been established during the last forty years, and more. It took two days to read aloud the royal ordinance.[18]]

184 Rebellion at Châlons-en-Champagne, 1418

Choix de pièces inédites, I, pp. 399–400; Arch. nat. JJ. 170, no. 269.

Charles, etc. Let it be known, etc. that we have received the humble supplication and request from the wife and close friends of Regnault le Moqueur, a poor man, manual worker, and labourer in the vineyards, responsible for three children.

He has been arrested and imprisoned at Châlons by the order of our friend and loyal knight, councillor and chamberlain, Jean of Neufchatel, lord of Montagu, a great officer of France and our captain of Châlons. Certain information was brought against Regnault concerning many riots [*sédicions*] and many assemblies he engaged in, which were comprised of commoners [*de petit peuple*] and those of the lower estate at Châlons. And on many occasions he delivered many words, evil speeches, and threats against this captain, his lieutenants, the governors, council, and many notables of this place. He and his accomplices endeavoured to overthrow the government and to replace it with new laws. They threatened and scorned the present rulers and their government, decisions, and deeds, saying they would kill them and spill a great amount of blood. And they sounded off with many other wicked words intended to persuade the people to believe that they have been badly governed and advised, even though this government had been good and had handled well its responsibilities and [public] works. And also for the past five or six years he has committed [...] [A long enumeration of robberies follows, then the remission for all these crimes, addressed to the chief officer of the Vermandois.]

Issued at Paris, October 1418.

18 On the ordinance, see Famiglietti, *Royal Intrigue*, pp. 123–5.

Southern France

185 Raids and illicit agreements with the enemy in the war-torn mountains above Saint-Flour, 1391

Letters of remission for an inhabitant of Saint-Flour; *Histoire générale de Languedoc*, cols. 1814–16; Arch. nat. JJ. 140, n. 14. Although the word 'Tuchin' never arises in this document, little seems to have changed in the mountains of the Auvergne around Saint-Flour from the 1360s and 1370s, that is before the duke of Berry supposedly smashed and drove out these bands of rustics and small townsmen, who profited against the crown, merchants, and the enemy during the Hundred Years War and its half-kept truces.

Charles, etc. Let it be known, etc. that we have been informed humbly on behalf of Jean Taffanel of the town of Saint-Flour in the mountains of the Auvergne. This town is and has been for a long time on a major frontier with our enemies, near the forts of Alleuze, Saillant,[19] Turlande,[20] Carlat, and many other fortresses, which our enemies occupy and have occupied in this district and in others around it. The town consuls and inhabitants of this town have made and agreed many pacts, ceasefires, and other treaties with these enemies, to which the petitioner has consented. Further, he has received many of them into his home, offering them food and drink. He has authorised the sale of and sold provisions, clothing, horses, and other things to them, and has associated with them in their garrisons. He has purchased, received as gifts, and by other means acquired from them horses, other animals, and other property, which he has taken through the countryside. Moreover, the petitioner, who was accustomed to arm himself at our expense for the defence of the country against these our enemies, has been living in the town of Brioude with certain other men of arms under the leadership of Poinchon de Langhac, esquire. And during the truces reached and agreed between our adversary, England, and us, these men have many times violated the truces with our enemies in this region. He discovered one of our enemies named Jean le Breton of the garrison of Carlat, who was passing through the countryside near the town of Brioude and, according to what was said, was on a pilgrimage to Avignon, carrying with him a certain payment. And when the plaintiff found out about him, he and other of his comrades and accomplices pursued this Jean le Breton and found him on the road, dressed

---

19 In the region of Saint-Flour.
20 In the commune of Verrières and region of Rouergue [Aveyron].

in a pilgrim's habit and saying that he was on a pilgrimage. They seized him and led him into a wood, where they relieved him of sixty-six écus and six nobles of gold,[21] which they used for their own purposes. And the petitioner was present and aided the company of this Poinchon and many others to plunder and capture many of our enemies. Up to eight or ten or thereabouts were put to death, wherever it was necessary, near the village of Mentière in this region of the Mountains. In addition, the petitioner ran many raids against our enemies in the fortresses they held and elsewhere, capturing and imprisoning them, putting many up for ransom, and stripping them of their horses, equipment, cattle, and other property, which he used for his own purposes. He engaged in all manner of war during these truces. And in this village we billeted some of these enemies with their horses and goods in the castle quarters under our control. The petitioner and others broke into the houses of this place and robbed the inhabitants of their necessities without paying anything. Because of these things [...] we have been beseeched to consider that our enemies during these truces had greatly troubled and damaged the region of the mountains and other areas around it. And this petitioner has served us well and loyally in our wars, as has been reported. Thus we wish to enlarge our grace and mercy to include him ...

Issued at Paris in January 1390[1].

Italy

186 The Ciompi try to restore their revolutionary guilds, 24 January 1382

Stefani, *Cronica fiorentina*, r. 905, p. 397. How various scuffles took place in the square of the priors, between guildsmen and others.

In this year [1382] on 24 January, with the two guilds now smashed,[22] those who had been members of these two guilds went about trying to stir up those belonging to the fourteen minor guilds and said they would again take to the streets. Although few in number, it is said that those barred from office [*gli smoniti*] had a hand in it.[23] Also, some

21 An écu, a gold coin, was initially worth 10 shillings Tournois (1266); a noble was an English gold coin minted during the reign of Edward III (1327–77), worth 6s 8d.
22 That is, the two revolutionary guilds of the dyers and doublet makers and their various constituent members.
23 These would have included disgruntled magnates and other citizens.

among the minor guildsmen armed themselves and went into the town square. Certainly had the butchers been armed and they had come into the Piazza in an orderly way, I believe things would have turned out differently. Instead like animals, they did not wait for their ranks to form but dribbled into the square, chanting: 'Long live the Twenty-four guilds'. The retinue [*famiglie*] of the city rectors and those of the wool bosses were already in the square armed and with many rustics [*villani*]. With little sense of order, these insurgents entered the square, hopping this way and that. They were beaten quickly, leaving three of them dead. They were chased out of the square as far as [the church of] Orsanmichele. And those of the Emergency Council [*balìa*] who were among the armed soldiers of the Palace [of the Signoria] went to ask for the banner of the [Guelf] Party and that of the [Ordinances of] Justice. They went into the square, and others followed. With these banners in the hands of two of the guard, they marched around the town square and stayed there until dusk. The priors sent for the banners of the guilds and had them put on the rostrum and then unfurled them from the windows of the Palace. And for this they closed all the shops of the guilds so the craftsmen could no longer assemble.

187 Another failed attempt by the Ciompi and the successful counter-revolution by the old families

Stefani, *Cronica fiorentina*, r. 913, p. 403.

How the city of Florence again rose up in arms with rioting through the streets; a new meeting of citizens [*parlamento*] was held and a new Emergency Council was created, composed of those previously on it and others.

On 15 February 1381[2], those of the Emergency Council wished to confirm their authority and to give their programme the force of their authority, which provoked a large number of people to assemble; that is, several from the principal families of Florence,[24] magnates, and the Ciompi joined together. First, they seized the flag of the [Guelf] Party and ran across the square; one had never seen such a sorry bunch of soldiers, some on foot, others on horseback. Lord John Hawkwood,

---

24 In other words, those with known family names such as the Strozzi, Pitti, Medici, etc. At this time only about 12 percent of Florentines had family names and far fewer in the countryside; see Cohn, *The Laboring Classes*, p. 45.

EPILOGUE: AFTER THE CLUSTER, 1382-1423

captain of war[25] assembled in the square 1500 cavalry and Genovese crossbowmen along with a number of other soldiers. Those Ciompi with the flag of the Party comprising perhaps fifty poorly armed men, entered the square and without any contest ran away. The city armed itself, and in the New Market all those from the principal families and many others gathered, who would force those in the Palace to hear what they wanted; that is, four from the emergency council should talk with them, and it was agreed. They deliberated in the Palace of the Guelf Party and ordered that forty-three men be signed on to join the existing priors and members of the emergency council for all of February. This is what they wanted and a meeting of citizens [*parlamento*] was called. The decisions of this meeting were read out on the rostrum of the Palace to the priors, the colleges, and captain of the people, who were listening at the windows, and to the armed people in the square. And the names of the forty-three who would enjoy emergency powers with the other previous 103 members [of the emergency council] were announced. And from the streets others came forward such as Lord Giovanni del Ricco, a judge, Carlo Strozzi and Bonaccorso di Lapo Giovanni with other documents containing many other matters, which they would read out to those below. And the forty-three elected along with a notary approved these motions without soliciting the opinions of the others on the emergency council. From the windows, the priors listened and understood little; they remained silent as had been requested. And thus the flag of the Guelf Party and that of the justice were whisked away, that of the Party in the hands of Lord Donato di Iacopo Acciaiuoli, that of justice, in the hands of Benedetto di Iacopo dal Buco, a vintner. And they ran through the city with those from the prestigious families, the people, and the armed soldiers. And before returning home, they ran through the countryside and brought the flags back to the Palace of the Priors.

These are the laws put forward by the town meeting.

First the above-mentioned forty-three will comprise this emergency council together with the other 103. They will control [the councils of] the people and commune of Florence until the end of February.

Item, all those bad apples[26] must be cleared from the town hall between today and tomorrow, and if any have not left by that time, it is

---

25 A principal condottiere of the Italian city-states from the 1370s to his death in 1394. He was now employed by the Florentines.

26 In Italian, bad beans [*male fave*].

understood that the above-mentioned forty-three will have the authority to throw them out. By bad apples is meant those who the college or the emergency council have barred from office [*smoniti*] and others who are suspect.[27]

[p. 404 Stefani then lists the measures passed by this emergency council, such as freeing all those who were banished during the past three years, restoring their property, and bringing more magnates into the government through various means.]

Item, sixty magnates are to be granted popular status [*popolani*].

Item, the prohibitions against holding government office [*il divieto*] are lifted for those magnates who had been made into *popolani* but must wait twenty years before being elected as a prior or as a member of the Colleges.

Item, those [with taxes in arrears] will have five months to pay what they owe the commune. Those with property worth 2 florins or more will have to pay a forced loan [*prestanze*] at a rate of 20 shillings on the florin and no more.

Item, anyone who committed any crime during that day [the day of the upper-class counter-revolution, 16 January, 1382] should be freed and absolved, and they added another thing that was diabolical: anyone who had committed a crime that day until midnight would be freed, and by this they included homicide ...

Item, the crossbows should be returned to those poor men from whom they were taken. And by this was meant those Ciompi whose bows were taken in September 1378 when they were chased out of town. These were the crossbowmen of the Ciompi, who had their crossbows lifted.

[Stefani then lists the forty-three new members of the Emergency Council. Although the majority came from the prestigious *popolani* and magnate families of Florence – de' Bardi, de' Rossi, degli Strozzi, Machiavelli, Peruzzi, da Ricasoli, degli Spini, de' Medici, etc. – the list begins with a worker in the wool industry, a *tiratore*, a tenterer, one who stretched out the cloth to let it dry. In addition, several minor guildsmen were appointed – a carpenter, cobbler, vintner, and cabinet maker, pp. 404–5]

27 This also meant any of those associated with the earlier governments of the Ciompi and the Minor Guilds.

EPILOGUE: AFTER THE CLUSTER, 1382-1423

188 How rioting again erupted in Florence with the Ciompi and those recently recalled from exile arming themselves, March 1382

Stefani, *Cronica fiorentina*, r. 916, pp. 406-7.

On 1 March [1382] the newly elected priors took office and began to draw the names for offices inside and outside Florence. Some of those who had been barred [*smoniti*][28] were elected for several lesser offices. Since some among the ruling class [*il reggimento*] were unhappy that they might be included among the 'admonished', they began to grumble amongst themselves. And because of this, those recently freed from exile roused up the Ciompi and other gangs, and on Saturday night, 8 March, they gathered in [the church of] San Michele Berteldi and held rather large public meetings [*parlamenti*]. The guards of the Signoria tried to remedy matters: first they went unarmed but their soft touch was useless. Late Sunday night the insurgents armed themselves again and rioted through the city with the insignia of the Guelf Party. They went to the house of one called Ciardo, cut off his head, sealed his door shut, and burnt him. They then went to the house of another rich one, who had been admonished, Maso di Neri, a rope merchant; they would have finished by burning all those who had been barred,[29] had the guild of the wool bosses and the neighbourhood militias [*Gonfaloni*] not armed themselves and come into the Piazza to put a stop to these things ...

189 How the Ciompi and the exiles re-armed, hoping to bring about a new order [*nuova cosa*], March 1382

Stefani, *Cronica fiorentina*, r. 917, pp. 407-8.

In 1381[2] on 11 March, that is, on the day following the public meeting, the Ciompi armed themselves all over again and, it is said, yelled: 'Long live the 24 guilds'. That is, they wished to bring back their three guilds, that of the *Popolo minuto* or the Ciompi, which had been outlawed in September 1378, and the two others, which had been disbanded in January 1381[2]. This aroused groups from the Florentine

---

28 These would have been magnates and others barred from holding office when the Ciompi and Minor Guilds were in power.

29 Here, I suspect Stefani intends those of the old Guelf Party members who had been barred but were now back in power.

prestigious families and the merchants to arm and march on the Palace of the Commune. They assembled behind the flags of justice, the Guelf Party, the captain of the people, and the captain of war. After a while, none of the insurgents were to be found; evidently they had disarmed and had gone home to hide; at any rate, they did not reassemble. The insignia were returned to the town hall, and the troops disarmed. However, the podestà was called in because a large number of newly freed exiles with a great number of other men were armed in the New Market and were parading with the insignia of the [Guelf] Party. They did not want to give the insignia back, but the podestà negotiated with them and persuaded them to do so. The troops of the exiles and the others put down their weapons. The following night the podestà indicted four of their leaders and the next day sentenced them to exile for disturbing the peace ...

[For another attempt by these new exiles to overthrow the government; see r. 952, p. 425, in May, 1383.]

190 How a conspiracy was planned in Florence solely by those of the lower orders [*gente minuta*], July 1383

Stefani, *Cronica fiorentina*, r. 954, p. 426.

In July this year [1383] a conspiracy was planned solely by the lower orders. Noticing that the plague [*mortalità*], of which we will say more later, was at first much worse in the city of Florence [than in the countryside], many citizens fled the city for at least a day or two or more, some to the *contado*, others outside the *contado*. Then they [the insurgents] judged the moment opportune and thought they would be supported by those who had been admonished [by the government] and by other malcontents. And certainly, every time they suggested this to the aforementioned malcontents, they thought it would come about. But they did not join them; nor did they have any intention of doing so. They wished only to bring the city and its people to ruin. This conspiracy was uncovered in the following way: as we have said, although the citizens had fled the city because of the plague, the lower orders remained. They got together with several of those recently freed from exile and agreed to go about robbing at the risk of being banished again if their deeds were uncovered. And truly they went about this business in a polite fashion, asking permission to do their misdeeds and without the powerful families around to get in their way, since they had fled the plague into the *contado* or beyond. But they began to be discovered when they ceased to behave with decorum. First, some (but not all of them) began to revolt, marching from Sant'Ambrogio, passing through Belletri for the gate of Ognisanti.[30] They gathered at the bridge of le Carraia.[31] [But] those on the other side of the Arno were not in cahoots with them and did not respond to their calls. As a consequence, they disbanded and achieved nothing. And the people became indignant and went after them. None were captured, but several were banished.

191 Perugia rioted, March 1383: a contemporary version from Siena

Perugia riots, March 1382[3]: Paolo di Tommaso Montauri, *Cronaca senese*, in *Cronache senesi*, p. 695. Little is known of this continuator of the Sienese chronicle between 1363 and 1431. He flourished in the first half of the fifteenth century and like Donato di Neri and his son came from a family of middling status, in Paolo's case, an old Sienese family of goldsmiths.

Perugia rioted: certain ones of the *popolo minuto* who stayed in the neighbourhood of the gate of Sant'Angelo rebelled to bring down the regime of the Raspanti.[32] The armed forces of the government came into the town square, fought and defeated them, capturing forty; some were beheaded, others hanged. Little by little, they pruned them and thus cleaned up their garden. Many artisans and people of the lower orders [*gente minuta*] fled town; those who remained swore oaths of solidarity [to the Raspanti]. And this happened in March [1383].

192 Perugia rioted: a later version from Perugia

Cronaca della città di Perugia dal 1309 al 1491 nota col nome di Diario del Graziani, ed. A. Fabretti, in *Archivio Storico Italiano*, 16 (1850), pp. 69–750, p. 288.

1382[3]. In Perugia at this time, one could hardly avoid a riot [*novità*]. Giacomo d'Odda of the neighbourhood [*porta*] of S. Angelo united

---

30 This was the same cross-neighbourhood march through the working-class districts of the city seen in the revolts of the Ciompi; see [121; 25 August 1378].

31 Built between 1218 and 1220, it was the second bridge over the Arno; it lay to the west after Ponte Vecchio; in 1252, a third bridge, Santa Trinita was built between the two; see Giovanni Villani, *Nuova Cronica*, I, pp. 272–3, and 343–4.

32 The ruling faction of Perugia at this time.

many of the youth of this neighbourhood to rid the city of all those of the Raspanti faction. The Raspanti had their suspicions and organised well the night watch, that night, Thursday, 11 April, with the large guard of the guild of the cobblers. But Giacomo waited until morning, after the guard had left the town square, and then suddenly rioted [*fece subito tumulto*], shouting from outside the gate of San Cristofano, 'To arms'. And together with many other youths, they took up weapons in the square of Borgo, where they killed Giovanni called Franghello and Bisgaro, a cobbler. Afterwards, they came into the town square, shouting, 'Long live the People and death to the Raspanti'; and they killed several citizens ... But against this revolt, the people took up arms. Giacomo became terrified and tried to flee by the above-mentioned gate of Sant'Angelo together with these youngsters, his followers. Many were captured and killed; others were forced to jump over the city walls to save themselves. Fleeing they killed Cristofano del Polzelletta of the Raspanti faction. Many from the neighbourhoods of S. Angelo and the basin [*della Conca*] left town without being chased out. Because of the riot, Vagne di Messer Bartolo and the sons of the della Nobile family, of the Monina, della Mozza, and Mosina were beheaded. Marin, a shield maker and the son of Tetto of the neighbourhood of S. Angelo were hanged.

193 A riot in Perugia to change the regime and in support of the Church, July 1392

Cronaca della città di Perugia, pp. 257–9.

On 30 July [1392] the People rioted; first they yelled: 'Long live the Church and death to the Raspanti'; afterwards: 'Long live the Church and death to the thieves'. It did not take long for the battle in the main square to break the noblemen [*i gentiluomini*], leaving sixty dead. [Graziani then describes several who died in battle, including three noblemen, who] stayed for three days locked up in the tower of Lord Ranieri with nothing to eat or to drink. They would not give themselves up without certain agreements, and the commune did not wish to negotiate. Finally on Saturday morning they turned themselves in as dead men [*per uomini morti*] and were led before the court of the podestà. But he would not execute them; they were then led back to the house of Lord Ranieri, where immediately they were bound, murdered, and thrown out of the windows ...

In these days the nobles of Perugia, with many wounded and others killed, were chased out of town with all their followers.

The government of the nobles had lasted nine years and three months, that is, from 1384 to 1 April 1393, with people constantly crying out: 'Death to the Raspanti'. In this period, they [the Raspanti] ruled in this poor city by deceit, plunder, murder, assassination, pillaging, thievery, adultery, violence, sacrilege, and every sort of licence for evil.

194 Art and co-optation of the people's victory, Perugia, 1392

According to the *Annali Decemvirali*, Biordo, the leader of the Michelotti faction, celebrated the people's victory over the nobles as though it was his own success. Immediately afterwards, he commissioned a statue of himself to this end; the *Annali* contains the Latin commission for the statue. It is cited in *Cronaca della città di Perugia*, p. 259, the original document is in the Archivio di Stato, Perugia.

Item, for perpetual memory, in the custom of the major events of Roman history, and to illuminate and distinguish the deeds of the abovementioned Biordo, an illustrious statue of him is and ought to be made and ornamented with various carvings and engravings. It is to be and must be put in a prominent position that can be clearly seen in the frontispiece of San Lorenzo [the cathedral of Perugia] or some other notable place. This statue is be funded by the commune's money, and the present lord priors are to elect certain treasurers to be responsible for overseeing the statue's completion with the prerequisite carvings, engravings, and sculpted ornamentation and [ensure] that it is placed in a worthy, prominent, and honourable place of their choice. And the commune of Perugia should spend a suitable sum to bring about the realisation of this project (Ann. 1393, f. 30). [There is, however, no evidence that the statue was ever executed, but perhaps it was the statue that in March 1448 stood in the private chapel of Biordo, when on orders of a Friar Roberto it was thrown out into the cemetery.]

195 How the Captain of the Emergency Council [*Balía*] in Florence cut off the heads of several artisans and hanged others, 1393

Giovanni Minerbetti, ed. Elina Bellondi in *RIS*, XXVII/2 (Città di Castello, 1915–18), pp. 181–2.

The captain of the emergency council then captured two of those citizens, who'd yelled out: 'Long live the People and the Guilds'; one was a tavern-keeper, named Domenico di Tancheri, the other a goldsmith, named Lorenzo. They were beheaded; then another twenty-three were charged and condemned. If they came into the hands of the commune, they would be hanged. [Minerbetti lists them: none came from a prestigious Florentine family. Except for a wool washer, who would have been a disenfranchised worker, and a furrier, who might have been an upper guildsman, the others appear as solid members of the minor guilds – two used clothiers, two oven operators, a boot maker, a purse maker, a baker, a tavern-keeper, and a shop clerk. In addition, another tavern-keeper was fined 200 florins. Of those deprived of holding office and sent into exile only one bore a family name.]

196 Peasant revolt in Parma, 1385

Conforto da Costoza, *Frammenti di Storia vicentina [AA. 1371–1387]*, ed. Carlo Steiner, RIS, XIII/1 (Città di Castello, 1915), pp. 35–6.

On the eve of the feast day of the Virgin Mary, 14 August, at least two thousand peasants [*rustici*] of the district of Parma,[33] by their own malice, plotted and conspired amongst themselves and went to the city of Parma in the silence of night. Here, a group of them[34] boldly invaded through a postern [*pusterlam*] of the city that ran to a city gate.[35] With swords they killed all the guards of the gate and with force broke it down. From here the rest of the armed crowd invaded the city and went to the town square searching to kill the tax collectors [*daciarios*][36] and to commit even more dreadful crimes. From fear, neither the captain [of the people], nor the podestà, nor any other citizens of Parma dared to oppose them openly, seeing that they were grossly outnumbered. But, by chance, a cavalry of three hundred

---

33 According to *Istoria di Parma, additamenta*, Muratori, XII (Milan, 1728), col. 752 (probably written in the late fifteenth century), four thousand peasants invaded Parma.

34 Other sources say a hundred rustics; see note 39.

35 According to *Istoria di Parma, additamenta*, it was in the gate of Santa Maria Nuova a capo di Ponte, which 'for many years had been walled up'.

36 According to the early sixteenth-century Milanese historian Bernardino Corio, *Storia di Milano*, ed. Angelo Butti and Luigi Ferrario (Milan, 1855–6), II, pp. 324–5, the peasants rebelled because of town's failure to supply them with salt.

EPILOGUE: AFTER THE CLUSTER, 1382-1423 361

lances in the service of the count of Virtù[37] on its way from Romagna came to the citadel of Parma to be quartered on this feast day. Immediately, they rushed against the peasants, killing over three hundred of them in armed combat and forcing the others out of the city.[38] Thus, it is believed that had not the hand of God intervened by bringing this army, the peasants would have furiously looted and sacked the entire city, exacting great carnage.[39]

197 A peasant revolt outside Ferrara, April 1395

Cronica volgare di ... Minerbetti, p. 194. This anonymous chronicler from the patrician Minerbetti family is the most exacting and detailed chronicler of Florence from 1385 to 1410. In many of his reports it is clear that he had access to government documents. His accounts ranged over northern and central Italy with particular detailed attention to Rome.

In April [1395], many rustics [*villani*] of the area of Puleggio di San Giorgio,[40] which was near Ferrara,[41] rose up, armed themselves, and came towards Ferrara shouting: 'Long live the house of Este[42] and death to the gabelles and the *dazi*.[43] As soon as this ruckus was heard about in the city, the soldiers who were there rushed out against them. They fought and soon the rustics were defeated: more than a

37 Giangaleazzo Visconti, duke of Milan.
38 According to *Istoria di Parma, additamenta*, three hundred of the citizens of Parma defeated and chased the peasants out of town.
39 In describing this peasant revolt Angelo Pezzana, *Storia della città di Parma*, I: 1346–1400 (Parma, 1837), pp. 153–4, relies on contemporary chronicles of Parma by Giovanni del Giudice and Giovanni Balducchini, which are unpublished and may no longer exist; they are not cited in the *Repertorium fontium historiae medii aevi*, (Rome, 1962–). According to Pezzana, the peasants' plot to invade the city involved previous planning with 'the *plebes*' of Parma; once in the city the peasants gathered in the neighbourhood called the '*malcantore*' with three hundred of these *plebes*, and together they attacked and killed noblemen of Parma along with tax collectors. The battle cry of the revolt clearly marks it as a tax revolt: 'Long live the *Plebes* and down with the taxes'. The much shorter Parmense account, *Istoria di Parma, additamenta*, makes no allusion to why the peasants revolted.
40 Today Polesella.
41 Also see the shorter entry in the Ferrarese chronicle, *Annales Estenses Jacobi de Delayto cancellarii D. Nicolai Estensis ... an MCCCXCIII usque MCCCCIX*, Muratori, XVIII (1731), cols. 923–4; Delayto identifies the rebellious villages as Villa Confandali, Villae Milliarii, and Masse Fiscaliae. Perhaps the last is Polesella, about 13km north east of Ferrara.
42 The ruling family of Ferrara for most of the period from 1212 to 1597.
43 Various excise taxes on commodities.

hundred of them were killed and many more taken captive. All the others fled, crowding other villages in the region of Puleggio. When the Marchese Azzo,[44] who was behind this uprising, heard about these matters, he left Lugo immediately for Ferrara with three-hundred cavalry and 1,200 foot soldiers and with a great quantity of grain and other supplies for these peasants.[45] But the Marchese of Ferrara soon made these matters known to Astore at Faenza[46] – where Marchese Azzo was and how many men he had. Together with Florentine soldiers, Astore then left immediately from Faenza with 1,200 specially selected men, two-hundred crossbowmen on horseback and a large number of foot soldiers. They went towards Argenta and reached the region of Puleggio di San Giorgio on 16 April. All the soldiers then in Ferrara attacked their enemies, and Astore with the Florentine soldiers fought against the Marchese Azzo, his soldiers, and the rustics. With little effort Astore defeated them and captured Marchese Azzo. His entire army was either killed or captured; no one was spared. Similarly, all the rustics were either killed or captured. Marchese Azzo was made a prisoner of count Currado, and the Marchese of Ferrara gave permission to his army and all those who had come with Astore to rob all they wanted from the rustics of Puleggio, and they did so immediately. All these peasants were rich, because they had never been wars here and the land was fat. Thus the booty was great, so much so that no one could estimate it. In this battle six hundred or more were killed, not counting those who drowned but are believed to have survived, and two thousand were taken captive. Then, after staying for a few days, Astore and the Florentine soldiers returned to Faenza, all wealthy.

198 Mountain peasants lay siege to the Florentine stronghold of Firenzuola, 1402[47]

ASF, Podestà, no. 3886 [1402], 9r–10v. This is an unpublished document.

Our Battista [son of lord Simone, count of Piacenza] count and

---

44 Azzo IX, Marchese d'Este, 1344–1415.
45 Ferrara was then under the Signoria of Niccolò II d'Este.
46 Astorgio I of the old Faentine ruling family, the Manfredi, gained control over the region after John Hawkwood sacked Faenza in 1376 on behalf of the Church.
47 This was a new town built in 1332 to defend Florence from the Ubaldini lords.

EPILOGUE: AFTER THE CLUSTER, 1382-1423   363

potestà of this court [of the Quarter of Santa Maria Novella], sitting at our usual bench:

Lord Galeotto of Pignole [Pignuole]⁴⁸ ⎫
Troncha di Giovanni d'Ugolino of Caprile
Guido di Guido of Pignuole
Baldinaccio d'Albisio of Cardaccia
Ceccho d'Ugolino di Francesco of Caprile
Nanni d'Antonio d'Ugolino of Carda   all from the Ubaldini
Activiano di Tanutio of Carda   family clan
Nascinbene di Federico
Cristofano di Francesco
Ubaldino di Guido
Scarpecata of Città di Castello
Antonio d'Actaviano of Visano   ⎭

Giovanni di Guadino of Coderoncho [Coderonco] ⎫
Ser Vannino di Cenni
Lippo di Ser Gini
Giovanni di Maestro Martino   from Caburaccia
Silvestro, called Totto di Ser Niccolai
Ser Francesco di Ser Niccolai, a priest
Biagio di Lorenzo
Giovannino di Magnino   ⎭

Bonono di Bertolo   ⎫
Cante and his brother
Tonno and his brother   from Cornacchiaia
Stefano di Fanutio   ⎭

Antonio d'Ugolino di Tani from Carda of the Ubaldini
Guido di Vannino, a cobbler from Rapezzo
Francesco di Nuccio, called Barile from Santerno

Tango di Guido   ⎫
Dominico di Chino   ⎬ from Rapezzo, living in Tirli
Nanni di Tonio   ⎭

Banbo, his son   ⎫
Giovanni di Soccino   ⎬ from Pignuole

---

48 Most of these villages – Caburaccia, Castro, Cornacchiaia, Pignole, Rapezzo, Santero, and Tirli – are in the Alpi Fiorentine. Carda, Caprile, Coderonco, and Visano were to the east, in the mountains of Romagna.

Angelino del Merla
Azzino di Babbino

Cinaccio ⎱
Giusto   ⎰ di Bertino

Stefano di Viviano, called Tanaya ⎫
Giovanni, alias Tacchone ⎱ his sons ⎪
Viviano, alias Nasso   ⎰   ⎬ from Castro
Guidoccello di Simone   ⎪
Guiduccino di Betti and   ⎪
Tonio di Mascio, alias Gnacchio[49] ⎭

Traitors and rebels against the magnificent and glorious people and commune of Florence, men of evil habits, associations, life, and reputation ... the above-stated in this inquest, each of them, and many others whose names at present it is better to keep silent, in the present year [1402] during the months of July and August, have been spurred on by the spirit of the devil ... to commit and perpetrate the rebellion [*rebellionem*] and betrayal described below. That is, this Galeotto Troncha of the Ubaldini clan and Cinuccio with many of the others listed above went to the city of Bologna on many, many occasions on various days, in the day time and at night to talk, negotiate, and plot with Lord Jacopo del Verme, the duke of Milan's lieutenant in the city of Bologna and the leader of the duke's armed forces. To overthrow and rebel against the castle town of Firenzuola in the *contado* of Florence on the river Santerno surrounded by walls and moats and located in the *vicariatus* of Firenzuola, Ser Vannino, along with Cinaccio and many others of those indicted, gave orders, saying to this Lord Jacopo, the lieutenant and captain: 'We have organised a plot for the take-over of this district [*vicariatus*] of Firenzuola and its Alpine region, which should proceed as follows: when the bell-tower chimes, you are to have your army of foot soldiers and cavalry ready at the [entrance of] the *castrum* of Firenzuola'. Ser Vannino, Cinaccio, Nasso, and many others of those listed above, in whom the *vicarius* of Firenzuola had placed great trust, went to this walled town with many others, their friends, whom they had enlisted. Armed with defensive and offensive weapons, they openly entered the town at the planned

---

49 Many of the indicted can be traced in the surviving tax surveys [*estimi*] of the late fourteenth century. For the most part they were mountain peasants with property and families to support; see Cohn, *Creating the Florentine State*, pp. 159–62.

time as though everything was normal. And Ser Vannino, Cinaccio, and the others named above thought that their forces were stronger than those of the *vicarius* and the soldiers of the commune of Florence permanently posted there. With their swords, they planned to kill the *vicarius* and the Florentine soldiers; then they would lead a revolt [*rebellabunt*] in this walled town against the commune of Florence and for the Ubaldini clan. But this time the orders and plans of Ser Vannino, Cinaccio, and the others failed to achieve these most depraved plans, plots, and intentions. They ordered the above-mentioned army [of Jacopo del Verme] to come near the walls of this walled town to rebel against the Florentine troops inside Firenzuola with Ser Vannino saying to the Florentine soldiers: 'And with street fighting and skirmishes, we will push you out of this town, one after another, starting with the soldiers of Florence, and we will allow you to follow us to the main gate of the town, to lay down your weapons and then flee quickly. We will then enter with all of our troops to take over the guard of this gate; we'll kill the *vicarius* of this town and any soldiers of the commune of Florence who remain here. Once this *vicarius* has been murdered, we will charge through this town of Firenzuola, causing it to rebel against Florence, its dominion, power, and authority. We will further commit and perpetrate many other crimes and murders against foreigners and friends of the commune of Florence'. With all these orders, plots, decisions, and efforts firmly agreed amongst them, the Highest One, who can repair all evil for the greatest good and bring about a favourable remedy, came forth and intervened: with the mediation of divine grace and with foresight, astuteness, and diligence, this lord *vicarius* of Firenzuola discovered each and every one of their plans and decisions so that they were unable to carry out their depraved and wicked plans ...

Not content with what they had done, this Vannino, Lord Galleotto, Troncha, and Cinaccio, together with many of the others indicted, realised that this lord *vicarius* had become aware of their iniquitous plans, and so they deliberated, plotted, and ordered an alternative and more effective plan to bring off their rebellion. They went to the city of Bologna for discussions with Lord Jacopo del Verme, lieutenant and military captain, and between them conducted discussions, plans, and deliberated. Then Ser Vannino, Lord Galeotto, Troncha Ubaldini, Cinaccio, and many others of the indicted, with the good wishes of this Lord Jacopo del Verme, lieutenant and captain, took a great quantity of weapons, cavalry, and foot soldiers of the duke [of Milan] into Firenzuola, including many cannons [*bonbardis*],[50] battering rams, and many other constructions built to overthrow the town of Firenzuola. They transported these things to a place called the hilltop of Montecoloreto, which is in the Alps above Firenzuola, near the villages of le Pignuole, Brento, and Brento Orsanio. And here on the summit of this hill, the indicted along with many others, whose names for the present are best kept quiet, made, formed, and built a bastion built of wood and stone, where they remained for many days as the enemies and rebels of the city of Florence. At the urging and with the support of the Ubaldini and the lieutenant of the duke of Milan, they inflicted maximum damage, injury, and shame on the people of the commune of Florence.

Not content with this but wishing to add even more evil deeds to those already committed, Cinaccio together with the above-indicted Bonomo di Bertolo and many others of the foot-soldiers and cavalry of the duke came down from the hilltop of Montecoloreto and invaded a certain place called the bastion of Castro in the Florentine Alps, near the villages of Cornacchiaia, Casanuova, and le Valli, which these rebels and enemies held for the Ubaldini. They also went to a certain place called the hilltop of Castle Giurino in these mountains, near the villages of Casanuova and Cornacchiaia. And on the summit of this hill, they built a bastion out of wood, which they held for many days at the request of the Ubaldini and the duke of Milan's lieutenant. And from this bastion, they committed and perpetrated many acts of robbery and extortion against subjects of the commune of Florence. Further, they captured and preyed on many messengers, who were sent to the lord *vicarius* with many letters from the lord priors of the guilds, the standard-bearer of justice, and the magnificent lords, the Ten of War of the commune of Florence. On these mountaintops and from their bastions, the indicted built and set up siege weapons to invade and take over the walled town of Firenzuola. And although they were not able to execute each and every one of their commands, they brought grave damage, injury, and maximum shame to the magnificent people and commune of Florence ...

[None of the indicted appeared before the court; they were to be led to the usual place of justice in the city of Florence, where each was to be beheaded, their property confiscated, and their names entered into the Book of Rebels (*Libro malabratorum*). The sentence was promulgated on 9 December 1402. A year later, many were absolved of their crimes and granted special privileges from the Florentine state; see 199.]

50 It could also mean catapults.

199 The Florentine state makes major concessions to the mountain rebels of the Alpi Fiorentine, 1402–3

ASF, Provvisione, register 92, fols. 87v–90v: Concerning Cavrenno [Caprenno] and Pietramala. This an unpublished document.

The magnificent and powerful lords of the Signoria, etc. have been informed by the Ten of War of the commune of Florence as decreed by the Officials of the Castles and Fortifications that Cavrenno and other places surrounding it with its men and women must come into the hands of the Commune of Florence ... And according to the petition negotiated by the Ten of War, the following are to be expedited ... decided on 22 June 1403:

First, the commune of Pietramala in the commune of Bologna,[51] from the day it becomes subject to the commune of Florence by a public document, along with its men and women will be exempt, liberated, and immune from paying each and every tax, fee, and gabelle of the commune of Florence for fifteen years...

Sabato
Falco
Ugo and } brothers and sons of Giannetto
Piero
Stefano di Nanni
Menico d'Andreole
Antonio called Capacchio di Michele and
Nanni di Matteo

all from this commune of Pietramala and their descendants forever down the male line are understood to be exempt, liberated, and immune from all taxes, fees, and gabelles of the commune of Florence ...

Item, that the commune of Pietramala and the men and women of this commune cannot at any time be forced or charged to pay to any official of the city, *contado*, or district of Florence any debts they may owe to the commune of Bologna or to any other organisation, place, or any individual, except for those debts incurred between them [the people of this commune]...

Item, that Antonio di Salvo
Nutello di Matteo

---

51 Individual villages could have communal statutes and were called communes as were large Republican city-states such as Bologna or Florence with hundreds of rural parishes and communes under their dominions.

Zaglia di Gratinello

all from the commune of Pietramala, who were condemned and banished as rebels by the commune of Florence can and should be reinstated, absolved, and liberated from these condemnations ...

Item, that any person of the commune of Bologna, who wishes to come and live in the commune of Pietramala should be understood to be exempt from taxes as are those of the commune of Pietramala and for the period of exemption stated above.

Item, that every year on the feast day of John the Baptist in June, the commune of Pietramala must make an offering of a silk palio,[52] costing about five gold florins, to be presented at the church of Saint John in the city of Florence.

Item, that:
Bononia[53]
Antonio called Fantaccio } brothers and
and Cante } sons of Bartolo } Cornacchiano[54]
Stefano di Fanuzio

Cinaccio and Giusto, brothers and sons of Bertino
Stefano called Tanaio di Viviano
Giovanni called Taccone di Stefanino } of Castro[55]
Angelino called Merlo

Tome called Nacchio called Maffaio de Faggiola, living at Castro

Francesco called Banle of Santerno

Piero called Melano

Bartolo called Pagnone } brothers and son of
Bonagio di Bini } Pagnuzzo of dale Valle
Corsino of Corella

Dombruno of the commune of Colognole in the *contado* of Florence

Domenico di Bartolomeo di Naccio of Florence

are to be reinstated [from previous exile] and absolved...

Item, that Bononia

[52] See [39].
[53] Condemned to death as a rebel leader; see [198]
[54] Both brothers were condemned to death as a rebel leaders; see [198]
[55] All the listed from Castro were condemned to death as a rebel leaders with Cinaccio as the principal strategist and negotiator with the Jacopo del Verme and the Milanese forces in Bologna; see [198]

EPILOGUE: AFTER THE CLUSTER, 1382-1423   369

Antonio
Cante and | brothers and sons
Domenico | of Bartolo and
Stefano di Bonnome   } of Cornacchiano and
Cinaccio and | sons of Bertino
Giusto | of Castro⁵⁶

cannot be forced to pay or in any way charged for any debt, which they may have incurred up to the present day with the commune of Florence, the commune of Castro, or the commune of Cornacchiaio⁵⁷...

Moreover, beginning with these ones and then their descendants down the male line forever, these men are understood to be exempt and freed from each and every tax, gabelle, property and personal tax, and any other burden owed to the commune of Florence or to any of its parishes or villages...

Item, that Stefano, Guiduccio and Ugolino, brothers and sons of Pino of Cornacchiaia, who have been living in the *contado* of Bologna for the last thirteen years and have just returned two months ago with their families into the *contado* of Florence are understood to be exempt ... from all taxes, gabelles ... for fifteen years ...

Item, that each and everyone of the communes of Cornacchiaia and Castro who left in June 1402⁵⁸ and went to live beyond the borders of the commune of Florence and who have been selected by the above-mentioned Bonomia, Gianotto, and Stefano or a majority of them ... may return to stay and live in peace in the city, *contado*, or district of Florence regardless of any acts of arson, robbery, or any extortions, excesses, or crimes they may have committed in this month of July [1402] until the present day.

And, moreover, any one of the commune of Pietramala who has committed or perpetrated any crimes, excesses, or delinquencies against any commune, parish, village within the Florentine Alps [*Alpi fiorentine*] or Firenzuola from this month of June [1402] until the present day, cannot be prosecuted or tried by any rector or official of the city, *contado*, or district of Florence, and especially concerning the murder

---

56 The three above were ringleaders in the revolts against Florence and to take over Firenzuola the year before; see [198].
57 This would mean that they were absolved from paying their back taxes and the heavy fines that accompanied late payments.
58 The beginning of the peasant revolts in the Florentine Alps.

of Jacopino di Nutello or di Michele of the commune of Friene[59]...
[This *provvisone* continues with many more 'items', extending rights and privileges to those of Cornachiaia and Castro, such as the rights to bear arms and to elect those who should enjoy such privileges. These specially privileged men included Cinaccio, Bonomia di Bartolo, Giusto di Bertino, and others, who were condemned to death a year before for their part in the siege of the Florentine Alps and the Florentine stronghold of Firenzuola; see 198.]

200 Giovanni di Pagolo Morelli's version of the mountain rebels, 1402

Morelli, *Ricordi*, in *Mercanti Scrittori*, pp. 262–3.

News of all these matters [the build up of the duke of Milan's forces and the encirclement of the Florentine territory] reached Florence [in the summer of 1402]. Everything seemed lost without any remedy. No soldiers remained at all, and in Florence there was nothing for two months.[60] The harvest was all in sheaves in the sheaving lofts. The country was deeply divided because of heavy taxation and because of discord [*novità*] among the citizens as can be in part understood. The countryside was more exhausted, impoverished, and more deeply divided than the city: there was not a peasant [*contadino*] who would not have gone happily to Florence to burn it down. Pistoia was in great conflict because of the Cancellieri and Panciatichi factions. Lord Ricciardo Cancellieri had been banished and Giovanni Catansanti[61] had his head cut off allegedly for things he had done for himself and deals he'd cut with the duke [of Milan], which were not true. Thus Ricciardo went and seized Sambuca[62] and held it along with other castles in the mountains. He devastated the countryside to such an extent that the rural officials retreated to safety within the walls of Pistoia. Nearby, many of the Ubaldini clan, who we thought we had finished off, came forward and took over the Podere[63] and sparked

---

59 I do not know who this man was, but he probably was a local rector of his commune responsible for keeping Florentine law and order and arresting criminals and rebels.

60 No shipments of food.

61 A rich citizen of Pistoia, who was a part of the Cancellieri faction.

62 District capital of the Montagna di Pistoia.

63 A region consisting of sixteen parishes in the mountainous northeast corner of the Florentine state bordering the region of Romagna.

uprisings throughout the Mugello.⁶⁴ And many of these villagers rose up in their support. And similarly, in Arezzo, Prato, Volterra, and everywhere, the exiled Ghibellines rose up across the countryside in whatever district or castle. And as you can imagine, had the duke ridden out, leaving Bologna well fortified as he could have done, he could have seized the entire harvest and then taken all the Florentine *contado* for sure. The country would have been his, and it would not have taken him too long to get it.

But God did not desire that so much evil should happen; we were not ridden over, and matters were remedied as rapidly as could be expected. First, the harvest was gathered in eight days, and with that Florence and the walled villages recovered for the most part: the gabelles on grain, wheat, and oil were lifted.

201 Gregorio Dati's version of the same

L'Istoria di Firenze di Gregorio Dati dal 1380 al 1405, ed. Luigi Pratesi (Norcia, 1902), p. 49–50 ch. 54. Dati was a merchant historian and according to Hans Baron, *The Crisis of the Early Renaissance*, 2 vols. (Princeton, 1955; revised edn, 1966), represented a new republican consciousness at the beginning of the fifteenth century.

[1402] The city of Florence is situated in a very well fortified place. Thus, anyone who might wish to enter its *contado* from whatever direction must first pass through the narrowest mountain passes, which are guarded by massive [*spesse*] castles and marvellous fortifications. And if a man or an army were permitted to enter through one of these passes, they would not know how to get out. For this reason, it takes few to guard these passes and fortresses or to attack an enemy who is trying to pass through. And cavalry will be even less successful than foot soldiers in these places, and, as you can understand, the Florentines have a great abundance of men in their *contado* and territory, and the castles and villages are thick on the ground, and one on his home ground is worth two foreign soldiers in these hard and bitter places.

I am happy to have made this clear: but if things are such, why have the Florentines not broken the invading enemies, especially since these enemies are so frightened?

64 The region within the *contado* of Florence north of Borgo San Lorenzo to the borders of the Florentine Alps.

202 Village rivalry near Monte San Savino, 1406

ASF, Provvisione, Registri. n. 96, 183r–4r: Petition of the commune of Marciano[65] on behalf of many of its men, 7 July 1406. This an unpublished document.

The petition below has been reverently placed before your magnificent and powerful lords of the Signoria, the priors of the guilds, and the standard-bearer of justice on behalf of the men and persons of the walled village [*de castro*] of Marciano in the *contado* of Florence ... named below:

Pagno di Jacobo alias Bertolla
Francesco di Vannuccio alias Balestra
Angelo di Francesco
Lorenzo di Francesco
Ghezzo di Giunte
Angelo di Ghezzo
Antonio di Ture
Cristofano di Antonio alias Vanza
Qeus alias Ciotto di Cristofano
Antonio d'Andrea alias Caffei
Jacopo d'Andrea alias Caffei
Piero d'Angeli alias Razino
Niccolò d'Angelo alias Strataza
Dominico di Corpo alias Aquarello
Santese d'Angelo
Antonio di Pagno
Donato d'Ugolino alias Gallo
Antonio di Fei
Nanni di Carbone alias Magazino
Paulo di Muccio
Cecco di Jacopo di Meus di Donato alias Gallo
Donato di Pieruccio and
Niccolò di Cristofano alias Danza.

All of these are from the walled village of Marciano in the *contado* of Florence and were sentenced by Nigio di Angerio of Florence for the magnificent commune of Florence and the podestà of the territory of Monte San Savino in the district of Florence and for other places subordinate to this podestà, etc., that is this Pagno di Jacobi alias Bertolla was fined 55 pounds [the next four are named with the same

65 The criminal case is found in ASF, Guidice, n. 98, 150r–61r.

fine] and each of the rest named above is fined 55 pounds to be paid to the general treasury of the commune of Florence...and if these sums are not received within ten days, the penalty is to be quadrupled. And they were thus sentenced because they had knowingly and deliberately with the worst of intentions and an iniquitous spirit come into the district [*curiam*] of Monte San Savino, where they destroyed and tore up a boundary marker placed and constructed there to delineate the boundary line of the district of Lucignano [with Monte San Savino]. The noble and egregious knight Lord Rinaldo de' Gianfigliazzi,[66] then a Florentine commissioner, has given the following report to the magnificent commune of Florence: with spades, hoes, pick-axes, clippers, and hammers, these men devastated and cut up this boundary marker and threw the stones and wood, which had walled it up and fixed it in place, into the river Esse. And each one of them along with many, many others from Marciano filled up this river Esse in this district of Monte by throwing many pieces of timber, brushwood, and rubbish into the river. From this they made a dam, which prevented the water flowing past, thus changing completely the course and flow of this water. This dam, its impediment to the flow of the river, and the subsequent changed course of the river devastated the grain and wheat, which was just sprouting at this moment in the curia of Monte. These actions were against the statutes and ordinances of the communes of Monte and Florence and provoked grave damage and harm to the men and women of the commune of Marciano and could have destroyed the peace and tranquillity of the communes of Marciano and Florence... [The podestà made these condemnations on 7 July 1406. The condemned claimed to be innocent of the charges, and because 'they were powerless and poor men and agricultural labourers', they beseeched the commune of Florence to approve their petition for clemency on 17 December 1407. With a vote in the Council of the Commune of 240 white beans (pro) and 26 black beans (against) they were absolved.]

66 An important and ancient family of Florence.

203 Village vigilantes seek justice after a monstrous murder of a baby in its crib, 1423

Paolo di Tommaso Montauri, [a. 1423], in *Cronache senesi*, p. 800.

Someone took a baby boy still at the breast being two months old from his crib, put him on the floor in an open room, took his bindings off and then gutted him open; his intestines were extracted and the liver taken from the body. He was left like this until his mother found him. People believed that his excrement and bile had been extracted [for some purpose]. No one knew who did it: it happened at Viteccio.[67] The baby had not yet died. Still at his mother's nipple, he was taken to Siena, where physicians examined and tried to cure him but failed. The baby died in the house of Cardo the barber on 28 September. When the mother arrived, after having gone to get wood, and saw the baby on the ground, a riot broke out, drawing many people into the streets. A poor man was captured and led to the executor [of justice] in Siena. That night and into the following night, he was tortured with the rope around his neck. Finally he pleaded: 'Stop torturing me; tomorrow morning I will tell you everything that happened'. The following night he was found hanging from a trap in his prison cell. People thought that he must have killed himself with the cord used by the executor to lead him to Viteccio. Here he was hanged [officially] at 6 in the evening.

204 The people of the city and countryside of Siena curse the city rulers, 1423[4]

The people of city and courtryside curse the Captain and city rulers of Siena during the Church Council of Siena,[68] because of their destruction of the Duomo's ornamentation, 1423[4]; Paolo di Tommaso Montauri, in *Cronache senesi*, p. 803.

Lord Malatesta of Pesaro came to Siena in the middle of March as an ambassador of Pope Martin to see how the church council was progressing. But nothing had happened, because there were many in Siena from many nations who wanted it to proceed according to their

---

67 Viteccio is in the Val di Merse, near Sovicille and today called Barontoli.
68 In 1423 Pope Martin V transferred the council to deal with reforms, principally taxation and benefices, from Pavia to Siena. Because of inadequate attendance, it was dissolved in 1424.

plans. The ambassadors of the king of Aragon, the archbishop of Toledo, and many other prelates were in Siena, who wanted to bring in Pope Benedict,[69] then in Catalonia. Many were of this persuasion, and Pope Martin was held in great suspicion. For this reason, this ambassador [Malatesta] with many others went many times to the Palace of the Commune of Siena to support the party of Pope Martin in Siena and tried many times to get the [church] council going but were unable to get it off the ground. And seeing that it was going nowhere, these governors began to destroy the ornamentation and beautification of the Duomo. And with this, the people [*gente*] in both city and countryside were upset and cursed the captain and the city rulers. And those foreigners who stayed around shared this anger because of the heavy expenses they were obliged to pay and because of the heresy which Pope Martin and the Florentines had imposed on the whole world.[70]

69 Benedict 'XIII' was the opposing pope during the papacy of Gregory XII (1406–15).

70 Although the 'Great Schism' had ended with the Council of Constance in 1417, this document illustrates that the council did not bring an uncontested unity to the church and that rival national parties of cardinals and clerics sponsored by monarchs and city-states continued to quarrel and present their claimants to the papacy. Clearly, the chronicler, expressing Sienese patriotism and therefore anti-Florentine sentiments saw the Florentine-sponsored Pope Martin as the anti-pope and thus as a heretic. He was, however, from 1417 the officially recognised pope and would begin restoring papal power and stability. Nonetheless, the conciliar movement and the opinion that a representative council was the best means for pursuing church reform continued into the second half of the fifteenth century or even to the Reformation; see *The Popes: A Concise Biographical History*, ed. Eric John (London, 1964), pp. 289–91; John A. F. Thomson, *The Western Church in the Middle Ages* (London, 1998), pp. 178–91; and Anthony Black, 'Popes and Councils' in *The New Cambridge Medieval History*, VI, ed. C. T. Allmand (Cambridge, 1998), pp. 65–86.

SUGGESTED READING

Boudet, Marcellin, *La Jacquerie des Tuchins 1363–1384* (Riom, 1895).

Bowsky, William, *A Medieval Commune: Siena under the Nine 1287–1355* (Berkeley, 1981).

Brucker, Gene, 'The Ciompi Revolution', in *Florentine Studies: Politics and Society in Renaissance Florence*, ed. N. Rubinstein (London, 1968), pp. 314–56.

——, *The Civic World of Early Renaissance Florence* (Princeton, 1977).

——, *Florentine Politics and Society 1343–1378* (Princeton, 1962).

Cazelles, Raymond, 'The Jacquerie', in *The English Rising of 1381*, ed. R. H. Hilton and T. H. Aston (Cambridge, 1984), pp. 74–84.

Chéruel, A., *Histoire de Rouen pendant l'époque communale 1150–1382*, 2 vols. (Rouen, 1843–44).

Chronicles of the Tumult of the Ciompi, trans. Rosemary Kantor and Louis Green, Monash Publications in History: 7 (Victoria, Australia, 1990).

Cohn, Samuel, *The Black Death Transformed: Disease and Culture in Renaissance Europe* (London, 2002).

——, *Creating the Florentine State: Peasants and Rebellion, 1348–1434* (Cambridge, 1999).

——, *The Laboring Classes in Renaissance Florence* (New York, 1980).

Coville, Alfred, *Les premiers Valois et la Guerre de Cent Ans (1328–1422)* (Paris, 1902).

Dean, Trevor, ed., *The Towns of Italy in the later Middle Ages* (Manchester, 2000).

Delachenal, Roland, *Histoire de Charles V*, 5 vols. (Paris, 1909–31).

Dino Compagni's Chronicle of Florence, trans. Daniel Bornstein (Philadelphia, 1986).

Dobson, R. B., ed., *The Peasants' Revolt of 1381*, 2nd edn (London, 1983).

Dyer, Christopher, 'The Social and Economic Background to the Rural Revolt of 1381', in *The English Rising of 1381*, ed. R. H. Hilton and T. H. Aston (Cambridge, 1984), pp. 9–42.

Epstein, Steven A., *Genoa and the Genoese 958–1528* (Chapel Hill, N.C., 1996).

Flammeront, J., 'La Jacquerie en Beauvaisis', *Revue Historique* 4 (1879): 123–43.

Fourquin, Guy, *Les campagnes de la région parisienne à la fin du Moyen Age* (Paris, 1964).

Fryde, E. B., 'The Financial Policies of the Royal Governments and Popular Resistance to them in France and England, c. 1270–c.1420', *Revue belge de philologie et d'histoire* 57 (1979): 824–60.

Green, Louis, *Chronicle into History: An Essay on the Interpretation of History in Florentine Fourteenth-century Chronicles* (Cambridge, 1972).

Guenée, Bernard, *Un roi et son histoire. Vingt études sur le règne de Charles VI et la chronique du religieux de Saint-Denis* (Paris, 1999).

Hilton, Rodney, *Bondmen Made Free: Medieval Peasant Movements and the English Rising of 1381* (London, 1973).

Horrox, Rosemary, *The Black Death* (Manchester, 1994).

Luce, Siméon, *Histoire de la Jacquerie d'après des documents inédits*, 2nd edn (Paris, 1894).

Martines, Lauro, ed., *Violence and Civil Disorder in Italian cities, 1200–1500* (Berkeley, 1972).

Medeiros, Marie-Thérèse de, *Jacques et Chroniqueurs: Une étude comparée de récits contemporains relatant la Jacquerie de 1358* (Paris, 1979).

Meek, Christine, *Lucca, 1369–1400: Politics and Society in an Early Renaissance City-state* (Oxford, 1978).

Miskimin, Harry, 'The Last Act of Charles V: The Background of the Revolts of 1382', *Speculum* 38 (1963): 433–42.

Mirot, Léon, *Les insurrections urbaines au début du Règne de Charles VI (1380–1383): Leurs causes, leurs consequences* (Paris, 1905).

Mollat, Michel and Philippe Wolff, *Popular Revolutions of the late Middle Ages*, tr. A. L. Lyttonsells (New York, 1973).

Najemy, John, 'The Dialogue of Power in Florentine Politics', in *City-States in Classical Antiquity and Medieval Italy*, ed. A. Molho, K. Raaflaub and J. Emlen (Ann Arbor, 1991), pp. 269–88.

Nicholas, David, *Medieval Flanders* (London, 1992).

Ottokar, Nicola, *Il Comune di Firenze alla fine del Dugento* (Florence, 1926).

Pirenne, Henri, *Histoire de Belgique: des origines à nos jours*, 6th edn, vols. I–II (Brussels, 1948; first edn, 1900).

Radding, Charles M., 'The Estates of Normandy and the Revolts in the Towns at the beginning of the Reign of Charles VI', *Speculum*, 47 (1972): 79–90.

Rubinstein, Nicolai, *The Palazzo Vecchio, 1298–1532: Government, Architecture, and Imagery in the Civic Palace of the Florentine Republic* (Oxford, 1995).

Salvemini, Gaetano, *Magnati e popolani in Firenze dal 1280 al 1295* (Florence, 1899).

Simonsohn, S., *The Apostolic See and the Jews*. vol. I, *Documents: 492–1404* (Toronto, 1988).

Stella, Alessandro. *La révolte des Ciompi: Les hommes, les lieux, le travail* (Paris, 1993).

Sumption, Jonathan, *The Hundred Years War*, Vol. II, *Trial by Fire* (London, 1999).

TeBrake, William H., *A Plague of Insurrection: Popular Politics and Peasant*

Revolt in Flanders, 1323–1328 (Philadelphia, 1993).

Trexler, Richard. 'Follow the Flag: The Ciompi Revolt Seen from the Streets', *Bibliothèque d'Humanisme et Renaissance*, 46 (1984): 357–92.

Waley, Daniel, *The Italian City-Republics*, 3rd edn (London, 1988).

INDEX

Abruzzo 83–5, 112
abuses, of the crown 268, 348–9
Agnolo di Tura del Grasso 56, 112
Aigues-Vives 333–5
aldermen 20, 26, 36, 108, 197, 327, 331, 336, 338–9, 347
Alès 331–2
Amiens 147, 162, 164, 197–8, 275, 296
Ancona 5, 68
Anjou, duke of, brother of Charles V 270–1, 275, 277–8, 283, 286
Anomimalle Chronicle 144, 172
Antichrist 235
anti-Semitism *see* Jews
Antonio, count of Bruscoli 140
apprentices 258
Aquitaine 35
Aragon 88, 375
archives 340–1
Arezzo 65, 371
Armagnacs 300, 338, 344–8
armies *see* soldiers
Arras 12
art 375
  see also coats of arms; paintings; sculpture
Artevelde, Jacob van 4
Artevelde, Philippe van 4, 240, 265–6, 285–7, 302
Ascoli-Piceno 85, 141–2
Asserbroek 29
assemblies 15, 20, 130, 166–7, 180, 185–91, 197–8, 228, 243–6, 248, 283, 285, 299, 305, 312–13, 329–30, 332, 349, 353
asylum 311–12
atrocities 100–1, 107, 151–5, 158, 171–5, 178, 181, 185, 219, 236, 254–5, 277, 287, 340, 374
Aubriot, Lord Hugues 280, 290, 295, 301
Auvergne 99, 101–2
Auxerre, treaty of 345
Avignon 79, 350

Ball, John 148
banishment *see* exile
banners *see* flags
Barberino Valdelsa 87, 109–10
Barga 136
barricades 5, 30, 54, 70–1, 154, 158, 209–10, 300
Basilicata 85
Beaucaire 325, 332
Beaumont-sur-Oise 170
Beauvais 164
Beauvaisis 8, 143–200 *passim*
Bégue of Villaines 165
Bentivoglio family 87, 110
belfries *see* bells
Bella, Giano della 5, 16, 42, 49–53
bells 27, 49, 56, 60, 98, 131, 139, 191, 215, 233, 241, 248, 256, 265, 281, 298, 329
Bercé, Yves-Marie 11, 13
Bertelli, Sergio 201
betrayal 161–2, 175–6, 194, 244
Béziers 327
Biella 55
bishops 97, 104
  see also clergy
blacksmiths 58
Black Death 1–3, 7, 11, 15, 17–18, 43, 87–8, 93, 266
Boccaccio, Giovanni 82n.146

Boccanegra, Simone di 68
Bois de Vincennes 281, 296–8, 303, 324
Bologna 18, 44, 50–1, 60–1, 87, 91, 110, 120, 136–41, 364–5, 367, 371
University of 60
bonnes villes 175, 184, 198
Boucicaut, Jean le Meingre, Lord Marshal (the elder), called 194–5
Boucicaut, Jean II le Meingre, Lord Marshal, called, 313
bourgeois 20, 147, 151, 164–5, 170, 172, 176, 182–3, 193, 198–200, 268, 274, 283, 293–4, 303, 308–11, 323
Brandini, Ciuto 3, 17, 74–5
bread *see* grain
Bride, Jehan 25, 28
Brienne, Walter of, duke of Athens 68–71
Brioude 350
Brucker, Gene 201
Bruges 4, 15, 20, 25–30, 37–40, 94–5, 265–6, 302, 304
Bruscoli 137
buckles 180, 193
Bundschuh 15
Burgundians 300, 338, 344–8
butchers 57–60, 338, 344–6

Caboche, Simon 339, 345–6
Cabochiennes 7, 300, 338–9, 344–9
Caen 89, 189–90, 322–3
Caggese, Romolo 82–3
Calabria 83–5
Cale (Calle, Carle, Charles), Guillaume 144–6, 159–62, 164, 166, 168, 185, 192
calendars 14
Campidoglio 64, 80
Campo (Siena) 58, 114, 116
Canterbury, archbishop of 277

Captal of Buch, Jean de Grilly 156–7
Carcassonne 18, 41–2, 107–9, 334
carders (wool) 70, 73–4, 231, 249, 257
cardinals, cardinal legates 124, 138–9, 140–1, 226, 328
see also clergy
Cassel 38
Castiglionchio, Lapo da 211, 227, 234, 252
castles *see* fortifications
Castracani, Castruccio, 62
Castro 364, 368–70
Cathars 55–6
cattle raids 104–5, 333–5
Cazelles, Raymond 146–9
Cento 136–7
Châlons-en-Champagne 156, 298, 339, 349
chamber pots 12
chants 29, 48, 51, 57–9, 69, 71–6, 79, 85–6, 98, 110, 113–15, 124–8, 131–2, 134–6, 140–1, 161, 209, 217, 229, 236, 240, 244, 247–8, 252, 255–6, 288, 302, 331, 352, 358, 360
chapels 343
Charenton, bridge of 155–6, 198, 280, 296
Charles, duke of Savoy 341–3
Charles, king of Navarre 143, 148, 150–1, 153, 155, 160–2, 164–5, 168, 171, 174, 176, 178, 192–3, 198
Charles IV of Bohemia, Emperor 81, 112–13, 115–16, 126
Charles V, king of France 150, 155, 158, 163, 174–5, 182, 261–2, 264, 318
Charles VI, king of France 99, 262, 264, 266–7, 287, 322, 342–3, 346, 348–9
Charles VII, king of France 300
charters 265, 293, 296, 307

INDEX

Chartres 301
Chéruel, Alfonso 264
children 12, 19, 35–6, 44, 86, 98, 107, 116, 151, 163, 165, 170, 173, 176, 236, 274, 316, 322, 326
chronicles 6, 143–4, 204–5, 262–3, 300
Chronique des quatre premiers Valois 158
Chronique normande 163
Chronographia regnum Francorum 288
Church *see* papacy
Cilly 167–8
Cinaccio di Bertino 364–6, 368–9
Cino da Pistoia 60n97
Ciompi 2, 6, 8, 91, 143, 201–60, 263–4, 267, 303, 339, 351–5
citizenship 43, 45, 94
city walls 156
clergy 11, 32–5, 41–2, 55–7, 63–4, 84, 92, 100, 102, 115, 140–1, 144–5, 148, 150, 182–3, 188–9, 195, 208–9, 224, 227, 290
Clermonte de Lodève 329–31
Clermont-en-Beauvaisis 15, 23–4, 155, 162, 168, 170–1
clubs, workingmen's 17, 66–7, 74–5, 82
Club of the Caterpillar (*Compagnia del Bruco*) 6, 90, 133–4, 340
coats of arms 115, 129, 250
cobblers 95, 358
Cochon, Pierre 93, 265
Cohn, Samuel, Jr 201
Cola di Rienzo 79–81
Colonna family 64, 80
common good 23
communal privileges 265, 281, 292, 298, 310–11, 322–3, 341
communication 9, 199, 263–4
companies *see* clubs; soldiers
Compiègne 163–6, 170, 197, 268

confraternities 180
conspiracy 23, 59–60, 76, 121, 131–2
Cornacchiaia 363, 366, 369–70
Cortona 135
Couchy, lord of (Enguerrand, 1342–98) 153, 158
Courtrai, 37, 286–7
Cousinot, Guillaume I 300
criminal records 5, 77–9, 110–11, 130–2, 137–9, 205, 245–8, 317, 341, 362–6, 372–3
Cronaca prima d'anonimo 240, 244
crossbows, crossbowmen 54, 60, 69, 71, 122, 135, 203, 211, 221–2, 226, 228, 230–4, 236, 241, 244–5, 247–8, 320, 353–4, 362
crusades 19, 35–6, 100n28, 106, 156n44, 160n56

Damme 20, 29
Dampierre, Guy de, count of Flanders 4, 21–2, 25
Dante, Alighieri 55, 62n104
Darcy, Regnault, Lord 180
Dati, Gregorio 341, 371
debt 239
demography 266–7
de Roover, Raymond 201
Deschamps, Eustache 176, 324
devil 99, 130, 153–4, 173, 364
diaries 204
Dieppe 321–2
Dijon 301
dinner parties 343–4
Dobson, R. B. 1–2
documents, destruction of 114, 222, 295
doge, office of 68
dogs 12, 123–4
Dolcino, Fra 55–7
Donati, Corso de' 51–2
Donato di Neri 112
Doria family 68
Dormans, Lord Miles de 271–2

Douai 15, 20–1, 98
dress 67, 190, 285–6, 288, 291, 304
drunkenness 31, 149, 265, 292
Duby, Georges 145
Duchesse of Orléans (daughter of King John II) 170
Dunkerque 38

Edward III, king of England 39n50
Eight of Santa Maria Novella 203, 205, 234, 243–9
elections 12, 15, 109, 114, 184–5, 202, 214–15, 220, 222, 226, 230, 239–40, 242, 249–52, 255, 257, 353–5
England, the English 39–40, 157, 160–1, 164, 174, 262, 266–7, 298, 304, 329, 350
English Peasants Revolt (Uprising) of 1381 1, 9, 148, 202, 267, 277
Enguerrand de Monstrelet 341
Ermenonville 165, 171
estates general 195n108, 197
evil, evil spirits 56, 166, 364
excommunication 224
execution 37–8, 38, 73, 87, 93, 110, 125, 129, 132, 192, 203, 210, 216, 219, 236, 241, 253, 282, 297–8, 327, 331
exile, exiles 20, 234, 239, 241–2, 253, 259–60, 343, 355–6

factions 62, 370
famines, food shortages 11, 16–18, 64–6, 72, 150
fear 26, 29, 33, 45, 48, 51–2, 58, 62, 69–72, 76, 94, 103, 105–7, 114, 119, 151, 156, 164–5, 172, 175–6, 185–90, 192, 197, 199–200, 208, 210, 217–18, 228, 235, 258, 269, 272–3, 277–80, 286, 290, 301, 303, 310, 315–17, 321–5, 330–1, 333–5, 344, 360, 371

Fermo 137, 142
Ferrara 224, 340n5, 341, 361–2
festivals, festivities 113, 118, 216
feudalism, feudal relations 9, 340
fines 20, 82, 105, 107, 187, 232–3, 251, 257, 310, 320, 343
Firenzuola 364–6
fires 63–4, 113, 128, 153, 166, 170, 172, 174, 176, 181, 217, 230, 252, 254–5, 355
fisticuffs 62–4
flagellants 88, 92
flags 27, 29, 33, 45–6, 49–50, 52, 54, 67, 69–70, 80–1, 86, 113, 129, 134, 161, 207, 211, 219, 221–2, 227–30, 233, 240–1, 243–5, 253–4, 256–7, 267, 286, 339, 347, 352, 356
Flammeront, Jean 149–50
Flanders 4, 11–2, 15, 17–18, 22, 25–30, 36–40, 95–6, 147, 153, 177–8, 265–6, 277, 285–7, 302–5, 316, 320
Flemings (as foreigners) 210, 253
Florence 12–13, 16–17, 43–6, 49–55, 65–75, 80–2, 92, 121, 124–5, 133, 136, 201–60, 340–1, 351–7, 359–60, 372–3
  churches and monuments: Cestello 215; Hermit Friars 215; Orsanmichele 65, 352; Palace of the Priors 125, rostrum 215–16, 227, 230, 255; San Frediano 230; San Giovanni 223; San Marco 246; Santa Maria Novella 223, 247–8; Sant'Ambrogio 357; Sant'Apollinare, 229; Santo Spirito, 209; Servites 215; Settimo, 215; Stinche 209, 240
  councils and committees: 206–7, 212–4, 225, 259, 215, 352, 359–60; *Otto di Guardia* 232–3

INDEX 383

Government of the Minor
  Guilds 203–4, 258–9, 339
Neighbourhoods, districts:
  Belletri 216, 357; Cafaggiuolo
  215; Camaldoli 216, 245;
  contado 221, 224–6, 242, 356;
  Oltrarno 210, 357;
Florentine Alps 366–70
foreigners 78, 140–1, 312, 375
  see also Flemings
fortifications 24, 46, 48, 94, 104–5,
  107–8, 112, 127, 156, 164,
  170–1, 173–4, 180, 329–30,
  366, 371
  provisioning of 163
Fossier, Robert 145
fountains 123–4
Fourquin, Guy 145
fraticelli 47
French Revolution 8, 143, 263
friars *see* clergy
Froissart, Jean, 2, 143, 149, 155,
  265, 301, 341
fullers 17, 35, 87n3, 88, 94, 95–6

gabelles *see* taxes
Galliano 91, 135–6
Galluzzo 225
Gambacorti family 121
games 233
Gaston Phoebus, count of Foix 153,
  156–7, 159, 168, 178
Genoa 59, 67–8, 91, 236, 313n92,
  340n5, 341, 353
Gentien, Pierre *see* Pierre des
  Essars
German Peasants' War 1524–25 2–3,
  15, 203
Germans, Germany 61, 88, 235
Ghent 4, 15, 20, 26, 39, 265–6,
  285–7, 302, 304–5
Ghibellines 44, 213–14, 371
gifts 231, 321
  see also palio

Gilles, Pierre 159, 167–8, 180
Giovanni d'Andrea, Lord 60
Giovanni di Mone 239, 243
God 171, 209, 218, 225–6, 231, 248,
  255, 284, 287, 324, 361, 365,
  371
golden spurs 286
grain 64–6, 72, 124–5, 224–6, 242,
  373
Great Flood 235
Great Schism (1378–1417) 92,
  375n70
guards 135, 313
Guelfs 44, 50, 340
  Guelf Party 52, 129, 202, 206–7,
  211, 213–14, 216, 228, 231,
  236, 240, 339–40, 352–3, 356
Guenée, Bernard 7, 9
Guicciardini, Luigi di Messer Piero
  217, 240, 254
guilds 117–18, 197, 202–3, 206,
  209, 213–14, 217–18, 221,
  228–9, 236–8, 244, 249–51,
  255–9, 297, 351–2
Guillaume l'Aloue 261n1
Guinigi family 129, 131
Guyenne, duke of 346–7

Hammer men (*Maillotins*) 8, 11–12,
  263–6, 278–82, 294–303,
  311–18, 322
Hangest, John, lord of 168
Harelle 7–8, 263–5, 289–94, 306–11,
  322
Harfleur 312
Harkwood, John 339
harvest 148
heresy 18, 41–2, 44, 55–7, 92, 226
hierarchy 14
Hilton, R. H. 8–9, 83
Holy Ghost 196
honour 103
hoods 193, 198
Hospitallers 160

Huizinga, Johan 1
humanism 263, 270
humiliation 96, 114–15, 139, 151, 183, 258, 266, 274, 319
Hundred Years War 39, 90, 146, 150, 262, 338, 350
Hungary 235
Hussites 2–3

ideology 9–11, 201
Île de France 146, 164, 172, 175
images 326
Imola 44, 61
Impruneta 235
infants 173, 340, 374
inns 110, 343–4
Inquisition 41–2
insignia *see* flags
insults 335–6
internecine conflict 95, 372–3
see also factions
Isabel of France, Madame 167

Jacopo del Verme 364–6
Jacquerie (Jacques) 7–8, 12, 89, 93, 143–200, 202–3, 261–2, 264
James of Saint-Pol 25–7, 29–30
Jean, duke of Berry 19, 89, 99, 101, 104, 182, 327–9, 338
Jean des Marès 275, 280, 282, 284, 300, 313
Jean de Troyes 240, 345, 347
Jean de Venette (so-called) 1, 19, 144–5, 170
Jean le Bel 7, 25, 143–4, 149
Jews 19, 35, 88, 92, 266, 274, 279, 287–8, 292–3, 295, 300, 311–16
Joanna I, Queen of the Kingdom of Naples 86
John the Fearless, duke of Burgundy 338, 345
John II, king of France 150, 167–8, 172, 193–6

John XXII, Pope 60n97
Joyous Entry (of king) 284, 291, 308
judges 57–60, 70

knights, knighting 201, 254, 313, 348
see also magnates; nobles
Knolles, Robert 317

ladies 151, 153, 167, 171, 173, 179, 346
see also nobles
Lanfranchi clan 61–2
Languedoc (southern France) 3, 8, 41–2, 90, 99–109, 182, 261–2, 325–37
Laon 194–5, 298, 318–20
la Roncière, Charles de 201
laws 69–70, 111, 117–18, 122, 148–9, 206–40 *passim*, 268, 310, 353–4
anti-magnates (Ordinances of Justice) 49, 52–4, 206
lawsuits 306–7
L'Ordonnance Cabochienne 338–9
natural law 269, 271–2
lawyers 290, 293–4
leaders, leadership 11–2, 16, 28, 146, 150–1, 184–6, 190, 192, 204, 216, 279–80, 286
leprosy 80
Le Puy 325–7
Lescot, Richard, continuator of 145
letters 177–8, 216, 226, 317
letters of remission 11, 90, 93–4, 99, 145–7, 179, 182, 262, 265
liberty 69, 99, 263, 269–71, 275, 292, 296, 305–6, 323, 340
lies 195
Lille 98
loans 320
Louis, of Nevers, count of Flanders, 39–40

INDEX

Louis IX (saint) 19, 295–6
Louis de Male, count of Flanders
   87n3, 88, 96, 266
Lucca 91, 129–32, 135–6
Luce, Siméon 145, 149–50, 179
Ludwig of Bavaria 81
lust *see* sex
Lyon 336–7

Machiavelli, Boninsegna 204, 208, 241
Machiavelli, Niccolò 6, 62n104
Mafia 89
magnates 5, 42–3, 47–9, 51–5, 61–2, 68–70, 114–16, 206–7, 224, 237, 240, 243, 257, 354
Maillotins see Hammer men
Marcel, Étienne 146–7, 149–51, 165, 173, 177, 180, 185–6, 193, 199
Marciano 372–3
Maremma 65
markets 95–6, 308
Marne river 157, 169
marriage 334
  see also weddings
Martin V, Pope 374–5
Marxist historiography 9
massacres *see* atrocities
Massa Marittima 58
mayors 22, 197, 292, 306
Meaux 152–4, 156–9, 163, 165, 167, 169, 177–8, 180–3, 283, 296, 299, 319
  Marché of 157, 159, 165, 167–8
Medici, Salvestro de' 201–2, 206–7, 211, 239, 243, 254
meetings *see* assemblies
menu peuple 31–2, 190, 289–94, 349
Mello 171, 185
merchants 268–9, 316–17
  see also bourgeois
Merchants' Court (*Mercanzia*) 114, 237

Michele di Lando 204, 220, 228–9, 231, 240, 243–4, 256
Michelotti, Biordo 340, 359
migration 188
Milan 4, 7, 120, 340–1, 364
militias, citizen 45–6, 48, 50, 57–8, 73, 147, 244, 276, 280, 297, 299, 313, 347, 355
Mirot, Léon 264
Mollat, Michele 3, 7–9, 91, 201, 261, 264
money 14, 181, 239
monks *see* clergy
Montalcino 122–3
Montdidier 171
Monte 238, 242
Monte San Savino 372–3
Montpellier 262, 327–9
mountains, mountain men 55–7, 139–40, 340–1, 350–1, 362–71
Mugello 370–1
Muratori, Ludovico 118n57
Mussis, Giovanni de' 91

Najemy, John 201
Naples 7, 18, 44, 64, 86
Narbonne 105
neighbourhoods 45, 62–4, 67, 76, 90, 111, 116, 124, 127, 134, 203, 205, 211, 230–1, 241, 340, 357–8
Niccola della Tuccia 48
Nîmes 276n32, 325
Nine, government of (Siena) 17, 56, 58, 60, 63, 76, 90, 112–17, 126–8
nobles, nobility 84, 94, 107, 116, 119, 143–200 *passim*, 269
  obligations to peasants 163, 169
  see also magnates
Normandy 152, 309, 322
notaries 52, 307, 331
Novara 57

Noyon 152
Nuremberg 88
Nuto, Ser (Pieri) 216–19, 254–5
oaths 246–8
obedience 192, 195–7, 272, 310
occupations 203, 214, 317–18, 360
Oise river 178
old age 186
Orléans 4, 296, 343–4
Orsini family 64, 80, 87
Oudenberg 37
Ovile, neighbourhood of 76–7, 79
paintings 82n146, 115
Palermo 86n157
palio 67, 113
Panzano, Lord Luca da 227, 234, 243, 245
papacy 79–80, 112, 123–4, 224–6, 374–5
war with, 1375–78 7, 136–42, 208, 215, 254
pardons 297
see also letters of remission
Paris 4, 7, 11, 13, 19, 29–32, 35, 37, 87, 147, 152, 154, 157, 159, 163, 165, 167–8, 175, 177, 180, 182, 192–6, 198–200, 263–6, 275–6, 278–85, 287–8, 294–303, 305–6, 311–19, 324–5, 344–8
monuments and institutions: Châtelet 106, 200, 263, 270, 274, 278, 280, 282, 294, 297, 311–12, 314–16, 324; Fifteen Score 317; juifverie 311; les Halles, 278, 300, 314; Louvre 159, 180; Sainte-Geneviève 295; Saint-Germain-Auxerrois 317; Saint-Germain des-Près 279, 295, 325; University of 175, 281, 341–3

Parma 92, 341, 360–1
peace 86, 142, 209, 215–16, 223–4, 254, 334
peasants 81–6, 143–200 *passim*, 221, 261, 268, 283, 335–6, 341, 360–75
protection of 145, 163, 169
Pellini, Pompeo 123
Pere III of Catalonia 88
Perthois 190
Perugia 80, 132–3, 340, 357–9;
neighbourhoods: Sant'Angelo 357–9
Peruzzi family and firm 28
Peter the King, 16, 25–6, 28, 240
petitions 213, 243, 247–8, 253, 255, 259
Petrarca, Francesco 60n97
Philip, the Bold, duke of Burgundy 301, 303, 341
Philippe le Bel (the Fair), king of France 25, 262, 295–6, 301, 305–6
Picardy 147, 174–5, 177–8, 190, 288–9
Piccolomini clan 113
Piero di Ciro 245–8
Pierre de la Bruyère 100
Pierre des Essars 345–8
Pierre de Villiers 275, 283
Pietramala 367–70
pilgrims 327, 350–1
Pintoin, Michele, 6, 90, 99, 262–3, 266
pirates 68
Pirenne, Henri 3
Pisa 61–2, 92, 121
Pistoia 370
Pitti, Buonaccorso 11, 302
plague of 1383, 356
see also Black Death
Podere 370
podestà 45, 51–2, 73, 141
Poitiers, battle of 172

INDEX 387

Polenta, Lord Bernardino da 119
Ponte-de-l'Arche 290–1, 298
poor, poverty 65–6, 143, 146, 149, 187, 279, 288, 292, 326–7, 338
Poperinge 15, 20–1, 37–8
popolani 68–9, 71
popolo 16, 42–3, 49–50, 61–2, 67–8, 137, 173, 207
popolo minuto 2, 16, 28–9, 42, 51, 53, 58, 68–9, 71–7, 80, 90, 112–14, 119, 121, 127–8, 144, 174, 201–60, 302–3, 351–9
Prato 371
prayers 326
priests *see* clergy
primo popolo 4, 16, 42, 44–5
prisons 106, 315
  see also Paris: Châtelet
processions 342, 356
prophecy 204, 235
provosts of merchants 97–8, 167, 181, 345–8
  see also Marcel, Étienne
provvisioni registers 205, 249, 341
Prussia 156, 178
Puglia 83–5

rape 151, 268
Raspanti 133, 340, 357–9
Ravenna 118–19
reforms, governmental 116–17, 128, 131, 137, 141, 202, 238
Reims 267, 296, 298, 338
Religieux de Saint-Denys *see* Pintoin, Michele
remensas (Spain) 3
rents 31
repression 13, 146, 166, 169, 172, 177, 203, 216
restraint 187, 191
rhetoric 6–7, 9, 28, 33, 79–80, 99, 190, 207, 240, 269–73, 280–1, 284–6, 347–8

rights of barony 265, 293
rings 139–40
rioni see neighbourhoods
robbery 114–15, 128, 153, 189, 209–10, 217, 253, 274, 311, 316, 349, 356
Robert, king of Naples 82–3
Robert de Clermont, Lord, Marshal of Champagne 180
Robert de Lorris 164
Robert le Coq, bishop of Laon 152, 194–5
Rocca di San Casciano 340n7
Rodolico, Niccolò 201
Rome 18, 64, 79–81, 87, 111–12, 123, 340n5
Rouen 4, 7, 13, 22, 24, 40–1, 87, 89, 94, 263–5, 275–7, 281, 284, 289–94, 298–9, 302, 306–11
  monasteries: Nôtre-Dame 265, 290, 292; Saint-Catherine, 293; Saint-Ouën 265, 277, 289–90, 292, 306–7; Saint-Godart 293; Saint-Lô 293
Rouergue 329
Rudé, George 10
Rutenburg, Victor 201

Saint-Denis, abbey of 19, 143, 145, 288
Saint-Dizier 191, 320
Saint-Flour 102–5, 350–1
Saint-Leu-d'Essérent 145, 159, 166, 170–1
Saint-Omer 20
Saint Peter (Rome) 80
Saint-Quentin 289, 320–1
Saint Sylvester, Pope 80
salaries *see* wages
Salimbeni clan, faction, *Monte* 126–8, 134
Salutati, Ser Coluccio 255
Sambuca 370
Sanuto, Marino, the younger 46

Saracens *see* Turks
Savelli, Luca 87, 111
Scali, Giorgio degli 208, 231, 236
sculpture 56, 359
Secousse, Denis-François 179
secret meetings 121, 174, 180, 193, 244, 295
Segher Jonssone (Sigerus, son of John) 37–8
Seine river 169
senators 111
Senlis 147, 162, 165–6, 301
Sens 167
Sercambi, Giovanni 129
Sercot, Richard 160
servants 98, 135
sex 60, 103, 171
shepherds 19, 35–6
Sicily 65
Siena 6, 17–18, 57–60, 62–4, 75–9, 87, 90, 112–18, 122–3, 126–8, 133–4, 357, 374–5
Simone Martini 82n146
sociologists 13, 16
Soissons 152, 298–9
soldiers 69, 120, 131, 135, 140, 157–8, 160–1, 164, 218, 283, 342, 350–1, 361–2, 365, 371
Somme, river 178
songs 98
Soulaz, Jehan 167–8
Spinola family 68
Stefani, Marchionne di Coppo 66, 204
Stella, Alessandro 201
street theatre 9, 265, 276–7
strikes 7, 10–11, 15, 17, 20, 23, 27, 81–2
Strozzi, Andrea degli 13, 71–2
Strozzi, Pagnotto d'Andrea degli 72
students 8, 60–1, 341–4
stupidity 336

Tarquinia (Corneto) 81

taverns *see* inns
taxes 13, 18, 23–4, 26–7, 32–4, 36, 40–1, 43, 46, 70–1, 83–5, 87, 92, 96–8, 111, 115, 118–20, 152, 221, 223–6, 233, 239, 250, 261–337 *passim*, 340–1, 354, 360–73
Templars 31
terms 5
threats 103
Tilly, Charles 10
Tolomei clan 17, 60, 75–8, 122, 126
torture 37–8, 133, 374
Toulouse 35, 106, 332–5
Tournai 15, 20, 22–3, 32–5, 96–8, 261n1, 298
town councils *see* aldermen
treason 180, 279, 310, 332
Treviso 92
Trexler, Richard 201
Tristan, Gentian, provost 181, 194
Troyes 301
trumpets 134, 139, 216, 330
Tuchins 7, 89–90, 99–107, 148, 203, 338
Turks 235, 325
Tuscany 3, 18, 65, 339
Twelve, government of, faction or *Monte* of (Siena) 112, 116–18, 123, 126–9
tyranny 340

Ubaldini clan 260, 362–6, 371–2
Uberti clan 44–5
Uguiccione de la Faggiuola 62
unions 17, 74–5
  see also clubs
Urban VI, Pope 328

vagabonds 327
Vaillant, Jehan 167
Valois 157
Vanderkinde, Léon 3
Vannino di Cenni, Ser 363–6

Velay 335–6
Venice 18, 46–7, 55
Verona 224
Veurne 38
Vexin 178
Villani, Giovanni 12, 28, 42, 66
Villani, Matteo 66, 94, 144
Visconti, Bernabò, Lord 120, 223
Visconti, Giangaleazzo (count of Virtù) 361, 365–6, 370
visions 19, 33
Viteccio 374
Viterbo 12, 47–8, 123–4
Volterra 225, 371

wages 23, 133, 241
wealth 362
weapons 63, 78–9, 95, 100, 103, 109–10, 138, 209, 211–12, 234, 291, 344
weavers 22, 87n3, 94, 95–6
weddings 96
White Hoods 265

wine 31, 300, 321–2, 324
Winstanley, Gerrard 252
Wolff, Philippe 3, 7–9, 91, 201, 261, 264
women 10–12, 29–30, 56–7, 60, 103, 107, 123–4, 163, 171, 176, 236, 274, 302, 315, 321
wool
  guild 227, 237–8, 259, 355
  industry 202–3
  production quotas 242, 258, 267
  shops 237
  workers 132–3, 232
  see also carders; fullers; weavers
Wrawe, John 148

youngsters 48, 358
  see also children; infants; students
Ypres 20–2, 37, 39, 96, 304

Zannekin, Clais (Colin) 37–8, 40
Zeeland 37

EU authorised representative for GPSR:
Easy Access System Europe, Mustamäe tee 50,
10621 Tallinn, Estonia
gpsr.requests@easproject.com

www.ingramcontent.com/pod-product-compliance
Ingram Content Group UK Ltd.
Pitfield, Milton Keynes, MK11 3LW, UK
UKHW021832140426
5217IPUK00021B/1407